THE TRANSFORMATION OF LEGAL AID

THE TRANSFORMATION OF LEGAL AID

COMPARATIVE AND HISTORICAL STUDIES

Edited by

FRANCIS REGAN
ALAN PATERSON
TAMARA GORIELY
and
DON FLEMING

OXFORD
UNIVERSITY PRESS

OXFORD
UNIVERSITY PRESS
Great Clarendon Street, Oxford OX2 6DP
Oxford University Press is a department of the University of Oxford.
It furthers the University's objective of excellence in research, scholarship,
and education by publishing worldwide in
Oxford New York
Athens Auckland Bangkok Bogotá Buenos Aires Calcutta
Cape Town Chennai Dar es Salaam Delhi Florence Hong Kong Istanbul
Karachi Kuala Lumpur Madrid Melbourne Mexico City Mumbai
Nairobi Paris São Paulo Singapore Taipei Tokyo Toronto Warsaw
with associated companies in Berlin Ibadan
Oxford is a registered trade mark of Oxford University Press
in the UK and in certain other countries
Published in the United States
by Oxford University Press Inc., New York

First published 1999

British Library Cataloguing in Publication Data
Data available
Library of Congress Cataloging in Publication Data
The transformation of legal aid: comparative and historical studies/
edited by Francis Regan [et al.].
p. cm.
Includes bibliographical references and index.
1. Legal aid. 2. Legal aid history. I. Regan, Francis.
K133.T73 1999 347′.017—dc 21 99–27431
ISBN 0–19–826589–1
1 3 5 7 9 10 8 6 4 2
Typeset in Times
by Cambrian Typesetters, Frimley, Surrey
Printed in Great Britain
on acid-free paper by
Biddles Ltd, Guildford and King's Lynn

Preface

This book has been a genuinely global production. Not only have eleven people contributed from eight different countries, but the editorial work has been distributed between Australia, Scotland and England. Wthout e-mail the book would simply not have been possible.

The contributors are all members of an offshoot of the ISA Research Committee on the Sociology of the Legal Profession. This Research Committee, chaired by Rick Abel of UCLA and Philip Lewis of All Souls College, Oxford, produced the Lawyers in Society trilogy (Los Angeles: University of California Press, 1989). Thereafter the Committee spawned a series of sub-groups including the Legal Aid and Legal Services group.

In the past five years the Legal Aid group has pursued three objectives. The first has been to conduct genuinely comparative studies of legal aid in developed western jurisdictions. Cyrus Tata discusses one such study—on criminal legal aid expenditure—in Chapter 6 where he also talks about the benefits and problems with this kind of work.

Secondly, members of the Group have taken part in a series of conferences with senior policy-makers from the leading legal aid jurisdictions. The conferences in the Hague (1994), Edinburgh (1997) and Vancouver (1999) grappled with the common problems confronting highly developed legal aid programmes and examined the options available to legal aid policy makers and reformers. It has, to date, been an unusually fruitful process of collaboration between these two groups who otherwise have few opportunities to learn from each other.

Finally, members of the group have worked on this volume of comparative, historical, and thematic essays. The monograph eschews the traditional formula for comparative works where a series of national reports are combined with two or three chapters in order to integrate the often disparate content. Instead, in this collection we have sought to include comparative elements, to some extent, within all the chapters, to try to understand better this complex and rapidly changing phenomenon. How far we have succeeded is for the reader to judge.

I commend this research to you, warts and all. I have no doubt it will be developed further in the future but I am also sure it extends what we know about and how we understand legal aid. I believe, also, that it demonstrates the value of an international group of scholars conducting related research. I look forward to an opportunity in the future to present further research by the Legal Aid and Legal Services Group.

Glasgow, 1999
Professor Alan Paterson
Chair, Legal Aid and Legal Services Group

Acknowledgements

The research presented in this book is the work of many people. The contributors have worked long and hard over these essays in a time when very little original research was being published about legal aid. While this allowed a degree of freedom to test fresh ideas it also put pressure on the contributors to delve into relatively uncharted waters. As editors we are very grateful for the patience and perseverance displayed by all our contributors in what has been a long and fairly drawn-put process.

A number of other people have provided much needed 'behind the scenes' assistance at different stages. Mary McKenna, at Flinders University, provided very capable research assistance as well as undertaking much of the work to produce the consolidated bibliography. Amanda Nixon in the Law Library at Flinders University also located references for a number of pesky items for the bibliography.

Finally, staff at OUP, including Mick Belson, Dominic Shryane and Myf Milton were very helpful in guiding the book through the different stages of the production process.

Contents

Part Three: Emerging Themes

List of Contributors

Earl Johnson, Jr
Justice, California Court of Appeal (1982–).

John C. Kilwein
Associate Professor, Department of Political Science, West Virginia University, USA.

Frederick H. Zemans
Professor of Law, Osgoode Hall Law School, York University, Toronto, Canada; and Founding Director, Parkdale Community Legal Services, Toronto.

Aneurin Thomas
Director of Policy, Legal Aid Ontario, Canada.

Tamara Goriely
Research Fellow at the Institute of Advanced Legal Studies, University of London; and Partner in TPR Social and Legal Research.

Erhard Blankenburg
Professor of Sociology of Law, Free University, Amsterdam, The Netherlands.

Cyrus Tata
Lecturer in Socio-Legal Studies, The Centre for Sentencing Research, Law School, University of Strathclyde, Glasgow, Scotland.

Mel Cousins
Independent researcher, Dublin, Ireland.

Francis Regan
Senior Lecturer in Legal Studies, Flinders University of South Australia, Adelaide, Australia.

Jon Johnsen
Professor of Law, Department of Public Law, University of Oslo, Norway.

Alan Paterson
Professor of Law and Chairman of Strathclyde University Law School, Scotland; Chair of the International Legal Aid Group.

Avrom Sherr
Woolf Professor of Legal Education at the Institute of Advanced Legal Studies of the University of London.

Don Fleming
Senior Lecturer in Law, Law School, University of Canberra, Australia.

Introduction

Legal aid has undergone several transformations in the post-World War II era. The first change, from charity to large-scale, publicly funded schemes, began to be reversed in the 1980s and 1990s when governments lost faith in public welfare programmes and began to cut legal aid budgets. Private profession charity is once again back on the agenda and more individuals are once again being forced to fend for themselves in court. Legal aid it seems is in a continual process of flux.

In this book we examine the ongoing transformation of legal aid in the industrialised societies in the post-war period and attempt to explain why it occurred. We argue that this process of expansion and decline has been well documented but not well understood. As a result many important questions remain. We do not really understand why the post-war expansion and decline took place. Did legal aid just 'evolve' over time or were the changes related to broader social and political influences? If the latter, what does legal aid tell us, for example, about the power of the legal profession, the impact of religion, or the rise and fall of the welfare state? And were the traditions of different legal 'families' also important? Were similar forces at work in different societies? In order to attempt to answer these questions, we examine the post-war transformation of legal aid from historical and comparative perspectives. Before sketching the contents, however, we summarise the process of change in more detail and highlight some of the gaps in the literature.

There can be little doubt about the scale of legal aid reform in the rich societies in the post-war period. In one society after another the inadequate private legal profession 'charity' was replaced by large, national, publicly funded and co-ordinated schemes. While the charitable schemes helped only the poorest citizens for a narrow range of serious criminal and matrimonial cases, the new publicly funded schemes offered a comprehensive range of services for a wide variety of legal problems to the poor, and in some societies to the non-poor. They often used publicly employed salaried lawyers alongside the private profession to provide services (Cappelletti *et al.*, 1975). Between 1950 and 1973 similar reforms were undertaken in the UK, the Netherlands, the USA, Canada, Sweden and Australia, while several other societies, including France, introduced more limited reforms.

It seemed for a while that the liberal vision of equality before the law was about to be realised in practice. The 1970s legal aid literature was optimistic about the impact and longevity of these changes. Cappelletti argued, for example, that 'equal justice for the poor' was finally becoming a reality and that, while an implementation gap existed, the recalcitrant societies would, in time, follow suit and reform their schemes (1975). Other commentators were also optimistic when they documented national reforms. Johnson (1978), for example, sketched the developments in the USA, while the studies in Zemans (ed.) (1979) examined the major reforms in a number of other societies including Scandinavia, England and Australia. Finally, optimism was reinforced by Cappelletti *et al.*'s identification of global waves of 'access to justice' reforms involving not just legal aid but the 'full panoply of institutions and devices personnel and procedures used to process, and even prevent, disputes in modern societies' (1978:49).

But did legal aid simply evolve as Cappelletti suggested? Evolutionary explanations were regarded as naïve by other commentators. Abel, for example, argued that the 'politics of legal aid' were central to legal aid reforms (1985). He saw the post-war expansion of legal aid as an essential part of capitalism's social control, designed to ameliorate class struggle by the working class and the poor. This was achieved in part by granting a range of welfare rights, including income support, health care, and housing as well as legal aid. At the same time, the reforms were a result of 'demand creation' pressures from private legal professions attempting to stimulate new legal markets in a period of oversupply of lawyers, according to Abel. Rather than equal justice for the poor, the expansion of legal aid had more to do with the politics of welfare states and the private legal profession. But while Abel criticised the evolutionary account, his explanation was also lacking. He did not explain, for example, why eligibility criteria varied between different types of welfare states, nor why the legal profession in most societies actually resisted rather than promoted legal aid reforms (Goriely & Paterson, 1996). Finally, while he noted that religion and legal families appeared to influence some aspects of legal aid schemes, these relationships were not explored in detail (1985). By the time publicly funded legal aid began to decline in the 1980s, major gaps therefore existed in the literature.

The decline of legal aid in the 1980s and 1990s has also been well documented in the literature (Goriely & Paterson, 1996). The details will be depressingly familiar to many readers. Despite growing demand most societies progressively tightened eligibility tests and cut budgets. Means and assets tests became steadily more restrictive and client financial 'contributions' levied on the cost of their cases were introduced or increased. Finally, 'policy guidelines' were used to restrict the range of cases for which legal aid was available. In one society after another legal aid was, as a result, increasingly targeted at the poor, and increasingly restricted to serious criminal cases. In some important respects, eligibility provisions in the late 1990s bore a striking resemblance to those of the charitable schemes prior to World War II.

A number of comparative studies have recently attempted to explain the post-war transformations. Blankenburg (1991) and Cousins (1993), for example, offered partial explanations of the post-war expansion in terms of welfare state influences and the power of the bureaucracy, respectively. Meanwhile, other studies identified links between the simultaneous decline of welfare states and legal aid (Goriely, 1994; Regan, 1994). But these and other factors, including the impact of interest groups, religion and legal families, have not been considered in detail. In other words, significant gaps remain in the literature, not just concerning the expansion, but also the decline of legal aid.

The contributions start from the premise that descriptive studies of national schemes are of limited value in explaining what are undoubtedly international patterns. The essays in this volume attempt, by contrast, to use comparative and historical perspectives to shed new light on the post-war transformations of legal aid. As a result they constitute a 'next step' towards, rather than the final word on, post-war legal aid.

The essays are grouped into three sections, but these reflect different emphases rather than hard divisions. The essays in the first section concentrate on historical material, while those in the second section focus on comparison and less on history. Finally, the essays in the third section examine issues that promise to shape the ongoing process of transformation of publicly funded legal aid into the next century.

The first two essays together document the rise and fall of a legal aid scheme that was regarded as a world leader in the 1960s. They also explain why it has gone terribly wrong. In the mid-1970s Earl Johnson published his account of the rise of the US legal services programme. In Chapter 1 he looks back and asks why civil legal aid in the US flourished for only a few short years and then apparently went into terminal decline. Drawing on historical evidence he argues that US judges and politicians have often spoken about the importance of equal justice for the poor. This passion has not, however, been shared by American governments which have never accepted equal justice as a 'fundamental obligation'. As a result, the OEO Legal Services Program, and later the Legal Services Corporation (LSC), always led a tenuous existence.

John Kilwein takes up the US story, focusing on the 1980s and 1990s. While acknowledging the lack of government commitment to legal aid, Kilwein also stresses the role and power of the LSC's adversaries. He argues that the slow decline under the Reagan, Bush and Clinton administrations is understandable if legal aid is seen as an 'interesting anomaly' in US social welfare history. While civil legal aid gave power to individual Americans to defend and assert their rights in divorce, debt and social security cases, it also funded a small amount of collective legal work that attempted to change causes of poverty. According to Kilwein, the attacks on the LSC were primarily designed to extinguish these collective actions because of the threat they posed to 'basic American political sensibilities'. The restrictions in the 1990s, for example, have focused on strictly limiting legal aid work to individual cases. Kilwein's analysis of the power of interest groups not only examines opposition to legal aid: he also acknowledges groups, such as the American Bar Association, that have vigorously supported the LSC. Ultimately he suggests that the LSC's decline cannot be explained in terms of the fiscal conservatism that drove funding cuts in other societies. Rather, the US decline is the result of conservative groups' ideological opposition to the poor having access to the legal system.

Fred Zemans and Aneurin Thomas focus on the often overlooked community-based legal aid sector, or 'clinics', rather than the large public schemes. By means of a survey of Australia, Ontario and England they describe the 'clinics' unique features including the variety of legal services offered, the unique community management traditions and their role in the overall legal aid schemes. Zemans and Thomas also describe recent developments in each society and in the process they pose the question: can community clinics survive? They demonstrate that clinics in the three societies face similar pressures including declining budgets, increasing work loads, demands from funding agencies to undertake more case work, and government reviews recommending more 'efficiency', 'cost-effectiveness' and 'rationalisation'. Nevertheless, they conclude on an optimistic note. Drawing particularly on lessons learnt in Ontario they argue that clinics can survive into the next century if they adapt to external pressures including that for improved efficiency. But they must also retain their unique features, such as community management.

Tamara Goriely points out that legal aid has a dual relationship with the welfare state. It is a form of welfare provision, and also a mechanism for enforcing welfare rights. Using Britain as an example, she considers how far legal aid has been used as a means to ensure that welfare is distributed in the way that the legislature intends. She argues that the individual legal enforcement is only one way of delivering social rights. In the immediate post-war world, social rights were seen as a collective matter. More recently, the emphasis has been on consumer choice in a public quasi-market. Consumers are to use their power to discipline providers by 'exiting' inefficient services and—where exit is not a possibility—by 'voicing' their concerns through a plethora of new complaints procedures. As enforcement mechanisms have changed, so has the role that legal aid is required to play. She concludes that British legal aid, founded during a collectivist era, grew to maturity during an individualistic age, in which individuals were expected to enforce their own entitlements through courts and tribunals. The result is a highly expensive scheme, stuck in a traditionally legal mould. It has not yet met the challenge of the consumerist era. It is too legalistic, too court-dominated, and does little to help people participate in the new forums.

In the first of the comparative essays Erhard Blankenburg analyses why legal aid expenditure varies between schemes in Europe, North America and Oceania. He argues that differences relate partly to three twentieth-century legal aid 'movements', the most developed being those established as part of welfare state reforms. He argues that the differences between schemes can therefore be partly explained in terms of the prosperity of welfare states. But the legal profession's ability to lobby in order to protect their professional privileges has also played a crucial role in legal aid developments. Weak or fragmented legal professions were unable to resist governments intent on the legal aid reforms that inevitably resulted in the profession losing control of legal aid.

Comparative legal aid studies are of course not limited to comparisons of schemes. They can also explain differences between particular types of legal aid work funded by different schemes. In the first part of his essay Cyrus Tata examines the extraordinarily high expenditure on criminal legal aid in Scotland compared to that in the Netherlands and in England and Wales. After assessing the strengths of a variety of explanations, including differences in adversarial and inquisitorial procedure, expenditure per head of population, and the number of legally aided 'cases', he concludes that a variety of factors are at work. In particular, Scotland grants a large amount of legal aid in relatively minor cases. Tata also reflects on the difficulties of legal aid comparisons. How, for example, does one compare numbers of 'cases' when the very concept of a 'case' relies on culturally specific but unarticulated understandings? He points out, however, that there are similar problems with conducting research within a single jurisdiction. He concludes that comparative research should not be avoided, but that, as with all research, it should be undertaken carefully.

Mel Cousins also compares schemes, and he focuses, not on the most developed, but on what he refers to as two legal aid 'laggards', Ireland and France. Cousins asks initially if religion is responsible for the less well developed legal aid in these two societies. He demonstrates by means of a historical summary, however, that while the influence of Catholicism is partly responsible for developments in Ireland the same cannot be said for France. He proceeds to examine a number of reasons which might explain why these schemes are laggards, including the wealth of the society and the size and power of the legal profession. He concludes that the development of legal aid in these two societies can be explained in terms of the capacity of the legal profession to limit interference by the state in the legal services industry. Finally, Cousins suggests that legal aid development appears also to be related to the type of legal system in the society.

Francis Regan takes up the question of the impact of welfare and legal systems on legal aid. He focuses on the small group of 'first-tier' schemes where substantial legal aid reforms were undertaken in the post-war period. He asks why legal aid's effectiveness increased in very different ways in two groups of schemes. He argues that to different degrees these schemes assist individuals to defend and assert their legal rights in two desirable ways, by way of 'inside' and 'outside' litigation services. The effectiveness of these services is no accident, but is shaped by welfare states and legal systems respectively. Northern European societies, for example, generally offer most welfare programmes, including 'in litigation' services, to most of the population. But because dependence on the state is also at the core of the traditions of the civil law legal systems, legal aid schemes offer little assistance in the form of 'outside litigation' services for individuals to resolve their other legal problems. The English-speaking societies, by contrast, discourage dependence on the state and instead target most welfare programmes, including 'in litigation' services, to the poor alone. But the common law emphasis on individual rights often results in legal aid schemes offering extensive assistance in the form of 'outside litigation' services for individuals to respond to other legal problems. Regan concludes that, while ideally legal aid schemes should assist individuals in and outside court, the international pressures for small government make this unlikely in the foreseeable future.

While the essays in the first two Parts of the book examine legal aid reform in the post-war period, those in the final section consider issues that are likely to influence future developments. Jon Johnsen argues that while 'legal needs' studies have often been criticised for methodological and conceptual weaknesses, they can nevertheless provide a foundation for future legal aid policy development. Johnsen draws on Norwegian and other legal needs research to argue that careful design is crucial. What is needed, according to Johnsen, is a comprehensive or 'systematic' approach that combines subjective accounts from the individuals about their experience of legal problems with expert evaluation of legal remedies by legal personnel. While systematic studies of legal needs are not cheap to conduct, Johnsen argues that this level of sophistication may be essential in order to convince governments and policy-makers of the ongoing role for publicly funded legal aid.

The remaining two Chapters examine the impact on legal aid of broader changes in legal systems. Alan Paterson and Avrom Sherr consider the recent international concern with maintaining, enhancing and measuring the quality of legal services. After summarising the recent debate over quality of legal services, they ask why it emerged as an issue so late. Furthermore, why has it been so hotly debated in some jurisdictions but not in others? Again, the Chapter highlights the differential power of legal professions through the developed world, as providers wrestle with the change from traditional views of professional services ('only other professionals can judge') to others more responsive to bureaucratic demands.

Legal aid is also being buffeted by other international developments. As Fleming explains, the trend to allow group or 'multi-party actions' to proceed to court has now spread from the USA to a number of other societies, including England and Wales and Australia. While he stresses the importance of groups being able to press their claims, he argues on the basis of a study of Australian developments that these claims have profound implications for legal aid schemes. Not only do eligibility criteria have to be rethought in terms of the group rather than the individual applicant, but also the significant allocation of personnel and financial resources required by these cases promises to restrict aid in other types of cases. While these multi-party actions pose difficult adjustments for legal aid schemes, however, the alternative also poses problems. If they are excluded by legal aid schemes, for example, the claimants will have to rely on the vagaries of contingency, or 'no win, no fee' arrangements. While they may be sufficient in clearly winnable cases, contingency fees do not solve the problem of bringing borderline group claims to court. In the future, the pressures on legal aid schemes arising from multi-party actions are likely to increase rather than disappear unless alternative sources of funds are made available.

Part One

Historical Studies

1

Justice and Reform: A Quarter Century Later

EARL JOHNSON, JR

In 1973, a quarter century ago, I completed a history of the early years of America's first government programme supplying lawyers to poor people in civil cases, *Justice and Reform: The Formative Years of the OEO Legal Services Program*. The final paragraph of the book asks a question:

> And so, America's poor await a verdict. Properly perceived, it is one that involves the quality of justice they receive as much as their chance to enjoy a better life. Are they to be entitled to equal justice only when their causes are minor or consonant with the philosophy of the ruling political party? Or will they be able to pursue any legal objective through any lawful means in keeping with the ideals of the legal profession? In the long run this question will be answered by the American public. The response most certainly will be the measure of the poor man's opportunity for justice in this nation and his right to seek better conditions through the orderly processes of the law. It may also determine, in large part, the quality of American democracy in the last quarter of the Twentieth Century (Johnson, 1978:284).

Justice and Reform was published the following year, coincidentally within a month of the day President Richard Nixon, in his last official act before resigning office, signed the Legal Services Corporation Act into law (Garment, 1997:148[1]). With that signature he assured what everyone assumed would be a permanent institutional structure for this new government programme of civil legal services for the nation's poor.

Unfortunately, the verdict mentioned at the end of *Justice and Reform* remains as much in doubt today as it was when I shipped the manuscript to the publisher almost a quarter century ago. Indeed, at the close of the twentieth century many would insist that the answer is clearly in the negative. At this point in history poor people in the United States are 'entitled to equal justice only when their causes are minor or consonant with the philosophy of the ruling political party'. And, they are no longer 'able to pursue any legal objective through any lawful means in keeping with the ideals of the legal profession' but instead are effectively

[1] Leonard Garment was legal counsel to President Nixon during most of his administration and 'became the reigning White House expert on the legal services program' who helped 'to persuade Nixon, for his last bill signing in office, to create an independent Legal Services Corporation' (Garment, 1997:148).

denied many 'lawful means' of achieving their legitimate goals, including class actions, administrative representation, and legislative advocacy.

In this Chapter I hope to explain how and perhaps why the American civil legal aid experience has been so different from that in most other industrial democracies. On one side, it has had a more colourful history and produced more profound social benefits for its clients than any legal aid programme anywhere in the world. On the other hand, the American programme remains one of the smaller (by comparison to the nation's size at least) among Western democracies. Even more disturbing, during the past two decades while many other countries have seen their legal aid investments expand several times over, the American programme's budget has actually shrunk by over half in real terms. Its very survival has been in jeopardy during most of those two decades and even now remains in question. Why this is so and what might be done about it dominates most discussions among legal services policy-makers in the United States.

I. Another path: America's very different approach to legal representation of the poor

Just as England both gained and lost from being an island a few miles off the coast of rather than a part of the European continent, the United States has gained and lost even more by being on another continent over three thousand miles away. Both countries have gained when they remained outside the realm of bad influences and improvident policies and free to pursue their own better, often more innovative solutions and to create their own, often superior institutions. Both have lost when they failed to heed some of the better traditions and principles born on the European continent. The United States, of course, is an ocean away from England too, and despite our historical connection and membership in the common law world we have, for good or ill, ignored much of the good as well as rejecting the bad in English governmental and legal institutions.

This helps account for this nation's failure to follow the path which England and most countries on the European continent have trod towards guaranteeing counsel for their low-income citizens in civil cases. There is an almost universal pattern in these countries. In the first stage the legislature passes a statute giving poor people a right to free counsel to be provided by lawyers serving without compensation; in the second stage, a few years, decades, or centuries later, the legislature appropriates public funds to pay lawyers representing poor people. In nearly all of these countries, most of this representation was and continues to be provided by the same private practitioners who represent the rest of the population on a fee-for-service basis. If there is a third stage of development, it is the addition of a layer of salaried lawyers either to lower the costs of supplying representation or to give specialised services which the regular private bar is ill-equipped or unprepared to offer. And now, with *Airey* v. *Ireland*, the European

Court of Human Rights has secured the principle that government-provided counsel is a matter of right for poor people in civil litigation across the European Community.[2]

I realise that in the details and at the fringes the English and continental European pattern is not so simple or uniform as portrayed above. But it is a close enough representation of reality for purposes of contrasting it with the American experience. At no time in this nation's history has a state, local, or the federal government enacted a *statute* conferring a right to counsel in *civil* cases. A few state courts have interpreted the *constitutional* guarantees of due process or equal protection of the laws as requiring the appointment of free counsel in certain narrow categories of civil cases, generally involving the threatened loss of parental rights (e.g. *State* v. *Jamison* (1968)) or in one state the involuntary declaration of paternity (*Salas* v. *Cortez* (1979)). But in 1971 the United States Supreme Court effectively slammed the door on any hope that it would follow the lead of the Swiss Supreme Court[3] or anticipate the European Court of Human Rights and declare a general right to counsel in civil cases[4] under the US Constitution. The Swiss Constitution's guarantee that 'All Swiss are equal before the law' may sound a lot like the US Constitution's promise that all our citizens shall have 'equal protection of the laws'. And the European Convention's requirement that courts provide a 'fair hearing' may sound nearly identical to the requirement to provide all civil litigants 'due process' found in the US Constitution. But in *Lassiter* v. *North Carolina* (1981) the Supreme Court ruled by a margin of five to four that this nation's Constitution only mandates state governments to supply free counsel to civil litigants in cases satisfying a rigid, nearly insurmountable standard.[5] Our high court found that the US Constitution permits a poor woman to lose her parental rights forever in a court proceeding

[2] In *Airey* v. *Ireland* (1979), the European Court of Human Rights was called upon to construe Article 6 of the European Convention on Human Rights which guaranteed all citizens of member nations the right to a 'fair hearing' in civil cases. The Court held that an indigent litigant could not receive a 'fair hearing' in the regular civil courts without the assistance of a lawyer and thus imposed that duty on the governments of the member nations to supply free lawyers to those litigants.

[3] In 1937, some quarter century before the US Supreme Court got round to declaring a right to counsel in criminal cases, the Swiss Supreme Court found a right to counsel in civil cases based on that nation's constitutional guarantee that 'All Swiss are equal before the law' (*Schefer gegen Appenzell A. Rh. Ragierungsrat*, Judgment of 8 Oct. 1937, BGE 63 I 209.) This decision is discussed in *O'Brien*, 1967.

[4] See *Airey* v. *Ireland*, supra n. 2.

[5] '[T]he Court's precedents speak with one voice about what "fundamental fairness" has meant when the Court has considered the right to appointed counsel, and we thus draw from them the presumption that an indigent litigant has a *right* to appointed counsel only when, if he loses, he may be deprived of his *physical liberty*. It is against this *presumption* that all the other elements in the due process decision must be measured . . . [T]hree elements [are] to be evaluated in deciding what due process requires, viz., the private interests at stake, the government's interest, and the risk that the procedures used will lead to erroneous decisions. We must balance these elements against each other, and then set their net weight in the scales against the *presumption* . . .' (*Lassiter* 1981:26–7, emphasis supplied).

where she could not afford, and was compelled to go without, the assistance of counsel.[6]

What all this means, of course, is the United States has not even reached the first stage of providing a formal legal guarantee of some form of legal representation, compensated or uncompensated, in most civil cases. England and most other European countries entered this stage a century or more ago.[7] The US has relied on charity—private charity for ninety years and legislative charity for the past thirty-two—to furnish the limited supply of free legal representation available in the civil law. Things would be even worse except for another difference

[6] The mother in *Lassiter* was a convicted murderer serving a 25–40 year sentence. The social welfare authorities sought to terminate her parental rights to have the child taken away from her several years before because of neglect. At the rather brief, simple three-witness court hearing, the welfare department was represented by counsel but the mother wasn't. When the court issued an order terminating her parental rights the mother appealed on the sole ground that she was indigent and denied appointed counsel in violation of the due process guarantee of the US Constitution.

The Supreme Court applied the balancing test described in n. 5 above and denied that due process required appointment of counsel for Ms Lassiter in this parental termination case. Even the majority, however, conceded some such cases might involve complex issues of procedure, fact, or evidence where unrepresented parents would bear an undue risk of an erroneous deprivation of their parental rights. In that instance, due process indeed would mandate appointment of counsel (id. 31). The court then highlighted the informality of the proceedings below (the government was often represented by a social worker not a lawyer), the absence of complex legal, factual, or evidentiary issues in the *Lassiter* trial itself, and affirmed the trial court's denial of counsel in this case.

In an interesting conclusion to the majority opinion, Justice Stewart takes note that 33 states had already created a right to counsel in parental termination cases as of 1981—usually by statute but sometimes by constitutional decision. The majority then observes, 'A wise public policy, however, may require that higher standards be adopted than those minimally tolerable under the Constitution. . . . The Court's opinion today in no way implies that the standards increasingly urged by informed public opinion and now widely followed by the States are other than enlightened and wise' (id. 34).

The 4 dissenting justices first dispute the 'presumption' that the constitution only requires appointment of free counsel for litigants when they risk loss of *physical* liberty. They then argue parental rights constitute a fundamental interest implicating liberty interests and thus demanding the provision of free counsel to indigents when government seeks to take away those rights. The fundamental nature of this right simply overwhelms the other factors in the balancing equation the *Lassiter* majority established.

Neither the majority opinion nor the 4 dissenting justices mention *Airey* v. *Ireland* 1979 decided by the European Court of Human Rights just 2 years earlier. Indeed it is doubtful the justices were even aware of this decision and its very different definition of fundamental fairness in civil cases. This is yet another example of how the geographic distance between the United States and Europe and the near-isolationist attitude of our legal system has worked to the disadvantage of the right to counsel and access to justice for low-income people in non-criminal proceedings. It is interesting to speculate what might have been the result and rationale in the *Lassiter* case had this nation been bound by the *Airey* decision and its reasoning.

[7] The English statutory right dates back to a 'Statute of Henry VII' enacted in 1495 which provided free counsel and waived litigation costs for poor people in civil cases (II Hen. VII c.12 1495). The statue expected attorneys appointed for this purpose to serve without compensation. This statute is reproduced in full in Pollock 1975:10. The common law courts construed this right to apply only to indigent plaintiffs, not defendants, but the courts of equity granted the right to both (*Oldfield* v. *Cobbett* (1845) 41 Eng. Rep. 765). This legal right to counsel may have been implemented in a niggardly fashion for several centuries, as is common when enforcement of the right depends on uncompensated lawyers. But it nonetheless existed and created a tension between right and reality which could only be cured by something like the Legal Aid and Advice Act of 1949.

Germany's right to counsel in civil litigation dates to Bismark and the creation of the German nation in the 1870s (Cappelletti *et al.*, 1975:48–52), France's to 1851 (ibid. 39–41).

between the American legal tradition and Europe: the contingent fee system. This is an important source of representation for poor people in certain limited categories of civil cases: those where the probability of victory and the potential monetary recovery are enough to persuade a lawyer to make the required time investment (Johnson, 1981:584–91).[8]

Why should the United States, of all countries, lag so far behind the European countries in implementing this essential element of the social contract, and democratic government in general? Indeed by this time America is so far behind that were it part of the European Community it would be out of compliance with the Community's 'fair hearing' guarantee as declared in *Airey* v. *Ireland*,[9] and required somehow, with government funds or by drafting private lawyers or otherwise, to provide free counsel to the millions of poor people it now asks to shift for themselves in the civil courts.

A quarter century ago, I noted this apparent paradox only briefly in *Justice and Reform* (Johnson, 1974, 1978:3–4). It formed part of the background for an account of the legal aid movement and the government's legal services initiative here in this country. That it is still true twenty-five years later is both surprising and—to me at least—alarming. During those years the gap has widened as not only most European countries but most Canadian provinces and several other nations elsewhere in the world have taken major strides towards making equal justice a reality for their lower income citizens.[10] For America's poor the historical phenomenon threatens to become a permanent predicament—and for millions of them each year a tragic one. While we judges and lawyers and academics may decry the lack of abstract rights and the implications for our democracy, to poor

[8] Since lawyers only get paid if they win, they can only afford to take cases where the recovery discounted by the probability of success exceeds by a substantial margin the predicted investment required to litigate the action. This means contingent fee lawyers are often unavailable to lower income people even when the relief they seek is a monetary recovery. Furthermore, the lawyer cost side of this equation is subject to manipulation by the opposing parties, typically insurance companies and other institutional litigants. They can run up the costs of litigation through multiple pre-trial motions, extensive discovery, etc., thereby discouraging contingent fee lawyers from taking any but the most promising cases. Thus the contingent fee system is an imperfect and only partial substitute for a government-subsidised right to counsel even for the limited class of cases in which it is theoretically available. Furthermore, recent legislative changes and proposed changes threaten to reduce still further the proportion of legal problems contingent fee lawyers can afford to take for low and moderate income people (see below).

[9] See n. 2 above.

[10] The middle class has fared less well than the poor in most European countries and Canadian provinces over the past 30 years. England is typical. At the beginning that nation's legal aid programme not only provided free legal representation to its poorest citizens but a partial subsidy, on a sliding scale, to those further up the income scale. Indeed at the beginning fully 80 per cent of the population was entitled to at least some subsidy for their legal representation. That percentage has drifted lower almost every year since, as the government deliberately failed to adjust eligibility standards to take account of inflation. At this point, less than half the English population is eligible for free or subsidised legal services. (While this may appear a low point to those concerned about the English legal aid programme it is extraordinarily generous by comparison with the US, where less than *twenty* per cent of the population is financially eligible to even attempt to receive the limited ration of free legal services available in civil cases.)

people the lack of counsel often costs them more concrete things—food, housing, children, jobs, even their dignity as human beings.

This time I want to turn more attention to this question of why: why neither the national Congress, a state legislature or any court has recognised that lower income people cannot get equal justice unless the government provides them with lawyers. What was obvious to Parliament in the days of Henry VII, to Bismark in 1877, to the Swiss Supreme Court in 1937, and to the European Court on Human Rights in 1979 seems to have escaped our nation's legislative and judicial leaders.

In *Justice and Reform* I speculated that the simplicity of America's frontier society and an early widespread antipathy to lawyers might explain how the colonies formed a nation without creating an express constitutional right to counsel in civil cases. So, curiously, the first nation designed largely by lawyers, not by kings or warriors, seems to have ignored the critical importance of that profession to the 'justice' the new nation promised to establish.[11] This temporary simplicity and anti-lawyer sentiment, I ventured, might also account for the failure of national and state legislative bodies early on to enact statutory guarantees similar to those found across Europe. While these factors may have a great deal to do with why the United States entered the nineteenth century without a statutory or constitutional right to counsel in civil cases, I no longer think they fully explain why we entered the twentieth century in this same posture, and doubt they can be given much credit—or rather blame—as this nation enters the twenty-first century still denying this fundamental right to its citizens. The United States has not been a simple frontier society for a long, long time. And lawyers, while their popularity ebbs and flows, have become more and more essential to anyone, rich or poor, who hopes to gain justice in our courts or in our society.

I shall return to this question after recounting the history of civil legal services in the United States, including the past twenty-five years. There are hints in that history which may help explain this nation's continuing failure to follow the European path, especially the Northern European path,[12] towards guaranteeing

[11] 'We the people of the United States, in Order to form a more perfect Union, *establish Justice*, insure domestic Tranquility, provide for the common defence, promote the general Welfare, and secure the Blessings of Liberty to ourselves and our posterity, do ordain and establish this Constitution of the United States of America' (Preamble, Constitution of the United States of America (emphasis added)).

[12] Some countries in Southern Europe—esp. Italy, Spain, and Greece—remain at 'stage 1' of the general pattern of development on that continent. That is, they have created a statutory or constitutional right to counsel in civil cases but still depend largely on uncompensated lawyers to supply the required representation. Thus far reformers in these countries have been unsuccessful in moving their legislators forward to the next stage. (See e.g. Proposed Law no. 453, Institution of State Aid for the Poor, introduced in Italy in 1973 and passed by the Italian Senate on 24 May of that year. This bill would have moved Italy to stage 2 by providing compensation for counsel serving the poor as well as streamlining the process. Unfortunately it died when the then ruling Italian government fell before the House of Deputies could act on the proposal. The details of the proposed legislation are explained in Capelletti, *The Emergence of a Modern Theme*, in Cappelletti, *et al.*, 1975, 1981:36–8.

lawyers to those unable to afford their own in civil cases. For now it is enough to know American politicians and judges have spoken much about the importance of equal justice but American governments have never accepted that as a fundamental obligation.

The desire to guarantee equal justice to all citizens was not the primary impulse behind the two key events in American legal aid history. Both the first local legal aid programme and, some ninety years later, the government's first funding of civil legal services for the poor were inspired by something else: a hope that lawyers and the law could be used to improve the lives of poor people.

It was exactly a hundred years after the Declaration of Independence and its axiom 'all men are created equal' and endowed with 'certain inalienable rights' before anyone anywhere in this new land decided it was time to give poor people legal counsel. In the nation's largest city a small group, not of lawyers or judges but of businessmen, gathered in 1876 to consider what to do about a growing social problem affecting their ethnic community. They were all German-Americans who had come to this country many years earlier and prospered. But they saw the latest wave of immigrants from their original homeland suffering exploitation at the hands of 'runners, boarding-house keepers and a miscellaneous coterie of sharpen'. They decided lawyers could do something to help these victims, and on March 8, 1876 formed Der Deutsche Rechtsschutz Verein. The founding businessmen contributed funds, opened an office, and employed a lawyer to represent impoverished German-Americans, who at that time were arriving in New York City by the thousands.

Within a few years Der Deutsche Rechtsschutz Verein evolved into the New York Legal Aid Society serving the city's poor without reference to ethnic background. But it had already established the basic format of legal aid in the United States for the next ninety years: (1) funding through private charitable donations, (2) representation provided by salaried attorneys, (3) attorneys based and services delivered at special legal aid offices, (4) administration by local non-profit organisations, usually called legal aid societies, rather than the courts or government, and (5) services limited to the number of clients who can be handled by the limited number of salaried lawyers the local society can employ with the funds donated. Not only this first legal aid venture in New York but several other pioneer societies were started by social service agencies—the Ethical Society in Chicago, for instance, and settlement houses in several other cities—rather than bar associations.

Some of these features characterise the delivery of civil legal services to America's poor even today. Indeed, for the most part only the sources and level of funding have changed, along with the development of more sophisticated forms of advocacy. As is obvious, this 'American pattern' of civil legal aid differs from the 'European pattern' in every one of these characteristics. In most of

He left for a position at the White House, which later led to his appointment as Secretary of Defense.

While the regionalisation controversy occupied centre-stage in Washington, back in California Governor Reagan launched a further assault on CRLA. This statewide programme supplied most of the legal representation available to farm workers and other poor people in the state's rural areas. The Reagan administration found a point of vulnerability in the gubernatorial veto included in one of the OEO Act's more curious provisions. This section allowed a state governor to 'veto' an annual grant to any OEO-funded operating in that state. The same section, however, contained a safety valve. The OEO Director had the power to 'override' a governor's veto and commit the agency's funds to the grantee despite the governor's objection.[25]

In 1970 Governor Reagan announced his veto of CRLA's refunding grant for the coming year. He accompanied the veto announcement with a massive report lodging dozens of separate charges alleging CRLA lawyers had acted illegally or unethically. This veto and the supporting allegations presented the Nixon administration with a serious political challenge. Ronald Reagan was already a powerhouse within the Republican party and chief spokesman for the conservative wing of the party. He even posed an outside threat to challenge Nixon for the 1972 nomination if the president lost too much credibility with those same conservatives. It was politically costly to override Reagan's veto. At the same time, however, to honour that veto and close down CRLA invited a firestorm of criticism in Congress, the press, the ABA, and the legal profession in general. So the decision whether to override this particular gubernatorial veto could not be left with the OEO Director. The issue quickly escalated to the White House and the President's chief policy advisors.

OEO and the White House eventually devised a tactical solution. They appointed a blue-ribbon commission to examine Reagan's charges against CRLA. This commission consisted of three retired state supreme court justices, all Republicans, and was asked to conduct open hearings to consider the charges and recommend whether CRLA should be refunded. If Reagan's charges stood up, no one in congress or the media could object to defunding CRLA. But if those charges proved meritless, Governor Reagan could not seriously object to an override of his veto.

Governor Reagan's office refused to co-operate with the inquiry, but the commission proceeded anyway. The three retired justices took their assignment very seriously. They spent months gathering documentary evidence as to each of the charges. Then they held twenty days of hearings, taking sworn testimony from over 100 witnesses (George, 1976:684–6). Shortly thereafter, the commission issued its report completely exonerating CRLA of each and every allegation. The report included a sharp rebuke of the Governor's office for having 'unfairly and irresponsibly subjected many able, energetic, idealistic and dedicated CRLA

[25] Public Law No. 88–452 sec. 209(c), 78 Stat. 508 (1964). N. 1983:599.

attorneys to totally unjustified attacks upon their professional integrity and competence'. (OEO, 1971:83–4).

After the Administration's hand-picked commission issued this report, the new OEO Director Frank Carlucci (also destined to become a Secretary of Defense), had no choice but to override Governor Reagan's veto (George 1976:687). But the whole political debacle—the CRLA confrontation on top of the regionalisation fight and the Lenzner firing—only served to reinforce the administration's resolve to rid themselves of responsibility for this controversial programme. Even while the CRLA inquiry was still underway OEO and the White House had made overtures to the small group of legal services supporters who had been working since early 1969 on a proposal to create an independent quasi-public corporation or foundation to assume control of the Legal Services Program. Those first overtures came in late 1970. It was a tortuous three-and-a-half years later before the Legal Services Corporation became a reality.

I have told the story of the origins of the Legal Services Corporation legislation before (Johnson, 1978, ix–xxiii), and others have completed that story elsewhere (see e.g. Note, 1983: 600–4; Buck, 1976:616–23). Thus I will only provide a capsule version here, enough to suggest the LSC had a tempestuous birth just as it has had a tempestuous life.

It all really began in January 1969 with the legislative committee of the National Advisory Committee to the OEO Legal Services Program. I happened to chair the committee which also included Jerome Shestack and Bill McCalpin, who then and now were respected leaders in the organised bar and firm supporters of the legal services programme.[26] The committee developed a proposal for a new independent entity to rescue the Legal Services Program from what it perceived to be a sinking Office of Economic Opportunity.[27] While originally called the 'National Justice Foundation', the proposal contained all the essential features eventually embodied in the first Legal Services Corporation bill,[28] and indeed committee memoranda used the term 'corporation' interchangeably with 'foundation'.[29]

[26] Shestack was the President of the American Bar Association for 1997–8. Earlier he was one of the founders of the ABA Section on Individual Rights and Responsibilities and chaired the ABA Standing Committee on Legal Aid and Indigent Defendants. (See note 14 above, and accompanying text about creation of this committee.) Over the past 3 decades McCalpin has been Secretary of the ABA, President of the National Legal Aid and Defender Association, Chair of the ABA Standing Committee on Legal Aid and Indigent Defendants, and twice a board member and once a Chair of the Legal Services Corporation itself.

[27] See Memorandum from Earl Johnson, Jr to NAC Legislative Committee, dated 3 Jan. 1969. (Memorandum in Archives of the National Equal Justice Library, n. 20 above.)

[28] The initial 'National Justice Foundation' proposal called for an entity completely independent of any government department or agency. It created a board combining Presidential appointees with members serving by virtue of office in the legal profession or by way of appointment by other elements of the justice system. It gave the Foundation the affirmative responsibility to ensure no one interfered with the independence of lawyers serving the poor. (Draft proposal accompanying 9 Jan. 1969 memorandum from Earl Johnson, Jr to NAC Legislative Committee.)

[29] See e.g. Memorandum, n. 27 above.

President's decision when he 'came out for Nixon's resignation. I made clear in my statement that it had nothing to do with Watergate' (Strober, 1994:469).

Passage of the Legal Services Corporation ushered in a second era of expansion for the legal services programme. Far too short, however. In the five years from 1975 through 1980 the budget increased fourfold, bringing it to its zenith (in real terms) of $321 million[30] during fiscal year 1981. This brought what LSC called 'minimum access' (one lawyer for every 5,000 poor people) to every one of over 3,000 counties in the land. At this peak, there were over 6,000 legal services lawyers serving the poor: still only about a quarter of what would be required to meet the full estimated need, but far closer than this nation has ever come before or since.

One can only speculate what might have happened had the political climate remained the same. Who knows, the United States might have continued increasing its investment in equal justice for the poor. And this country might have begun recognising that the legal needs of the near poor and the middle classes also required some government subsidies for legal representation. We might even have moved in the direction of a guaranteed right to justice in civil cases.

But none of this was to be. The 1980 election brought another change in Presidents. The Legal Services Corporation went from administration favourite to administration nemesis. Possible elimination, not expansion, was in the future. Survival, not growth, was the best legal services could hope for.

III. The continuing ordeal: 1981–98

Another Chapter of this book (Kilwein) describes in great detail the political travails the Legal Services Corporation has had to endure over the last quarter century. I do not propose even to attempt to duplicate that impressive undertaking. But I do want to underscore what I view as the nearly unique nature of the opposition America's legal services programme has faced during both the OEO Legal Services Program and the Legal Services Corporation eras.

Other chapters of this book describe a common theme—the shrinking of the welfare state in most countries and with it shrinking budgets for legal aid programmes (or at least attempts to slowdown the growth in those budgets). The American experience is very different, however, on at least three counts.

First, the budget of the US programme at its height was minuscule compared to England and many other European countries. At the peak, the annual LSC budget was $1.65 *per capita*, and is now only a few pennies over $1 *per capita*. With a population more than five times England's, the current LSC budget is not

30 This is equivalent to roughly $650 million in 1998 dollars. The LSC budget in FY 1998 is $283 million.

even one-sixth what the English Legal Aid Board spends on civil representation for that nation's poor people.[31] In other words, England spends over *thirty times* more *per capita* than does America's Federal government on equal justice for its low-income citizens. If the US Congress were as generous as the English Parliament, the Legal Services Corporation's annual budget would be nearly *nine billion* dollars instead of 283 *million*.

Civil legal services expenditures also represent a much smaller component of the government's total justice system budget in the United States than many other countries. The United States has fifty state court systems as well as the Federal courts, so national statistics simply don't exist. But according to best estimates Federal and state governments in this country invest something between 13 and 15 billion dollars on their court systems.[32] This means the US is only spending on its LSC budget roughly *two per cent* of the amount the nation spends on its court system. Even if we add in the 50 to 90 million dollars currently devoted to civil legal services through state IOLTA programmes and another roughly 100 million spent for this purpose by a miscellany of federal and state government programmes, the combined governmental commitment remains *below four per cent* of the government investment in its court system. In contrast, the English civil legal aid budget is larger than its current annual expenditures on the judiciary. Even in Quebec Province, Canada, which spends only a quarter as much *per capita* on civil legal services as England, the civil legal services budget is *sixty per cent* as large as that jurisdiction's judicial budget.[33]

What this means is the LSC budget simply is not a factor in the overall governmental budget—or even the total justice system budget. Complete elimination of the programme would not accomplish meaningful savings. Thus budgetary restraint is not a real motivation or realistic explanation for the ongoing attempts

[31] In 1997, the English government spent over £985 million—the equivalent of over $1.5 billion—on civil legal services for its lower-income citizens (information from Legal Aid Board). That is nearly $33 *per capita* compared to the $1.08 *per capita* the US government spent on the same function. (The figures supplied from LAB are the gross civil figures, prior to recoveries from the other side or contributions by the assisted parties being factored in.)

[32] Robert Tobin, an authority on court financing at the National Center for State Courts, Williamsburg, Virginia, estimates total funding for state courts at between $10 and $12 billion annually. Mr Tobin's estimate appears in a letter dated 7 July 1997 from the Director of Information Services at the Center, Kenneth G. Pankey, Jr. The National Center on State Courts compiles an annual report of state court statistics and Tobin states as yet there exists no aggregate study of funding for all state court systems. Meantime the Federal government spends slightly over $3 billion on the Federal court system (US Bureau of the Census, Statistical Abstract of the United States: 1996 116th edn. Washington DC, 1996). Thus, combining state and federal courts it appears the United States spends something between $13 to $15 billion dollars annually on its judicial system.

[33] In 1996–97 Quebec spent 73.15 million Canadian dollars on civil legal services ($9.75 *per capita*) and 123 million ($16.40 *per capita*) on total judicial expenditures (legal aid expenditures from Annual Report (1997), Commission des Services Juridiques. Judicial expenditure figures provided via 13 March 1998 Electronic Mail Letter from Jeannine Lahaye, Direction des Communications, Ministere de la Justice du Quebec).

to reduce or phase out the Legal Services Corporation. Furthermore, the comparatively tiny size of the US programme also means any cutbacks—or slowdowns in growth—of legal aid budgets in other nations seem a rather minor inconvenience from this side of the Atlantic. A reduction from $33 *per capita* to $30 *per capita* or even to $10 *per capita* arouses little sympathy in a country that never got up to $2 *per capita*, is now at $1 *per capita* and which has powerful political opponents who would like to reduce it to fifty cents *per capita* on the way to zero.

Secondly, unlike most countries the budget has not been growing—dramatically or otherwise—in the past decade or two. In real terms, the LSC budget reached its peak in 1980, at $321 million, or about $1.25 *per capita*. In 1994, the budget which had fallen as low as $241 million during the Reagan years rose to $400 million. But that represented less than $200 million in 1980 dollars. While many so-called 'welfare state' programmes were seeing their budgets double, triple and even quadruple from 1980 until the present day,[34] federal government spending on legal services moved in the opposite direction—cut to less than half the 1980 level.[35]

As a result, unlike England and perhaps some other European countries, legal services expenditures are not and cannot be viewed as an out of control item in the nation's balance sheet. For the same reason, budget considerations obviously have nothing to do with the opponents' antipathy to the programme.

Finally, we come to what I view as the true reason for LSC's unhappy experience with the current Congress and before that with Governor and then president Reagan, and with others along the way. Unlike the budget concerns behind proposed cutbacks in legal services funding in other countries, in the United States the opposition has nothing to do with expanding government budgets and everything to do with a complex combination of factors which may be unique to this country—political, philosophical, and economic.

This array of problems begins with a repeat of the cycle the private legal aid societies went through from their vigorous reformist beginnings in the last quarter of the nineteenth century to their timid performance during the middle third of the twentieth century. In both instances, lawyers representing the poor eventually fell victim to opposition from those who held the purse strings and felt threatened by what those lawyers were capable of doing for their clients. In the case of the legal aid societies—as suggested earlier—those purse strings were held by local businesses whose donations supplied the revenues needed to operate the societies.

[34] From 1980 to 1994 Medicare expenditures (health care for the elderly) increased 451.2 per cent, MedicAid (health care for the non-elderly poor) increased by 464.4 per cent, Social Security expenditures (retirement income for the elderly and disabled) increased by 262.9 per cent and Aid for Dependent Children (primary income supplement programme for poor) increased by 183.3 per cent (Statistical Abstract, 1996: pp. 111, 181, 74, 381 and 483).

[35] The $321 million budget of FY1981 is the equivalent of $624 million in 1997 dollars. Thus, in real terms the current budget of $282 million is only 45 per cent of the 1980 budget.

Now once again businesses control the purse strings. Only this time it is their generous political donations to key congressional leaders which put them in a position to stop legal services lawyers from providing vigorous representation to poor people.

More than one wag has explained this phenomenon by pointing out the difference between government-paid health services and government-paid legal services: 'Defeated germs don't make political contributions, but losing litigants do.' If germs did, those wags continue, many of the politicians who are currently committed to ending the legal services programme, or at least stopping its lawyers from using the most effective legal tools like class actions and legislative advocacy, would also be clamoring to eliminate Medicare and to prevent government-paid physicians from using antibiotics and vaccines and any other truly effective cure for disease.

There is real question whether other countries can take any important lessons from the recent unhappy history of civil legal services in the United States. That is because the nature and strength of the opposition appears unique to this nation.

A common explanation begins with the observation that for a variety of reasons, well documented in recent years, the United States political system is far more susceptible than European democracies to the preferences of major private donors. Campaigns cost exorbitant sums. Public funding is not available, except for presidential races and local elections in a few communities. In common with most elections, senate and house races must be funded entirely with private donations. Different legislators and other office holders are beholden to different donors, often depending on the dominant economic interests in the geographic district from which they were elected. Of particular relevance to legal services history, those coming from rural areas of Florida, Texas, Georgia, Mississippi, and California, for instance, receive much of their financial support from major agricultural interests—generally large farming enterprises, often corporations, who also happen to be the nation's largest users of migrant farm labour.

Before the Federal government started funding legal services lawyers those migrant workers had *no* legal representation and thus no way of enforcing legislation enacted to protect them. That all changed with the creation of California Rural Legal Services, Florida Migrant Legal Services, Texas Rural Legal Services, and similar programmes. These legal services lawyers soon began bringing lawsuits to enforce labour and safety and housing laws. As a result, farm enterprises perceived their labour costs were increasing and they might lose markets to foreign producers.

Thus, most legal services supporters point out, from the beginning many agricultural businesses saw legal services lawyers as their enemies and committed their considerable political resources to removing this threat from their fields. As the dominant political contributors in many rural areas, they were immediately able to assemble a determined band of Congressmen and Senators to oppose the OEO Legal Services Program. At first they lacked the power to do more than snipe and threaten. For a variety of reasons unrelated to legal services itself, however, during the past two decades many politicians whom agribusiness has long supported have assumed leadership positions in both political parties, but especially the Republican party. Ronald Reagan moved from Governor of the largest agricultural state and the biggest user of migrant labour to eight years as President. For most of the past five years both the United States Senate and the House of Representatives have been headed by men elected from Southern agricultural states. Many of their chief lieutenants also come from those same states.

As a result of these political developments, legal services supporters emphasise, agribusiness's unique level of hostility toward legal services lawyers—shared by no other powerful national interest group—rises much higher on the political agenda than its comparative influence would otherwise warrant. Most other economic and political power groups have remained neutral or completely disinterested in agribusiness's war against legal services lawyers. Indeed many legal services supporters ask the question: if agribusiness were out of the equation, would the OEO Legal Services Program and the Legal Services Corporation have enjoyed a smoother relationship with Congress and the executive branch this last quarter century? I am not at all certain about the answer to that question. In any event, it is only a hypothetical issue in the United States. But for other countries seeking to learn from our experience, it may have some considerable relevance.

In recent years, however, another political development unique to the United States has worsened the prospects for an adequate legal services programme in this nation even further. That phenomenon is the rise of a highly organised, well financed campaign advocating 'civic justice reform' or 'tort reform'. This movement enjoys a very broad base of support among economic power groups: not just agricultural interests, but manufacturers, major retailers, insurance companies, bankers, the health care industry, and the like. To its supporters, this movement represents an attempt to eliminate abuses which threaten the prosperity, the competitiveness, and even the survival of the American economy. To opponents, it is a plot aimed at reducing the individual citizen's ability to hold major economic institutions accountable for their actions or to obtain redress for the harm they suffer when these institutions misbehave. This bundle of legislative proposals includes at least the following:

- changes in contingent free arrangements to reduce the availability of contingent fee lawyers to represent individuals seeking redress for the injuries they suffer;
- arbitrary 'caps' or limits on the amount of monetary compensation injured people can recover no matter how much harm they actually suffered, thereby further limiting access to contingent fee lawyers, as well as reducing the cost to economic enterprises;
- elimination or severe restriction of 'punitive damages' which otherwise provide economic institutions a strong incentive to change behaviour harmful to the public;

- a shift from the 'American Rule' to a 'loser pays' allocation of legal fees and litigation costs in order to dissuade individuals from suing institutional opponents;[36] and
- a forced transfer of cases out of the public courts which offer trial by jury, a broader range of remedies, and public exposure of misconduct, and into private arbitration which offers individual litigants none of these.

Thus far, the 'civil justice reform' movement has achieved success only in some states and generally only in favour of some industries. In California, for instance, the Legislature enacted legislation embodying several of these 'reforms' but primarily only for the health care industry. For injury resulting from negligent health care, this legislation capped 'pain and suffering damages' at $250,000 (even for a lifetime of quadriplegia or its equivalent), cut contingent fee percentages to as little as 15 per cent of recoveries above $600,000, and specifically authorised health care providers to require patients to surrender their right to jury trial and substitute private arbitration of their claims.[37] Recently, however, there have been experiments with 'loser pays' fee-shifting for all forms of litigation in certain California counties, and many banks and financial institutions now require their customers to give up their right to jury trial in any disputes with those institutions. And every year the civil justice reform forces introduce bills which would make all these changes for litigation involving any industry.

Reserving entirely any comment on the merits of these proposals, it is obvious they have profound implications for lower-income litigants. Some of these measures affect legal services lawyers directly because they change the rules for cases those lawyers are handling just as they do for other lawyers. And others affect them indirectly because they decrease the availability of contingent fee lawyers to serve the poor in certain types of cases. When no contingent fee lawyer can afford to take an injured person's case, that person has no recourse but to seek representation from a legal services office. If the office responds, it must divert resources from other clients and cases to undertake representation that in an earlier time would have been provided by another type of lawyer not paid out of government funds.

But the even more important consequence for the legal services programme is more subtle—and political. The 'civil justice reform' movement is extraordinarily well financed, as one would expect, and because of that and the power of its sponsors carries enormous political clout. The campaign has spent hundreds of

[36] Although justified as a means of discouraging 'frivolous' litigation, in reality most analysis and empirical research indicates individuals are risk averse, justifiably so since as 'one-shotters' they can't balance losses with wins (see e.g. Zander, 1975; Rowe, 1984). Institutional litigants, on the other hand, as repeat players with deep litigation pockets can afford the risk. As a result, a 'loser pays' system discourages individuals from filing any lawsuits except sure winners especially against the institutions that can afford to invest whatever it takes in the litigation game (Galanter, 1974).

[37] These provisions are found in California's Medical Injury Compensation Reform Act (MICRA) enacted in 1975 (Stats. 1975, Second Extraordinary Session, Chapter 2).

millions publicly criticising contingent fee lawyers, the jury system, punitive damages, frivolous lawsuits, overly generous jury awards, and the like. Although not aimed directly at legal services for the poor, this movement has generated a hostile political climate wider and deeper than its primary legislative goals, a climate that says litigation is *bad* and anything which might increase litigation is *bad*. It also is an anti-lawyer climate, ironically focused entirely on lawyers representing individuals and who are characterised as greedy sharks and worse. It is easy for politicians in any way influenced by the powerful civil justice reform coalition to see appropriations for legal services as just using public money to do a bad thing—more *bad* lawyers to file more *bad* lawsuits. As a result, this civil justice reform movement and especially the climate it has created is yet another political obstacle, perhaps unique to the United States, which legal services lawyers must face in coming years.

These are the political realities facing proponents of civil legal services for the poor in the United States—at least for the near future and maybe well into the next century. A powerful core opposition in Congress focused directly on the goal of ending government-funded legal services for the poor, many of whose members are financially beholden to an interest group with an economic stake in the achievement of that goal. Secondly, a well orchestrated and well financed anti-lawyer, anti-litigation climate produced by the nation's most powerful interest groups that threatens to envelop the Legal Services Corporation and government-funded representation of the poor along with all other lawyers representing individual citizens.

What has saved the Legal Services Corporation from utter destruction, thus far, is a group of Republicans in the House and Senate not beholden to agricultural interests or to an extreme political philosophy opposing government funding of legal representation for the poor. Although many of them probably support the civil justice reform agenda itself they have also avoided confusing that message with funding of equal justice for the poor. These Republican legislators have broken ranks with their leadership and voted to maintain federal funding of legal services for the poor, even though admittedly with restrictions which are incompatible with true equal justice for this population.

IV. The non-government sector

The American experience may differ from most other countries in another way. Here the national government's programme, in this instance the Legal Services Corporation, is not the only source of legal representation for poor people. They can also look to contingent fee lawyers, *pro bono* (volunteer, uncompensated) lawyers, and those attorneys willing to work for the prospect of earning court-awarded legal fees. All three of these augment the supply of civil legal services available to the poor in the United States.

Contingent fee lawyers. Although statistics are hard to come by, it is entirely possible that in the United States contingent fee lawyers currently provide as much legal representation to poor people as government-paid lawyers do, given the paucity of public resources presently committed to the latter. This does not mean half the legal problems poor people face are of a type sufficient to generate a recovery attractive to lawyers working on a contingency basis. Rather it reflects the fact that poor people can usually get legal representation for the types of cases that generate fees, but can seldom get representation for those that don't. Were adequate public funds devoted to the latter, contingent free lawyers would still be handling the same quantity of cases they are today. But that would amount to far less than the roughly fifty per cent of the total representation available to poor people which this contingency fee sector provides today.

Nevertheless, no one can dispute poor people in the United States have access to a source of free legal representation unavailable to their compatriots in most other countries where contingent fees remain illegal. Whether America's poor can look to contingent fee lawyers to take care of 5 per cent of their legal problems or 25 per cent—or something in between—is difficult to calculate. No cases in which poor people are defendants offer any possibility of fees. Nor do family law cases between poor people, even if the client is a plaintiff. The same is true of landlord–tenant, consumer, government benefit, and most others in the 'poverty law' category which form the grist of a practice serving poor people. Indeed except for auto accidents, medical malpractice, workers' compensation, and similar cases involving physical (or sometimes psychological) injuries, poor people seldom have cases which would appeal to lawyers on a contingent fee basis. So at best the contingent fee system offers free representation to poor people in a discrete, although admittedly important, segment of their universe of legal needs.

Ironically, current trends threaten to shrink the contingent fee sector at the same time as government-funded legal services remain woefully inadequate to the need for legal services in areas contingency lawyers could never serve. On its face, the contingent fee approach seems the exemplar of a 'market-based' solution to the need for legal representation among poor people. After all, it draws not one dollar of government subsidy. Nor does it require one iota of government regulation. One would expect free-market advocates, in and out of the legislature, to seek out and endorse anything calculated to increase the supply of this form of legal services. Yet as we have already seen, the contingent fee system is a prime target of the 'civil justice' (or 'tort reform') movement, itself a product of those who, for the most part, are otherwise among the most fervent 'free marketeers' in the country. By capping recoveries and fees in high damage cases, these proposed reforms reduce the economic cushion that makes it possible for contingent fee lawyers to take on smaller and riskier cases. The inevitable result is less contingent fee legal services for poor people.

Pro bono *lawyers.* Even disasters can yield some benefits. Just as 'necessity is the mother of invention', so political disaster can be the mother of social responsibility. The 1980s brought the threatened extinction and the actual decline of government-funded legal services for the poor. Those years also gave birth to a new national movement—*organised pro bono* legal services. What had started in a few cities in the 1970s as a way of matching volunteer private lawyers with the still unmet legal needs of the poor evolved quickly into a massive effort to enlist members of the private bar and organise their donated services to respond to the LSC's reduced funding. Encouraged and co-ordinated by the American Bar Association, many local bar associations or local legal services agencies, and sometimes both, took the lead. They formed *pro bono* projects and *pro bono* organisations and *pro bono* partnerships. By the 1990s most cities of any size had a *pro bono* programme staffed with salaried lawyers who recruited, trained, and co-ordinated volunteer private lawyers to serve some of the unmet legal needs of the poor. Through these programmes, scores of thousands of lawyers donate hundreds of thousands of hours to representation of the poor.

These *pro bono* lawyers compensate for some of the LSC's loss of financial resources by taking on some of the routine legal representation the reduced force of legal services lawyers can no longer handle. But in recent years their most important role may have been to take on cases LSC-funded lawyers are no longer permitted to undertake. As pointed out above and documented in Chapter 2 of this book, Congress has imposed restrictions on what legal services lawyers can do in representing their clients: no more class actions, no more legislative advocacy, no more representation at all of certain clients, e.g. aliens, or in certain types of cases, e.g. abortion rights. It makes no difference the clients are too poor to hire anyone to do any of these things.

Some private law firms are especially well equipped to take on the precise kinds of representation Congress has told LSC-funded legal services agencies they can no longer provide to their clients. Major corporate law firms make their living performing these very functions for their well-heeled business clients. So it is not surprising these firms find they can contribute most to the poor by doing the very things for them that they have been doing all along for the rich—test cases, class actions, legislative advocacy, and the like. While no replacement for legal services agencies in these fields, the *pro bono* programmes help ease the pain flowing from congressional enactment of these restrictions.

Court-awarded fees. Although *mutual* 'loser pay' fee-shifting is the norm elsewhere in the world, the prevailing model in the United States—the so-called 'American Rule'—expects winners as well as losers to absorb their own legal fees. This allows legislatures and sometimes courts to promote socially desirable litigation through *one-way* fee-shifting—that is by awarding one side, usually successful plaintiffs, their legal fees if they win but not allowing defendants to recover if the case goes the other way. By offering this bounty, court-awarded fees make it economically feasible for private lawyers to supply legal representation to classes of clients and in categories of cases they could not otherwise consider taking on.

Some statutes simultaneously define a legal right and provide the incentive of one-way fee shifting to encourage enforcement of that particular right. But it is not uncommon for a legislature to create a 'catch-all' law authorising court-awarded fees for any lawsuit which both advances the public interest and would not be brought unless clients and lawyers were offered this bonus. California's statute is typical. To earn a court-awarded fee, a client must demonstrate (1) that the case vindicated an important public right, (2) benefiting a large number of people, and (3) did not bring the client enough personal financial benefit from the victory to warrant absorbing the legal fees.[38]

Court-awarded fees augment the supply of legal services for poor people, but only in class actions or cases where the legal issue in dispute affects thousands of individuals. So the existence of this system for compensating private lawyers offers some relief in some cases from the restrictions Congress has imposed on LSC grantees and their lawyers. If California is any measure, however, it represents only a modest source of legal representation for the poor. As of 1994, court-awarded fees accounted for less than 3 per cent of the total universe of legal services provided to the poor in that state.[39]

The fact that poor people in the United States sometimes have recourse to legal services not dependent on government funding should not obscure their desperate situation in the vast majority of cases. After deducting the legal problems for which they can look to lawyers satisfied with a contingent fee, *pro bono* satisfaction, or court-awarded fees, there remains a huge residue of unfulfilled need. As discussed above, present levels of government funding barely begin to meet that need. Without a dramatic turnaround in this nation's commitment to government-paid civil legal services, the nation's low income citizens are doomed to a continued denial of the equal justice our political rhetoric seems to guarantee.

V. The future of equal justice in America

The American legal services programme seems destined to enter the twenty-first century with an uncertain future. In some respects it is like a small craft floating on the open seas: whether it survives and where it goes depends on the course of

[38] '. . . A court may award attorney's fees to a successful party . . . in any action which has resulted in the enforcement of an important right affecting the public interest if: (a) a significant benefit, whether pecuniary or nonpecuniary, has been conferred on the general public or a large class of persons, (b) the necessity and financial burden of private enforcement are such as to make the award appropriate, and (c) such fees should not in the interest of justice be paid out of the recovery, if any' California Code of Civil Procedure Section 1021.5.

[39] Access to Justice Working Group, 1996:23; see Table 7.

powerful political waves and currents far beyond its control. Tell us how far and high the present conservative wave continues before it crests and falls, and we will know a great deal about the existence and budget of the Legal Services Corporation in the year 2000 and beyond. Indeed it is entirely possible this will have more to do with LSC's fate than anything legal services supporters can do to improve its political prospects. One can paddle prodigiously and artfully against a powerful current and still succumb. Conversely, one can ride a favourable wave with little effort other than a few well placed strokes to maintain the proper course.

In my view, it is easier to set the proper course than to calculate how to get there should the ill winds continue to blow. Somehow civil legal services in the United States must achieve the status it has in the United Kingdom and most European countries—a matter of right, not charity of either the private or legislative variety.[40] That should be the goal. In my view, this should be the goal no matter what the direction of the political waves and currents. Unless and until legal representation of the poor in civil cases earns the status of a legally enforceable right its future will *always* remain in jeopardy.

To most legal services supporters in the United States this sounds like a terribly ambitious, maybe unreachable, goal. Meanwhile, to almost anybody in any other industrial democracy, it probably appears but a modest first step. But America is like an infant who has barely learned to crawl—and very late at that. To such a tardy baby the prospect of standing up and walking, even to totter unsteadily, seems impossible. Worse, the current political situation has people trying to knock this crawling infant off his knees and flat on the floor, thus turning the notion of actually standing up and walking into pure fantasy. The only thing that may keep the baby trying is the realisation that all these other smaller children are already walking around on their own two feet, maybe stumbling now and then, but walking nevertheless. So it *must* be possible, after all.

[40] Obviously, the right we are talking about is not absolute in the sense it means any person would have a right to free counsel for any case he or she might want to bring or defend. All the European and Canadian jurisdictions with such a right, of necessity, require the person to be financially eligible and for that person's case or defence to have some potential merit. For a discussion of the various formulas different countries use and a critique of their possible implications in the appellate context, see Cappelletti *et al.*, 1975, 1981:184–5, n. 105.

2

The Decline of the Legal Services Corporation: 'It's ideological, stupid!'

JOHN KILWEIN

Introduction

In the run-up to the 1992 American presidential election between incumbent George Bush and challenger Bill Clinton, Clinton campaign advisor James Carville was asked to explain the surprising success of his boss. After all, the campaign had highlighted Bill Clinton's past problems with marital infidelity and his avoidance of the draft during the Vietnam War, just one of which would have normally doomed a presidential candidate to defeat. The Bush campaign was baffled that its candidate was not connecting with the electorate, given his leadership during the Gulf War, his stable marriage, his past service in the military, and his conservative position on the moral and ideological issues that had been used in the past to appeal to a generally conservative American electorate. In declaring: 'It's the economy, stupid!' Carville concluded, correctly, in hindsight, that most Americans were less concerned with ideological wedge issues like abortion or the constitutionality of burning a US flag, and more concerned with their own economic well-being. No matter how hard the Republicans tried to focus the 1992 election on these ideologically divisive issues, the electorate resisted, focusing instead on what many perceived to be a stagnant economy. The presidential elections of 1992 and 1996, and the general shift to the right by President Bill Clinton, have led some to conclude that ideology will play less of a role in national politics in the United States in the next decade. For the most part, leaders of the Democratic and Republican parties agree that the focus of national government should be on retrenchment, i.e. cutting taxes, balancing the budget, and shifting power to the market and the states. The remaining battles deal, not with whether this retrenchment should occur, but with how it will be implemented.

Viewed comparatively, this consensus around retrenchment makes the United States part of a more general pattern observed in many of the industrialised nations where the welfare state developed and flourished. In Britain, France, Germany, Canada, and even the Nordic states, political parties on the right have convinced middle-class voters that they pay too much in taxes for government programmes that do not benefit them. The popularity of this 'let me keep mine' message has forced many left-of-centre parties to move to the right in a bid to attract these important voters. Jean Chretien's Liberals in Canada, Tony Blair's 'New' Labour Party in Britain, and Bill Clinton's Democrats have all appropriated substantial portions of their opponents' fiscal conservatism to gain, or retain, power. Rather than trying to convince voters that the principles of the social welfare state can be adapted to handle new and difficult demographic realities, e.g. an older population, these ersatz leftists argue instead that they will bring about a 'kinder, gentler', albeit inevitable, retrenchment than that offered by their conservative opponents.

One social welfare programme where this rush to reduce has had a particularly significant impact is legal aid. A number of liberal democratic governments are testing the political feasibility of reducing, or eliminating altogether, their role in providing legal assistance to those who otherwise cannot afford it. Leading this slashing of legal assistance was the United States, where the 1980s brought significant reductions to the federal government's support of the Legal Services Corporation (LSC), the federally funded agency charged with supporting a network of staffed legal services offices that provide legal assistance in civil matters.[1] Substantial cuts in government funding of legal aid have also been proposed or implemented in Australia, Britain, and many of the provinces of Canada. These changes add a renewed sense of urgency to ongoing comparative questions of definition, need, and purpose associated with legal aid.

Clearly, an understanding of the American experience with government-funded legal services should be an important part of trying to answer these larger questions. But, when placing American legal services politics and policy into a comparative context, it becomes clear that the United States is somewhat unique in terms of the general contraction of legal aid observed worldwide. Unlike the cuts to government-funded legal aid in many countries, the primary impetus behind cuts to the Legal Services Corporation is political ideology, rather than fiscal conservatism.

With these political realities in mind, this essay examines the state of legal aid in the United States at the close of the twentieth century, by focusing on the status of the Legal Services Corporation. First, the essay presents a brief review of how the legal services system developed in the United States, connecting that development to the general American welfare state. Next, the essay explores the political interests involved in American legal services policy debates. Thirdly, the essay describes the policy outcomes that have resulted from these debates: funding levels and rules of operation for the Legal Services Corporation and its grantees. The essay concludes by analysing the connection between legal services policy debates and practice, using a comparative perspective. By making comparisons with legal aid politics and practice in Ontario, Canada, this essay will highlight how American legal services fits into, and differs from, international

[1] Legal Services programmes are prohibited by law from representing criminal defendants.

patterns. The general conclusion of this essay is that the decline of the Legal Services Corporation and government-funded legal services in the United States is unique in that it is inspired not by fiscal conservatism, but instead by a thirty-year ideological battle waged by radical conservatives opposed to the idea of effective access for the poor to the legal system.

Legal aid in the American welfare state

In the United States, two systems have provided legal aid or assistance to those who otherwise could not afford counsel: legal aid and legal services. In the American context, legal aid refers to a system of legal aid societies that began to develop in the late 1800s in large metropolitan areas (see Smith, 1919; Brownell, 1951). By the mid-1960s these societies had spread to a substantial portion of the country and they were its only systematic providers of legal aid. Legal aid societies were private entities that relied on private funds to operate. They operated independently of each other and utilised staff attorneys to provide legal assistance to their clients.

The legal aid societies were heavily dependent on local bar associations and business leaders for support. As a result of this funding reality, societies pursued a practice that focused almost exclusively on providing individual services to clients in legal areas that would not offend their 'main street' sponsors. For example, legal aid societies were heavily involved in family issues, while they eschewed activities like debtor–creditor or landlord–tenant disputes, that might put them directly at odds with local business leaders. In addition to these substantive restraints, legal aid societies were required to establish extremely restrictive eligibility criteria, lest they rob private attorneys of potential paying clients. Although many legal aid societies continue to operate, their relative importance declined substantially with the advent of government-funded legal services in 1967.

Its design and style of practice made the legal aid movement a perfect complement to the American welfare state that existed prior to the creation of President Franklin Roosevelt's New Deal in the 1930s (see Fox Piven & Cloward, 1971; Katz, 1990; Patterson, 1994; Trattner, 1994). During this period, the social welfare needs of the poor in the United States were addressed, if at all, by an unorganised collection of programmes operated by state and local governments, private charities, and religious groups. These programmes were operated with the belief that the American economy provided opportunity for all citizens, and, therefore, each individual was responsible for his or her own welfare. Based on this belief, poverty was viewed as a personal failure, which the society had no responsibility to mitigate. Using this world view, subsistence-level social welfare assistance was targeted at the 'worthy' poor, people with special characteristics that made them unable to partake in the 'American dream', for example the severely handicapped or widows with children. There was no right or entitlement to these benefits; they could be expanded, contracted or eliminated as their providers saw fit.

Some argue that the first real American welfare state 'regime' was created as a response to the Great Depression of the 1930s (Quadagno, 1994:196–7). President Franklin Roosevelt's New Deal was unique in American history in that it set up national programmes, funded by the state, that sought to insulate some working-class Americans from certain types of financial insecurity. Specifically, the New Deal targeted workers who were temporarily unemployed, through the Unemployment Insurance programme. It provided elderly Americans with a greater opportunity to retire through the Old Age Assistance and Old Age Insurance (more commonly referred to as Social Security) programmes. And, through the Aid to Dependent Children (ADC) programme, the federal government, for the first time, provided funding to state programmes, developed earlier in the century, that assisted widows who were raising young children and who were, therefore, unable to work outside of the home. It should be noted that the New Deal did not affect the nature of legal aid in the country; aid in the courts was strictly within the purview of the local bar associations and the legal aid societies they sponsored, and bar leaders worked tenaciously to maintain this status quo.

While the creation of the New Deal welfare programmes is generally regarded as the birth of the American welfare state, Quadagno and others (see Lubove, 1986; Nelson, 1969; Patterson, 1967) show that these programmes essentially excluded black Americans, by exempting the agricultural sector of the economy. This exclusion was the result of a political compromise struck by the Roosevelt Administration with Southern members of Congress, in order to secure their support for New Deal legislation. These senators and representatives from the South sought to maintain the large pool of cheap farm labourers, most of whom were black. Unfortunately this shortsighted failure to deal with the country's most difficult and consistent social problem, the exclusion of black Americans from effective and equal participation in economic and political life, consigned the United States to continued racial unrest in the face of grinding *de jure* and *de facto* segregation and racism.

The post-World War II period brought major social and demographic changes to American society. Important among these was the large migration of Southern blacks to the industrial cities of the North. In most cases, these host cities did not deal well with their new reality, increasingly diverse populations. Racial tensions in the nation's urban areas were compounded by increased competition for the very industrial jobs that had lured the migrants north in the first place. These troubles encountered by blacks in the North and the continued existence of state-sanctioned segregation in the South gave greater impetus to the development of the civil rights movement, and began to raise the consciousness of some white Americans that the continuation of American *apartheid* was untenable. Politically, the Democratic Party, outside of the South, recognised that urban blacks comprised an important block of votes, and began to court this electorate with, among other things, a second American social welfare state regime, marked by President Kennedy's Great Society, and President Johnson's War on Poverty (see Haveman, 1973; Zarefsky, 1986). This second social welfare regime sought to complete the work left unfinished by the New Deal, namely to give the traditionally excluded—black, Hispanic, American Indian, and rural citizens—a chance for fuller participation in American society. An important part of this effort was the Office of Economic Opportunity, which funded and managed a number of anti-poverty programmes, including the precursor of the Legal Services Corporation, the Legal Services Program.

Two important characteristics made the OEO programmes innovative in terms of American social welfare policy. First, the programmes were designed to bypass state and local officials and labour union leaders (see Moynihan, 1970:145,182–5; Fox Piven & Cloward, 1971:ch. 9). These actors were viewed as hostile to the goal of serving OEO target populations, seeking instead to divert OEO dollars to middle-class constituents and union members. Unfortunately, this political move engendered substantial hostility among these excluded actors towards the War on Poverty programmes, thereby creating enemies who would haunt these programmes in the future.

The second innovation attempted by the OEO was its goal of seeking the 'maximum feasible participation' of its client communities in the design of specific programmes. Community Action Agencies, local programmes funded by OEO, were charged with seeking and implementing the goals of citizens who lived in poor communities (see Moynihan, 1970). For the most part, attempts to increase client participation, like the direct election of client councils that would affect programme management, were unsuccessful (ibid. 137). Still an important legacy of this experiment in administrative pluralism was the development of a politically aware cadre of urban activists, who would go on to populate many of the nations' city halls and state legislatures (Quadango, 1994:41–2).

It certainly cannot be argued that War on Poverty was a total victory; far from it. The collection of 1960s anti-poverty programmes did reduce hunger, improved education in some parts of the country, increased the poor's access to the organs of government and to health care (through the Medicaid programme) and broke down some artificial barriers to welfare benefits. But in the final analysis, the United States' other war in Vietnam saw to it that the anti-poverty effort would never come close to being fully funded. Still, for a brief period of US history, the American welfare state was better funded and the poor had a greater voice in its design.

It was during this unique period of the American social welfare state that the experiment with government-funded legal services was developed. Building on the experience of several private demonstration projects (see Weisman, 1969), the Office of Economic Opportunity funded the Legal Services Program in 1969.

The legal services experiment

In many ways, the Legal Services Program was a reaction to the perceived failures of the legal aid approach to serving the legal needs of the poor. The legal services movement brought with it a more activist approach to improving the poor's status before the justice system (see Cahn & Cahn, 1964). As envisaged by its creators, this style of poverty law demanded that a lawyer not only sought to address the individual problems of the poor, but also attempted to change governmental systems when they adversely affected the poor, by making policy. This policy change was to be pursued in all forums that might affect the status of poor clients. In the court-room, the lawyer was to seek broader change through test cases and class action suits. The creators of activist legal services also expected the poverty lawyer to expand his or her activities beyond the walls of the court-room. Legislative bodies and administrative agencies were to be confronted and lobbied by legal assistance agencies on issues that were likely to affect the client community. And an activist agency also was expected to be involved in organising citizen groups within the poverty community that sought to empower that community.

The American Bar Association (ABA) was heavily involved in this developmental stage of the Legal Services Program and greatly affected the nature of the implemented Program (Johnson, 1978:39–70). The ABA itself had recognised the need to expand the level of legal assistance available to the poor prior to the creation of the Office of Economic Opportunity (ibid. 55) and gave its support to the proposed Program in February 1965. That support was contingent on the ABA being given a formal role in developing the new agency's agenda. The agreement mandated local bar association approval of proposed local legal services programmes. In addition, the ABA won assurances that existing legal aid societies would be eligible to apply to be local legal services grantees if they so desired, provided they changed their policies to match those of the OEO Legal Services Program. OEO leaders also agreed in their negotiations with the ABA to a requirement that lawyers would comprise a majority on the local projects' boards of directors.

The American Bar Association was involved in one other critical decision involving the design of the Legal Services Program: determining who would actually provide legal services to the client community. A coalition of OEO administrators and officials of the ABA thwarted an attempt by state and local bar associations to develop a judicare system like that which existed in England and Wales at the time, and would be established later in Australia and many of the Canadian provinces (Johnson, 1978:ch. 5). The administrators of the new programme viewed a judicare system, i.e. paying private attorneys directly for services rendered to individual clients, as a threat to the activist conception of poverty law behind the legal services project. Their opposition was based on three basic concerns: most private lawyers lacked any significant poverty law experience; there existed a serious potential conflict of interest between a private lawyer's judicare and non-judicare clientele; and a judicare system would not allow for an exchange of knowledge among programme participants that might lead to a more strategic response to the legal problems of the poor (ibid. 118). Instead, OEO administrators sought to staff local legal services programmes with salaried lawyers who would dedicate their professional work to an activist poverty law practice.

American Bar Association officials opposed a judicare system of legal aid for a different set of reasons. First, many of these leaders had experience with failed attempts at increasing the private bar's *pro bono* efforts to deal with the legal needs of the poor. These ABA officials feared that reliance on private lawyers, even with federal reimbursement, to provide legal aid was destined to fail. Other bar leaders were concerned that the lure of federal judicare dollars would attract the more marginal elements of the bar and result in a feeding frenzy that could tarnish the image of the entire legal profession (ibid. 118–19).

In the end, OEO administrators and ABA leaders were able to resist the calls for a judicare system by agreeing to fund several judicare demonstration projects, which would be monitored by the programme for their effectiveness. Other than these four demonstration projects, the initial local legal services programmes were all designed around a staff attorney model (ibid. 121). These programmes were, and still are, independent contractors, which are governed by local boards of directors drawn from the local legal and general communities. Daily operations are handled by programme managers, and legal services are provided by salaried staff attorneys.

Unlike the legal aid system, the OEO Legal Services Program grantees were connected to each other through several channels of communication established by the national Program, thereby increasing the likelihood of a more strategic and co-ordinated national poverty law effort (ibid. 176–7). The Legal Services Program produced a national newspaper, *Law in Action*, and a law review, *Clearinghouse Review*, for its programmes, both of which were designed to create a national legal services community and create a new field of poverty law. The Legal Services Program also created national training programmes and the Project Advisory Group, a body made up of local programme directors designed to provide the advice to the national programme. Finally in the sprit of activist poverty litigation, the OEO Legal Services Program created and, until 1996, the Legal Services Corporation continued to fund specialised law reform units designed to change law in specific substantive legal areas that affect the client population, e.g. youth law, immigration law, and senior law. These national support centres are staffed by attorneys who develop an expertise in the substantive area of the law that is the focus of the centre. Prior to 1996, the support centres pursued cases that were drawn from all of the local recipients of the Legal Services Corporation, choosing those cases best able to effect legal change. In

1995, at the urging of conservative groups and legislators who found the support centres too activist, Congress cut off their Legal Services Corporation funding. And in 1996, Congress created a 'gag' rule that forbade the Corporation, its recipients, and their personnel from referring cases to the national support centres.

In a move intended to depoliticise the provision of civil legal services, the Legal Services Corporation was created by Congress in 1974 (The Legal Services Corporation Act) as an independent corporation funded by the federal government to support financially the same local programmes that had been funded by the OEO Legal Services Program. Today the Legal Services Corporation is responsible for funding and supporting over 320 local programmes that provide actual client services. The Legal Services Corporation is not involved in directly serving the needs of clients. Instead, the Corporation enters into contracts with individuals, law firms, organisations, and state and local governments for the provision of legal assistance to the poor. Also, it is charged with setting income guidelines that must be used by the local projects when determining client eligibility. The Legal Services Corporation is required to audit its grantees to determine whether they are utilising their grants properly and following LSC managerial and litigation regulations. In addition, LSC provides training and research for its grantees' personnel and serves as a clearing-house for new information on poverty law.

Statistics complied by LSC show that in 1994 the local programmes served the great majority of their clients without resorting to litigation (Legal Services Corporation 1994). Only 15 per cent of the 1,686,313 cases closed in 1994 by LSC recipients involved litigation. Far more common reasons for case closure were: providing counselling and advice (35 per cent), brief legal service without litigation (22 per cent), and referring a client to another attorney (10 per cent). The four most common substantive case types dealt with by LSC grantees in 1994 were family law (33 per cent), housing issues (22 per cent), income maintenance (16 per cent), and consumer law (11 per cent). From a budgetary perspective, the Legal Services Corporation is quite a bargain; in 1996, LSC received $278 million in federal funds, and in 1997, $283 million, slightly more than a dollar *per capita* for civil legal assistance.

From the inception of the OEO Legal Services Program until about 1973, legal services attorneys won important victories in courts that reshaped the American welfare system, especially the programme that replaced the Aid to Dependent Children programme, Aid to Families with Dependent Children (AFDC). Beginning in 1969 with *Shapiro* v. *Thompson*, the local programmes won a series of constitutional decisions at the US Supreme Court that curtailed the ability of the welfare system to limit benefits through difficult eligibility criteria (Houseman, 1991). Both conservative and liberal observers agree that the litigation of Legal Services Program's grantees between 1967 and 1974 greatly increased the number of people receiving social welfare benefits (Murray, 1984:182; Fox Piven & Cloward, 1971:308). Legal services attorneys also won judicial decisions by asserting their clients' rights to benefits under federal social welfare statutes and administrative regulations, in essence forcing the government to live up to its Great Society promises to the poor. In addition, programme attorneys won important common law victories during this time period, e.g. giving renters greater rights under landlord–tenant law.

As the welfare system began to contract in 1974, local programmes found that they faced a more conservative federal judiciary less amenable to their calls for change. Gradually, programme attorneys have had to shift their practice to the state courts as the federal government has delegated more and more social welfare responsibilities to the states. No longer expecting to win cases that expand the provision of social welfare benefits, legal services programmes are engaged in actions designed to minimise the negative effects to the poor of the 1990s version of welfare retrenchment, which in 1997 includes the elimination of AFDC (Coyle, 1995).

In retrospect, most legal services programmes did not achieve the activist goals their foreparents envisaged for them, either by design or because excessive demand for individual services forced them to fall back to a more traditional individual client-centred approach (Katz, 1982). Still, the minority of programmes that did utilise a more activist approach to legal services tended to alienate powerful political, religious, and business leaders, and drew these powerful enemies into active participation in American legal services politics (Besharov, 1990).

Legal services politics

The experiment with government-funded civil legal services for the poor that the Legal Services Corporation embodies is at the centre of a set of very stormy political debates in the United States. These arguments deal with contentious intersections between law, the welfare state, racial, gender, and generational politics, and policy. Given this connection to so many important domestic issues, legal services politics in the United States have attracted the attention of a number of vocal actors and interest groups, who in turn have affected the nature of legal services in the United States. This section examines these players in American legal services politics, by looking first at supporters, and then opponents of government-funded legal services.

Supporters of legal services

Throughout its existence, the national legal services programme has had four important sets of supporters: the American Bar Association, client groups, public interest law groups, and Democratic politicians. In addition to a general concern about the availability of legal aid, each of these groups has had unique reasons for their support of the programme.

Without a doubt, the American Bar Association has been the most consistent and powerful non-governmental ally of the Legal Services Program/Corporation. A thirty-year review of Senate and House hearings dealing with legal services indicates that representatives of the ABA appeared at nearly every hearing, providing uniformly supportive testimony (Kilwein, 1997). By using its communications network, the ABA has also been at the forefront of mobilising political support from within the legal profession to defend the Legal Services Corporation from its opponents. The following call to arms contained in a flier distributed by the American Bar Association's Governmental Affairs Office, 6 April 1996, is typical of the group's mobilisation efforts on behalf of legal services:

LSC ALERT. The *real* battle over LSC has begun! Opponents of the program are organizing to end LSC once and for all. It is critical that we again reactivate all LSC Steering Committees and other advocacy groups and make contact with *all* Members to urge them to fund LSC in *'97 and beyond.*

Throughout the history of the programme, the ABA's main concerns have dealt with issues of funding and professional independence. With regard to funding, the ABA has called for continued increases in the budget for legal services, arguing that LSC recipients' staff lawyers provide expert, effective, and efficient service to the poor (see e.g. Cooper Ramo, 1996). Further, the ABA has argued for the need of private attorneys to live up to their professional responsibility to do *pro bono* work for the poor. Yet, recalling the woeful state of legal aid prior to the creation of the OEO Legal Services Program, the ABA has argued consistently that *pro bono* efforts must act as supplements to the work of legal services programmes, rather than as replacements of LSC and its grantees (see e.g. Bushnell 1995).

In addition to concerns over adequate LSC funding, the American Bar Association has been tenacious in its attempts to guard the independence of LSC and its recipients' staff attorneys to choose the strategies they feel best meet the needs of their clients, including the activist approach to service provision (see Johnson, 1978:124–6). The ABA has been especially concerned with the incremental diminution of permissible activities imposed on LSC and its grantees by Congress throughout the programme's history.

Clearly, the organised bar's concern over the continuation of government funding for legal services is motivated by more than an altruistic concern for the legal needs of the poor or a desire to maintain an independent legal services programme. Rick Abel is correct when he points out that 'private lawyers fear they will be called upon to render *pro bono* services in millions of cases if the federal funds are terminated, and many support staffed offices as a means of avoiding that obligation' (1985:508). It is for this reason that conservative critics have called on Congress, in legal services debates, to drop its traditional deference to the ABA in matters that affect the legal community (US Government, 1995:261).

When examining the underpinnings of the ABA's support of legal services it is impossible to untangle mercenary motives from a general concern for more equitable access to society's civil courts; clearly both are at play. If government funding of legal services ceased, the organised bar would undoubtedly feel strong pressure to make up at least part of the loss in services. There is no question that the continued existence of LSC enables most private attorneys to focus on their paying clients and their balance sheets. But this financial interest in the continued existence in government-funded legal services is different from that which exists in a judicare system of legal aid, where the financial link between many private lawyers and government-funded legal aid is direct: lawyers are paid by legal aid schemes for the work they provide to eligible clients. For a substantial portion of the bar in countries utilising a judicare system, this legal aid work makes up an important part of their income.[2] When the organised bar lobbies for increased funding of a judicare scheme, it is lobbying for, in addition to a more equitable civil justice system, direct benefits for its members, undoubtedly as a result of lobbying it has received from these members.

In the United States, on the other hand, the vast majority of lawyers receive no fees from the Legal Services Corporation. In fact, throughout the existence of the programme, some marginal private attorneys have argued, without strong supporting evidence, that the Legal Services Corporation's grantees were competitors for potential clients. For most private lawyers in the United States, their financial interest in government-funded legal aid is indirect. The Legal Services Corporation is insurance against a worst-case scenario, a scenario where private attorneys would see their profits reduced or eliminated through some type of forced *pro bono* legal aid system. Given the distant nature of this financial consequence, most private lawyers in the United States are indifferent to issues of legal services. This indifference gives the ABA freer rein over its legal aid policy, but it also requires that ABA resources be expended to call its membership into action to protect legal services.

The Legal Services Corporation has developed a long roll of supporting organisations throughout its history who have echoed many of the sentiments of the American Bar Association. Testimony before congressional committees over the last thirty years shows that supporters of legal services have praised the programme for the work it has accomplished, demanded increased funding for the programme, sought to maintain LSC independence, and made pleas for increased service in particular areas of the law affecting certain parts of the poverty community. Foremost among these allies are client groups representing broad interests, like the National Clients' Council, and groups representing specific portions of the client community, e.g. the National Council for Senior

[2] E.g. the Law Society of Upper Canada reports that almost 40% of Ontario's 17,000 lawyers participated in the Ontario Legal Aid Plan in 1996. Over 56% of those lawyers received more than CDN$10,000 from OLAP for services rendered (Law Society of Upper Canada, 1997:11).

Citizens. These organisations have appeared at nearly every legal services hearing, providing testimony on the importance of legal services to their members and calling for increased support for their members' special needs with the law. In addition, certain religious charities that serve the same client community as LSC, have come before congressional committees to argue that the elimination of LSC would make the already difficult position of the nation's poor and the private charities attempting to assist them unbearable, as the comments made by the President of Catholic Charities on behalf of LSC underscore:

> While individuals and communities can help to heal and minister to the poor, government's role must be to ensure a just society for everyone, including people in need. Without free legal advice and access to the civil courts, poor people simply cannot get justice in this country. Without the Legal Services Corporation and adequate Federal funding of it, there will be no justice (US Government, 1995:596).

Other consistent supporters of the programme are public interest law groups like the National Association for the Advancement of Colored People (NAACP), which represents the interests of African-Americans, and the American Civil Liberties Union (ACLU), a group dedicated to maintaining the individual civil liberty protections found in the US Constitution. Personnel from both organisations have often co-litigated impact cases with legal services staff over the years. Representatives of these law reform groups have focused their testimony on the importance of Legal Services Corporation impact litigation in securing the broader rights of the poor.

In general, Democratic legislators and presidents have been supportive of the Legal Services Corporation. This is in keeping with the Democratic Party's marginally greater concern, *vis-à-vis* the Republican Party, for the needs of poor in American society. The programme is especially popular in many urban districts that make up the bedrock of Democratic support. Carter and Clinton Administration officials consistently appeared before Congress to defend the programme. Representatives of federal and state administrative agencies have provided testimony praising the work of legal services attorneys with whom they have come into contact. For example, John P. Carey, General Counsel for the Federal Emergency Management Agency, came to the House to provide testimony that praised the swift and effective work of legal services workers in helping the poor deal with the effects of a series of natural and man-made disasters (US Government, 1995:124–32). And with time, big city mayors, a predominantly Democratic lot, have shifted their view of local grantees from that of external agitators to valued social services providers that cost their city budgets nothing.

It is worth noting that during its existence, legal services has faced criticism from observers who support its mission, but criticise the style of legal services practice in the United States. These critics complain that the programme is overly bureaucratised in its delivery of service. They contend that many local programmes handle clients' needs in an assembly-line fashion, often ignoring the uniqueness of each individual's problems (Bellow, 1977; Sarat, 1990). Others have doubted the legal system's capability to effect real policy change (Scheingold, 1974; Horowitz, 1977; Rosenberg, 1991). For example Stuart Scheingold, referring specifically to impact lawyering in legal services, suggests that legal services lawyers should focus less on appellate work and more on political activities like coalition building.[3] Anthony Alfieri (1987–8) argues that poverty lawyers who rely on impact lawyering and client lawyering actually help to perpetuate the existing power structure that works against the poor. Still, given the decreasing level of funding directed to the Legal Services Corporation and the rather conservative state of legal services politics in 1997, one might question the practicality of a call to move scarce legal services resources from litigation efforts to a greater focus on mobilisation efforts. For example, Paul Tremblay (1990) argues that, although the legal services lawyer would benefit from a better understanding of his or her clients and efforts to strengthen the sense of community among them: '. . . defects in poverty lawyering are structural, institutional, political, economic, and ethical. Teaching poverty lawyers to change their attitudes may be critically important, but those attitudes and the resulting behavior are largely products of the conditions under which poverty lawyers work' (1990:1132).

As Tremblay's comments indicate, the debate over the utility of a more activist legal services style in bringing about real change in the poverty community is in many respects an academic one. Creating and funding a system that allows legal services attorneys to engage in activities with the transformative impacts that Alfieri seeks is politically impossible in the present American political climate. And while it may be true that impact litigation was oversold in terms of its transformative potential, it has effected some change in some governmental systems and programmes that affect the legal services client community. Given the sustained attacks on the Legal Services Corporation, it has been the work of the ABA, Congressional Democrats, Democratic presidents, and other allies that have allowed the programme to continue to exist, albeit with incremental cuts to its budgets and discretion.

Opponents of legal services

Strong and vocal opposition to the idea and practice of government-funded legal services has been a constant element of the legal services environment in the

[3] For Scheingold and others, impact lawyering might actually work against the elimination of poverty. He argues that impact litigation contributes to a 'myth of rights'. Impact litigation victories change little in society and actually affect the poor negatively in that these ineffective solutions, impact cases, add a veneer of fairness and respectability to an unfair structure. Fundamental change in the condition of the poor will only come about through policy adopted in the legislative, executive and administrative branches of government which was brought about with pressure from a mobilised client community (Scheingold, 1984)

United States. Opponents to legal services fall into a number of groups with somewhat different motivations for their opposition.

Some conservatives oppose the programme on basic ideological grounds. They view the Legal Services Corporation and its recipients as nettlesome refugees from what they believe to be the failed leftist policy of the 1960s' War on Poverty. For example, Samuel Brakel, an attorney who headed the Reagan LSC transition team, argues that the legal services movement has failed to serve the true needs of the poor and should be replaced with a new system of legal assistance delivery (Brakel, 1982). To Brakel, legal services' failure is rooted in its focus on impact lawyering, ignoring, as do most conservative critics of legal services, that the vast majority of legal services work is individual care. Other conservative critics make the argument that the legal services experiment has in its thirty-year history actually worsened the status of the nation's poor and harmed society as a whole. For example, Howard Phillips argues that legal services litigation in the welfare arena has created a permanent class of welfare recipients who drain resources from the rest of society (US Government, 1995:261). In a similar vein, Ralph Reed, former Executive Director of the Christian Coalition, has argued that the Legal Services Corporation must be eliminated because it provides representation in divorces to over 200,000 poor citizens every year and in the process threatens basic American 'family values' (Pittsburgh Post-Gazette, 1995).

Other critics of legal services begin with the assumption that there probably should be some federal support to meet the legal needs of the poor and that, possibly, the Legal Services Corporation should be retained as the mechanism to serve that need (Besharov, 1990). But they argue that the focus of the Legal Services Corporation and its recipients must be shifted from the classic activist approach of the original OEO programme to one that focuses on the individual legal needs of individual clients, again ignoring the realities of legal services practice in the 1990s. For example, conservative policy analyst Douglas Besharov calls for even greater oversight by Congress over the Legal Services Corporation, and by LSC over its recipients, to ensure the nation that programmes are complying with the restrictions created by Congress (Besharov, 1990:ch. 2). Besharov also calls for greater client control over the development of the recipient programmes litigation priorities (ibid. ch. 3). Besharov and others have argued that the past work of legal services represented the interests of the leftist, middle-class attorneys who staff the programmes rather than those of the client community. Ironically, conservatives like Besharov have called for an increase in client participation in programme management, something programme originators lost in OEO's agreement with the ABA.

Probably the most threatening opponents that the Legal Services Corporation has developed in its history are those powerful actors in society that its local programmes have consistently prevailed against in the court-room. In the early years of the programmes, local and state government officials, who were often the targets of local projects' impact litigation, were vociferous opponents of the programme. Politically, the creators of legal services failed to consider, or chose to ignore, the ramifications of federally funding a programme that had as a principal goal the restructuring of the legal system, including state and local courts and administrative agencies. For example, one of the most vehement opponents of legal services was Ronald Reagan who, in his role as the Governor of California, lost a number of prominent cases to legal services programmes. He retained his animosity to legal services, and after his election in 1980 he tried, but failed to eliminate legal services. With time, though, many mayors and governors have come to view legal services as more of a benefit than threat, as the local programmes have developed their own local constituencies. More recently representatives of the agricultural industry have been frequent witnesses at congressional hearings alleging that Legal Services Corporation recipients' litigation on behalf of migrant workers was in reality a forbidden labour union organising activity.

Legal services policy

From 1974 through 1995, the Legal Services Corporation was able to count on support from powerful political actors. Democrats in Congress were consistent protectors of legal services, especially during the Reagan presidency. And for the last thirty years, the American Bar Association has thrown its considerable support behind the programme. These and other allies have kept a threatened Legal Services Corporation alive over a difficult period. But during this same time period, critics of the programme, Republican legislators, conservative think-tanks, and powerful opposing litigants, were able to narrow, through the Legal Services Corporation Act of 1974 and its later amendments, what LSC recipients could do to provide legal representation to the poor (see Dooley & Houseman, 1984). These efforts were based on ideological, economic, and political motivations (see Besharov, 1990). By affecting the statutory law that governed the Legal Services Corporation, foes were able to restrict the programme and its recipients from participating in demonstrations, involvement in political campaigns, lobbying legislatures unless requested to do so by legislators, initiating class action suits without the prior approval of the local project's managing attorney, and participating in criminal cases. The Legal Services Corporation Act and its amendments have also prevented legal services attorneys from participating in cases involving political issues, minors without the consent of their parents, desegregation, abortion and the Selective Service System. Lawyers employed by a Legal Services Corporation grantee are barred from holding outside employment. These limitations developed incrementally over twenty-two years. They were significant, but they did not threaten the basic structure of legal services in the United States.

The congressional election of 1994 fundamentally changed the nature of this political arrangement. For the first time in over forty years, Republicans controlled both Houses of Congress, and saw in Bill Clinton an easy target for defeat in 1996. With real power to effect change in the federal government through Congress's budgeting responsibilities, Republicans sought to eliminate the Legal Services Corporation once and for all. But thanks in part to the excessive manner in which they attempted to implement their 'Contract with America', Clinton regained some power and vetoed legislation that would have eliminated the programme. But the legal services compromise yielded by this new federal dynamic was a very different animal than those the legal services community had come to know between 1974 and 1995.

On 26 April 1996 President Clinton signed into law PL 104–134, the Omnibus Continuing Resolution. PL 104–134 brought an end to the protracted battle between the Republican-controlled Congress and Clinton over budgeting for most of the US Government. One small part of the PL 104–134, ignored by the national media transfixed by the Act's significance in ending the larger budget battle, dealt with funding levels for the Legal Services Corporation. PL 104–134 provided for a payment of $278 million to the Legal Services Corporation. That the Corporation was funded at all was a victory for the Legal Services Corporation and its supporters. During the struggle over the federal budget, representatives and senators who opposed the Legal Services Corporation and its mission, sought to eliminate the programme completely. Instead, programme opponents in Congress proposed a block grant scheme that would have divided a portion of the eliminated programme's budget among the states to support legal aid efforts as they saw fit. Although the passage of PL 104–134 was yet another example of the Legal Services Corporation belying premature notices of its death, it brought with it the most stringent restrictions ever placed on the programme in its history. The Legal Services Corporation defied death, but just barely. PL 104–134, to all intents and purposes, guts the LSC of its fundamental elements.

The Act prohibits the ability of recipient programmes to accomplish one of the fundamental goals of the legal services programmes: affecting policy, wherever it is produced, that affects the poor as a group. The Act defines policy as any output of federal, state, or local government that has a '. . . general applicability and future effect'. In a related manner, local programmes are specifically prohibited from attempting to influence '. . . the passage or defeat of any legislation, constitutional amendment, referendum, initiative, or any similar procedure of the Congress or a State or local legislative body'. This bar includes seeking to testify at legislative hearings.

The most radical change bought about by PL 104–134 is its bar on class action suits. The Act allows recipient programmes to conclude class action suits that were undertaken prior to its passage, but forbids them from pursuing any new suits. With this prohibition, legal services attorneys lose a critical tool for effecting policy change in the courts, arguably the most fundamental goal of the

American legal services experiment. In the wake of this ban, policy change through judicial decision-making must occur in the context of cases argued on behalf of individual clients.

Another new and difficult restriction placed on local programmes by PL 104–134 is a ban on claiming attorney fees in cases where federal or state law allows or requires such awards. This new restriction has two important impacts on local legal services programmes. First, it essentially limits or prevents local programmes from becoming involved in important types of cases, e.g. civil rights and discrimination, where attorneys fees are often required by statute. Secondly, it eliminates a non-LSC source of revenue that had become important to some local programmes.

The Act creates a new ban on representing any person incarcerated in a federal, state, or local prison, thereby eliminating the ability of local programmes to challenge the unhealthy and dangerous conditions found in many American prisons. Prior to the passage of the Act, legal services programmes, along with public interest law groups like the American Civil Liberties Union, were often at the forefront of pursuing prison reform in the United States, much to the consternation of government officials overseeing the targeted institutions.

The Act prohibits LSC recipients from attempting to affect, in any way, efforts by federal and state actors to change the welfare system. Specifically, Sec. 504 (a) (16) of the Act permits the local programmes to represent an eligible client who is '. . . seeking specific relief from a welfare agency if such relief does not involve an effort to amend or otherwise challenge existing law in effect on the date of the initiation of the representation'. This is another example of the Act shutting down an area of legal activity where legal services attorneys have had, in the past, a fundamental impact. This section was added to meet the demands of conservative members of Congress who alleged LSC lawyers were stifling their version of welfare reform. Finally, PL 104–134 prohibits local programmes from defending a tenant of public housing in eviction proceedings, if the tenant is charged with, but not convicted of, illegal drug activity by law enforcement officials.

If fully implemented[4] the overall impact of PL 104–134 should be clear: a complete repudiation of the ideals of the legal services practice developed by the pioneers of the programme thirty years ago. Gone is the notion of pursuing policy change to benefit the overall status of the poor in multiple governmental forums. Eliminated is the more fundamental practice of impact litigation through target

[4] Ironically, the American penchant for relying on judges to resolve difficult policy issues is observed in the legal services debate. But interestingly, 2 circuits of the US Courts of Appeal have ruled differently on whether the restrictions violate the First Amendment speech rights of LSC attorneys. In Legal Aid Society of Hawaii *et al.* v. Legal Services Corporation USCA, 9th Cir., 97–16567, the court ruled that restrictions do not violate speech rights. But the Second Circuit, in Velazquez *et al.* v. Legal Services Corporation USCA, 2nd Cir., 98–6006, ruled that restricting LSC lawyers from litigating cases that challenge welfare reform was not constitutionally permissible, while upholding all the other restrictions. Given the discrepancy between these two decisions, it seems very likely that the US Supreme Court will choose to review and settle the issue in the not-too-distant future.

cases and class action suits. Whole areas of the civil law are now off-limits to legal services providers. Legitimate sources of non-LSC funding have been cut off or drastically reduced. And the *raison d'être* of the national support centres has been severely hampered, thanks to the 'gag' rule that prevents local programme staff from forwarding relevant cases.

With PL 104–134, what remains for any recipient of an LSC grant is the provision of individual care, to individual clients, in a limited numbers of substantive legal areas. If successful, the Act will have brought organised provision of free civil representation in the United States back almost full circle to the late 1950s. In essence, PL 104–134 creates government funding for a national network of legal aid societies, docile providers of individual legal services to the poor. The activist and transformative elements of the legal services agenda will either be abandoned or carried on in a more limited way by individual cause lawyers (see Sarat & Scheingold, 1998) or public interest law organisations.

Putting American legal services into a comparative context

The retrenchment of government-funded legal assistance is not unique to the United States. Significant cuts to legal aid systems are also either proposed or in place in England, Wales, Scotland, Canada, and Australia. While it is true that the US took the lead in cutting its spending on legal assistance in the early 1980s, governments in these other nations are clearly moving towards reducing, or eliminating altogether, their role in providing legal assistance to those who otherwise cannot afford it. This international reality forces those interested in government-funded legal assistance to re-examine ongoing fundamental issues surrounding its existence. What is legal aid? What sort of politics surround legal aid? Can the retrenchment of legal aid be reversed? Can government shed its role in the funding of legal aid? Are there viable alternatives to government-funded legal assistance? Clearly, an understanding of the American legal services experience should be an important part of trying to answer these larger questions. But, when placing American legal services politics and policy into a comparative context, it becomes clear that the United States is unique in terms of the general contraction of legal aid observed worldwide.

First and most important, in the United States the drive to cut or eliminate government-funded legal aid is exclusively driven by ideology and economic self-interest; conversely, cuts in the predominantly judicare legal aid systems of Australia, Britain, and Canada are primarily motivated by fiscal concerns over growing government budgets. A comparison of recent legal aid budget battles in the Canadian province of Ontario and the United States highlight this underlying difference.

In the United States, the $278 million in federal funds spent to support LSC represented just over 0.00001 per cent of the US Government's outlays in 1996, or a national commitment to civil legal aid of about one dollar *per capita*. By contrast, in 1996 the Ontario Provincial Government funded the Ontario Legal Aid Plan (OLAP) at just over CDN$192 million to reimburse private attorneys for criminal and civil legal aid (the Canadian Government also contributed CDN$59.7 million). OLAP records show that reimbursement for civil legal aid represented over half (51 per cent) of the programme's reimbursement to lawyers (Law Society of Upper Canada, 1997:6–11). This means that Ontario dedicated .17 per cent of its provincial budget to, or spent about CDN$9.72 *per capita* on, civil legal aid, clearly significantly more than its southern neighbour.

The battles to eliminate the Legal Services Corporation in the United States are inspired by a conservative ideology that goes beyond reducing government spending. The Corporation is targeted for elimination for what its creators had envisioned (the activist plan of the Cahns and others), not for what it does (primarily individual casework) or what it costs.

In Ontario provincial governments, faced with growing budget deficits and an electorate strongly opposed to tax increases, have targeted a wide range of 'big-ticket' social programmes, including legal aid. Given its overwhelming focus on judicare, cuts to OLAP are not based on concerns over the activities of allegedly leftist lawyers. Instead, legal aid has been targeted, like education and health care, because that is where much provincial money is. The fact that the original OLAP caps were established in 1993 by a left-of-centre New Democratic Party government underscores the less ideological nature of legal aid cuts in Ontario. While they are driven by an underlying fiscal conservatism, debates over cuts to legal aid in Ontario, Britain and Australia more resemble American discussions over Medicare and Medicaid funding—i.e. can we afford to continue pay these escalating entitlements?—rather than the ongoing and ideologically charged American legal services debate.

A second factor that makes the American legal aid experience unique is its method of service provision. Given its staff lawyer delivery system, LSC creates a different type of bar politics than is found in judicare countries. As was discussed earlier, the average private lawyer in the United States has an attenuated financial link to LSC and legal services politics, i.e. the distant and negative possibility of increased *pro bono* expectations. Given this reality, most private lawyers in the United States are indifferent to issues of legal aid. This indifference is a double-edged sword for the American Bar Association as it develops and pursues its legal aid agenda. The ABA is relatively free to develop its legal aid policy and to lobby Congress in pursuit of that policy. But as the call to arms cited above indicates, the ABA must also expend significant resources in rallying rank and file attorneys to support that policy. The fact that the ABA's voice on American legal aid policy has been minimally affected by the average American lawyer has a number of important consequences. First, the Legal Services Corporation and its programmes have benefited from greater independence and minimal threats from judicare competitors. But on the other hand, without rank and file interest and support, the Legal Services Corporation has been more vulnerable to conservative opponents. These actors portray the ABA's legal services policy as a product of elites, rather than the average attorney, again heightening the ideological nature of American legal aid debates.

In jurisdictions with a judicare delivery system, many lawyers have an immediate financial interest in the state of legal aid. Rank and file members lobby their professional organisations to guard and defend legal aid from budget cuts. As the bar and government bargain over budgeting for legal aid, the debate centres around fiscal priorities and proper payment levels for professional services, and not over ideological debates over whether legal aid should exist.

Finally, American legal services politics is unique because, unlike its counterparts in Australia, Britain, and Canada, the Legal Services Corporation and its grantees are prohibited from dealing with criminal matters. Although there have been significant cuts to criminal public defender services in the federal and state systems in recent years, their total elimination would require a very difficult constitutional change. Civil representation, on the other hand, is not constitutionally protected, making the job of legal services opponents that much easier.

Conclusion

James Carville appeared to be correct when he argued that Americans and their politics are somewhat less concerned with ideological wedge issues like abortion or defining appropriate patriotism. There especially seems to be a growing consensus among the electorate and elected officials from both major political parties that the role of national government should be reduced. Many Americans are focused on the reduction of the budget deficit, the national debt, and tax reduction. With the elimination of the Aid to Families with Dependent Children (AFDC) programme, the national government has severed its direct responsibility to provide for the welfare needs of the nation's poorest citizens. Conservatives point to the relatively modest programmes of the Great Society and argue that this brush with American 'socialism' was a complete failure and definitive proof that market-place solutions must replace those of the welfare state, and again many voters agree. For now, the majority of Americans have clearly opted for a conservative, market-oriented view of society. But within this conservative consensus, some ideological battles of old are trotted out by leaders of both political parties intended not for general consumption, but instead to energise the party faithful. The politics of legal services is one such 'golden oldie'.

Legal services has never been a salient issue for the general American public. Most Americans probably know little, if anything, about the Legal Services Corporation and grantees. Instead, legal services politics pitted urban Democrats, the American Bar Association, and liberal public interest groups against

Republicans, conservative and religious interest groups, and some businesses in a battle that since 1974 has been played out within the confines of Washington, DC.

The committed supporters of legal services—the ABA and groups working with the Corporation's client community—have consistently fought hard for the programme. But alone, their power to protect the programme was limited. Critical to the health of legal services was a Democratic majority in Congress during much of the programme's history. Congress's constitutional role in determining the national budget makes it a crucial actor in the life of any federal programme, including the Legal Services Corporation. Committed supporters like the ABA had played a significant role during this period by convincing Democratic caucuses in Congress that legal services was a programme worth maintaining, a job made easier by the programme's small budget. Congressional majorities funded the programme while allowing their conservative colleagues in the opposition to make incremental diminutions to the agency's power. Still, the fate of the Legal Services Corporation was a very minor issue for Congressional Democrats. From their perspective, this was a low-cost programme that did not engage their electorate, and they were relatively unenthusiastic supporters.

The same cannot be said of the Congressional Republicans. During their time as opposition legislators in Congress, conservative Republicans focused heavy criticism on programmes, like the Legal Services Corporation, created in the 1960s. The budget battles to eliminate LSC, or the National Endowment for the Arts, or the Corporation for Public Broadcasting, in the United States have been used by conservative legislators and interest groups to rally their constituencies. For example, the manifesto of the Conservative Action Team, a group of seventy House Republicans who represent the extreme right wing of their party, contained the following agenda items:

> [W]e will work to eliminate funding for the National Endowment for the Arts (NEA). We will also eliminate funding for the Legal Services Corporation (LSC), a reckless agency that under the guise of helping poor people with legal assistance, uses tax dollars to advance a radical, left-wing agenda. We intend to pull the plug on these programmes not simply because it is the fiscally responsible thing to do, but more importantly because we believe in reinstating the proper limits for government and respecting the values of the American people (*Washington Times,* 1997).

For these members of Congress, the political gain that comes from slaying what they perceive to be one of the last remaining dragons spawned during the dark ages that were the radical 1960s cannot be underestimated. The ability to point to the carcasses of 'leftist' federal programmes like the Legal Services Corporation, the National Endowment for the Arts, or the Corporation for Public Broadcasting would enable conservative Republicans to declare to their committed core of voters that the era of American 'socialism' is truly dead. It matters little that the budgets of these programmes are paltry, or that the substance of their missions are viewed as mainstream and essential in nearly all liberal democracies. Their elimination would cement the political support of a minority of Americans, politically active radical conservatives, who have achieved significant power within the Republican Party in the last twenty years. As a result, the Corporation's critics scour its huge caseload searching for unusual cases that allegedly highlight the programme's true radical nature. Republican legislators, searching for campaign donations, then point to these cases as they seek to convince supporters that a fairly conservative federal government is, in fact, infested with leftist elements that threaten American 'family values'.

The Congressional election of 1994 upset the twenty-year legal services status quo of continued funding with incremental cuts to the LSC budget and discretion. In that election voters gave the Republican Party control of Congress and the federal purse. Now committed supporters of the Legal Services Corporation had to count on the negative constitutional power of the presidential veto, rather than the positive power of congressional budgeting. Given this environment, supporters like the ABA fought even harder than they had in the past to protect the Legal Services Corporation from elimination. But the battle now shifted to convincing a President, who felt that the American public had sent him a message in the 1994 election to move to the right, that LSC was worth protecting. In the end, President Clinton did make it clear to the Congressional Republicans that he would veto any bill that eliminated funding for the Legal Services Corporation, the National Endowment for the Arts, or the Corporation for Public Broadcasting, and Congressional Republicans, sensing that they had overplayed their hand, backed down and funded these programmes. But underscoring the significance Congress's power to shape the federal government through its control of the budget, this funding came with the significant restrictions outlined above. While very troubling to legal services supporters, these restrictions were not significant enough for President Clinton to veto the budget compromise reached with the Republicans and continue the unpopular shutdown of the federal government. The allies of the Legal Services Corporation worked diligently for the programme, but in the new political environment, funding with severe restrictions on activity was the best they could achieve.

In the final analysis, one is forced to consider whether the legal services experiment was an interesting anomaly in US social welfare history, destined to die because its basic mission, giving the poor an active and effective voice in the civil courts, is so controversial and threatening to basic American political sensibilities. Debates over the utility of litigation notwithstanding, legal services has given poor Americans power. There is no better proof of that statement than the amount of time and money powerful interests have invested in convincing Congress to limit the ability of legal services lawyers to take them to court. It is irrelevant that LSC programmes were dedicating an overwhelming amount of their work effort to meeting the individual needs of individual clients. That 5, 10, or 20 per cent of the legal services work effort that could be labelled activist, threatened significant opponents who appear to have eliminated the threat. In fact, if anything is surprising about the American experiment with government-funded legal services, it is that it took thirty years to impose on LSC restrictions like those found in PL 104–134.

Given its past death-defying feats, it would be foolhardy to predict that the end is near for the Legal Services Corporation.[5] Still, it seems clear that the United States is headed towards an even more dramatic retrenchment away from federal involvement in maintaining access to the civil courts. Given the nature of American federalism, where the states act as fifty different policy 'laboratories', this detachment might lead to a patchwork system of civil legal assistance. In a few cities and states, government and private funding would probably allow some of the former LSC recipients to return to a more activist approach to legal services, freed from the restrictions tied to present federal funding. More likely, state and local government and private foundations will fund former LSC recipients to provide civil legal assistance using the legal aid model. And in a few areas of the country, one is likely to see the return to the days where no formal mechanism existed to provide the poor with civil legal assistance.

[5] In fact the LSC has had small budget increases in Fiscal Years 1997 ($283m., a 1.8% increase) and 1999 ($300m., a 6.0% increase). These incremental increases indicate that conservative members of Congress, who continue to seek the LSC's elimination, have been abandoned by their more moderate colleagues. These moderate Republicans, satisfied that the litigation restrictions imposed on the LSC significantly reduce its ability to cause problems, have joined Congressional Democrats to approve small increases in funding. However, these do not nearly make up for the dramatic cuts of 1996. More importantly, the Republican Congressional majority has no plans to revisit the litigation restrictions imposed in 1996. Yet again, LSC and its supporters anxiously await another national election in 2000 to determine what political actors will chart their future.

3

Can Community Clinics Survive? A Comparative Study of Law Centres in Australia, Ontario and England

FREDERICK H. ZEMANS AND ANEURIN THOMAS

Introduction

This Chapter grows out of the authors' research into contemporary developments in legal aid in Canada and the international environment. It focuses particularly on community clinics and their equivalents in Australia, Ontario and England. All three jurisdictions have adapted the American store-front legal clinic model to the needs and legal cultures of their society. In Ontario and England, legal aid has been dominated by the judicare system, emphasising the case-by-case delivery of legal services by private members of the legal profession (Zemans, 1994). Australia has a mixed model, in which over half of individual casework is dealt with by salaried lawyers in legal aid commissions (Fleming, 1994; Crockett, 1994). However, community-based organisations, variously called 'community legal centres' in Australia, 'legal clinics' in Ontario and 'law centres' in the United Kingdom, have made a contribution to legal aid services that is out of proportion to the resources devoted to them (Kuras, 1994; Stephens, 1991; OLAFS, 1991).

Here we look at each jurisdiction in turn. We start by examining the history of these clinics and their progressive roots. We then consider their present activities and future in a world in which governments increasingly emphasise centralised decision-making and control. Governments now speak the language of priorities, cost-effectiveness, financial and operational accountability, quality assurance and co-ordination. Centres perceive such demands for accountability as a threat to their independence. They fear a profound change, that will jeopardise their community roots and hamper innovation. We ask whether strategies are available to allow clinics to retain their independence and uniqueness in the face of these pressures to 'bureaucratise'.

Australia

Out of the three jurisdictions, Australia has the most generous provision. In 1997, there were 151 community legal centres, or 8.1 centres for every million people

(NACLC, 1997).[1] This compares to 6.4 centres per million population in Ontario and a mere 1.1 in England.[2]

The first centre, Fitzroy Legal Service, was established in 1973. At the heart of the movement to develop community legal centres was a fundamental disenchantment with the manner in which traditional legal services dealt with the disadvantaged of society which was placing a particular emphasis on individuals and a case-by-case approach (Basten *et al.*, 1983; Chesterman, 1996). Inspired by a commitment to equality before the law and a belief that social and structural change could be achieved through the legal system and community-based activism, centres sought to dismantle the barriers faced by the poor in securing access to justice. Consequently, their work has focused on disadvantaged individuals and groups within Australian society.

Australian community legal centres may be defined as community-based and community-managed organisations, structured to provide 'free, accessible and easy to understand legal services . . .' (NACLC, 1996). To combat the economic barriers, the early legal centres offered free legal advice to their clients. Although community legal centres lacked sufficient resources to provide extensive litigation services, they provided support in the form of advice and education for clients engaged in litigation. Some centres were able to finance public interest or test cases with legal aid funds from the state Legal Aid Commissions. Cases were selected on their capacity to benefit the greatest number of people in a client group and on the requirement of a reasonable chance of success.[3]

Client involvement was central to the community legal centre movement's ideology. It was intended to overcome the sense of powerlessness of those confronting the legal system. The community legal centres also established networks of people facing similar problems, with the intention of relieving the sense of isolation felt by many disadvantaged clients and facilitating a view of their problems which encompassed the broader social context.[4] Leaders of the community legal centre movement saw the formation of community groups and organisations as a vehicle for solidarity with the capacity to create community campaigns and social movements addressing the social problems facing their clients. As well, the community legal centre served as a resource for the community, providing assistance and advice.

[1] This does not include the 23 Aboriginal and Torres Stait Islander legal aid services, which are managed and funded entirely separately and tend to concentrate on criminal law issues. These particular services are outside the scope of our study.

[2] However, English law centres are larger. While Australian centres have an average of 6.2 full and part-time staff per centre, English law centres have 8.9 (NACLC, 1997; personal communication with Law Centres Federation, London).

[3] This practice has generally been limited to some of the specialist centres such as the Consumer Credit Legal Services, the Disability Discrimination and Welfare Rights services and the Environmental Defenders Office. See National Association of Community Legal Centres, 1996.

[4] For example, landlord–tenant disputes were a common class of problems faced by clients of community legal centres. These disputes arose from the fact that in many jurisdictions in Australia there was inadequate low-cost housing and furthermore, tenancy laws generally were overwhelming in favour of the landlord. See Basten, Graycar and Neal, 1983:180.

Many of their features were perceived as radical at the time of their development, including informal physical surroundings, accessible opening hours, group work, community legal education, law reform and a heavy reliance on volunteers. They have been typified as adhering to notions of 'grass-roots level organization, community control, empowering the recipient, de-professionalisation, human rights . . . free access to services' (Basten *et al.*, 1983:179). In the 1970s and 1980s, the community legal centres' programme roots and radical style of delivery prompted conflict with the private profession due to fears of loss of work and income (Chesterman, 1996). Relations with governments have also been heated at times. Nevertheless, although conflict persists over funding levels to community legal centres, they have finally been accepted by the profession and governments as integral to the legal aid infrastructure.

Commonwealth and state governments provide the overwhelming majority of funding.[5] Despite this, centres have always stressed their independence, from both government and the legal profession. Originally, decisions were made by the membership, a broad concept that included not only volunteers and employees but also members of the community. During the formative stages of Fitzroy Legal Services, for example, extensive open meetings were held for all members (Chesterman, 1996). However, the ideal of community control, central to the centres' original mandate, has not been fully realised (Basten *et al.*, 1983:180). Centres have progressed from relying almost entirely on volunteers to being employing organisations. As a result, the character of centres has changed and paid staff have become the dominant decision-makers. Despite this, there continues to be a strong reliance on volunteers, including not only volunteer lawyers, but also social workers, paralegals and students. The National Association of Community Legal Centres (1997:31) calculates that on average each centre has two to three solicitors, three or four other paid staff and 21 volunteers.[6]

Centres have been defined by two different notions of community. Generalist centres are organised with reference to communities defined by geographical boundaries and offer services covering most areas of non-commercial law. Specialist centres are organised around communities of common interest (such as tenants, young people, refugees, women or consumers) and provide services designed to deal with problems in these areas. While generalist centres tend to concentrate on referral, information, advice and education, the specialist centres conduct more test cases and carry out significant law reform activities (OLAFS, 1991).

[5] In 1995/96, community legal centres' income totalled approximately AS$19 million of which the Commonwealth contributed AS$15 million and state governments most of the remainder (Parliament of the Commonwealth of Australia, 1997:33).

[6] Data is drawn from a survey of 140 centres for a professional indemnity scheme. Between them the 140 centres employed 316 full or part-time solicitors, 554 full or part-time other staff and used 3,004 volunteers. The involvement of volunteers is much greater than in the UK, where law centres use on average only 5 volunteers each (Law Centres Federation, personal communication, 1998).

Table 3.1: Legal Centres across Australia in 1992

State	No. of centres	No. of centres per m. pop.	No. of specialist centres
Victoria	38	9.0	15 (39%)
New South Wales	24	4.1	16 (67%)
Queensland	18	6.0	10 (56%)
South Australia	7	4.8	1 (14%)
Western Australia	10	6.1	5 (50%)
Tasmania	5	10.7	1 (20%)
Aust. Capital Terr.	1	3.4	1 (100%)
Northern Territory	1	6.0	0
Total	104		49 (47%)

Source: Williams (1992: 293)

The various Australian states differ markedly in their mix of specialist and generalist centres. Table 3.1 shows the distribution of community legal centres in 1992, illustrating the differing state traditions when it comes to funding centres.

Victoria leads the way, though Tasmania is generous in proportion to its small population. In New South Wales the specialist tradition predominates. South Australia, on the other hand, has little in the way of specialist provision, and lacks the same culture of educational or reform work. In Western Australia, centres take what has been termed a 'social-work' approach, motivated by a strong suspicion of lawyers.

Despite these differences, however, there are many common threads. Across all centres, assistance to individuals is a major, and often predominant, aspect of centres' work. Centres estimate that, collectively, they assist approximately 300,000 people annually (NACLC, 1997). A government study of four centres carried out in the 1990s found that 26–48 per cent of time was spent on advice, representation and referrals to other agencies. Community legal education took 8–16 per cent of time, law and administrative reform 6–14 per cent and administration and service development 19–54 per cent (OLAFS, 1991: 100–1). However, although the time allocation was relatively low, all four centres carried out an impressive range of community education work. They prepared guides and newsletters, gave local talks and courses and even produced radio programmes. Increasingly, centres are co-operating in such activities and implementing programmes through State Federations and working groups.

The pressing question is how far community legal centres will be able to survive the change of political cultures implicit in the rise of the 'New Right'. Centres developed as part of the expansion of the welfare state, whereas now: 'The ideology of the "neo-conservative" New Right rejects the concept of the welfare state, takes the rhetoric of individualism literally and downplays the probable adverse social and political consequences of the "conflictual order" it advocates' (Jayasuriya, 1996:19–20).

With a growing focus on economic rationalisation, the desire of governments to 'balance the budget' seems to apply regardless of which political party is in power. Social spending has been cut and programmes abandoned, reduced or transferred to the private sector. With cuts to welfare and other social programmes, the gap between the rich and the poor in Australian society has increased and more and more fall below the poverty line (Jayasuriya, 1996; Noone, 1997).

Despite the rise of the New Right, however, community legal centres have fared reasonably well for most of the last ten years, securing increased official recognition. In 1987, for example, the Labor Commonwealth Government created the National Legal Aid Advisory Committee (NLAAC) to advise the Minister responsible for legal aid. The Committee, which undertook a comprehensive review of the Australian legal aid system, published its final report in 1990 calling for the Commonwealth Government to take a more active leadership in the provision of legal aid (NLAAC, 1990). It was positive about the role of centres, and recommended improved access for the socially excluded, such as social security claimants, homeless young people and prisoners.

Shortly thereafter the Minister of Justice and the Commonwealth Attorney-General formed the Access to Justice Advisory Committee to 'make recommendations for reform of the administration of the Commonwealth Justice and legal system to enhance access to justice and render the system fairer, more efficient and more effective' (AJAC, 1994). When, in 1994, this Committee released its report, it also affirmed the notion that the Commonwealth should play a leadership role as the major funder of Australian legal aid. It endorsed the work of community legal centres and called for more programmes designed to provide community legal education, telephone advice and legal training for community and social workers (AJAC, 1994).

Alongside these endorsements came a steady increase in funding. The number of centres rose from 104 in 1992 to 151 in 1996. The Labor Government responded to the report with the Justice Statement of May 1995, by announcing that national funding of legal aid would increase by $68 million over a four year period, including an additional $14 million for law centres. The introduction stated that: 'The Commonwealth will also assert its proper role and authority as the major provider of legal aid funding. It will ensure that community needs regarding legal assistance are addressed fairly and efficiently, and that legal aid policies are oriented to meet community expectations' (Government of Australia, 1995:1).

It recognised the importance of community legal centres and endorsed the principle of community control: 'The government recognises that community legal centres' close links to their communities are an important part of their effectiveness and accessibility and will continue to support and foster this fundamental characteristic through community participation and development' (Government of Australia, 1995:109).

Implementation of the new package, however, was interrupted by the election of a new Conservative Government in March 1996. At first, the legal aid system seemed reasonably secure but the climate soon changed. Regan explains that:

> In the election policy statements the then Opposition pledged to 'maintain current levels of legal aid funding as well as funding to community legal centres'. Legal Aid Commissions were therefore shocked when, in the August budget, the new government announced its decision to cut legal aid expenditures. The proposed $33 million cut for each of the following three years represented approximately 20% of the Commonwealth expenditure, a drastic reduction by any measure. Surprisingly, instead of Attorney General Daryl Williams arguing that legal aid was ineffective, or inefficient, he argued that the cut was part of his Department's contribution to the new government's debt reduction strategy (Regan, 1997).

While the brunt of the cuts fell on the official legal aid commissions, community legal centres experienced a smaller but significant cut of 4 per cent of commonwealth funding over the next two years. The additional monies promised by the Justice Statement were also cut. Needless to say, the cuts created difficulties for many centres, though none was forced to close.

Governments are not only reducing funding, but are also increasing managerial control. So far, the main effect has been felt within the legal aid commissions but pressure is also mounting on community legal centres. In 1995, the Attorney-General of Victoria introduced legislation which transformed the state legal aid commission into Victoria Legal Aid, a body which is corporate in structure and function. The old commission included representatives from a wide range of those concerned with legal services: the legal profession, community legal centres, salaried legal aid staff and the Council for Social Services. These were removed from Victoria Legal Aid, which was structured to provide greater efficiency and control (Noone, 1997:27). Meanwhile the Commonwealth and state governments have begun joint reviews of community legal centres in three states 'with a view to increasing the efficiency and effectiveness of their operations' (Keys Young, 1997). Governments may, in the future, rationalise centres and intervene in their activities more than they have to date.

Australian community legal centres are a success story. Until very recently, they have managed surprisingly well in the darkening economic and political climate. However, things are now taking a distinct turn for the worse. While the Commonwealth Government may endorse community participation in community legal centres, recent developments in the legal aid system indicate that the measure of success is the quantity of legal services purchased for every dollar (Noone, 1997:28). Community legal centres will have to compete for decreasing funding with the private profession, with commissions, with other welfare organisations and with each other. At the same time, poverty is increasing and legal aid commissions have fewer resources to help people in need. Community legal centres find their workloads rising at a time when their own resources are declining. Finally, the movement towards both more 'corporate like' structures for the administration of legal aid and to national planning, threatens the community basis of the legal centres' movement. This restricts the voice of the community and lessens the ability of the disadvantaged to express their views and to effect change through the system (Noone, 1997:29).

Ontario

If Australia's community legal centres have been successful, Ontario's have been even more so. Ontario's 1967 Legal Aid Act established a statutory right to legal aid and acknowledged the obligation of the government to individuals who could not afford a lawyer. The Act was premised on a desire to make the same legal services available to the poor as were already available to 'fee-paying' clients. Legal services were to be delivered through the judicare model, using private lawyers as service providers. The Act effectively established legal aid as a government-funded social programme for the poor.

The Act also set out the basic governance and management structure of the Ontario Plan, specifying that the Law Society would administer and determine policy for the Plan, and establishing with accompanying regulations, its coverage and basic financial eligibility criteria. The Plan was embraced by the profession. Approximately half of all Ontario lawyers registered their names on legal aid panels to be called if their services were required. The Plan was also embraced by the public, and both the number of certificates issued by and the total costs of the Plan grew considerably during this period.

Despite the growing number of certificates, in the late 1960s and early 1970s many lawyers and social activists concluded that poor people often had much different legal needs from 'fee-paying' clients. These analysts believed that judicare lawyers were not qualified to address the legal needs of the poor (Taman, 1971:9). As a result, a different delivery model was required: the community legal aid clinic, a model based on the American neighbourhood legal clinic. As in Australia, early community clinics were guided by five principles: a strong focus on the legal needs of the poor; community involvement in decision-making; independence from government and the Law Society-controlled Ontario Legal Aid Plan (OLAP); a broad definition of 'legal services', including law reform, public legal education and community development; and reliance on staff lawyers and non-lawyers to deliver services.

The early clinics' radical focus was reflected in their governance structure and staffing policies. Clinics were governed by 'community boards of directors' and were staffed by a combination of salaried lawyers and salaried 'community legal workers'. The community legal worker concept was new to the province. Neither lawyers nor administrative staff, 'CLWs' were primarily community organisers whose focus was community legal education, law reform and community development.

The first community legal aid clinic in Ontario was established in 1971.[7] The early clinics were established outside of the existing OLAP management structure and funded by a variety of charitable and government grants. As a result, the clinics had a considerable degree of independence. At this time, the clinics were not formally organised into a 'clinic system'.

As the number of clinics grew, pressure mounted on the provincial government to provide them with funding. As a result, the provincial Attorney General appointed a Task Force on Legal Aid in 1973. Officially recognising the validity of the clinic approach to legal services for the poor, the 1974 *Task Force Report on Legal Aid* (the *Osler Report*) recommended a 'mixed' delivery system for legal aid in which the existing judicare system would be supplemented by staffed neighbourhood legal clinics funded by the provincial government. Mr Justice Osler noted that 'the poor have many problems peculiarly their own . . . [the poor] are tenants not landlords, debtors not creditors, purchasers not vendors' (*Osler Report*, 1974:39). More precisely their needs have been seen as relating to housing law, income maintenance law (including welfare, family benefits, employment insurance, Canada Pensions, and workers compensation); work-related issues (including employment standards and occupational health and safety); and consumer and debt problems. Like other areas of law, the interpretation of the complex statutory and regulatory schemes in these fields often depends on legal assistance.

The provincial government accepted the *Osler Report*'s clinic recommendations. In 1976, a regulation under the Legal Aid Act established funding for the existing twenty-two legal aid clinics in the province (Ontario Regulation, 1976).

In 1978, Mr Justice Samuel Grange conducted another provincial inquiry into legal aid, intended to examine the relationship between the clinics, OLAP, and the private bar. Like the *Osler Report*, the *Report of the Commission on Clinical Funding* (the *Grange Report*) affirmed the mixed delivery system of legal aid in Ontario, concluding that community clinics played a significant role in Ontario's legal aid system. (*Grange Report*, 1978) The *Report* found that the clientele and legal issues addressed by the certificate programme and clinic programme were very different. As a result, the *Report* viewed the relationship between clinics and the private bar as one of co-operation, not competition, encouraging the growth of clinics to complement the services provided by the private bar under judicare. Importantly, the *Report* concluded that clinics should have 'autonomy with respect to policy and administration, subject only to accountability for the public

[7] Parkdale Community Legal Services was a pilot project funded by the Federal Department of Health and Welfare, the Council for Legal Education for Professional Responsibility, and York University (Zemans, 1997).

funds advanced and for the legal competence of the services rendered' (*Grange Report*, 1978:22). Policy and administrative autonomy were considered necessary to ensure community control and preserve the clinics' law reform mandate.

In 1979, the *Grange Report*'s recommendations were incorporated into a regulation of the Legal Aid Act establishing the structure of provincial funding for clinics. The 'Clinic Funding Regulation' attempted to preserve clinic autonomy by effectively dividing the governance of community legal clinics between the Law Society's Clinic Funding Committee (CFC) and volunteer, elected community Boards of Directors specific to each clinic. The CFC, like the Legal Aid Committee, is a Standing Committee of the Law Society, separate from the Legal Aid Committee, responsible for establishing policy and guidelines in respect of the funding of clinics and administering the clinic funding programme (Ontario Regulation, 1990). The clinics' operational policies—including determination of case priorities, other activities and financial eligibility—are intended to be determined by democratically elected, volunteer Boards of Directors. The Regulation attempts to preserve clinic autonomy by establishing a complicated series of checks and balances between the CFC and the clinic funding staff (CFS). Initial funding decisions are made by the CFS but are ultimately determined by the CFC (Ontario Regulation, 1990). Distanced from the application process, the CFC hears appeals of funding decisions (Mossman, 1983).

There are currently seventy clinics in Ontario, serving over 100 communities; there are two main categories of clinics: general and specialty clinics. Fifty-six clinics are general service clinics, offering services in core areas of poverty law practice. Fourteen clinics are specialty clinics which specialise in a particular area of law or in the legal needs of a specific client group, such as the Advocacy Centre for the Elderly, the Advocacy Resource Centre for the Handicapped, Justice for Children and Youth, the Centre for Spanish-Speaking Peoples, the Canadian Environmental Law Association and university clinics.[8] Ontario also has three clinics affiliated with university law schools in the province: the Correctional Law Project (Queen's University), Legal Assistance of Windsor (University of Windsor) and Parkdale Community Legal Services (Osgoode Hall Law School).[9]

In 1996, clinics carried 37,097 files, provided summary advice in 147,636 poverty law matters, made approximately 70,000 referrals to social services, community agencies or private lawyers, conducted 2,055 public legal education sessions (reaching more than 72,000 people) and presented 792 briefs or

[8] The list of specialty clinics also includes: Aboriginal Legal Services of Toronto, Community Legal Education Ontario, Correctional Law Project, Industrial Accident Victims Group of Ontario, Injured Workers' Consultant, Landlord's Self-Help Centre, Metro Tenants Legal Services, Metro Toronto Chinese and Southeast Asian Legal Clinic, Pay Equity Advocacy and Legal Services, Metro Toronto Chinese and Southeast Legal Clinic, Pay Equity and Legal Services and Toronto Worker's Health and Safety Legal Clinic.

[9] Law students in these programmes complete a one-term placement in the clinic, earning academic credits while undertaking practical clinical work.

submissions in court or tribunal cases.[10] They also produced videos and pamphlets, pursued law reform initiatives and launched community development projects which assist clients to organise and to form self-help groups focused on low-income issues, including injured workers and tenant associations (Law Society of Upper Canada, 1992:7). Simple case totals, however, may not reflect the relative complexity or impact of a single case. One clinic may specialise in complex test-case litigation, another in high-volume case representation. Clinics have always operated under capped budgets and their funding has been frozen since 1993. In 1995/6 the clinic system cost slightly more that 10% of the total legal aid budget (Ontario Legal Aid Review, 1997; Clinic Funding Submission).

As not-for-profit corporations, clinics are managed by elected boards of directors who are responsible for clinic administration, personnel management (boards are the employers of the staff of each clinic), financial management, the determination of legal services to be provided (both the choice of area and the methods or strategies to be used) and the evaluation of services.[11] The day-to-day management of each clinic is the responsibility of the executive director (a member of the staff).

The practices of most geographically based clinics are heavily weighted in the areas of social assistance (family benefits, general welfare assistance), workers' compensation, employment insurance, Canada pensions, housing (landlord and tenant, homelessness), and consumer problems: those areas of law which impact pervasively upon the lives of poor persons. The specialty clinics address a range of other legal issues of particular significance to their communities. Casework is the predominant activity of most clinics. Over the more than two decades of clinic operation, some clinics have offered limited services in criminal, family and other civil matters on an exceptional basis. Such assistance, however, has generally been provided only where clients have little access to other legal services, primarily in remote areas.

Two recent reports prompted by the fiscal crisis in OLAP's certificate programme strongly supported the goals and operations of Ontario's community clinic system and recommended the clinic system as a model for Ontario's legal aid system as a whole. The first, *From Crisis to Reform: A New Legal Aid Plan for Ontario* (Zemans and Monahan, 1997) was a privately funded report written

[10] See Community Legal Clinics Statistics Discussion Paper, 1996, and letter from Clinic Funding Staff to Boards and Deans of Law Schools (29 Nov. 1996) [unpublished]. The clinic funding staff have stated that there are many problems in the processes used to gather the information reported by these statistics. For example, there is a lack of consistency between matters identified as case files and those identified as summary advice; the swearing of affidavits may be counted as summary intake in one clinic and as a case file in another. The clinic funding staff have finalised a new scheme for data collection, based upon new (and defined) categories to match actual clinic practices better, and this new system was put in place in 1998.

[11] These responsibilities are spelled out in the Clinic Funding Operating Manual for clinics and in Clinic certificates.

by Osgoode Hall Law School Professors Frederick Zemans and Patrick Monahan.[12] The second, *A Blueprint for Publicly Funded Legal Services* (Ontario Legal Aid Review, 1997) (hereinafter *McCamus Report*), was a report by an independent task force funded and appointed by the provincial government. The *McCamus Report* stated that:

> The community clinic model meets many of the goals we have identified for the larger legal aid system. The community clinic system can run on a capped budget; it works to understand and respond to individual and community needs; it utilizes lawyers, non-lawyers, public legal education initiatives, and other delivery systems in order to deliver services cost-effectively; it prioritizes needs and attempts to meet them strategically; it has developed linkages to nonlegal service providers; and it has recently adopted a quality assurance program (*McCamus Report*, 1997: vol. 1, c. 11).

Both reports strongly endorsed the principle of community governance as fundamental to the success of the clinic system and the delivery of poverty law services. Each noted the importance of community-elected boards to the independence of the clinics, to identifying and prioritising community needs and to ensuring accountability to the clinic community.

Both reports also noted that the present division of responsibilities between the Legal Aid Committee and the Clinic Funding Committee does not work very well. The *Zemans-Monahan Report* stated that the two committees exist as 'two solitudes', with decisions by each committee often, if not usually, being made without reference to the other. Despite this strong statement, both reports ultimately recommended comparatively modest efforts to improve co-ordination between clinics and the overall system.

The *Zemans-Monahan* study recommended that the provincial community clinic system should be integrated into the same regional board structure they recommended for the system as a whole (Zemans and Monahan, 1997:167). The study stated that these regional boards should eventually assume the duties and responsibilities of the current CFC. The formal relationship between a community clinic and its regional board should be established in a detailed operating agreement or an equivalent of the current clinic certificate issued by the clinic Funding Committee. The *McCamus Report* recommended even more limited structural reforms. Rather than recommending a full integration of the clinic system, the *McCamus Report* recommended that individual clinics and the overall clinic system should initiate a multi-year strategic planning process and that the Executive Director of each clinic and the Area Director of each OLAP area office should sit on each other's boards. Both reports recommended clinic representation on the Board of Directors of the proposed new statutory agency.

The more controversial recommendation of each report was that the clinic budget and the system's overall budget be integrated. The current Legal Aid Act explicitly separates the certificate programme budget and the clinic programme

[12] The study was funded by The Donner Canadian Foundation.

budget. Each programme has its own distinct statutory funding regime. As a result, monies designated for one programme cannot be transferred to the other.[13] The two reports came to the same conclusion. The *Zemans-Monahan Report* argued that clinics face grave threats to their funding if they remain dependent upon direct grants from the provincial government. They thought that the current funding structure, organised around dedicated grants to the Clinic Funding Committee, did not sufficiently protect clinics from potentially severe budget cutbacks initiated by a provincial government which was intent on cutting costs across the board or one which might be resentful of the clinics' law reform activities. They argued that the current funding structure, organised around dedicated grants to the clinic structure, unnecessarily narrows the political constituency supportive of clinic funding (Zemans and Monahan, 1997:105).

Implicit in both reports was the conclusion that the present funding structure has contributed to the 'two solitudes', separating the clinic and certificate programmes. Both reports recommended that the budget integration be phased in over a period of years.

The public, legal aid stakeholders, and the provincial government were very supportive of the *McCamus Report*'s recommendations. Seeing the writing on the wall, and itself fed up with the constant headaches of administering a large social welfare programme, in February 1998 the Law Society voted overwhelmingly in favour of a motion to transfer responsibility for the administration of the Legal Aid Plan to an independent statutory corporation (Makin, 1998). They proposed that the Board of the new agency should be made up of provincial government appointees, Law Society appointees, and a Chair appointed from names recommended by a nominating committee comprised of the Attorney-General, the Treasurer of the Law Society, and a mutually agreed third party. In contrast to both the *Zemans-Monahan* and *McCamus* recommendations, the Law Society model did not explicitly include a clinic representative on the Board of the proposed agency.

Clinic representatives were alarmed by the Law Society model's lack of a dedicated clinic or consumer representative on the Board, interpreting the Law Society's proposal as a major regression from the McCamus model. Moreover, the model obviously ignored many of protections built into the McCamus model, including a Board-level clinic committee with dedicated staff. By way of contrast, the Association of Community Clinics of Ontario recommended a Board and agency structure which would considerably dilute the perceived power of judicare

[13] This separation was intentional. The authors of the original Clinic Funding Regulation feared that 'pooling' the clinic and certificate programme budgets would give the Law Society the opportunity to systematically divert clinic resources to the certificate programme. This fear—which many, if not most, contemporary clinic supporters share—is founded on a belief that the Law Society's commitment to private-bar delivery of legal aid would take precedence over its commitment to clinics, especially during times of fiscal restraint. According to this view, the formal separation of the two budgets is absolutely critical to the continued survival of the clinics.

lawyers to restructure or reduce funding for community clinics. It recommended that the Board should have as many non-lawyers as lawyers; that the Law Society should be obligated to appoint at least one clinic staff person; and that at least three members of the Board should be consumer representatives. It also recommended the establishment of a Standing Board-level clinic committee with dedicated staff and that the agency should have a dedicated clinic budget, expressed as a minimum percentage of the overall legal aid budget.

To date, the provincial government has not made any final decision on legal aid reform, although legislation is expected in the near future. In the present environment, clinic representatives are extremely wary of what they fear may be significant changes to the long-standing rules governing relationships between independent community clinics and the funding authority. They have repeatedly stated that the basic governance and funding structure set out in the *Grange Report* were fundamentally sound. They are suspicious of efforts to introduce system-wide statistical collection, quality assurance measures, performance measures, or service priorities and consider such initiatives as infringements on clinic independence.

Clinic resistance to contemporary provincial government social programme management techniques (quality assurance, performance measures, co-ordination of services, etc.) has led many commentators and stakeholders—including the authors of the *Zemans-Monahan* and *McCamus Reports*, clinic funding staff, administrators of the certificate programme, and representatives of the provincial government—to criticise the community clinic system as being inefficient or lacking accountability. The debate has intensified with the capping of certificate programme funding and the pressure on government and legal aid administrators to improve the cost-efficiency and financial accountability of the entire system.

The ongoing debate about integration, co-ordination and independence is often reduced to a recital of the merits of clinic system 'centralisation' *versus* the merits of relatively unfettered clinic 'autonomy'. Some analysts argue that the CFC's funding power gives it authority and responsibility to take a more assertive role in co-ordinating clinic planning and operations in the name of promoting accountability, efficiency and system-wide co-ordination. Others stress the importance of clinic independence, arguing that the CFC's funding power is limited by the power of community boards to determine individual service priorities and clinic operations.

More than twenty years after the promulgation of the original Regulation, the debate remains vibrant. The paradox of the 1970s Grange model is that the same governance structure which has historically protected the clinic system against intrusions from judicare lawyers and the provincial government has also led to significant criticisms of clinics. The same transformative activities (law reform, community development) which make the clinic system successful also render it politically vulnerable. In fact, the clinic system is in a bind. Community clinics cannot easily embrace the ethos of cost-effectiveness and co-ordination or integration within the larger system without significant consequences; any attempt to justify law reform or community development initiatives on the ground of cost-effectiveness, however valid, is a hard sell to the same politicians and funders who are often the focus of the clinic's political organising.

Opponents of the clinic model often criticise the focus on law reform. They argue that law reform activities are not strictly 'legal', that law reform diverts attention and resources away from individual clients, and that it is inappropriate to spend public money on 'political' activities. This latter argument is particularly common within the halls of government. By way of contrast, community clinic supporters have argued that law reform is an integral and inevitable part of the clinics' work. As Janet Mosher has argued, 'The law reform work of clinics, particularly in situations where clinics act as a resource to low-income communities to facilitate their direct participation in law reform activities, enhances justice. At a more pragmatic level, participation of low-income communities will result in better laws' (Mosher, 1997:935). Our view is that the long-term success of the community clinic model depends upon community clinics retaining their law reform focus. The original justification for the law reform mandate remains as valid today as in the early 1970s, perhaps even more so.

Clinics such as the Advocacy Resource Centre for the Handicapped, Justice for Children and Youth, the Correctional Law Project, and the Advocacy Centre for the Elderly, the unquestioned experts in their respective fields, have made invaluable contributions to the development of laws and policies for the betterment of all Ontarians. These specialty clinics have been able to devote more resources to law reform activities than general service clinics. As well, they are more likely to have well established links to social/political movements with the same goals. Finally, specialty clinics have been able to develop larger strategies, working with others in a larger social/political movement, in order to target resources and skills effectively. The Advocacy Resource Centre for the Handicapped, for example, is often viewed as the legal arm of Ontario's disability movement. In contrast, while general service clinics often assess and litigate cases based upon their view of the long-term strategic impact of that case on a class of individuals or group, as a matter of necessity and mandate they are often required to restrict the scope of their law reform analysis to local activities and circumstances. As a result, the impact of their law reform activities is often localised. Most importantly, limited funding and the dire needs of their clients put incredible pressure on general service clinics to focus on individual casework.

Important challenges confront the community clinic system's ability to benefit persons with low incomes through law reform. First and foremost, law and litigation is a limited, discrete tool. Political change generally requires a broad-based political strategy, of which legal work and litigation may be but one component. Political change also requires development of broad-based community support, media, lobbying, etc.—all of which requires more diverse skills than clinics are likely to be able to provide. Secondly, law reform often draws unwanted attention to the clinic system, raising the obvious potential for a government to cut off funding for clinics in order to silence political critics. In Ontario this potential has not been realised to date, despite the grumbling of successive provincial governments. Thirdly, it is not yet clear how law reform activities can be assessed, quantified or evaluated within 'modern' legal aid administrations which emphasise business planning, quality assurance, cost-effectiveness and management accountability.

Although the Provincial Government has not formally announced its plan for legal aid reform in Ontario, both the Attorney-General and staff in the provincial Ministry of the Attorney-General have been consulting with community clinic representatives on the basis that the community clinic system will continue to be an important component of the 'new' legal aid system in Ontario; amendments to the Province's Legal Aid Act will preserve independent community boards; the new legislation will require the new legal aid agency to deliver 'poverty law' services and that, at the very least, the board of the new agency will include consumer representatives.

The Government has, however, also announced its intention to improve the cost-effectiveness and co-ordination of all the Ontario Legal Aid Plan's services, including community clinics. To date, the Government has not announced details of these measures. The Government's commitments have been clearly been influenced by, and are consistent with, the recommendations of the McCamus Commission. If Ontario's new legal aid legislation matches these commitments, the community clinic system in Ontario will have retained an enviable measure of legislative protection and stability.

England and Wales

English law centres, like their Australian counterparts, have faced many challenges, first from the profession and secondly from their principal funders. Unfortunately for them, they have never managed to attract the all-round support afforded to Ontario community legal aid clinics. Yet it all began so optimistically. The introduction of judicare in the United Kingdom in the early 1950s contained provision for state-salaried lawyers (albeit appointed and controlled by the Law Society) to complement the efforts of the private profession in poorer areas. However, although retained in the legislation to the present day, the provision was never implemented. As a result the law centre movement in England and Wales, as in Australia and Ontario, owed its origins to a dissatisfaction with judicare as a means of addressing the legal needs of the poor. With the notable exception of the very first law centre to be set up in England and Wales in 1970, in North Kensington, the early neighbourhood law centres were attracted by the model of the community law centres in the United States. They focused strongly on the legal needs of the poor, favoured community involvement and independence from the private profession (including the professional bodies), were prepared to handle test cases in pursuit of law reform, engaged in public legal education and relied on a mix of staff lawyers and lay workers. North Kensington, however, sought to restrict its efforts largely to individual casework, seeing itself as closely akin to private practice.

Soon after the first law centres were established the Government bowed to the pressure of the Society of Labour Lawyers, the Conservative Lawyers Group, the National Consumer Council, and the Law Society, by introducing a greatly expanded advice and assistance scheme, known as the 'Green Form' scheme. With a simple financial eligibility test and covering any area of English law, it was hoped that the Green Form scheme would encourage the private profession to use it in poverty law areas, rather than crime and family cases which had dominated judicare since its inception. While law centres found imaginative ways of using the scheme, e.g. by combining multiple applications with extensions to fund the acquisition of experts' reports (Paterson, 1979) the private profession showed no similar flexibility. Payments for social welfare law cases rose painfully slowly from 10.7 per cent of Green Form accounts in 1975/76 to 16.6 per cent in 1985/86 and 21 per cent in 1990/91 (Goriely, 1994; Smith, 1997b). During the same period it was estimated that nearly 60 per cent of the work of English and Welsh law centres concerned housing, welfare, employment and immigration matters.

In 1986, the Legal Aid 'Efficiency Scrutiny', established by the Government, recommended that large sections of the Green Form scheme be transferred to the voluntary advice sector. Fierce debate arose and the recommendation was never implemented, although it did set the stage for future Government intervention. The Scrutiny made another suggestion, subsequently implemented with little protest. In 1988, the Government passed the Legal Aid Act 1988 which transferred the administration of legal aid from the Law Society to the newly created Legal Aid Board (LAB) (Lord Chancellor's Office, 1986). In the past, the Law Society had wanted control over the administration of legal aid, but by 1986 it was somewhat relieved to be absolved of responsibility, given the amount of criticism it had received from its members (Smith, 1997b:154).[14] (We noted a similar response in 1998 by The Law Society of Upper Canada.)

Unfortunately, the transfer had no impact on law centre financing. Contrary to the position in Australia and Ontario, funding for United Kingdom law centres has never been part of the mainstream of publicly funded legal service. Many centres were funded initially from Urban Aid, a partnership between central and local government concentrating on inner-city rejuvenation, or by charitable foundations.

[14] In one experiment involving microfiche, a legal aid office was paralysed and unable to administer itself. After the Legal Aid Board took control, the Law Society would not have to worry about such embarrassments.

These grants were time-limited, so every centre sooner or later faced major financing problems. In 1975 the Labour Lord Chancellor extended central government funding to seven law centres with financial problems but this concession was never expanded. Surprisingly, the concession was continued under Conservative governments but only for those seven centres. From 1982 onwards governments took the view that law centres were for local authorities to support. The result was an unequal funding base for law centres across England and Wales: law centres located within the jurisdiction of Labour councils generally received better funding than those in Conservative jurisdictions. Such funding inequities were exacerbated by the allegedly 'political' activities of some law centres (e.g. community organisation or challenging the policies of the local authorities) which tended to upset Conservative councils more than Labour ones. Nor was it just the local authorities. As early as 1973, the Law Society had begun to criticise law centres for 'stirring up political and quasi-political controversy far removed from their principal mandate of ensuring equal access to the protection of the law' (Smith, 1997a:905). By 1979, the Labour Government's Royal Commission on Legal Services was adding to that criticism (Royal Commission on Legal Services, 1979). The 'Commission appeared hostile to any role for the centres beyond increasing provision for casework in social welfare law'. Particularly averse to the activist role asserted by the law centre movement, it recommended a new era of non-political citizens' law centres (Smith, 1997a:907). The Commission also advised that law centre funding should be provided entirely by central government, rather than from a variety of funders which included local governments. This advice was never heeded since the Conservatives took office shortly after the publication of the report.

The Law Society's opposition to political activities by law centres was symptomatic of their understandable suspicion of the early law centres. The centres espoused progressive forms of lawyering which were unsettling to traditionalists, and the fact that they offered their services free of charge was perceived as unfair competition. Operating a law centre required a waiver from the Law Society of the professional rules against advertising and sharing fees. This gave the Society the ability to control where and when a new centre could be established. In 1975 a group of local practitioners in Hillingdon, outraged by the imminent funding of a local law centre, pressed the Law Society into refusing to grant waivers to lawyers working in the centre. The Government intervened on the side of the law centres, threatening legislation. Eventually an accommodation was reached under pressure from the Labour Lord Chancellor. In future, provided centres agreed not to compete with private practitioners in such areas as adult crime, matrimonial and personal injury litigation, probate and conveyancing,[15] the Law Society would no longer use its powers to grant waivers as a means of controlling the setting up of law centres (Smith, 1997b:152). In truth this compromise suited

[15] This division of labour parallels that in Ontario between clinics and the certificate scheme.

both sides since few centres saw their mission as requiring them to invade the traditional areas of private practice. Moreover it soon became accepted that UK law centres, by referring such work to the private profession, generated income for the private profession rather than taking it from them.

However, the division of labour did not solve the long-term funding crisis facing the law centre movement. Gradually they were forced to turn more and more to individual casework funded by legal aid rather than the more innovative forms of poverty lawyering which they had espoused in the early years. Indeed, the amount of casework a law centre pursues is largely determined by the existence of other sources of legal aid. Following the deregulation of the profession in the 1980s the Law Society lost its ability to curtail the work of law centres through waivers. This has created the intriguing scenario of law centres moving into the areas of work previously colonised by the private profession. It remains to be seen to what extent the dependence on casework encourages moves in that direction. To date, most centres have tried to maintain a broader concept of 'access to justice': 'Use of the [Green Form] scheme by Law Centres is indeed regarded with a certain ambivalence by the people who work in them . . . [W]hile 'Green Form' work (and other legally aided work) provided a useful source of revenue, it was not regarded as a mainstream activity of Law Centres. It was even in some respects viewed as representing something of a diversion from the main work that staff wished to undertake [sic]' (Baldwin and Hill, 1988:102).

The Law Centres Federation, the voice of the law centre movement, views casework as merely one aspect of the function of a law centre. Indeed, as reflected in the Federation's definition of a law centre, casework is often considered only a minor aspect in the provision of services by law centres: 'Law Centres aim to make the most efficient use of their resources and so have developed several methods of work to achieve the best results. These include case work, participating in the process of legal reform, campaigning, education work, development work and resourcing (providing a valuable source of information and support for all sorts of agencies and groups)' (Law Centres Federation, 1991).

Law centres have structured themselves to deal with the need for flexibility, by generally encouraging horizontal power structures, self-servicing, skill-sharing and community control. Nonetheless, these values are not all manifested in every centre. As in Australia, community control has proved elusive in the UK, either because the salaried staff take *de facto* charge of policy or because some local authorities insist on a hierarchical management structure as a requirement for funding.

Despite financial difficulties, the number of law centres grew from 28 in 1979 to 56 in 1986. The number of citizens' advice bureaux (CABx), lay advice centres grew from 473 in 1966 to 869 in 1986. In the same time period the volume of enquiries at CABx had grown from 1.3 million to 6.8 million. In the 1970's, CABx had also experimented, on a pilot basis, with the employment of solicitors; in some cases they also combined efforts with law centres. Between 1990/1 and 1995/6, the amount of money received by law centres for 'Green Forms' increased from £1 million to £1.9 million. However, 'Green Form' payments to the private profession in social welfare areas increased by a greater margin in the same period. Similarly, funding to advice agencies that employed lawyers increased from £202,000 to £1.2 million (Smith, 1997a:912). Moreover, in 1996, as part of a pilot project, the LAB dispersed another £2.6 million to advice agencies that did not employ lawyers. Since 1986, CABx and the private profession have come to attract an ever greater percentage of legal aid funds flowing towards social welfare law. Three principal reasons account for the shift in the delivery capacity of CABx and private practitioners. First, private practitioners—particularly those in niche social welfare firms (often near law centres and staffed by ex-law centre workers) began to use the 'Green Form' scheme extensively for social welfare work (Goriely, 1994). They also colonised special interest groups influential within the field.[16] Secondly, advice centres have overtaken law centres in terms of volume of casework. Finally, high-level test cases have become much more a specialty of national not-for-profit pressure groups such as the Child Poverty Action Group, Shelter (a housing campaigning organisation), and Liberty (formerly the National Council for Civil Liberties) (Smith, 1997a:897,913).[17] It must be remembered, however, that the law centre movement does not generally measure its success by its volume of casework or by the number of individuals served.

In recent years, legal aid policies have begun to change. The advent of franchising (see Paterson and Sherr, Chapter 10, below) offered new opportunities for funding for law centres. Franchising is a system that rewards providers who can satisfy criteria of competence in their work as well as adhering to key practice management standards (Legal Aid Board, 1989:6).

A number of law centres became franchised. However, in a White Paper (UK, 1996) published by the Conservative Government, franchising evolved into the concept of contracting. In future, only providers with quality assured contracts with the Legal Aid Board will be able to provide 'Green Form' work. The allocation of the contracts would be based on geographic assessments of need and competition between service providers. While franchises were not intended to be exclusive (i.e. any number of service providers could qualify to be franchised) contracting is effectively exclusive insofar as there are a finite number of contracts available.

Shortly after the publication of the Conservative White Paper, the Labour Party was voted into government. While the new Government adopted the Conservative plans for contracting, Labour has also made a commitment to a community legal aid service (Lord Chancellor's Department, 1998).

[16] Organisations such as the Housing Law Practitioners Group or the Immigration Law Practitioners Association, largely dominated by private practitioners, are very influential.

[17] In other jurisdictions, the function of these groups may be handled by specialty legal aid clinics. However, in England and Wales there exist both specialty clinics and lawyer-employing pressure groups.

While the proposals have not been passed into law at the time of writing, the Government seems committed to transferring 'Green Form' resources towards advice for social welfare law. This will result in opportunities for law centres and advice agencies to obtain exclusive contracts to provide advice on aspects of social welfare law (ibid.). While this will place them in competition with the private sector, it will only be with private firms specialising in social welfare law, of which there are relatively few.

Overview and conclusion

We return now to the questions that began this Chapter: can independent community clinics survive in a world in which governments increasingly emphasise centralised decision-making and determination of service priorities, cost-effectiveness, financial and operational accountability, quality assurance and co-ordination of service providers? Can clinic supporters adopt strategies to ensure that they are able to retain their independence and uniqueness in the face of countervailing pressures to 'bureaucratise' or centrally manage their operations? Our review of the clinic systems in Australia, England and Wales, and the Ontario case study demonstrate that there are no simple answers to these questions.

Law Centres in England and Wales have never been as significant an element in the legal aid system as the legal clinic in Australia or Ontario. The historic lack of substantial funding for Law Centres has considerably limited their development and effectiveness. Moreover, Law Centres are now being tempted to compete with the private bar and the advice sector for limited funds. Australian Community Legal Centres have not suffered the same lack of funding and central support as England's law centres. There are, however, major challenges which threaten to alter fundamentally the nature of Community Legal Centres, including the focus on centralised planning and the concurrent lack of consumer or Legal Centre representation on the bodies governing legal aid. Of the three jurisdictions, the Ontario community clinic system appears at present best placed to meet the current challenges effectively. Indeed, the reforms which have been suggested by the Ontario Government do not fundamentally change the governance or operations of the community clinic system. In fact, they may strengthen it.

To what can we attribute the comparative success of Ontario's community clinic system? Several factors can be identified. These include the Province's long, successful experience with community clinics; the size and the sophistication of the system; the protection afforded clinics by the Grange governance and funding structure; the fact that political attention in recent years has been focused on the 'crisis' in OLAP's certificate programme; the clinics' success at building community networks; continued support for clinics among legal and bureaucratic elites (many of whom worked in clinics as students); and the strong endorsement of Ontario's clinic system by domestic and international observers.

Ontario's experience offers valuable insights as to the conditions required for the continuance and future success of the community-based legal clinics. It suggests that community legal clinics can survive, and perhaps thrive, in the face of contemporary challenges, but that their chances of survival can be enhanced if certain prerequisites are present:

a. clinics should have networks of supporters within their communities, the legal profession, government bureaucracies and the governing bodies of legal aid programmes;
b. legal aid systems should maintain a clear division of labour between the private profession and the clinics;
c. funding sources should be stable and secure;
d. independent community clinic boards should be preserved;
e. legal aid plans should have specific administrative structures dedicated to clinic issues; and
f. community clinics should adopt new management techniques, including quality assurance programmes, performance measures, and strategic planning, despite expressed concerns about their relevancy to the clinic model.

In many respects, the issues defined above, though specific to the Ontario case, identify critical aspects of a continuing clinic movement whatever the jurisdiction. For this reason, it is interesting to examine the issues in more depth and to extrapolate as to the general applicability of the issues and concerns. Each of these issues is discussed briefly below.

Clinics should have networks of supporters within their communities, the legal profession, government bureaucracies and the governing bodies of legal aid programmes

The community clinic model has developed a wide range of supporters in each clinic's respective community, in the Province's legal profession, and in the justice system's bureaucracy. This network has been vital to preserving clinic funding throughout changes in governments and political philosophies. Community clinics, in both Australia and Ontario, have been effective in mobilising support at key moments to lobby in support of maintaining clinic funding. (By contrast, since 1995 Ontario's funding for most community service providers has been cut dramatically and welfare rates have been reduced by over 20 per cent.) Representation of clinics on state or national governing bodies drawn from local clinic boards ensures that clinic issues and perspectives will be heard by the legal aid authority's highest levels. Moreover, it ensures that the perspective of a person with experience in community-based service delivery will be integral to policy discussions.

From a clinic perspective, the appointment of a member (or members) either representative of, or associated with community clinics would obviously be the best governance model. As discussed earlier, the recent changes in Australia seem to be moving away from clinic or community leadership in legal aid administration. Unlike the previous state legal aid commission, the board of directors of Victoria Legal Aid does not include any nominee from community legal centres or the community.

Legal aid systems should maintain a clear division of labour between the private profession and the clinics

There are two straightforward reasons for ensuring a clear division between clinic services and judicare services: fear of being 'overwhelmed' by criminal and family cases, and fear of competition from the private bar. In Ontario, clinic supporters argue in favour of a clear division between clinic services and judicare services because of a fear that clinics could be overwhelmed by either criminal or family cases, effectively eliminating their poverty law focus. Hence, clinic supporters in Ontario have always argued for a 'bright line' dividing clinic and judicare practice. In Australia, England and Wales, and Quebec the situation is reversed. The governments of these jurisdictions have intentionally promoted competition between alternative services providers as a means to lower costs. Rather than being overrun by criminal and family cases, Community Legal Centres and Law Centres are facing competition from the private bar on their own terms. Increasing numbers of private lawyers and other service providers now provide poverty law services.[18]

One way to overcome the threat that this poses is to espouse a flexible, statutory definition of 'Poverty Law'.[19] Definitions which are overly specific run the risk that the board will refuse to authorise services being provided in areas not mentioned in the legislative definition. Just as importantly, a specific definition can be written and interpreted to preclude law reform activities. General definitions, on the other hand, give community boards the flexibility to respond to such local needs as they deem appropriate.

Funding sources should be stable and secure

Clearly the Australian and Ontario clinics started with the major advantage of central funding which has always been denied their English counterparts. However, as US legal services (see Chapters 1 and 2) have found, central funding can be lost where government and community support falter. Equally, hostility from the local legal profession or local government can jeopardise local funding, as several English law centres have discovered.

[18] As discussed above, the Commonwealth Government in Australia is increasingly shifting responsibility for social programmes such as legal aid to community legal centres and other social organisations. This has resulted in a greater demand on both the financial and personnel resources of community legal centres. It is anticipated that case-loads in community legal centres will increase.

[19] For example, the Association of Community Legal Clinics of Ontario proposed the following definition to the Ontario Government during the Government's legal aid consultation: 'legal issues which particularly impact on low-income communities, and which are identified by those communities as being of critical importance to them' (Ontario Legal Aid Review, 1997).

Independent community boards should be preserved

It is, or should be, axiomatic that the character of community clinics cannot survive without independent community boards. The recent Ontario Legal Aid Review in Ontario, like others that have examined community clinics, stated that 'community governance is of fundamental importance to the mandate and operations of the community clinic system and the delivery of "poverty law" services' (*McCamus Report*, 1997:193). The *Report* described the advantages of community governance succinctly: 'Community boards have historically been important in ensuring independence from both the [Ontario Legal Aid Plan] and the provincial government; in assisting the clinic in identifying and prioritizing community needs; in ensuring accountability to their communities for the nature and quality of services provided; and, through their board members, in providing vital linkages to other community services' (ibid. 193–4).

Moreover, independent boards offer several advantages to governments interested in saving legal aid costs: independent clinics hire their own staff, reducing government payrolls and operations; the government is not legally liable for lawsuits against the clinics; and community boards donate considerable time and skills which might otherwise have to be paid for.

Legal aid plans should have specific administrative structures dedicated to clinic issues

The experience in Ontario and Australia over the last 20 years has proven the immeasurable value of having an administrative structure within the larger legal aid system specifically dedicated to clinic issues and programmes. Clinic administration is fundamentally different to the administration of other parts of a legal aid programme, especially judicare. In the absence of a dedicated administrative structure, there is a real chance that clinic issues will be lost within the larger legal aid debate. A dedicated administrative bureaucracy can provide sophisticated policy analysis appropriate to, and reflective of, the community clinic system.

Adoption of modern management techniques

At this point, we must stress the distinction between adopting modern management techniques (such as quality assurance programmes, performance measures and business planning) and centralised, hierarchical control of service priorities and delivery mechanisms. In an era in which government and legal aid administrators emphasise the need for cost-effectiveness and financial accountability, clinic resistance to the adoption of modern management techniques is self-defeating. Future funding for clinics is clearly dependent upon clinics both being able to deliver their services cost-effectively and their ability to prove that they can do so.

Our consideration of the history and current developments in Australia, Canada (Ontario) and the United Kingdom have led to certain predictions concerning the future of the clinic movement. Despite current problems, we conclude on an optimistic note. Though judicare represents the predominant model of service delivery in the United Kingdom and Ontario, and despite the movement away from community-based social programmes, community legal clinics have generally developed strong roots and distinctive structures that have a unique capacity to respond to the needs and agendas of the three jurisdictions studied. We anticipate that these strengths will allow them to continue to develop and to respond to the expectations and needs of low-income citizens in each of the three countries.

4

Making the Welfare State Work: Changing Conceptions of Legal Remedies Within the British Welfare State

TAMARA GORIELY

Legal aid has a dual relationship with the welfare state. On one hand it is a welfare provision. The level and nature of help which legal aid provides will be influenced by general societal attitudes to welfare. On the other hand, providing legal help to the poor may also play a part in enforcing welfare provision and other social rights. It may be a mechanism to make the welfare state work.

This chapter focuses on legal aid as a mechanism to help the welfare state meet its own goals. Using Britain as an example, it considers how far publicly funded legal services have been seen as a means to ensure that welfare is distributed in the way that Parliament intends. For the purposes of this discussion, the welfare state is defined broadly. It includes the provision of social security, health, education, housing and physical care, whether through the state or private suppliers. It also encompasses social rights, through anti-discrimination or employment legislation, for example, designed to ensure that individual citizens receive the care and respect they deserve.

The existing literature tends to see the legal system as central in enforcing such social or welfare rights. Cappelletti and Garth (1978:7), for example, argue that social rights require individual legal enforcement, and individual legal enforcement requires citizens to have access to justice. They see legal aid as an important (though by no means exclusive) way of ensuring such access to justice. This establishes a standard which judicare schemes are frequently criticised for failing to meet.[1]

Here we argue that it is simplistic to assume that social rights automatically require individual legal enforcement. Cappelletti and Garth's mistake was to treat as universal and self-evident a proposition that is contingent and controversial. The belief that social rights require individual enforcement is dependent on both time and place. The time was 1965 to 1989. The place was individualistic 'liberal' welfare states of developed capitalist democracies. This Chapter

[1] See e.g. Society of Labour Lawyers (1968), National Consumer Council (1989) and Legal Action Group (1992).

argues that individual legal enforcement is but one model of how welfare may be delivered. Earlier, more collectivist societies believed in 'collective enforcement'—that social rights should be enforced by society as a whole. Meanwhile, as government re-invents itself as the contracted state, the tendency is towards a new quasi-market model based on the citizen as consumer.

Enforcing social rights: three conceptions

Here we explore three models of enforcing social rights—collective enforcement, individual legal enforcement and consumerism—by considering how ideas on the role of law have developed within Britain over the last fifty years. Each model is a response to specific social values and circumstances, and needs to be understood in its social setting. Changing methods of enforcing welfare rights have profound implications for the job legal aid is expected to do.

We begin with the period 1945–51, which marks the formation of the 'classic welfare state' in Britain. During the war, citizens had assumed collective responsibilities for defending the realm, and the experience of sharing risks led to a desire for shared security. The state assumed a new responsibility for ameliorating the consequences of misfortune, whether illness, unemployment or involvement in legal actions. Among the many new schemes—including a national health service and national insurance scheme—a state-financed legal aid scheme was established. However, social rights were thought to be primarily a matter for society as a whole, rather than for the individual. They should therefore be enforced politically rather than legally. The development of a welfare state required new statutes and regulations on a previously unprecedented scale, but they were considered 'planner's law' rather than 'lawyer's law'—and therefore of no concern to the legal profession. The role of the first legal aid scheme was extremely narrow: in practice it was dominated by divorce.

Inevitably, over the next twenty years the character of the welfare state changed. During a period of peace at home, the emphasis shifted from the responsibilities citizens owed to the state to the rights the state owed to individuals. It was no longer assumed that society had a common goal: instead, values became more permissive, with individuals free to pursue their own conception of the good. At the same time, the welfare state developed from an aspiration to an institution. Gregg (1967) points out that when the term 'welfare state' first entered the *Oxford English Dictionary* in 1955 it was defined as a 'polity so organized that every member of the community is assured of his due maintenance, with the most advantageous conditions possible for all'. By 1967 it had become a state 'having national health, insurance and other social services'. During the 1960s, all social services expanded, and legal aid grew along with other parts of the welfare state.

However, with the institutionalisation of the welfare state came bureaucratisation, leading to concerns over the power exercised by welfare professionals. The

1960s and 1970s saw increasing demands that individuals should have rights against those ostensibly concerned with their welfare. An active welfare rights movement inspired increasing legalisation of the welfare state. Citizens were given new remedies to enforce directly against welfare providers. In the process, the distinction between 'planner's' law' and 'lawyer's law' broke down. A new breed of welfare lawyer started to use the legal aid scheme to help the poor in their dealings with state officials.

Although originally inspired by the left, the trend towards welfare rights was taken up and developed during the first few years of the Thatcher Government. This government, anxious to curb the power of welfare bureaucracies, enacted significant new rights—in housing, mental health, child care and education. At the same time legal aid expanded, and one of its fastest growing parts was advice about welfare problems. The expansion, however, was not nearly sufficient to cope with growing needs. In practice, welfare recipients rarely knew about their new rights; if they did, they usually lacked the confidence or resources to exercise them; and if they did get as far as a tribunal, without skilled representation they usually lost.

By the mid 1980s, society's values underwent yet another change in emphasis. Welfare was no longer seen in a purely positive light. Instead, welfare states were blamed for creating passive, dependent citizens. The emphasis was neither on responsibilities nor rights but on self-reliance—a quality thought to be encouraged by the market and destroyed by the state.[2] The British Conservative Government made no secret of its contempt for welfare bureaucrats. Perkin (1989:486) commented that it 'believed them to be parasitic upon the creators of wealth and, undisciplined by market forces, almost by definition inefficient if not actually incompetent.' The solution was to minimise the social role of welfare by targeting it at the poor alone. As the market was best, such welfare services that remained were to emulate the market model wherever possible. It was thought that politicians were best confined to deciding what services should be delivered (the 'purchaser' role). The task of providing services was either contracted to the private sector or delegated to a series of special agencies or trusts.

Again, English legal aid was caught by these wider social trends. The money spent on legal aid came under increasing scrutiny; the means test was reduced so as to concentrate help on the poor, and successive governments extolled the virtues of 'contracting' with the private profession. But the ideological shift did not only affect the delivery of legal aid: it also affected the role it was required to fulfil.

Under the new market-emulating welfare state, the role of citizen mutated into that of consumer. Consumers' primary influence was to be exercised through choice. The intention was to provide a variety of services, so that consumers could 'exit' those with which they were dissatisfied and join those that more

[2] For a useful summary of writing in this area, see Kymlicka and Norman (1994).

closely met their wishes. In many services, however, competition proved unattainable, and a substitute was needed. This was provided by allowing individuals the opportunity to 'voice' their concerns directly to those in charge through a plethora of formal complaints systems. The role of lawyers was to maintain the constitutional and market framework. Within this framework, it was hoped that most people would be able to put forward complaints without legal intermediaries. The evidence is, however, that individual recipients—usually poor, often vulnerable, inarticulate, suspicious and overwhelmed—need advice and assistance in voicing their grievances. Legal aid, with its concentration on expensive lawyers and court cases, is ill matched to provide help with these lower-level procedures. The result is a gap between the assistance people need to participate in society by voicing their concerns and the help actually provided.

Although the discussion concentrates on Britain, the models have implications for other jurisdictions. High-spending collectivist societies are most likely to initiate legal aid. Such countries are used to spending money, and if they perceive a demand for legal aid (for divorce, for example) funds are likely to be made available. However, they are also likely to rely on the collective enforcement of social rights, which means they will make little use of civil legal aid except for family disputes. Individualistic societies, on the other hand, are more likely to distrust their welfare professionals. This means that they will be more prepared to enact legal rights for individuals to enforce against welfare providers, while simultaneously being more wary about funding yet another professional group. Resources will be granted more reluctantly, even though legal aid will be faced with a wider range of social issues to tackle.

The most generously funded legal aid schemes are those, like Britain, that have moved from collectivist provision towards individualism. Schemes established according to relatively generous criteria during a collectivist era have grown to respond to the demands made by a rights-oriented individualist society. However, at the start of the twenty-first century, any scheme dominated by private practice lawyers looks increasingly anachronistic. The challenge is to develop more broadly based provision to enable citizen-consumers to express their desires and grievances effectively to those with power over their lives.

1945–50: Collective enforcement in the classic welfare state

New social rights

The Labour government of 1945–51 was elected to attack the old giants of Want, Disease, Ignorance and Squalor and to create the 'classic welfare state', based on shared risks (Lowe 1994). A commitment to full employment underpinned the universal provision of social security, health and education.

The legal aid scheme was a very small part of this brave new world. It originated in the report of the Rushcliffe Committee, published in May 1945 during the VE Day celebrations, and was inspired by all the optimism of the period. The report recommended a generous and comprehensive scheme, covering 80 per cent of the population and including all courts, tribunals and coroners' proceedings. To ensure the full co-operation of the legal profession, it put control of the scheme in the hands of the Law Society (Rushcliffe Committee, 1945). Another committee recommended a separate but similar scheme for Scotland (Cameron Committee, 1946).

The Rushcliffe scheme set a new prototype for legal aid. This is not to say that it was the first scheme—far from it. Before the war, Germany, Sweden, Finland, and Poland funded municipal bureaux employing full-time staff to give legal advice. Furthermore, Sweden, Germany, Denmark and Switzerland provided some, albeit limited, payment to advocates to conduct cases (Cohn, 1943). Blankenburg (see Chapter 5 below) describes how in Germany bureaux were a response to Bismarck's highly legalistic welfare provisions: workers needed help in understanding their entitlement. Conservative politicians worried that without state-funded services, trade unions would exploit this information gap for their own purposes. Many commentators urged Britain to follow the bureaux model (though, during the war, they quoted the Swedish example rather than the German one).[3] The Rushcliffe Committee, however, rejected such an approach. The core of the English scheme centred around private practice. It funded lawyers to do what they already did, rather than establishing specific services to assist people in claiming their welfare entitlement.

The incoming Labour Government accepted the Rushcliffe report in principle, but it took another five years before the scheme was introduced. These were five austerity years in which much of the initial optimism evaporated. Legal aid was given a low priority. The first space that could be found for it in the Government's crowded legislative timetable was in the 1948–9 parliamentary session, and by then the money had run out. The scope of the scheme was drastically reduced. First libel was excluded, then tribunals, then coroners' courts. Finally, in 1950, both legal advice and legal aid for county courts were postponed indefinitely. The first scheme covered the High Court only, and was predominantly used for divorce. In 1955, 78 per cent of all certificates issued were for divorce. County court representation was not included until 1956, and then generated only a tiny number of cases. Legal advice was added in 1959.

It is easy to gloss over these compromises as the inevitable result of limited resources, but this begs the question of why some services were funded rather than others. Why was legal advice given such a low priority? And why was divorce favoured over tribunals dealing in social rights?

[3] See e.g. Cohn (1943) and Allen-Jones (1938). Among those giving evidence to the Rushcliffe Committee, municipal bureaux were urged by the Dr Cohn, Glanville Williams, and the Independent Labour Party (Rushcliffe, 1944).

'Lawyers' law' v. *'planners' law'*

It is often suggested that legal aid followed the law: only as law expanded into new areas of life did legal aid's role broaden. In fact, Britain during the late 1940s was more highly regulated than at any other time in peace-time history. Rationing continued long after the war and by 1947 the restrictions seemed worse than ever. The government regulated many basic tasks, from buying a loaf of bread to killing a pig (Cooper, 1963). Temporary restrictions were joined by new social provisions, requiring new primary legislation, new regulation-making powers and new tribunals to hear the resulting disputes. The difference between the 1940s and 1970s was not so much in the amount of law, nor in its intrusiveness into everyday life, but in the way law was regarded. During the 1940s it was common to draw a distinction between 'real law' (or 'lawyers' law') and the regulations that beset everyday life.

The distinction was drawn most sharply by right-wing commentators. For example, in 1947 Quintin Hogg, then a young Tory MP and later Lord Chancellor, drew a distinction between the 'immutable' natural law and 'the constant, restless and apparently limitless alteration' of regulations. Real law, he suggested was unalterable while ministerial regulations from a Socialist government were inherently unconstitutional (Hogg, 1947:69, 71). Hogg's views were clearly influenced by the right-wing philosopher, Friedrich von Hayek, whose polemic against socialist planning, *The Road to Serfdom*, was published in 1944.[4] Here Hayek drew a distinction between 'formal law', which was required by the rule of law, and the regulation of economic planners. Formal law was intended to last for some time and laid down general rules applicable to all, so that 'we do not know what particular ends these rules will further, or which particular people then will assist' (Hayek, 1944: 75). By contrast, 'planning' was specific, concerned with individuals, and temporary. It privileged one group over another and was thus antithetical to the rule of law. This was a distinction that Hayek elaborated at length in his later work, *Law, Legislation and Liberty* (1973).

A modern audience may have difficulty in grasping the distinction. During the 1940s, however, it resonated with the way lawyers thought. To solicitors and barristers returning from the war and trying to pick up the threads of private practice, the plethora of emergency regulations were not the 'real' law that they remembered. Complex, changeable, disagreeable and unprofitable, they were something best avoided. If ignored long enough, they would probably go away. The legal profession had neither the expectation nor the desire to help the poor in gaining their new social rights.

[4] Hogg (1947) quotes *The Road to Serfdom* twice, both times with approval: pp. 50 and 60.

The left's suspicion of lawyers

If lawyers distrusted socialist planners, the suspicion was entirely mutual. The main architects of the welfare state—Beveridge, Bevan and Morrison—came from different political perspectives but shared a desire to keep lawyers away from their creations.

The social security system was based on Sir William Beveridge's 1942 Report, which proposed a simple scheme in which those who paid contributions received payments as of right. There would be no more intrusive investigations of means; no more discretionary decisions to be challenged. Beveridge argued that under the new scheme claimants would not need independent advice.[5] Instead, advice should come from within the organisation itself. Every local Security Office should run its own Advice Bureau 'to which every person in doubt or difficulty [could] be referred' (Beveridge, 1942, para. 397). Beveridge thought that if the Ministry were properly run, by enlightened bureaucrats such as himself, a service could be created which was both efficient and humane. He gave little attention to the question of benefit appeals, a subject that did not interest him. In one short paragraph he recommended that the appeal system should be retained more or less as it was, but should be rationalised and made local and informal (para. 394). He did not foresee any role for lawyers within the scheme.

Aneurin Bevan, the minister responsible for the National Health Service, considered lawyers dry and cautious at best. At worst they would openly support the capitalist class (Campbell, 1987). When the British Medical Association, backed by the Conservatives, demanded that dismissed doctors should have the right to appeal to a High Court judge, Bevan spoke openly of the 'judicial sabotage of Socialist legislation'.[6] The National Health Service gave few legal rights to its recipients and staff. What should be granted, and to whom, was left to the discretion of public professionals.

Meanwhile, Herbert Morrison, a senior member of the cabinet and a stalwart of municipal socialism, declared himself alarmed at the scope of the proposed legal aid scheme. In 1948, when the proposals had to be reconciled with financial constraints, he proposed that the government should allow 'no legal aid before tribunals of any description'. This was not merely a matter of finance but of principle: 'we ought to work to a position in which a man can appear personally before a tribunal and we could then reserve for the Courts cases in which he

[5] He rejected suggestions, such as that made by the National Council of Social Service (1923), advocating a centre where people could go for independent advice about an increasingly complex and remote social security system.

[6] See Report stage of National Health Service Bill, *Hansard* 23 July 1946. This was despite the fact that during the forties senior judges showed themselves less prepared to interfere with the decisions of the executive than at any time since the First World War. Decisions such as *Liversidge* v. *Anderson* [1942] AC 206 and *Franklin* v. *Minister of Town and Country Planning* [1948] AC 87 are generally regarded as the low point of judicial review.

should be represented'.[7] Morrison had his way. The Lord Chancellor's Department, unable to distinguish between those tribunals where legal aid was needed and those where it was not, responded by withdrawing all mention of tribunals from the legal aid bill.

Public accountability rather than private action

Alongside an instinctive distrust of lawyers were more ideological objections to granting individuals legally enforceable rights. In 1949, as the English Legal Aid and Advice Bill was passing through Parliament, T. H. Marshall delivered his influential essay *Citizenship and Social Class*. He divided citizenship into three elements, each associated with a period of history. Thus civil rights were struggled for in the eighteenth century, political rights in the nineteenth century and social rights in the twentieth century. Marshall is rightly remembered for stressing the importance of social rights of citizenship, but it is also worth noting what he said about enforcing the new rights. The legal aid scheme, he suggested, merely completed the eighteenth-century project by ensuring that *civil* rights could be enforced through the courts. By contrast, social rights to education, health and economic security should not be enforced by individuals. Instead, they were a matter for society as a whole, in which 'individual rights must be subordinated to national plans'. It followed that social rights should be enforced through political institutions, not through courts or tribunals: 'The obligation of the State is towards society as a whole, whose remedy in case of default lies in parliament or a local council, instead of to individual citizens, whose remedy lies in a court of law, or at least in a quasi-judicial tribunal' (Marshall, 1949:109).

This view found expression in the practical policy of the era. In 1945 it was suggested to the Ridley Committee on rent control that local authorities should be made subject to the same rent-restriction legislation as private landlords. This the Committee firmly rejected. They argued that local authorities, unlike private landlords, were non-profit making organisations acting in the public good. Any sanctions against local authorities should be political rather than legal: '. . . the fact that actions and decisions of local authorities receive publicity and are open to criticism by the public and the Press provides a safeguard for their tenants against unfair treatment' (Ridley Committee, 1945, para. 23). Meanwhile, sanctions against private landlords should be enforced by rent officers.

In the employment field, individuals' primary safeguards were through the collective action of trade unions. As emergency legislation was slowly withdrawn, unions were keen to return to 'voluntarism', in which worker's interests were secured by free collective bargaining rather than by law (Davies and Freedland, 1993). Where legislation was passed to protect vulnerable workers, it

[7] Letter from Morrison to the Lord Chancellor, Lord Jowitt, 5 Nov. 1948: Public Record Office file LCO2/4625.

was enforced by government inspectors rather than by individuals. For example, the Wages Council Act 1945, which extended the powers of Trade Boards to set minimum wages for workers in low paid industries, gave government inspectors extensive powers to enter premises, inspect documents and bring criminal prosecutions. The Disabled Persons (Employment) Act 1944 went further and specifically precluded any legal action without the express authority of the Minister of Labour.[8] The idea that individual workers would require legal services to take their own actions for discrimination or unfair dismissal was not to arise for another twenty years.

Thus within the 'classic welfare state' established during the 1940s, there was little perceived need for legal aid to help individuals establish their welfare rights. This may be explained, not by the lack of social rights, but by the steps politicians took to minimise the role of lawyers. As we have seen, welfare professionals (such as National Health Service doctors or local authority housing officers) were given considerable discretion. This discretion was overseen through a system of political accountability rather than legal enforcement. Services were designed to be simple to use: one justification for the change from means-tested to universal benefits was to reduce the problems of claiming and the resulting disputes. At work, employees were intended to rely on strong work-place trade union representation, in which disputes were handled informally between representatives of union and management. In the 'sweated trades', where employer power was not balanced by unionisation, minimum rights were enforced by government inspectors. Although regulators received complaints from individuals they did not require their active participation.

So why introduce a legal aid scheme at all? The answer lies in the particularly British approach to divorce. In 1945 divorce remained a formal, expensive, difficult and highly adversarial procedure (Stone, 1990). In was politically unacceptable to simplify divorce procedures. Although the government made some efforts in that direction, the combined opposition of church and lawyers was too strong.[9]

[8] The Act required employers to employ a quota of disabled persons. It made it a criminal offence for an employer who was under-quota to employ someone who was not registered as disabled. Prosecutions required the authority of the Minister of Labour (s. 19 (1)). Before such authority could be given, the matter would have to be considered by a district advisory committee, who must have allowed the employer to be heard and submitted a report to the Minister. No disabled person had any right to bring an action against an employer, however serious the breach. Nor did they have the right to be represented before the committee.

[9] At a Cabinet sub-committee on 5 Apr. 1946, Lewis Silkin, Minister of Town and Country Planning, argued for transferring jurisdiction to the county court, and received some support: see Public Record Office file LCO2 3943. In June 1946, the Government asked Mr Justice Denning to chair a committee on the subject. However, the opposition to county court divorce proved strong. Both the Archbishop of Canterbury and the senior judge of the Probate Divorce and Admiralty Division made vigorous private objections: see PRO file LCO2 3951. The furthest Denning could go was to propose that county court judges should be able grant divorce by sitting as special High Court commissioners. They would wear High Court robes and sit according to High Court procedures and only barristers would have rights of audience (Denning Committee, 1946).

However, it was equally unacceptable to deny divorce to the increasing numbers of couples seeking it. Legal aid was the way in which the government reconciled these opposing forces. Divorce was to stay expensive, but applicants were to receive state help in meeting the cost.

The Rushcliffe scheme: how far was the model emulated elsewhere?

The English and Scottish schemes generated considerable interest—and influenced some other jurisdictions. They served as the prototype for the Ontario plan, established in 1951, which also put administration into the hands of the Law Society. During the 1950s the Ontario plan relied on the charitable work of lawyers, but in 1967 lawyers were paid for their work out of public funds. The English judicare model also had repercussions in the Netherlands. During the war, the Dutch government-in-exile in London was heavily influenced by the Beveridge Report and other social proposals (Van Kersbergen and Becker, 1988). The Dutch introduced their own judicare legal aid scheme in 1957. It is worth noting, however, that both the Dutch and Ontarian schemes were to prove unresponsive to the changing emphasis on rights. During the 1970s they were heavily criticised for failing to deal with social issues, and were supplemented by salaried centres specialising in the social welfare problems of the poor (Schuyt, 1980; Zemans and Monahan, 1997).

In the USA, however, the British approach was uncompromisingly rejected. Most American commentators regarded collectivist provision with horror. Writing in 1949, the pioneer of legal aid in the USA, Reginald Herber Smith, noted the widespread fears that English legal aid was a step towards the 'socialisation' of the legal profession: 'The Labour Government has socialized the railroads, coal mines and other basic industries and it has been assumed in the US that legal aid is another step towards complete socialism' (Smith, 1949).

Smith himself considered such fears to be exaggerated. After visiting the Law Society, he commented that the scheme was 'certainly intended to interfere as little as is really possible with the normal relations which exist between client, solicitor and counsel' (Smith, 1949). Elson (1946) went further in advocating such a scheme for the United States. However, these were isolated voices. Johnson (1978) notes that 'although public financing—and especially Federal financing—of legal aid was always considered to be relatively controversial in some quarters, until 1950 it remained a respectable alternative, one that could be urged before any bar association or legal aid society'. After 1950, the idea ceased to be politically acceptable. The English scheme was widely condemned, while during the McCarthy era ' "creeping socialism" became the great evil, the insidious enemy of American society' (Johnson, 1978:17–18). The USA was not a collectivist society and did not introduce a collectivist legal aid scheme. As Johnson points out in Chapter 1, above, American and British legal services provision rest on very different foundations.

Collective enforcement: an unsustainable approach

Collective enforcement has many strengths. It allows a strong-willed government to make effective change quickly. While individual enforcement requires people to learn about their rights, put themselves forward and cope with the complexities of legal procedure, public agencies can 'cut straight to the chase'. They bring the power of the state to bear against malfeasors. In the long term, however, neither the British classic welfare state nor the collective approach to law enforcement were to prove sustainable.

In Britain, full employment proved unattainable and, without it, contributory benefits were unable to replace means-tested ones. In 1950 around a million Britons relied on means-tested benefits and it was assumed the number would fall. In fact, by 1992, means-tested benefits supported six million people. Beveridge's vision of a simple and dignified benefits system could not be realised. Instead, most people found claiming benefits 'an unnerving and traumatic experience' (Baldwin *et al.* 1992). Esping-Andersen's work in classifying welfare states reveals how much Britain has changed since the war. In 1950 it was one of the most 'social democratic' states in Europe, in which many benefits were provided on a universal basis, irrespective of work status. By the 1980s it was one of the most 'liberal', in which the market was the dominant force, with most state benefits granted only on a means-tested basis for those whom the market had failed (Esping-Anderson 1990).

Meanwhile, public enforcement proved overly dependent on government will. When government stopped wishing to enforce laws, they sank into abeyance, long before they had been democratically repealed.[10] Furthermore, the public lost its faith in welfare professionals. Perkin (1989) argues that arrogance and condescension were inherent in the structural character of professionalism, and would inevitably inspire a backlash. When the public came to distrust discretion handed to welfare professions, political accountability no longer proved sufficient. The language changed in to a demand for welfare 'rights'. As we see below, this was to have profound implications for legal aid.

1965–72: The rise of individual legal enforcement

The 'welfare rights' movement

Cappelletti and Garth (1978) trace legal aid reform to 1965, the year when the United States established the Legal Services Program as part of the Office of

[10] In 1989, the Wages Inspectors brought only 10 prosecutions for failing to pay minimum wages despite widespread evidence of non-compliance (Low Pay Unit 1990). The Disabled Persons (Employment) Act 1944 was effectively moribund by 1980, although it continued to exist in name until 1995.

Economic Opportunity's War on Poverty. They show how the thinking behind the programme, carried around the world by the tides of the student protest movement, led to a 'wave' of legal aid reform in the early 1970s: 1972 saw new legislation in England, France, Sweden, Germany and Quebec; in 1973 the Australian Legal Aid Office was established; in 1974 the Dutch Government set up its first legal aid bureaux.

The changes to legal aid were part of a wider movement for 'welfare rights'. In 1970 Richard Titmuss identified a myriad of different lobby groups—from old-age pensioners, single mothers and tenants to student action groups and squatters. Although it was often difficult to say what such groups favoured, it was clear what they were against—the arbitrary exercise of power, discretion and moral judgements by welfare providers (Titmuss, 1970). A series of left-wing critics castigated welfare providers for being out of touch with their clients, putting their own interests first, and pursuing bureaucratic agendas (Illich, 1977; Robinson, 1978).

'Welfare rights' were not necessarily seen in legalistic terms. At a symbolic level, 'rights' gave recipients a measure of dignity and equality lacking under the old discretionary system. However, lawyers tended to take the language of rights literally. Several committed lawyers argued that lawyers had a particular role in championing the views of the poor (Cahn and Cahn, 1964; White, 1973). They pointed out that people could take their problems to lawyers without fear of stigma. Moreover, lawyers were trained to be partisan; they could use their legal knowledge and advocacy skills to express their clients' views to others. According to Clinton Bamberger, first Director of the US Legal Services Program, legal services could 'marshal the forces of law and the power of lawyers . . . to defeat the causes and effects of poverty' (Bamberger, 1966).

Within Britain, the ideological climate set in the 1940s started to change. The distinction between lawyers' law and planners' law began to break down. As the new generation of law students started to embrace social welfare law, it slowly came to be regarded as worthy of lawyers' study. At the same time, the existing legal aid scheme was criticised for putting too much emphasis on divorce, and too little on the social welfare problems of the poor.[11] Some, such as the Society of Labour Lawyers (1968), proposed 'neighbourhood law firms' similar to those in the United States, in which salaried lawyers set up new offices in the slums and proselytised for their cause. From 1970 onwards, groups of lawyers and community activists started to set up 'law centres' in inner cities to provide lawyers for the poor. By 1979 there were twenty-eight such centres in England and Wales.

It took much longer, however, to achieve institutional change. Labour lawyers failed to convince the new Conservative Government that legal aid should include

[11] The argument received powerful support from one of the first empirical studies of legal services, carried out in Birmingham in 1969, which revealed that over 80% of civil legal aid certificates and advice bills concerned family disputes (Bridges *et al.*, 1975).

a significant salaried element. Instead, it adopted the Law Society's plans to extend advice provision though private practice. A new advice scheme was established which later became known as the Green Form scheme.[12] Law centres remained a marginal service, outside the mainstream of legal aid.

It also took longer to change substantive law. In the early 1970s, the poor had few opportunities to bring individual actions against the welfare agencies that controlled their lives. In 1973 the newly formed Legal Action Group published a list of all the areas of life where lawyers could offer advice under the newly established Green Form scheme (*LAG Bulletin*, May 1973). It was broad, including immigration, education, welfare benefits, debt, housing, planning, mental health, and complaints against the police. Yet only rarely were lawyers able to assert specific legal rights. The suggestions for action show that usually lawyers could do little more than explain their clients' circumstances to the bureaucracy or, where this failed, explain the bureaucratic system to the client.[13] The Legal Action Group was several steps ahead of the legislation. It was putting forward a moral argument that the poor *ought* to have more rights against welfare providers rather than reflecting existing legislation.

As the decade progressed, however, governments started to enact more legislation that required individuals to bring their own actions, either to courts or to tribunals. Significant changes were introduced to employment law, with new rights to combat unfair dismissal and discrimination (Davis and Freedland, 1993). In 1975 the Labour Government's white paper on race discrimination argued that relying on a government agency to bring actions against discriminators was 'cumbersome, ineffective and unduly paternalistic'. Instead, individuals should be free to bring their own complaints before industrial tribunals (Home Office 1975).

Early Thatcherism and the rise of rights

When in 1979 a Conservative Government was elected under the premiership of Margaret Thatcher the emphasis on individual enforcement gathered momentum. In 1970, Titmuss had referred to a 'paradoxical alliance' between the 'new Diceyists' of the political Right, who wished to reduce administrative empires, and the welfare rights campaigners of the left who also distrusted state bureaucrats (Titmuss, 1970). During the 1980s it was an alliance that was to prove particularly powerful. The Thatcher Government was particularly keen to reduce what was seen as the unaccountable discretion of public professionals, and in its

[12] Legal Advice and Assistance Act 1972. For accounts of this period see Stephens (1991) and Zander (1978).

[13] For example, advice about choice of schools was a matter of 'writing to education authorities'; dealing with homelessness involved contacting social services and the housing department and advising on the 'points system of allocation'; council tenants facing possession summonses were to be 'advised about eviction'; while discrimination matters were 'referred to the Race Relations Board'.

early years it gave electors many new rights against them. In 1980 public tenants were given security of tenure for the first time.[14] In the same year, parents acquired new rights to appeal against local authorities' allocation of school places,[15] while the Education Act 1981 allowed them to challenge assessments of special education needs. The Mental Health Act 1983 increased the possibility of legal challenge to medical decisions, while parents gained extended powers to challenge social services departments who deprived them of access to children in care.[16]

An even greater upheaval occurred within the social security system. In 1980 the Conservative Government implemented previous plans to turn the discretionary allowances of supplementary benefit into legal entitlements. The reforms originated in poverty campaigners' attempts to make the system fairer, but the government thought they offered the opportunity to curb expenditure (Baldwin *et al.*, 1992). At first they succeeded: one-off payments for special needs fell from 1,129,000 in 1980 to 834,000 in 1981. Claimants were often mystified by the changes, and failed to understand how to bring their individual circumstances within the boundaries of the rules (Allbeson and Smith, 1984). Soon, however, advisers realised that they understood the scheme better than the poorly trained DHSS officers, and could use the rigidity of the rules to gain more money for their clients.[17] As the new system became better understood, the number of single payments soared, topping four million by 1985. This was accompanied by an increase in claims to tribunals.[18] Meanwhile, the old (and much criticised) supplementary benefit appeal tribunals became increasingly legalistic, culminating in the creation of new social security appeal tribunals in 1984.

Titmuss points out that the move towards welfare rights followed US experience, and reflected the values of a more individualist, liberal society. Often a rights approach was associated with greater selectivity, in which welfare was targeted at those in greatest need. As one of the war-time generation, he argued passionately against such selectivity in favour of a return to universal benefits, provided to poor and non-poor alike without the intervention of lawyers and advisers (Titmuss, 1970). His, however, was a lone voice in a world increasingly doubting the capacity of the old welfare institutions to deliver on their promises.

The pressures on legal aid

The 1980s saw a rapid expansion of the legal aid scheme, in terms of the number of solicitors participating, the money spent and the work done. In England and

[14] Housing Act 1980. This was a necessary first step towards allowing council tenants the right to buy their homes. Without security of tenure, hostile councils may have evicted those who attempted to purchase their homes.

[15] Education Act 1980.

[16] See Health and Social Services and Social Security Adjudication Act 1983 and Children Act 1989.

[17] One solicitor claimed that, by providing a benefit check for all his clients on supplementary benefit, he could gain additional income for 70% of them (Smith, 1989).

[18] The number of applications rose from 75,500 in 1980 to 202,000 in 1986 (Council on Tribunals 1981 and 87).

Wales, social welfare advice was one of the fastest growing areas, with the number of 'Green Form' bills for advice on housing, welfare benefits, debt, employment and immigration rising from around 63,000 bills in 1980/1 to 220,000 bills in 1990/1. But the expansion was not nearly sufficient to meet the increased demand. The change towards individual rights, coupled with more individual enforcement, put enormous pressure on the legal aid scheme. Empirical studies showed that individuals needed advice and assistance to take advantage of their new rights (Baldwin *et al.*, 1992). Those attending tribunals were more likely to win if represented (Genn and Genn, 1989). A series of commentators criticised the legal aid scheme for relying too heavily on private lawyers, concentrating too much on divorce and failing to provide adequate advice on social welfare law (National Consumer Council, 1989; Legal Action Group, 1992). The problems were compounded by the exclusion of tribunal representation from the scheme. As the decade closed, English legal aid was a collectivist scheme trying unsuccessfully to cope with a new individualistic age.

The 1990s: The age of consumerism— regulating bureaucracy through 'exit' and 'voice'

The new welfare rhetoric

By the mid-1990s a powerful change had taken place in the rhetoric of welfare. The word 'welfare', far from implying the positive aspiration of the 1940s, was now seen as essentially negative—becoming associated with dependency, passivity and unaffordable expense. Moreover, public services were seen as compounding the errors, but being overblown, unresponsive and inefficient. The solution was thought to lie in making welfare services as much like the private sector as possible. The new rhetoric imported the terminology of the market into the welfare debate, with talk of 'contracting', 'consumers' and 'choice'. As Harden (1992) points out, such words appeal to powerful symbols, suggesting individual autonomy and consumer sovereignty. In 1991, the Conservative Government's 'Citizen's Charter' provided an impetus to this debate (Cabinet Office, 1992).

Under collective enforcement, citizens' first remedy is political action; rights-holders' first remedy is legal action. To economists, however, consumer sovereignty is primarily exercised through 'exit'. That is, consumers have the option of leaving an undesirable supplier and joining one that more closely meets their needs. In a competitive market, managers will respond to the possibility of exit by more closely meeting demands. The Citizen's Charter argued that, wherever possible, consumers should be given a choice of providers. Poor quality providers would thus be subject to the discipline of the market. However, the nature of the public sector means that competition is strictly limited. In the end, we do not have a choice over who collects our taxes, who pays our social security payments or who takes our children into care. Despite the rhetoric of consumer choice, competition has only a limited effect on the public sector.

In 1970 Hirschman described a second mechanism by which consumers, members and citizens can exert influence over providers. He called it 'voice'. The Major Government of the early 1990s came to agree with Hirschman that, in the public sector, 'voice' is often as, if not more, important than 'exit'. The Citizen's Charter emphasised complaints procedures, through which assertive citizens would 'increasingly put pressure upon those responsible for providing services to deliver them to a higher standard' (Cabinet Office, 1992). In 1993 the Cabinet Office established a task force to encourage the development of internal complaints systems throughout the public sector. The decade saw an explosion of new adjudicators, commissioners and ombudsman (from the Revenue Adjudicator to the Prison Ombudsman) to provide some independent element to organisations' internal complaints procedures.

Complaints procedures are now seen as an essential mechanism by which to discipline public services. They are clearly an important form of voice—but a narrow one. Hirschman himself defined voice as: 'any attempt at all to change, rather than to escape from, an objectionable state of affairs, whether through individual or collective petition to the management directly in charge, through appeal to a higher authority with the intention of forcing a change in management, or through various types of action and protests, including those that are meant to mobilize public opinion' (Hirschman, 1970:30).

Thus Hirschman saw it as including both individual and collective action. The Citizen's Charter, however, considered only individual action. Barron and Scott (1992) comment that the Citizen's Charter reinterpreted 'citizens' as welfare 'consumers'. Furthermore, complaints procedures direct the brunt of criticism at managers (especially fairly low-level managers) rather than politicians. They are therefore quite different from the politically directed criticism that Marshall (1949) saw as the most appropriate way of disciplining public services in the 1940s.

The backlash against rights

Simultaneously, the British Government came to regret its previous emphasis on individual rights. Simply put, rights proved too expensive. Once individuals had been granted legally enforceable rights to a service or payment, they could not be denied because the budget was overspent.

Social security reforms led the backlash against rights. In 1988 the Government abolished the old means-tested 'supplementary benefit' with its elaborate single payments and additional allowances to meet particular needs. Instead, the new benefit of 'income support' paid fixed amounts with premiums based on easily identifiable attributes such as age and family status. This could be supplemented only in rare circumstances, by loans and grants from a new 'social fund' working within a cash-limited budget. Those refused social fund help were no longer entitled to appeal to a tribunal, for tribunals could not be required to keep within the budget. Instead recourse was to internal Social Fund Inspectors, as monitored by the Social Fund Commissioner. Similar approaches were adopted elsewhere. For example, the 1986 Disabled Persons Act established an appeal system for those disabled people denied services by their local authority. This, however, was never implemented. Instead, the 1990 NHS and Community Care Act emphasised internal complaints procedures.

Reducing legal aid

In the current climate, 'legal' is often seen as a term of abuse. Official speeches and reports frequently attack lawyers for being greedy and legal procedures for being slow, expensive and uncertain.[19] Instead, we are told to explore a variety of alternatives—such as ombudsmen, arbitration schemes and mediation (Lord Chancellor's Department, 1995b; Woolf, 1996; Lord Chancellor's Department, 1998).

The combination of public-spending restraints and attacks on lawyers do not augur well for legal aid. In England and Wales, the Conservative Government produced a White Paper that proposed to replace a demand-led legal aid system with one based on cash-limits. It suggested abolishing the traditional right to legal aid for those meeting the means and merits test. Instead, the Legal Aid Board would 'contract' with a range of suppliers to provide services (Lord Chancellor's Department, 1996). The Labour Government, far from reversing these policies, is continuing their implementation. As a first step, it has proposed cash-limiting the civil advice and assistance scheme from 1999 (Legal Aid Board, 1998a). In addition, legal aid for personal injury work will be replaced by conditional fees. As this volume makes clear, such cutbacks are an international phenomenon. It appears that the money has run out for all developed legal aid schemes. Australia, Ontario, Quebec, and the Netherlands have all experienced reductions in the level of resources spent on legal aid (see Chapter 5 below).

Amid this gloomy news it is important to remember that making oneself heard is not an optional extra: it is an essential mechanism to ensure responsive public services. It therefore has public as well as private benefits. The public have a vested interest in giving the necessary assistance to those brave and determined individuals willing to voice their grievances.

Are complaints systems accessible?

Complaints procedures appear to offer some solutions to the access problems associated with legal procedures. The government has stressed that, unlike

[19] For examples see Woolf (1996:2) and the views of the Lord Chancellor, Lord Irvine (*Legal Action*, Aug. 1997, 4).

welfare tribunals, the new entities should be well-publicised, informal, consumer-friendly and suitable for people to use by themselves.

The practice, however, is often different. Even the final social security safety-net for those in need, the 'social fund', is controlled by voluminous guidance and a complex series of reviews. We have already discussed the change from rights-based appeals to internal reviews by social fund inspectors, reporting to a Social Fund Commissioner (Baldwin *et al.*, 1992). The Commissioner has taken pains to establish the inspectors as an independent service: she stresses that their function is judicial, and that much of their function is to ensure the correct interpretation of law and directions.[20] Although they examine issues on the papers, the Commissioner emphasises that this is effectively a paper hearing which must accord with the rules of natural justice. Thus claimants are allowed to comment on what the local office says. While the system therefore has some of the advantages of the judicial model of decision-making, it also shares its weaknesses. Dalley and Berthoud (1992) found little to choose between tribunals and inspectors on grounds of cost or time taken. Moreover, applicants were frequently confused by the system: they had little knowledge of what was available or how the review system worked, and officers agreed that they were rarely able to present claims in the most effective way. All those involved thought that skilled welfare rights advisers were still enormously important in helping to prepare claims (Dalley and Berthoud, 1992:121).

Research shows that most people do not know about complaints systems, and those who do know about them do not use them.[21] A survey of complaints in one 'model' local authority showed that around two-fifths of citizens had a grievance. Yet only a third of those with grievances had even contacted the council—and only a tiny proportion used the formal channels, such as an authority-wide complaints scheme and the local government ombudsman (McCarthy *et al.*, 1992). Those who do use self-help systems are drawn disproportionately from the middle classes. Surveys consistently show that they draw their clientele from the top fifth of the population—the professional and managerial classes.[22]

This leaves two groups of unvoiced people: the poor (or bottom fifth of the population) and the middle-income group (the vital 60 per cent of the population on whose support the stability of the state depends).

[20] Department of Social Security (1993). Lewis and Birkinshaw (1993) comment that they are 'impressed by her efforts to ensure procedural fairness and efficiency in a much discredited scheme'.

[21] For example, a survey for the electricity regulator, OFFER, shows only 3% of all consumers would even think of contacting them about a problem (MORI, 1993); no more than 27% of the population claim to have heard of the private-sector ombudsman schemes, even when prompted (Office of Fair Trading, 1991); while the complexities of the National Health Services complaints schemes defeat two thirds of the population (Clarke *et al.*, 1988).

[22] See the recent study of small claims in Baldwin (1996). The AB social groups (professional and managerial workers) account for 18% of those dissatisfied with their holidays and 59% of those using the Association of British Travel Agents arbitration scheme (National Consumer Council, 1991). Similarly, they form 22% of mortgagors but 46% of those complaining to the Building Society Ombudsman about mortgages (National Consumer Council, 1993).

Access for the poor

It is important to remember just how vulnerable the poor are when it comes to expressing their grievances. Many are: 'financially poor, are dispirited and unwell; are lonely, isolated and inarticulate; cannot properly read and write; they are sometimes fearful and occasionally angry' (McCarthy and Simpson, 1993).

Furthermore there may be years of distrust to overcome, if people are to be persuaded that 'they' will listen to their grievances. As Doyle and Harding (1992) comment, agencies are at their most formidable when challenged, and users often need external help. The issue is particularly acute for the most vulnerable members of society—such as children and young people in residential care—who are dependent on those against whom they wish to direct their complaints (Lindsay, 1991; Plowden, 1993).[23] A major survey of local government complaints schemes found that they were usually 'woefully inadequate' as a way of protecting highly vulnerable client groups such as children or the elderly in residential care (Lewis *et al.*, 1987).

Access for middle-income groups

Meanwhile, middle-income groups have seen their access to justice decrease in recent years. In 1993 they were excluded from the Green Form scheme and only admitted to litigation aid on the payment of much increased contributions. Their access to advice agencies has also decreased. Citizens advice bureaux were established during the war as a broad-based service. Over the last fifteen years, however, the work of CABx has become increasingly concentrated on the chronic problems of the poor—debt, welfare benefits and housing.[24] Bureaux are less and less able to fulfil the role they once played—of offering accessible, one-off information about a broad range of issues to a wide variety of people. Research commissioned by the National Association of Citizens Advice Bureaux found that many people no longer regarded bureaux as a place to take general worries about health, education or discrimination (Petterson *et al.*, 1995). People commented that CABx were now a service for those 'with no choice and at the edge' or 'with nothing else and nowhere to go' (Petterson *et al.*, 1995:21).

A new strategy is needed to improve complaints systems and to make them accessible to a wider range of people. People need more varied help, through different forums, many of which are not strictly 'legal' in the traditional sense. This, however, is easier said than done. Politicians and administrators are caught

[23] The problem is not confined to Britain: van Vliet (1990) criticises Dutch children's home procedures on the grounds that children are rarely represented.

[24] In 1980, social security, housing and employment work accounted for some 36% of CABx' workload: by 1994/5, it had increased to 50%. When one adds in debt work (which in 1980 was hardly discussed and not recorded separately) the current proportion of social welfare work rises to 58% (Social Trends, 1994; National Association of Citizens Advice Bureaux, 1995).

within the confines of the existing system, in which legal aid is interpreted narrowly—as focused on lawyers and courts. Responsibility for improving out-of-court justice is relegated to the occasional committees—whose conclusions, however valuable, are too soon forgotten. It is still not seen as a mainstream activity of government.

Conclusion

This Chapter has argued that the task a society sets for legal aid depends on its attitudes towards welfare enforcement. This in turn depends on deeper attitudes towards welfare. We have identified three different approaches, each with their own implications for legal aid.

Collectivist states have the fewest problems. While they are likely to fund legal aid schemes reasonably generously, they make relatively little demand on them. The modern legal aid scheme that comes closest to the collectivist model is probably that of Sweden. Sweden is well known for its strong universalistic welfare state, consensual labour relation and active labour policies geared towards full employment. It has one of the highest rates of trade union membership in the world.[25] Generous social security provision coupled with no-fault liability schemes leave little room for personal injury tort claims.[26] Strong workplace organisations usually obviate the need for employment cases to be funded under legal aid.[27] Meanwhile consumer and other market regulations are enforced though strong agencies such as the Consumer Ombudsman. The result is that legal aid has little role in making the welfare state work. Instead the scheme is dominated by family problems—which account for more than 80 per cent of all cases brought under legal aid (Johnsen, 1994).

The English scheme, founded during a collectivist era, grew to maturity during an individualistic age, in which individuals were expected to enforce their own entitlements through courts and tribunals. The result is a highly expensive scheme, stuck in a traditionally legal mould, trying desperately to cope with the mass of individual case work. Attitudes are now changing around it for a third time, as individual legal redress is being replaced by a more consumerist model. New systems for complaints and reviews are being established, through which consumers are meant to voice their grievances so disciplining welfare providers. Yet legal aid does too little to give people the help they need to participate. It is too legalistic, too court-dominated, and concentrates too heavily on individual case-work at the expense of education and reform activity.

[25] In 1991, 77% of manual workers and 80% of white-collar members were trade union members.

[26] In 1992, legal aid funded only 2,000 such cases (0.25 cases for every 1,000 people, compared with 1.83 cases in England and Wales) (Johnsen, 1994).

[27] In 1992, legal aid funded only 335 such claims (Johnsen, 1994).

The Australian schemes appear to have progressed further towards the consumerist model. Regan points out that although Australian legal aid has lower levels of eligibility and expenditure than the Swedish scheme, it has some significant strengths. It offers a greater choice of providers, and a wider range of services (Regan, 1994b). More emphasis is placed on information and education, whether through pamphlets and kits or 'do-your-own divorce classes' (Regan, 1996:93–4). Furthermore, it is easier for people to find out about their options through advice 'which is comprehensive, universally available and free' (Regan, 1994b:35). Finally, law reform activity can voice the poor's concern on a collective basis.

Britain faces a challenge that it shares with other liberal welfare states. How can it equip its citizens with the means to voice their needs, interests and views to the bureaucracies that impact on their lives? Such 'voice' is an increasingly important part of democratic participation, to provide responsive public services and to restore public confidence in apparatus of government. The challenge is to switch from individual legal casework to provide the information, education, advice and support people need.

Part Two

Comparative Studies

5

The Lawyers' Lobby and the Welfare State: The Political Economy of Legal Aid

ERHARD BLANKENBURG

This Chapter analyses and accounts for the different amounts spent on legal aid in a selection of developed countries. It starts by describing the limits and success of three legal aid movements: the *right to counsel* codification in European Continental codes, the *peace of law movement* in Germany around the turn of the century and the *legal aid movement* in some of the welfare states of the 1970s. Explanations are sought for why legal aid grows in some countries but meets resistance in others under similar circumstances. As main factors, the prosperity of the welfare state and the success of lawyer lobbies in defending professional privilege are singled out. They provide the key to explaining why Canadian provinces or Australian states have, but American states have not (and why Scandinavian countries and the Netherlands have, but Germany or France have not) invested in legal aid infrastructures. The way legal aid institutions are embedded within the welfare system and in the legal profession also explains why current austerity politics have managed to put a ceiling on Dutch and Scandinavian expenditures but not on the British legal aid scheme.

1. Historical movements in the development of legal aid

1.1. The first movement: 'right to legal counsel'

My point of departure is the observation that legal aid has nowhere been pushed by the 'needs' of those groups for whom it is designed (Abel, 1985). The two movements for legal aid experienced this century occurred during times of relative economic and social growth in countries that could afford them, rather than in those that needed them most. Furthermore, the labelling of the poor's needs as 'legal needs' has never come from the needy themselves, but rather from professionals who took it as their task to care for them. Many of their good intentions have, however, foundered: some neighbourhood legal services, mediation centres and diversion projects had to close because of lack of demand, while others have been flooded with more clients than they could handle. Market research on the 'legal needs' of the poor[1] has not been able to bridge two gaps:

- the perception gap between 'needs' as perceived by professional researchers and those perceived by poor people themselves;[2] and
- the action gap between perceived needs and actual demand for action to be taken.[3]

Thus *legal aid* has become what lawyers think they can offer to those who have some acknowledged status of being poor, marginalised and discriminated against. Whatever legal aid recipes have been brought forward, they are shaped by the capacities (and sometimes the interests) of what the legal profession has to offer. They are supply-shaped, rather than demand-led.

This benevolent top-down approach to legal aid has a long tradition. It formed the principle behind the codifications of a 'poor man's law' in most Continental countries during the nineteenth century.[4] The 'right to counsel' established by such codes did not entail more than court fee waivers and the appointment of duty solicitors for very poor people. At first, attorneys were expected to act on a professional *pro bono* basis, though later (in most countries in the twentieth century) moderate fees were granted on a statutory basis. In the German *Kaiserreich,* for example, it took until after the First World War for lawyers to be remunerated and, even then, consultation in the early stages of a conflict was left to lawyers' charity—a limitation characteristic of the formal approach to legal services. To curb demand, the prosecutor fiscal was given the task of determining whether a claim was frivolous.[5]

Even today in civil cases the European Court on Human Rights restricts the *right to counsel* to lawyer costs in courts where representation by an attorney is mandatory. In trying to find an expression that is neutral between continental civil law and common law, it guarantees a *fair hearing*, which may mean a right to a lawyer where representation is required but could just as well be satisfied by simplified procedures without representation by lawyers.[6]

The strategy of anchoring a *right to counsel* as a basic, inalienable right proved successful in some common law countries with respect to criminal defence.[7] As

[1] See e.g. the repeated studies of Curran (1977; 1996).

[2] Extensively discussed in Blankenburg and Reifner (1981).

[3] See John Griffiths (1980) for a critique of 'legal needs' research.

[4] See Earl Johnson (1985). He attempts to establish a principle Right to Counsel independent of historical context by citing early codifications of the enlightened absolutism such as the Austrian Justizgesetzsammlung JGS 1781 and JGS 161, Hofdekret of 24.1.1791 together with the Spanish Reglamento por l'Administracion de la Justicia of 1835, the French Code procedurale of 1851, the German Zivilprozeßordnung 1877, etc.

[5] Arts.114–27 ZPO (civil procedural code).

[6] European Court on Human Rights, *Airey* v. *Ireland*, Judgment of 9 Oct. 1979, series A,32.

[7] The key US decision was *Gideon* v. *Wainwright* 372 US 335 (1963) in which the Supreme Court interpreted the Sixth Amendment to the US Constitution as requiring each state to make provision to provide counsel to all those accused of serious crimes who could not otherwise afford help. But see also the Canadian Charter of Rights, s. 10(b).

a principle, the right to defence counsel cannot easily be dismissed, but it invites cost-effective organisation outside private practice. When the United States Supreme Court granted a constitutional right to a defence lawyer in any criminal procedure, many states (especially in urban areas) quickly established *public defender* offices to satisfy the constitutional right without running into the costs of having to compensate full lawyer fees.[8]

However, most European countries have interpreted the right to legal aid restrictively. Applying a '*fair hearing*' criterion, duty solicitors are appointed wherever defence by a lawyer is mandatory. As most simple procedures before criminal courts do not statutorily require a lawyer, legal aid is not granted either. British and Dutch lawyers have suggested that the European Convention extends further than where representation is mandatory, and some case-law supports this.[9] However, most Continental European judges would be reluctant to grant free legal counsel as a human right in a way which goes beyond the legal aid schemes they are used to from their home countries. In Germany, France, most Latin countries and most Eastern European countries the *right to counsel* alone gives no guarantee of a criminal defence in either misdemeanour courts or in police or prosecutors' investigations.

Just as in civil and public law matters legal aid becomes effective only when established as more than a formal procedural right, it appears that criminal legal aid also needs an institutional infrastructure. If some court districts provide pre-trial legal defence and legal aid for early consultation, this is because lawyers have established such an infrastructure, either on the basis of some interest group organisation or in the framework of other social benefits. This renders it doubtful whether a strategy of demanding more effective legal aid schemes on the basis of human rights claims would be successful on a European level.

1.2. The second movement: legal aid to appease the class struggle

The approach was less formal when interest groups took the initiative to provide representation in their members' conflicts. At the turn of the century, trade unions in Germany invested in a network of legal advice and consultation bureaux, and they soon met with competition from city administrators and even church organisations. Trade unions instituted the first legal advice centres for their members as early as 1890. These were soon followed by charitable legal aid institutions established by churches and, later, by public institutions set up by local government.

8 A 1986 survey of US counties found that 52% used assigned-counsel schemes as their main provision; 37% used public defenders and 11% used contracts: Bureau of Justice Statistics (1988). Thus in terms of number of schemes, assigned counsel schemes are still the most common. However, larger cities tend to use public defenders; it has been estimated that around two-thirds of the population is now covered by public defender schemes: see Klien and Spangenburg (1993).

9 Art. 6.3 talks of free representation 'when the interests of justice so require' which seems wider than the 'fair hearing' criterion set out in Art. 6.1. For a discussion of the case-law, see Ashworth (1996).

All sides used them for binding a clientele to their social ideology. They mirrored political forces' fight for ideological dominance during periods of rapid industrialisation.

Legal aid movements generally emerge as a response to social issues. At the end of the nineteenth century, the German *Reich* was experiencing industrialisation and the rapid rise of a workers' movement. Compared with England, industrialisation came late to Germany and, especially in Prussia, it was characterised by the alliance of big landowners, big industry and the state. Both workers' unions and workers' parties were repressed by economic as well as legal means. When in 1878 Bismarck outlawed 'all associations which aimed at overturning the order of the state and society by social democratic, socialist or communist means', this was only the highlight of the legal repression of the workers' movement. At about the same time, however, he introduced the illness insurance law in 1883, the accident insurance law for industrial workers in 1884, and insurance for retired and handicapped people in 1889. All of these were attempts to prevent the industrial proletariat from organising in socialist parties and unions by paternalistically solving some of their social problems. When in 1890 the Social Democratic Party were successful in the general elections, the anti-socialist law had to be dropped, but the social security legislation remained as a feature of a welfare state that claimed to be above the antagonism of class interests. Thus, against its general conservatism, the Prussian state in the time of Bismarck became a forerunner in corporatist welfare policy.

The workers' union secretariats undertook the task of giving advice about these new rights, granted under the social security laws, the Instalment Credit Protection Act 1894 and the Labour Protection Acts 1891. In 1904, when 226,260 persons sought advice from the forty-eight workers' secretariats,[10] bourgeois politicians recognised that workers' legal aid would be a necessary part of their attempt to integrate the working class through social policy institutions. The former Minister of Trade, Möller, expressed this opinion publicly when he stated to the Prussian Parliament: 'The propaganda activities through legal counselling administered by the Social Democratic Party are exceedingly vast, exceedingly intensive and exceedingly effective, and we would be gravely negligent if we did not satisfy this need in a different way' (Brunner, 1906).

With the support of the Government, local communities and religious nonprofit organisations established legal aid offices to offer free legal advice to all citizens. In these legal advice centres, laymen worked with public functionaries, especially those who were concerned with legal affairs in public administrative courts. The legal advice was to be given in an objective and nonpartisan way and the goal was to maintain social peace and to prevent 'unnecessary litigation' (Radbruch, 1919).

[10] See *Reichsarbeitsblatt*, continuous reporting. The 1913 issue announces that data on similar legal services in the Netherlands and in Scandinavian countries would be published; this, however, was prevented by the outbreak of World War I.

Table 5.1: Legal aid in Germany 1912: number of offices and their activities

		Legal aid offices	Number of counsellings	Number of written actions on behalf of clients
I.	Public legal aid	119	337,071	57,563
II.	Denominational legal aid			
	1. Protestant	23	30,838	13,434
	2. Catholic	122	235,638	90,713
III.	Legal aid by workers' associations			
	1*a*. Workers' secretariats of the free trade unions	119	701,648	173,897
	1*b*. Legal aid by the trade union cartels	211	51,772	18,748
	2. Federations of artisans (*Deutsche Gewerkvereine*)	55	58,365	11,185
	3. Christian trade unions	55	40,056	22,490
	4. Polish occupational union	8	21,081	12,224
	5. Other workers' associations	6	3,166	1,516
IV.	Legal aid by associations of employees	23	58,703	1,319
V.	Legal aid by rural co-operatives	9	17,056	584
VI.	Legal aid by management	9	12,461	5,017
VII.	Legal aid by political associations	32	33,732	14,463
VIII.	Women's legal aid	93	45,485	8,859
IX.	Other non-profit organisations	32	194,292	36,016
Total		916	1,841,364	468,028

Source: 1913 *Reichsarbeitsblatt*, Beiheft

Within a few years, competition led to a legal aid infrastructure provided by three of the main societal forces: trade unions, churches and public authorities. Like Bismarck's policy of social insurance in the 1880s, this competition between private and public legal aid societies helped to appease social conflicts in the German Reich of the early 1900s. Even trade unions were not against such appeasement, as became clear from their policy of promoting bureaux under the label of the *peace of law* movement. The legal aid movement around the turn of the century even reached the United States where it was used to integrate German immigrants into the New World (Smith, 1919).

After World War I, however, these legal aid institutions experienced only a brief revival and they slowly died away during the economic and political breakdowns of the Weimar Republic. It did not take much effort to corrupt the surviving peace of law bureaux under the Third Reich and to integrate them into the corporative institutions of the Fascist state (Reifner, 1982).

The Federal Republic of Germany has not seen any revival in the *peace of law* movement. The only element left is the right of trade unions to give legal advice (exclusively on social and labour law matters) to their members—one of the rare exemptions from the advocates' monopoly. Trade union advice is significant in individual as well as collective labour conflicts: in 1989 the West German trade unions employed over 300 legal officials to give advice to their members, and they played a major role after unification when Communist infrastructures on the shop floor of East German companies were overturned.

But on the whole the unification of the German states in 1990 did not give rise to any serious investment in a legal aid infrastructure, although East German's legal needs were obvious to everybody: after all, they were shifted overnight to a legal system which was entirely different from what they had been used to. The same holds true for other post-Communist countries in Central and Eastern Europe. Despite academic relativism around the non-objectivity of research constructions of legal needs, the regime change from Communism to Western rule might be the long-desired social situation where researchers can legitimately talk of legal needs independent of subjective demand. Communist regimes did not cherish legal institutions, but they embraced the population with welfare provision. But while the post-Communist regimes propagate the rule of law together with privatisation of social risks, legal aid remains conspicuously absent. Lawyers are far too busy grasping the gains of the emerging market economy to care about professional charities.

1.3. The third movement: legal aid as part of the welfare state

Vitality was restored to the cause of legal aid when pioneers transformed the legal aid movement of the booming welfare state in the 1960s and 70s (Capelletti and Garth, 1978; Cappelletti, 1984). Enthusiasm spread among law graduates and young lawyers in both the English-speaking world and a few of the most developed European welfare states such as the Netherlands and Scandinavia. The movement went beyond *right to counsel* arguments by stating that effective access to law required not only representation in court but advice. After all, people did not arrive with law suits but with problems, and these required professional reformulation to be apt for legal pursuit. The welfare state was booming: fed by three decades of growing prosperity, welfare regulation had reached unprecedented levels of bureaucratic refinement. For progressive young lawyers this was reason enough to defend welfare consumers against too much government interference. Their arguments both relied on the welfare state and were antagonistic towards it. It was suggested the more that public provision took over the regulation of life risks, the more reasons existed to resist regulatory interventions in private spheres. The welfare state trend towards judicialisation evoked the reproach of 'colonisation of individual well-being by the law'.[11]

The in-built welfare contradiction, however, was not the main reason most countries on the European Continent failed to include legal services in the general growth of welfare state provisions. A more important factor lay in lawyers' reluctance to espouse the cause of legal aid. German and French lawyers' associations, in particular, pursued only a limited professional interest. The profession was concerned with duty defence schemes and in complementing court fee waiver schemes with sufficient remuneration of their fees. However, they remained reluctant to extend legal aid further. One might argue that they used the existence of a subsidized *right to counsel* scheme to hinder the establishment of specialised *social advocacy*.

The litmus test of a developed legal aid infrastructure is whether it helps solve the problems people experience in accessing traditional lawyers. This makes the active involvement of the legal profession a necessary condition for successful legal aid development. The professional involvement might be triggered by ideological movements (such as the student movement of the 1960s and '70s) or it might originate in political strategies, as occurred in the post-Bismarck era. But nowhere can it survive without satisfying some long-term interest of the legal profession itself. Perceived professional self-interests not only determine the willingness of lawyers' lobbies to go along with movements for legal aid: even more importantly, they shape lawyers' coping strategies once a market in subsidised legal services has been established. This leaves us with the conclusion that a more or less effective legal aid scheme is dependent on two factors: a generally high level of welfare state provision and the willingness of the legal profession to be included among its providers.

2. A country by country comparison

Our multi-country comparison sets out to compare only countries which were known to have developed an effective legal aid infrastructure for a wide array of problems, not just criminal defence. This implies that the comparison is restricted to the rich countries around the world. In some countries of the former British commonwealth like India or Bangladesh, we find admirable lawyer initiatives. Likewise, we find legal clinics in South Africa and at Latin American universities encouraged by development programmes. Lacking a welfare state environment, however, they remain isolated initiatives, sponsored by reform-minded groups, often from rich countries. As one would predict, without a welfare state covering basic poverty one does not find a developed legal aid infrastructure.

[11] Aptly brought under the umbrella of sociological theories by Habermas (1981).

Even by confining our comparison to rich countries, we find a range of provision, allowing ample opportunity to compare the effect of professional interests on legal aid. Only a few countries have historically been big spenders on legal aid: these are the United Kingdom, the well-to-do ex-Commonwealth countries and the Netherlands. The Scandinavian countries spend less money, but have developed encompassing criminal and civil schemes embedded in general welfare state provision. Several developed welfare states, such as Germany, France and their well-to-do neighbours have only reluctantly enlarged their traditional *right-to-counsel* provisions. Finally, there are rich countries with low welfare provisions such as the United States and Japan which have left (at least civil) legal aid largely to lawyers' *pro bono* initiatives.

We have used taxpayers' money spent on legal aid as a leading indicator for

Table 5.2: Legal aid provisions as dependent on welfare state levels

Legal aid provisions	Welfare state level extensive	Welfare state level limited
mixed delivery high expense	United Kingdom, all provinces in Canada, Australia, New Zealand Netherlands	
moderate expense	Norway, Sweden	
low expense	Ireland	
public offices		
moderate expense	Finland	
low expense	Austria	
right to counsel + *legal aid by lawyers* low expense	Germany, France	
right to counsel (civil + criminal) low expense	Eastern Europe Belgium, Spain, Italy	Switzerland Japan
few public civil aid with high spending on criminal defence		most states of the United States of America

Sources: Survey among members of the international working group on legal aid (see footnote 1). Questionnaires based on national data 1994/95. Data for Switzerland (Kanton Zürich) and Japan (National Association of Bengoshi) are based on personal communication. Ibem dito Austria which provides legal consultation at municipal offices (Volksanwälte), no budgetary figures available. Information on Spain and Italy from the report of the French Conseil d'Etat (1991).

The row criterion was set by delivery systems and the total amount of public legal aid expenditures; 'high expenditure' was set at a *per capita* total of US$10 or more, among them at least $5 civil aid per head of the population.

comparing various schemes, but this needs to be complemented by an assessment of the array of services available in different areas of law, both for out-of-court advice and court representation.

We start by considering common law countries before analysing the different approaches taken by the civil law world.

2.1. The common law world

As far as investment in civil legal aid is concerned, the United States of America rank lowest among common law countries, even though many of the concepts of the 1970s legal aid movement unfolded there. Lacking substantial public provision, welfare politics in the United Sates depend on semi-private initiatives. Legal aid initiatives were started by local and state bar associations, universities and community groups who set up legal centres. Meanwhile, charitable foundations funded programmes for special target groups. The federally funded Legal Services Corporation, established in 1974, helped finance such projects on a strictly time-limited basis. Although the Corporation's budget has depended on the ups and downs of political moods, it has never contributed much more than $1 per head of the American population. Its policy has always been to initiate programmes without creating permanent institutions. That has also been the effect of the inventive funding schemes of bar associations, which often used interest paid on lawyers' trust funds. However, as interest payments depend on the number of private transactions conducted, funding is cyclical and insecure. To take California as an example, in 1993 budgets for legal aid projects amounted to $3.6 per head, of which around 45 per cent came from federal, state and local funding, 28 per cent from bar associations and lawyer funds and 21 per cent from charitable foundations (State Bar of California 1996:6, 23).

These figures, however, do not include legal aid for criminal defence which is organised and budgeted for separately, primarily at state level. Unfortunately, few figures are available, and we have not been able to include them in our international comparisons of legal aid costs. In 1986, spending on criminal defence services ranged from 67 cents per head in Arkansas to $9.32 in California and $28.90 in Washington DC (Bureau of Justice Statistics 1988). The national average of $4.11 per head in 1986 is said to have doubled by 1996.[12]

Canadian provinces provide obvious neighbourhood comparisons with the United States. Their combination of American-style salaried criminal defence counsel with European-style welfare legal aid schemes supplemented by an array of community legal services and university clinics has been praised as 'the Cadillac of legal aid'. However, there are questions about how much longer the Cadillac will be affordable (Zemans, 1994b). The costs of public legal aid are

[12] Personal communication with Robert L. Spangenburg, Standing Committee on Legal Aid and Indigent Defendants, American Bar Association.

higher than in other Commonwealth countries outside the United Kingdom. For example, in 1994/5 Ontario paid CDN$111 million (US$8.78 per head of the population) for criminal defence cases and CDN$118 million (US$8.73 per head) for civil and public law cases. In 1996, however, the plan was severely curtailed, as a new Ontarian government sought to reconcile pledges to reduce public expenditure with rising costs per case and reduced federal funding. It appears that expenditure *per capita* might stabilise at around two-thirds of the pre-1995 level. Nevertheless, despite these problems, the focus on changing poverty needs is maintained by the activities of community legal clinics, and by university clinics that combine legal education with advice and case-work on public interest and poverty issues. As a whole, Canadian legal aid can still stand comparison with most schemes outside Great Britain.

Australian states possess a similar combination of Community Legal Centres and Legal Aid Commissions which provide in-house services and administer certificates for private lawyers. Special services for aboriginal peoples are provided by the federal government. In 1993/4, public expenditure was within the range set by Canada and the European countries: it amounted to AUS$288 million (US$217 million), or US$10.5 per head of the population (though if the rather costly aboriginal services were excluded it would be US$9.3). Some additional funding comes from community contributions and university legal clinics. More than half the budget is spent on criminal defence: in terms of cases, 82 per cent of all private-lawyer cases and 60 per cent of staff ones concern criminal law. Divorce and family law cover two thirds of the remaining private-lawyer cases and half of the remaining staff ones.

In New Zealand legal aid is largely provided by private practitioners, supplemented by some community legal centres. In 1991, a Legal Aid Board was established. Expenditures were rising until 1996, to NZ$59 million, or US$14 *per capita*. Of this, 54 per cent is spent on civil legal aid and 46 per cent on criminal legal aid, including a duty solicitor scheme.

However, the leader in the legal aid league measured both in terms of funding and institutional tradition is the United Kingdom. If Canada claims 'Cadillac legal aid', the British are seemingly driving a Rolls Royce.

British legal aid dates back to the welfare politics of the second World War and its aftermath. The war created a new institution, *Citizens Advice Bureaux*, to help the population deal with the disruptions of war. As the *Liverpool Echo* of 3 January 1940 put it, they dealt with 'every kind of domestic and personal worry ranging from what to do if one cannot keep up the instalments on a wireless set to how to obtain compensation if evacuees damage one's home'. Staffed with volunteer helpers, they later became constant providers of social consultations, among them simple legal advice. Currently about 1,000 such bureaux are actively providing services.

Of course, the lawyer lobby did not acquiesce with such unprofessional services. When the Legal Aid and Advice Act 1949 granted subsidies for solicitors and barristers representing poor people, the Law Society was charged with the administration of the scheme for England and Wales. They performed this task until the Legal Aid Act 1988 established a new Legal Aid Board.[13] Administering the scheme is a major bureaucratic undertaking: in 1991/2 the Board employed around 1,300 staff. Both the Law Society and the Board have lobbied effectively during successive reforms of the scheme. In addition, a multitude of public interest law issues are taken up by some fifty-five community financed Law Centres, which primarily address local issues and are loosely co-ordinated by the national Law Centres Federation.

Recent reform attempts present a remarkable story of failure to cut costs. In the 1980s British legal aid expenditure was substantially above European or Commonwealth levels. The Lord Chancellor's Department responded by substantial cuts in clients' eligibility and by attempting to reduce solicitor fees. The Law Society tried to challenge the cuts in court in a classical configuration of professional self-interest and client's representation,[14] but failed. While other countries have effectively curbed legal aid funds, in the UK they have doubled since 1990. In England and Wales the remuneration of solicitors and barristers for legal aid per head of the population amounted to almost $38 *per capita* (25 per cent of which was recovered from clients' own contributions and opponents' costs). In Scotland 1994 expenditure was even higher, standing at $40 per head of the population. Of this, $33 (£107.5 million) was spent on court representation by solicitors and advocates and $3 (£24 million) on legal advice and consultation. The additional expenditure in Scotland seems to be entirely due to higher criminal law costs: 63 per cent of Scottish fees were for criminal cases as against only 44 per cent in England and Wales. As criminal legal aid cannot easily be curbed by eligibility restrictions, Scottish observers fear that over time very little funding will be left for civil legal aid.

It is intriguing to ask why legal aid expenditure in Britain is so much greater than anywhere else in Europe or the Commonwealth. Is it due to the volume of cases, or to the complexity of the work done on them, or have lawyers simply exploited the scheme? Compared to the neighbouring Netherlands, British criminal legal aid sticks out on all measures: not only caseloads, but also average fees per case. Average criminal case fees amount to $938 in England/Wales and $634 in the Netherlands (Goriely, Tata and Paterson, 1997). In spite of similar rates of crime reported to the police, English courts (and, to an even greater degree, Scottish courts) are processing petty cases for which the Dutch—like other Continental jurisdictions—use out-of-court fines and penalties. Thus, it is not only legal aid which is more expensive in Britain: the entire penal procedure is less streamlined than on the Continent.

[13] The Law Society of Scotland administered a similar scheme in Scotland until 1986, when it was replaced by the Scottish Legal Aid Board.

[14] *R* v. *Lord Chancellor* ex parte *Law Society*, CA 1993 *The Times*, August 11.

Table 5.3: Legal aid expenditures 1994/5 per capita *in common law countries*

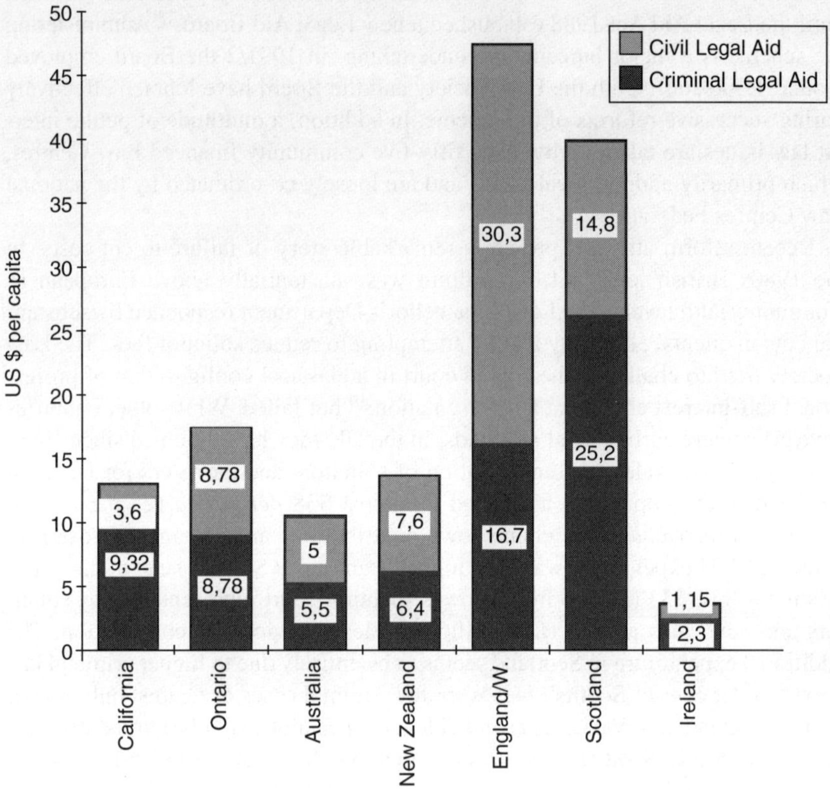

Source: International Legal Aid working group survey. Unpublished paper.

In sharp contrast to the British schemes, Ireland ranks lowest among the common law countries we have compared. Its legal aid scheme was introduced in 1980 and now spends an equivalent of $9 million, or $2.30 *per capita* on criminal and $1.15 on civil legal aid.

2.1. The civil law world

As with all comparisons of legal cultures, the Channel forms a conceptual split in the legal aid world. Historically, common law countries started out with the idea that parties and their lawyers mobilise their rights, and that adversarial presentation produces just outcomes. Civil law countries started out with the notion that *justice* is something like *truth*, which is there to be found by the best judge possible. Advocates are there to help judges find that true justice. This distinction means that legal aid is more vital in common law countries, where adversarial procedures lay the full responsibility for identifying, investigating and arguing issues on lawyers. By contrast, on the continent, judges are more active in searching out the facts of a case, allowing many parties to appear without being represented. Thus, it fits more easily into common law adversarial thinking that access to law rests on representation by a lawyer, while continental thinking was more easily satisfied with a guarantee that the poor may have an advocate when appearing in court. As a consequence, common law countries spend more on a variety of lawyer services to provide parties with equal arms. Civil law countries, by contrast, have developed legal aid around formal *right to counsel* provisions.

However, the clear distinction in the role of lawyers under common and civil law vanishes once we recognise that in both worlds court action is only a minor part of what lawyers do. First-line legal aid offices, in particular, handle most of their cases simply by giving information, advising on out-of-court actions and possibly writing a letter or negotiating on behalf of their clients. As in most lawyer offices, court action is used as a last resort, an implicit threat rarely to be acted on. In many civil law countries, a variety of public agencies offer legal services, including community centres, university departments and interest groups, such as trade unions, consumer organisations and renters' or houseowners' groups. Although outside the legal profession, they are close to the social fields where potential legal conflicts arise and are able to represent the interests of their clients in a number of ways rather than being restricted to the institutions of the legal system.

We have already highlighted the infrastructure of legal services provided by German trade unions, churches and community groups at the turn of the century. Little survived the First World War and the economic crises of the 1920s, although it may have served as a warning to the lawyer lobby that they needed to guard their professional monopoly more effectively in the future. A fresh start came to the continent from the common law legal aid movements of the 1970s. The Dutch, in particular, were influenced by North American ideas on legal services, which were closely tied to other welfare reforms. Legal aid has shared the ups and downs of welfare state provision from early optimism in the 1970s to the austerity of the 1990s.

The Netherlands stand out for their extensive legal aid infrastructure. Since the 1970s, public legal aid bureaux have provided first-tier advice, referring people to attorneys where court representation is required. Even though bureaux workers do not enjoy rights of advocacy, they co-operate effectively with social advocates for both individual cases and political lobbying. In the movement's heyday, the mixed system of legal aid advocacy (*sociale advokatuur*) and staff bureaux (*buros voor rechtshulp*) acted as a formidable pressure group for those on the margins of society. At the beginning of the 1980s, 16 per cent of all advocates worked predominantly on a legal aid basis (Klijn, 1981).

Since the mid-1980s, however, the government's austerity policies mitigated further growth and polarised the interests of bureaux workers and those of social advocates. In 1993 social advocates numbered the same as fifteen years earlier, but the overall growth in lawyers meant that they accounted for only 8 per cent of the profession (van Leeuwen *et al.*, 1996:76). By limiting eligibility and raising clients' contributions, the government managed to keep legal aid expenditure at a modestly rising level throughout the 1980s. However, this was not enough, and in 1994 the government took a drastic step. The scheme was put under the control of new regional units ('Legal Aid Councils') to audit the distribution of fees to lawyers. In addition, clients' contributions were raised prohibitively, in a way that the majority of Parliament came to regard as overkill. Thus contributions were slightly reduced again by 'repair legislation' in 1996. The result of these changes was that, by 1996, legal aid cases dropped by 39 per cent. Legal aid eligibility which had ranged up to 62 per cent of all Dutch households dropped to 43 per cent. The price paid by government for the more austere scheme was a rise in lawyer fees, which had previously remained stable for ten years (1984 to 1994). Social advocates were understandably demanding increases if they were to continue their participation. Overall costs, therefore, remained the same as before. In 1995 Dutch taxpayers spent about $11.7 per head of the population on legal aid, of which roughly one-third is spent on divorce and family problems, one-third on other civil and public law issues, and one-third on criminal defence.

We also find sophisticated legal aid infrastructures in Scandinavian countries, although they never reached the expenditure levels of The Netherlands. Sweden and Norway subsidise legal fees by attorneys and provide public legal aid bureaux in areas of special need (in isolated communities and for minority groups). Most of the cases concern divorce and family problems (in Sweden 82 per cent, in Norway 49 per cent). A sizeable part (24 per cent in Norway) also concerns immigration cases. Public expenditure on civil cases amounted to $4.7 for every Swede and $5.2 for every Norwegian. Additional sums were also spent on the criminal duty solicitor schemes. Finland has a country-wide system of legal aid, bound entirely into their public system of community offices. The subsidy amounts to $6.1 for every Finnish citizen (of which only 13.5 per cent is spent on criminal defence).

Other continental countries fall well below these levels. Similar to the constitutional arguments which established rights to criminal defence in the common law world, the *right to counsel* argument safeguarded representation in the civil courts on the European Continent. Though levels and institutional provisions for legal aid vary, most European countries have enlarged their provision under pressure from the *access to law movement*. However, they did so rather late, towards the end of the growth of the welfare state. For example, Germany did not do so until 1980 and the main French reforms were not until 1992. Thus expansion has been half-hearted, influenced by the public spending austerity which has affected all welfare expenditures since the late 1980s.

The neo-liberal ideology of public expenditure restraint has particularly affected legal aid in post-Communist countries. Although in Communist times these countries enjoyed a tradition of free access to legal advice, this did little to safeguard private rights, simply because in the Communist tradition public organisations were run according to political party lines, not rules of law. The breakdown of Communism allowed basic welfare provisions to survive—partly because the economic crisis did not leave a choice—but it did not encourage any new provisions. Thus the post-Communist turnover brought democratic rule and market economies—and with them courts and contracts—but did not introduce legal aid for ordinary people who have to come to grips with the host of legal problems which the regime transformation entails. It is quite obvious that the emerging lawyer professions under post-Communism are more involved in building capitalist institutions at the top than in transferring its benefits to people at the bottom.

The more typical pattern of legal aid in the Western part of the Continent is the result of lobbying by the legal professions to keep their monopoly in delivering legal services. It results in increases in right to counsel provisions, with some modest provision of legal advice outside of court procedures. In Germany and France policies have been implemented to prevent rather than stimulate innovation in legal services.

Germany with its century-old *right to counsel* tradition spends a total of $4.50 per head on legal aid. This includes $4 for a scheme to waive court and lawyers' fees for court representation (*Prozesskostenhilfe*) and a duty solicitor scheme for serious criminal cases which demand mandatory lawyer representation (which most ordinary crime cases do not). The waiver scheme, which entails a means as well as a merits test, is mainly used for divorce, which accounts for more than two-thirds of civil cases helped. In 1981, the Bar responded to the international legal aid movement by agreeing to a modest scheme for pre-court legal advice (*Beratungshilfe*). With eligibility being very restrictive (two times the social security minimum) and lawyer fees for first-hand consultation being unattractive, its expenditure amounted to a mere 80 Pfennigs ($0.40) per head.

The test of the system came with unification in 1990. The East German population clearly required information and assistance in coping with an entirely new system of law and legal institutions; but instead of forming a specialised service to help the new citizens with the social transformation, the West German chambers of advocates concentrated on maintaining their market monopoly. In spite of their higher legal needs, until 1995 expenditure on legal aid remained lower in the poor Eastern states than in rich western Germany.[15]

[15] Figures for the waiver and the duty solicitor scheme are taken from the 1994 budget of Nordrhein Westphalia. They can be assumed to be similar in other West German states. My unpublished budget comparisons in 1992 and 1994 show that all legal aid expenditures in the New States (*Neue Bundesländer*) of Eastern Germany remain well below the West German *per capita* level.

The situation is similar in France, except that expenditure is even lower. Until 1992 legal aid was mainly limited to a scheme of court fee waivers and limited lawyers fees in civil and penal procedures (*aide judiciaire*). In 1992 this was substantially improved, so that by 1994 the volume of admissions doubled in civil law cases and tripled in penal cases. At the same time, a scheme was introduced for advice and consultations, but this has proved less successful. In an attempt to reconcile the legal aid scheme with the interests of the profession, local legal aid bureaux were set up jointly by judicial officials and lawyer associations. These joint arrangements were also left with the arduous task of establishing special auditing bureaux (called CARPA) for the control of legal aid payments to lawyers. Considering the bureaucratic complexity of these provisions and the low fees involved, it is no wonder that some local chambers lacked the will to see them through. Only where active local initiatives took advantage of the central government's subsidy was legal aid supplied effectively. In many districts (among them Paris) so little legal aid was paid out in 1993 that the 1994 budget had be reduced according to cameralistic logic. In 1994 legal aid for pre-court consultation cost less than US$ 1 *per capita* (*Ministère de la Justice*, 1995). Adding an

Table 5.4: Legal aid expenditures 1994/5 in civil law countries

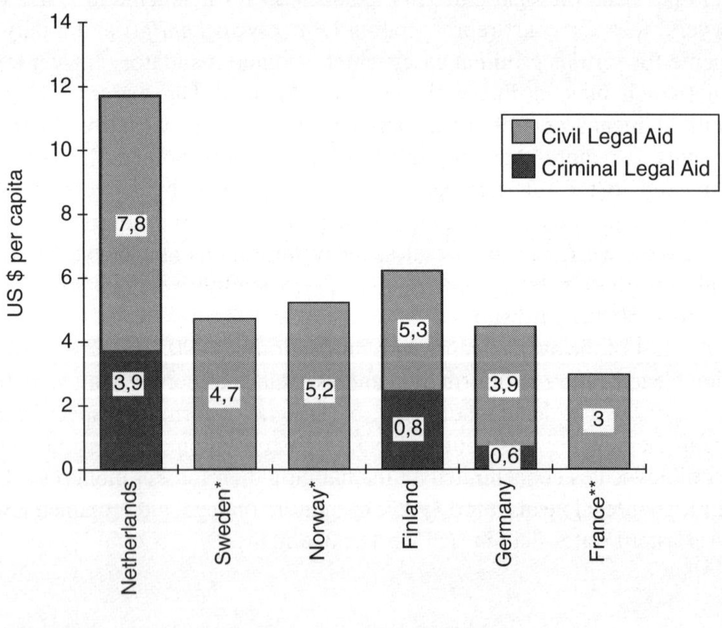

Source: International Legal aid working group survey. Unpublished paper.

* We do not have budget figures on legal aid for criminal law duty solicitor schemes for Sweden or Norway

** Figures for France are estimates.

estimated $2 for the waiver scheme,[16] French expenditures are still below the German level.

The survey of individual countries in Table 5.4 highlights that, despite the divergent institutional arrangements for legal aid, criminal legal aid is far more developed in the common law world than in civil law countries. In most countries civil legal aid is dominated by divorce and its follow-up, but some countries allow for a considerable clientele in public law issues (especially immigration law). The variation in overall expenditures does not seem to result from vastly different lawyer fees. Compare average legal aid costs of $661 per case in England and Wales (which includes contributions and costs) with $516 (plus $95 paid by clients' contributions) in the Netherlands. British average fees are lower than those in Sweden ($710) and Norway ($840). All of them, however, are much higher than the average costs of the municipal legal aid offices in Finland ($300 per case). It would be intriguing to see in what respect the kind and complexity of Finnish cases differs to enable their comprehensive services to work at such low rates.

3. Curbing legal aid provisions in the 1990s and the limits to austerity politics

Our country-by-country comparisons suggest that the correlation between welfare state expenditures and investments in legal aid is far from perfect. The comparison between the United States and Canada demonstrates that sizeable legal aid investments depend on a concomitant development of welfare state provisions. At the same time, the comparison of Germany and France with the Netherlands and Scandinavia illustrates the decisive role of the legal profession in blocking or furthering the inclusion of legal aid in these (equally developed) welfare states. Comparing these countries one is tempted to conclude that legal aid needs a strong welfare state *and* a weak lawyers' lobby. The ongoing growth of the British legal aid system, however, presents a legal profession successfully generating substantial income from the system. Here a fairly strong lawyer lobby has managed to exploit legal aid, and has institutionalised the profession as part of the welfare system. In any case, in Britain as in all other countries, two main factors determine the range of variations documented by the comparative survey: the institutions of the welfare state and legal culture.

The same factors shape the demise of legal aid in the 1990s. The enthusiasm of the founding years of the legal aid movement has been replaced by sober considerations of budgetary austerity. Exactly at a time when the number of the unemployed, refugees, asylum seekers and other marginalised people is growing,

16 As the French Ministry of Justice has not responded to our requests for recent budget figures, we have relied on *Counseil d'Etat* (1991).

legal aid is in retreat, together with the rest of the welfare state. Welfare expenditures behave cyclically with the distribution of prosperity, and thus anti-cyclically with respect to needs. While in the 1960s and 1970s full employment and social prosperity allowed for generosity, the growing numbers of poor and marginalised people in the 1990s call for austerity.

The pressures on legal aid lawyers are typical of those affecting all professions partly dependant on government subsidies. The mechanism has been studied exhaustively for the health services: with insurance schemes paying for the costs of most extensive treatments, neither patients nor doctors have any incentives to restrict services under cost considerations. Unrestrained investment in highly technological medicine has been the result. If the driving forces of professional supply coalesce with the interests of demand, there seems to be no limit to a spiral of services and their costs. It leads some analysts to proclaim a universal law of supplier-induced growth (Bellow, 1994; Cooper, 1994).

The experience of the 1990s, however, shows that such a vision of 'socialist professionalism' is nothing but an expression of ideological polarisation. First of all, the supply side of subsidised services is no self-service store for the professions, but rather a politically dependent, highly regulated collective negotiation system. The degree to which the professions can influence politics to extend the range of their subsidies depends on how urgently and how legitimately they can sell their services in the political arena. Doctors' arguments ('if you are poor, you have to die earlier') convince more easily than those of lawyers ('law protects the property of the poor as much as it protects the property of the rich'). Thus, lawyers have nowhere become as dependent on public insurance systems as medical doctors have. While legal aid fees are tightly regulated, lawyers prefer to engage in a rather wide array of non-regulated activities which open vast possibilities to individually negotiated prices. The subsidised sector of legal services is only a fraction of what lawyers do as a whole. On the other side, compared to overall health or welfare budgets, legal aid expenditures are very small. Both with respect to the overall income of most lawyers and to welfare state provision as a whole, even fully developed legal aid remains in a marginal position.

Nevertheless, there are 'creaming the poor' effects by recipients of services. Just as we find people living in subsidised housing long after receiving a comfortable middle-class income, we find legal aid clients who willingly pay for an array of divorce costs but ask for legal aid when a lawyer has to be paid. Also professionals are known to exploit creaming effects by stretching procedural costs when third-party payment is guaranteed.[17] Scandalisation of such misuse, however, is easily exploited far beyond the actual relevance of creaming effects.

[17] Stretching effects regularly occur when governments try to restrict lawyers services by introducing regulations and fee schedules. The Lord Chancellor Department discussed the problem in their Green Paper (LCD 1995).

Secondly: the demand side of legal services is not nearly as price-elastic as the thesis of supplier-inducement assumes. People in their private lives try to avoid lawyers and litigation for their social risks, which extend well beyond purely financial costs.[18] The extent to which low-income recipients and others use legal services depends largely on the alternatives they perceive to be available for their problems. In assessing the effect of legal aid on demand, the form in which legal aid is given turns out to be more relevant than mere budgetary indicators or eligibility criteria. The most wide-ranging effects are often engendered by the smallest sector of subsidised legal services. All legal services report that first-tier consultation and information forms a considerable part of their activities. The more clients they serve, the more demand increases. The next step of representing clients, first out-of-court and eventually in litigation, asks for a choice between courts and their alternatives.

Most countries restrict legal aid to paying fees for lawyers (which Americans term 'judicare') but some combine this with some institutional subsidy for additional kinds of service delivery. The criteria and the forms of these combinations vary with pressure groups and with institutional traditions. Research comparing delivery systems shows nationally as well as locally varying advantages. Legal cost insurers (in countries without lawyer privilege for legal advice) have been quite inventive in controlling lawyers' fees: by handling first-tier advice and routine cases though in-house staff or tendering with advocate groups for court cases, they use competition to find the most cost-efficient means of providing specific services. Community groups and universities have used similar strategies of cost control, and at the same time have innovated with different forms of delivery. Finally, there are historical examples of membership groups ranging from trade unions to company group schemes, from automobile clubs to immigration groups, which prove that subsidised markets can be extremely inventive in finding the most effective forms of services for different legal needs.

The history of legal aid shows social advocacy in many forms of delivery. Whilst it is clear that the most disadvantaged groups cannot afford legal aid without institutional subsidy, such subsidy can take many forms and come from diverse sources. Even though the level of spending for legal aid is far below that of other welfare costs, government-subsidised legal aid is dependent on the general mood for sustaining welfare state policies. At the same

[18] Our study of the litigation behaviour of Germans who are privately insured against all legal costs may serve as an example (Blankenburg, 1981). Evidence on the low price-elasticity of legal services among low-income groups has been systematically tested by van Tulder (1990). He shows that the effect of price on seeking lawyers advice is more similar to investment decisions than to consumption; it depends on overall available investment capacity as well as urgency of needs; as a result the elasticity is greatest just above the eligibility threshold—which is exactly in the 'creaming' crowd.

time, the forms that legal services delivery take are dependant on professional lobbies whose (legitimate) interests in adequate remuneration also determine the costs of legal services. Thus we need an analysis in terms of both the political economy of the welfare states and the sociology of the legal profession to understand why the supply side of legal aid offers such a diversity of institutional infrastructures.

6

Comparing Legal Aid Spending: The Promise and Perils of a Jurisdiction-Centred Approach to (International) Legal Aid Research[*]

CYRUS TATA

Public expenditure has become the key battleground where legal aid policy is contested (see e.g. Goriely, 1997b; Moorhead, 1998). Research examining current and projected costs of policy (both within and between jurisdictions) inevitably commands attention in government circles. Although the promise of comparing costs within and between jurisdictions seems immense, care needs to be taken in interpreting what the comparisons actually mean; and it is imperative that attention is paid to issues underlying comparative methodology. This Chapter reflects on some of the key issues in comparing criminal legal aid expenditure. It arises from a research study which compared criminal legal aid expenditure in three European jurisdictions. This paper first describes the origins, background and objectives of the study before reporting some of the main findings. The Chapter proceeds to examine key issues in comparative research of this nature. It uses the inter-jurisdictional study and its findings as a means of discussing the methodological issues underlying 'comparative' research.

Although the Chapter reports recent comparative criminal legal aid research, it necessarily raises questions for comparative civil legal aid research, as well as 'comparative' methodology more generally. It would be tempting to assume that inter-jurisdictional empirical research is necessarily far more problematic than single-jurisdictional research (e.g. Beirne and Nelken 1997). This Chapter

* Part of this Chapter discusses some of the findings of a study by Goriely, Tata and Paterson (1997). During the course of that study valuable assistance was received from the following people: Albert Klijn, Max Komer, Bert Berghuis, Peter Lavenkamp, Hans Shoenmakers, Julia Mints, B. Reimus, Rene van Koetsveld, A. E. Zunderdorf, Chris van Elk, B. F. F. Gosschalk, E. J. P. Nolet, Judge de Vries, Frits van Straelen, Robert Livingstone, Keith Marshall, Gillian Parmakov, Sue Warner, Andrew Fleming, Fred Thorne, Helen Rae, David Edwards, Kevin Dibdin, Tim O'Farell, Neil Mackay, Chris Jones, Margaret Ayres, and David Wall. In addition, I would like to acknowledge the important contribution of my co-authors to that report: Tamara Goriely and Alan Paterson. A previous version of this paper was delivered to the Biennial Conference of the British Society of Criminology. I am grateful to David Wall, Sue Warner, Simon Halliday, and to the Editors for their valuable comments on an earlier draft of this Chapter.

questions the view that inter-jurisdictional is necessarily more difficult than single- or 'intra'-jurisdiction research. Rather, it will argue that 'jurisdiction' (the legal limits of the state) and legality (i.e. legal doctrine and institutional legal obligations) are not the primary sources of the major challenges facing research on legal aid spending. The Chapter suggests instead that the key intellectual difficulties are located in the attempt to make any kinds of comparisons, whether over time; between organisations; between different populations; geography; cultures, etc. I will suggest that labelling only inter-jurisdictional research as 'comparative' is misleading and that instead we need to recognise that the essence of empirical legal aid research is necessarily comparative. First, however, the Chapter discusses the conduct and findings of recent research on the spending patterns of three European countries.

Criminal legal aid expenditure and constitutional requirements

Criminal legal aid expenditure is not solely a matter of political choice. In its 1995 Green Paper, the Lord Chancellor's Department of England and Wales acknowledged that 'criminal legal aid is different from family and other civil legal aid' (LCD, 1995a, para. 4.38). Thus: 'unlike most other forms of legal aid, demand is determined by the state. Defendants in criminal cases have no choice but to defend themselves against the power of the state ranged against them in the form of prosecuting authorities' (para. 4.40). Furthermore, the right of a criminal defendant to legal assistance is guaranteed under Article 6 of the European Convention on Human Rights. Article 6.1 guarantees the right to 'a fair and public hearing within a reasonable time by an independent and impartial tribunal established by law'. In the case of criminal trials, Article 6.3 sets out the following minimum rights:

(a) to be informed promptly, in a language which he understands and in detail, of the nature and cause of the accusation against him;
(b) to have adequate time and facilities for the preparation of his defence;
(c) to defend himself in person or through legal assistance of his own choosing or, if he has not sufficient means to pay for legal assistance, to be given it free when the interests of justice so require;
(d) to examine or have examined witnesses against him and to obtain attendance and examination of witnesses on his behalf under the same conditions as witnesses against him;
(e) to have the free assistance of an interpreter if he cannot understand or speak the language used in court.

However, it is not possible to say what level of expenditure would be necessary to comply with the Convention and the amount actually spent differs considerably over time, between, and within jurisdictions. So why might identical constitutional requirements give rise to differential levels of expenditure? For these purposes, the Convention's key provision is Article 6.3(c) which requires that defendants with insufficient means must be given free legal assistance 'when the interests of justice so require'. This, however, must be read in conjunction with the other provisions, which demand, for example, adequate time to prepare a defence and the chance to examine and cross-examine witnesses.

There is now an emerging body of case-law interpreting Article 6.3(c) (Ashworth, 1996). It has been held that when legal assistance is provided free the accused does not necessarily have the right to choose a lawyer,[1] but his/her wishes should be considered. Where the relationship between a lawyer and client has broken down, schemes should make provision for another lawyer to be assigned.[2] The key question is when and in what circumstances 'the interests of justice' require legal assistance. The determining factors appear to be: the complexity of the case; the seriousness of the charge; and the severity of the possible sentence. In *Quaranta* v. *Switzerland*[3] the accused received a custodial sentence and the court found that 'free legal assistance should have been afforded by reason of the mere fact that so much was at stake'. *Pham Hoang* v. *France*[4] suggests that the interests of justice may also require representation for a serious charge when the proceedings are '. . . clearly fraught with consequences . . .' even if the outcome was a large fine (Ashworth, 1996).

Expenditure levels

At one level, therefore, all the signatories of the Convention are bound by the same rules. It is clear, however, that these rules result in different levels of expenditure. Although there are no official figures on criminal legal aid expenditure within Europe, the 1994 International Conference on Legal Aid made the following estimates of 1992 *per capita* expenditure within the most developed legal aid schemes. They cover three signatories to the European Convention—the UK, the Netherlands and Sweden.

As the authors of that paper acknowledge, the figures in Table 6.1 are only estimates. They relate to different time periods; do not extract tax; and do not necessarily extract the criminal elements of combined expenditure (for example, on children or advice). However, the magnitude of these differences inevitably raises questions as to the different ways in which Scotland, England and Wales, the Netherlands, and Sweden interpret their obligations to comply with the European Convention in terms of *per capita* spending.

1 *Croissant* v. *Germany* (1992) 16 EHRR 135.
2 *Pakelli* v. *Germany* (1983) A 64.
3 (1991) A 205.
4 (1993) 16 EHRR 53.

Table 6.1: Estimate of expenditure per capita *on criminal legal aid 1992*

	US$
England and Wales	15
The Netherlands	3
Scotland	21
Sweden	9

Source: Klijn and Huls (1994)

A recent pilot study investigated some of the reasons for these apparent differences (Goriely, Tata and Paterson, 1997). In particular, it considered why Scotland appears to spend so much more on criminal legal aid than other signatories to the Convention. The pilot study did not aim to provide complete answers to these questions, but to provide some reasonably robust hypotheses which might be pursued by subsequent research. The study, commissioned by the Lord Chancellor's Department of England and Wales and by the Scottish Office, compared the spending patterns of England and Wales, Scotland and a third country: the Netherlands. The Netherlands was included because of its seemingly very low level of spending, the extent of information which is available, and the high-quality reputation of its scheme. The first Director of the American Legal Services Corporation, Clinton Bamberger, described the Dutch legal aid scheme as 'one of the best in the world: probably the best' (Bamberger, 1989). Like the UK schemes, it relies on private practitioners to provide criminal services: there are no salaried public defenders providing assistance in criminal matters. Furthermore, the Netherlands has a relatively high level of compliance with the Convention—at least equal to that of the UK (Swart and Young, 1995).

'Adversarial' and 'inquisitorial' models of criminal justice

It might be expected that differences in criminal legal aid expenditure between Britain and other European jurisdictions could be explained by differences between 'adversarial' and 'inquisitorial' models of criminal justice. In an 'adversarial' model, where the judge is a neutral umpire between prosecution and defence, it is clearly vital for both sides to be represented. Thus, it might be supposed that the interests of justice require more people to be represented. Furthermore, the defence lawyers must carry the burden of presenting evidence: they must therefore do more, and be paid more for it. In the typical 'inquisitorial' case the main burden of finding evidence relies on the judge. Defence lawyers may be needed in fewer cases, and may be required to do less.

However, empirical examination suggests that the varying assumptions behind the 'adversarial'—'inquisitorial' divide cannot provide the primary answer to the question of why international differences arise in criminal legal aid expenditure. There are four reasons for this. First, it cannot account for the differences between 'adversarial' systems. If anything, Scotland's system, with the important historical role given to the Procurator Fiscal in criminal trials, is more inclined towards the 'inquisitorial' system than that of England and Wales. Yet, as this Chapter explains, its criminal legal expenditure is significantly greater. Differences within Canada and the USA also show that even within the same legal family variations in culture and political preference can result in substantial differences in legal aid expenditure (Goriely, 1997b; Wall, 1996). Secondly, it is too easy for comparisons between 'adversarial' and 'inquisitorial' systems too concentrate on trials, especially the symbolic high-point of the British system, trial by jury (Darbyshire, 1997; Duff and Findlay, 1997). Although British jury trials are relatively slow and expensive, it should be remembered that in Scotland at least, the bulk of legal aid expenditure does not involve jury trials (or even their possibility) but rather summary procedures prosecuted in the lower courts. In addition, in most cases the accused pleads guilty, at least when the case comes to trial (Samuel and Adler, 1994; Samuel, 1996) and (in common with research findings in England and Wales) proceedings tend to be abrupt (McBarnett, 1979; McConville, Sanders and Leng, 1991). Therefore, although the assumptions underlying the Dutch and Scots approach may differ, it is by no means self-evident why the Scots's system should be so much more expensive in the way that these cases are handled. Thirdly, the easy invocation of 'adversarial' and 'inquisitorial' models of truth-finding underestimates the extent to which the Dutch scheme is increasingly relying on defence lawyers to cut investigative corners (Jörg, Field and Brants, 1995). The criteria governing when the court may refuse such requests have been relaxed by statute, resulting in a great increase in litigation on the issue. There is also more pre-trial contract between prosecution and defence in the Netherlands. Jörg, Field and Brants (1995:48) comment that 'the incidence of negotiations between defence and prosecution is on the rise: while not called plea bargaining yet, the terminology has emerged in official documents.' Finally, there are some aspects of 'inquisitorial' justice which may actually increase legal aid costs. For example, in an 'inquisitorial' system an uncorroborated confession does not necessarily dispose of a case in the same way as a plea of guilty does in the 'adversarial' system (Jörg, Field and Brants, 1995:50)

Therefore, in the study discussed here, it was recognised that the primary explanation for the marked differences in *per capita* spending does not lie in the differences between 'adversarial' and 'inquisitorial' models. To understand the dynamics of spending we must consider explanations other than simple constitutional requirements. Below I focus on the key findings of the comparative study.[5]

[5] There is not space here to describe the anatomy of the criminal process in the three jurisdictions (see Goriely, Tata and Paterson, 1977).

Criminal legal aid expenditure in England and Wales, Scotland and the Netherlands: analysis of spending by population

The initial task was to calculate expenditure on criminal legal aid by head of population in each of the three jurisdictions under discussion. Table 6.2 shows total expenditure by per head of population, broken down into its constituent categories.

Table 6.2 distinguishes between the cost of representation in cases dealt with in jury courts and in others. Thus, the category 'Representation in jury courts' relates to cases which go to the crown court in England and Wales, and those dealt with under solemn procedure within the sheriff and high courts in Scotland. These latter cases do not necessarily involve a trial, and include guilty pleas and cases where the Procurator Fiscal takes no proceedings. The Dutch do not have jury trials. The second category includes cases dealt with under summary procedure in the sheriff and district court in Scotland, the magistrates' court in England and Wales and, the Dutch district court.

How does Scotland compare?

In the year 1994/5 expenditure in Scotland was clearly the highest, with spending per head of population 52 per cent greater than in England and Wales, and more than nine times that of the Netherlands. The biggest differences are in payment for representation before summary courts, where Scotland's *per capita*

Table 6.2: Expenditure on criminal legal aid, per head of population (£ sterling) 1994–5

	England and Wales	Scotland	The Netherlands
Population (1991)	51,099,000	5,107,000	15,010,000
Representation in jury courts	£5.76	£4.79	nil[a]
Representation in non-jury courts	£3.16	£10.32	£1.41
Court duty solicitor schemes	£0.24	£0.18	n/a
Assistance at Police stations	£1.34	n/a	n/a
Advice	£0.47	£1.36	£0.16
Appeals	£0.25	£0.29	£0.20
Total	£11.22	£16.94	£1.77
less contributions	£0.08	nil	nil
Total net costs[b]	£11.14	£16.94	£1.77

Technical notes and sources for these figures are provided in Appendix B of Goriely, Tata and Paterson, 1997.

[a] There are no juries in the Netherlands.

[b] Figures may not add up exactly, due to rounding.

expenditure is three times that of England and Wales and seven times more than the Netherlands.

At first sight, the difference between England and Wales and Scotland seems surprising given that Scottish criminal procedure contains several features which have been proposed in England and Wales as money-saving devices. First, in contrast with England and Wales, accused persons in Scotland do not have the right to choose jury trial: the decision is that of the prosecutor alone. Decisions over who should be granted summary legal aid are made by the Scottish Legal Aid Board, rather than by the courts as in England and Wales. Secondly, Scottish solicitors also have more extensive 'rights of audience' than their counterparts in England and Wales, and solicitors in Scotland can appear in all Sheriff Court proceedings. Thirdly, the Scottish prosecutor has more powers to divert cases from formal court procedures, and fourthly, the Scottish criminal legal aid system appears to be less generous to those pleading guilty.[6] Finally, the Scottish system has not had to bear the high costs of city-related fraud trials which can be so expensive for the English and Welsh scheme. The finding that the Scottish system costs more than that of England and Wales is unexpected for another reason. Research by Samuel and Adler (1994) found a widespread perception among Scottish solicitors that, compared with England and Wales, the Scottish system offered good value for money.

So far I have identified differences in *per capita* spending. In an attempt to provide some further analysis and explanation, and given space constraints, the remainder of this Chapter concentrates exclusively on the element which appears to account for the vast bulk of spending, representation before non-injury courts, by examining first the number of cases and then the costs per case.

Representation before summary courts

A key question in understanding the differences identified by Table 6.2 in representation before non-jury courts is whether they relate to the volume or the price of cases. Do the Scots fund more cases, or does each case cost more? Do the Dutch fund fewer cases, or is each case cheaper?

The number of summary bills

The differences in volume in the three jurisdictions are striking. Per head of population, England and Wales pays double the number of summary bills as the Dutch, while in 1993–4, the Scots paid almost double the number paid by the English.

[6] Full criminal legal aid in summary proceedings in Scotland can be applied for by accused persons only after a plea of not guilty has been tendered. For further explanation of this point see Goriely, Tata and Paterson (1997:7–11).

Table 6.3: Bills for Representation before Summary Courts in England, Wales, Scotland and the Netherlands

	1993–4		1994–5	
	No. of bills	Rate per 1,000 pop.	No. of bills	Rate per 1,000 pop.
Scotland	68,480	13.41	65,839	12.89
England and Wales	355,787	6.96	392,577	7.68
The Netherlands	48,341	3.22	51,055	3.40

Source: England and Wales: Legal Aid Board *Annual Reports*; Scotland: unpublished information supplied by the Scottish Legal Aid Board; Netherlands: information supplied by the Ministry of Justice.

Table 6.4: The Number of Persons Proceeded Against in Court: Scotland, England and Wales and the Netherlands, 1994

	All	All except motoring offences
Scotland (No.)	178,667	112,545
Scotland per 1,000 pop.	34.81	21.92
England & Wales (No.)	1,847,200	1,088,500
England & Wales per 1,000 pop.	38.11	20.91
The Netherlands (No.)	99,500	n/a
The Netherlands per 1,000 pop.	6.63	n/a

Sources: Scottish Office (1997); Home Office (1995); Openbaar Ministerie (1994)

Finally, it must be remembered that, as the Dutch do not have jury trials, the summary figures include all the serious cases which in Britain would have been dealt with before the higher courts. All these factors make the high number of Scottish bills particularly surprising.

Numbers of 'persons proceeded against' through the summary courts

One possible explanation for the additional number of cases is that more Scots may be prosecuted through the courts. However, as Table 6.4 shows, this does not seem to be the case. In comparing Scotland with England, it appears that the difference lies in the higher proportion of cases which are legally aided rather than in the number of cases dealt with by the Scottish courts. The Dutch prosecute far fewer cases.

The explanation of the differences between England and Wales and Scotland can therefore be explained by the proportion of accused persons being granted legal aid rather than the number of persons passing through the courts. What factors might explain the larger differences found between the Dutch figures and those for Great Britain?

Why are fewer Dutch 'cases' legally aided?

Although comparing crime rates between countries is always fraught with problems, the numbers of crimes reported to the police in the Netherlands and in the UK appear to be similar (van Dijk and Mayhew, 1993). David Downes's in-depth comparison of the Dutch and English criminal justice system concluded that 'no obvious disparity emerges between Dutch and English victim surveys to suggest that Dutch police recording of crimes differs at all substantially from that of England' (Downes, 1988:12). The numbers of crimes recorded per 100,000 inhabitants are virtually identical (ibid. 34). Therefore, differences in the number of legally aided cases relate, not to the overall number of crimes, but to the way they are processed within the criminal justice system.

There are many reasons why the Dutch legal aid scheme funds a smaller proportion of cases. It is normal Dutch prosecution practice that, whenever possible, separate police reports against the same person are combined into a single 'charge sheet'. Each 'case' passing through the courts may therefore represent an aggregate of several crimes committed by the same person on different dates and in different places.[7] Using the official estimate of the number of police reports included in one charge sheet (Openbaar Ministerie, 1995:44–5), the number of 'cases' included in legal aid bills is 3.8 (rather than 3.4) per thousand of population in 1994–5. This suggests that case aggregation provides only a partial explanation for the difference. It is possible, however, that the official figures may not estimate the practice of 'adding' cases adequately. A second reason why the Dutch legal aid scheme appears to fund a smaller proportion of cases than the schemes operated in Great Britain relates to appearance in court. Dutch accused persons are not obliged to attend their own court hearings, but if they do not attend they cannot receive legal aid representation. There appears to be no official figures of exactly how many people do not attend their court hearings. However, a short period of court observation by the author in 1996 suggested that in the single-judge chamber District Court in The Hague around half of all trials may be completed without the presence of the accused. A third reason why the Dutch scheme appears to fund a smaller proportion of cases than the Scottish or English scheme lies in sentencing. Accused persons brought before the Kantongerechten (or sub-district courts) are not at risk of imprisonment. They are therefore not entitled to legal aid (save in the most exceptional circumstances regarding the possibility of loss of livelihood or exceptional legal complexity). Fourthly, Dutch

[7] Similarly, in Scotland it can be normal practice for the relevant agencies to conjoin police reports/charges where it is believed practicable so to do. It appears, however, that the scope of the practice of such policy may be far wider and more deliberate in the Netherlands than in Scotland.

courts are relatively informal. Even in the higher courts an accused person who decides to attend his/her trial may feel more comfortable about appearing without an advocate due to the informal atmosphere of Dutch courts compared with that in UK courts.[8] It is possible that Dutch fee structures may provide lawyers with some incentive to persuade their clients that representation is not necessarily crucial.[9]

A fifth and major reason for the difference in the figures, however, lies in the lower number of cases brought to court. Here the role of the prosecutor is crucial. Dutch prosecutors have significant powers to deal with cases out of court, and they are much more likely than British prosecutors to exercise them. Dutch prosecutors take only a third of all the cases they receive to court. In Scotland prosecutors take around half the cases, and in England around four-fifths of cases to court.[10] Although Scottish prosecutors share most of the powers of their Dutch counterparts,[11] they do not use them to nearly the same extent. The ability of the Dutch prosecution service to divert such a high proportion of cases from court (and thereby obviate the need for legal representation) appears to provide one of the most important explanations for the conspicuously low level of overall spending on criminal legal aid representation in the Netherlands. It may also reflect the powerful position of the prosecution service. The Dutch prosecutor enjoys a position as a key policy leader, or perhaps *the* key policy leader, occupying perhaps the most important position in the Dutch criminal justice process (van Swaaningen and uit Beijerse, 1993; 't Hart, 1988; Fionda, 1995; Holthius, 1993), or, as Van Dijk neatly expressed it 'the spider in the web' (Downes, 1988).[12]

Comparing eligibility for legal aid in Scotland and England

A major reason why the Netherlands has fewer legally aided criminal cases than the UK is that fewer criminal 'cases' are brought before the courts. This, however, does not account for differences between Scotland and England and Wales. As Table 6.4 showed, on the basis of population, the numbers of cases proceeding

[8] The architecture and design of the court appears to allow a rather more intimate atmosphere; accused persons may remain seated when being asked and replying to questions; and wigs are not worn by judges, prosecutors or defence advocates.

[9] For discussion of fee structures in the three countries see ch. 7, Goriely, Tata and Paterson (1997).

[10] However, the study was not able to compare the effect of police diversion schemes, such as cautioning in England and Wales. For further findings and more detailed discussion see Goriely, Tata and Paterson (1997), ch. 5.

[11] However, one important difference is that, unlike the Scottish public prosecutor, the Dutch public prosecutor is obliged to recommend a sentence to the court in all cases.

[12] It is worthy of note that public prosecutors in the Netherlands are formally part of the judiciary (referred to as the 'standing judiciary') and share a period of common training with those who later go on to a career as a member of the 'sitting judiciary' (i.e. judges).

through the courts in both Scotland and in England and Wales are broadly similar. Explanations, therefore, must lie in the way legal aid is granted. A number of criteria are used to grant legal aid for both guilty and not guilty pleas. The following section considers the decision-making process in granting legal aid. In particular, it focuses on the way in which decision-makers identify cases which appear to merit legal aid: the 'interests of justice' test.

The 'interests of justice' test

In both jurisdictions, in order to qualify for summary legal aid, the accused person must meet both a means and a merits test. In practice, legal aid applicants are predominantly unemployed and on low incomes and very few are refused help on financial grounds (Scottish Office, 1993a:59).

The merit tests in the two jurisdictions are similar. Under both the English and Scottish Acts the grant of legal aid must be 'in the interests of justice' and in deciding this question, a range of factors must be considered. These were first set out by the Widgery Committee in 1966 and are often known as the 'Widgery criteria'. They have now been enacted in the Legal Aid (Scotland) Act 1986 s. 24 and the Legal Aid Act 1988 s. 22 in similar but not identical terms. The wording of each section is set out in Appendix A at the end of this Chapter. In both jurisdictions, the criteria are not mandatory. They must be taken into account, but they do not decide the issue. The existence of one or more factors does not necessarily mean that a grant of legal aid must be made.

Detailed scrutiny of the two provisions suggests that (at least on paper) the Scottish test is slightly more generous. In Scotland, for example, legal aid may be granted where 'evidence is of a complex or difficult nature' while in England and Wales, complex evidence must involve 'the tracing and interviewing of witnesses or expert cross-examination of a witness for the prosecution'. Furthermore, in Scotland, legal aid may be considered if the defence 'does not appear to be frivolous', or, where 'the accused has been remanded in custody pending trial'. However, the exact words used are much less important than how they are applied. In both jurisdictions the words of the statute allow the decision-maker considerable discretion.

Several commentators on English criminal legal aid have noted that, although the words of the interests of justice test have remained similar since 1966, legal aid has been increasingly granted in magistrates' court cases. The number of grants has continued to increase, so that between 1970 and 1990 England and Wales experienced a tenfold increase in expenditure in real terms (Young, 1996: 139).[13] Richard Young has coined the term 'Widgery drift' to highlight the way

[13] This increase in expenditure has been almost matched by the volume of cases; there has been a steep increase in both the numbers and proportions of people receiving legal aid in the magistrates' courts (Young, 1996:138–9).

that magistrates' courts have interpreted the same statutory ('Widgery criteria') test increasingly generously (Young, 1996:138). The question of *who* makes the decision, and what incentives they work under, is arguably more important than the wording of the criteria themselves.

In England, the 'interests of justice' test is applied by magistrates' court clerks, and much of the responsibility for 'Widgery drift' has been attributed to them. In 1992, the National Audit Office pointed out that courts often make the decision on the basis of insufficient information. It also commented that allowing courts to make the decision when they had no financial responsibility for the outcome created difficulties in terms of clear lines of accountability. 'The Lord Chancellor's Department was accountable to Parliament for the expenditure incurred but could not exercise management and control over the operations and decisions within the courts which determine the level of that expenditure and its propriety and regularity.' (National Audit Office, 1992: para. 3.15). A further criticism of magistrates' court decision-making is that they act inconsistently. 'Using the 1990 figures covering 384 courts, for example, there were eight courts which refused at least a quarter of all applications, whereas, at the other extreme, 97 refused no more than one in 20' (Young, 1996:139). The main difference between Scotland and England and Wales is that in Scotland the 1986 Act took the decision about granting legal aid away from courts and gave it instead to the Scottish Legal Aid Board (Samuel and Adler, 1994:58). The Scottish Office has also concluded that moving the merits test from the Courts to SLAB has been successful. The Scottish Office has argued that '. . . there is not a problem with consistency of interpretation in Scotland and [research shows that] . . . a majority of defence agents have little difficulty in interpreting the criteria' (Scottish Office, 1993a:34).

Unlike magistrates courts' south of the border, the Scottish Legal Aid Board may have proved itself to be consistent and efficient. Whether nor not it has also been successful in avoiding a similar pattern to that produced by the English phenomenon of 'Widgery drift' is less clear. Within the Scottish criminal justice system, there appears to have been a drift from the district court (the 'lowest' criminal court) to the sheriff court (the intermediate criminal court). Crown Office figures show that between 1988 and 1995, the number of summary cases disposed of after the 'pleading diet'[14] in the district court fell by 27 per cent[15] (from 21,115 to 14,700) while the number disposed of in the sheriff court rose by 31 per cent (from 30,146 to 39,412). This shift has proved to be expensive for legal aid, first because sheriff court cases are much more likely to attract legal aid, and secondly because they are more expensive.

The effect can be seen most clearly if one looks at that most characteristic of

[14] The diet to which accused persons are called to offer a plea in response to the charges.

[15] In part this may be accounted for by the introduction in 1993 of police powers to issue conditional offers which may have had the effect of 'removing' a large number of road traffic offence cases from the district court.

Scots offences: breach of the peace. In 1991/2 legal aid funded 9,310 breach of the peace defences, of which around half (4,787) were in the sheriff court. By 1994/5 it funded 13,436 cases, of which two-thirds (9,034) were in the sheriff court. As a result, legal aid expenditure of breach of the peace cases rose from £5 million to £9 million.

There are no clear explanation for this change. Breach of the peace is, of course, a particularly elastic common law charge. Although normally used for minor public order offences (such as shouting and swearing in public, generally threatening behaviour, etc.) it can also been used to charge more serious offences, including 'stalking', and those relating to football hooliganism and prison disturbances. Although it is technically possible that breach of the peace is now more often used to cover more serious matters such as 'stalking' than in the past, it seems unlikely to have accounted for such a large change. Christie (1990:23) argues that, with the exception of mobbing, breach of the peace is 'essentially a minor offence'. However, relatively little is known about the kinds of criminal behaviour which breach of the peace is employed to cover and whether there has been a change over time in what it does cover.

Another possible explanation for the steep rise in the funding of breach of the peace cases is that behaviour once considered to be minor may now be seen as more serious, so that the 'public interest' demands that they should be dealt with by the sheriff court. For example, heightened public anxiety may mean that being drunk in a public place may be treated more seriously by both police and prosecutors to reflect that anxiety. This may mean that such behaviour is more likely to lead to arrest and prosecution in the Sheriff Court. Apparently heightened public anxiety about the 'growing threat' of public disturbances and generally 'loutish' behaviour may also lead to expectations that the courts will deal with such cases more punitively. Perhaps of all offences, breach of the peace is one of the most malleable and 'useful' in a variety of circumstances; it is therefore especially difficult to predict whether it will attract a custodial sentence or not. It may therefore be difficult to refuse legal aid on the grounds that a custodial sentence appears unlikely. However, these speculations can only be answered by further research examining the relative 'seriousness' of breach of the peace cases and how they are constructed in their organisational contexts by agencies in the criminal process (e.g. Duff, 1997; McConville, Sanders and Leng, 1991; Moody and Tombs, 1982; Tombs and Moody, 1993).[16]

The shift from district court to sheriff court, however, is not confined to breach of the peace matters. There has also been significant growth in two other offences which used to be thought of as suitable for the district court: 'vandalism' and

[16] Alternatives to the much-debated supplier-induced inflation thesis (e.g. Gray, 1994; Samuel, 1996), include the state-induced-demand thesis and client-induced-demand. Smith, for example, argues that the increased use of lawyers, courts and legal aid spending follows an overall trend towards people seeking advice and assistance from a variety of 'helping' organisations (Wall, 1996).

'other road traffic offences' (that is, traffic offences not involving drink or drugs). In 1991/2, legal aid funded 5,536 cases in these two categories. By 1994/5, the number had doubled to 10,832, of which 9,710 were in the sheriff court. 'Breach of the peace', 'vandalism' and, 'other road traffic' cases taken together have become an increasingly important part of the legal aid scheme. In 1991/2 they accounted for 24 per cent of all cases and 18 per cent of expenditure. By 1994/5 they accounted for 31 per cent of cases and 22 per cent of expenditure.

Overall, it seems that Scottish criminal legal aid is increasingly directed at offences which were once considered relatively minor. The explanations for this are far from clear. SLAB has not been granting a higher proportion of applications: the grant rate has stayed fairly steady at between 90 and 92 per cent of applications received. It has, however, been receiving more applications. The reasons appear to be linked with a shift in prosecution from the district court to the sheriff court, though why this should have happened is unclear. It is a subject which merits further investigation. However, the volume of cases is only one of the two questions posed at the beginning of this section. Let us now turn to cost per case.

The cost per case

Average case costs. Over the last few years, considerable concern has been expressed over the rise in the average cost of Scottish summary legal aid cases. The data in Table 6.5 charts this rise in Scottish spending.

Interestingly, the difference in case costs between England and Wales and Scotland is not caused by higher lawyer fees. Fee levels in Scotland have not been increased since April 1992, and are now lower than equivalent rates in England. Thus in England and Wales, the hourly rate for preparation ranges from £44 per hour for 'non-franchise holders' outside London to £47.25 per hour for London 'franchise holders'.[17] The Scottish equivalent is only £42.20 per hour. In England and Wales, routine letters and phone calls can be charged at between £3.40 and £3.60, while in Scotland they receive only £2.40. Scots' bills are, therefore, higher because solicitors bill for more work rather than because they charge higher fees. Why this should be is a question which requires further research.

Table 6.5 also shows average case costs in England and the Netherlands are practically identical. This is counterintuitive, as it is often stressed that under an inquisitorial system the role of the judge is more important and the role of the defence advocate less important. It must be recalled, however, that Dutch defence lawyers carry out work which under the English system might be expected to cost more. First, the cases are more serious and include all those which in Britain

[17] Legal Aid 'franchising' sets up a 'preferred supplier' relationship with firms of solicitors and other providers of legal services in which the quality of work is assured to the clients (Sherr, Moorhead, and Paterson, 1994:7)

Table 6.5: Average cost per summary legal aid case in Scotland, England and Wales and the Netherlands, 1991–2 to 1994–5

	1991–92	1992–93	1993–94	1994–95
Scotland	£595	£634	£684	£749
England & Wales	£445	£458	£450	£423
The Netherlands[a]	£418	£426	£411	£428

Sources: SLAB Think Tank—Case Costs—*Interim Report* 1996; Legal Aid Board, 1994/95 *Annual Report* p. 73; Unpublished figures from the Ministry of Justice, Netherlands.
[a] These figures for the Netherlands include all first instance representation, including cases which would be dealt with in jury courts in the UK.

would be dealt with by jury courts. Secondly, they often handle all the charges outstanding against their client together, rather than submitting several bills for the same person. In very broad terms, the Dutch system costs less because serious cases are dealt with more cheaply and less serious cases are not legally aided. Instead, they are dealt with out of court, through dismissals and transactions, or in the sub-district court (Kantongerechten, or cantonal courts) without representation because of the almost total lack of risk of imprisonment.

In conclusion, whatever the reason for the rise in criminal legal aid costs, it remains the case that, compared with the Netherlands and England and Wales, Scotland incurs a higher level of spending on criminal legal aid, with the bulk of the money spent on large numbers of 'ordinary' summary cases. A particular feature of the Scottish system appears to be the high number and cost of relatively 'minor' cases within the district and sheriff courts.

Nonetheless, the knowledge produced by this study of three jurisdictions is, of course, necessarily determined by its methodological assumptions. While the study may have succeeded in uncovering findings and focused on particular questions, it is only one small step along towards a fuller explanation of the determinants of legal aid spending. I began this Chapter by noting that comparative research of this kind is fraught with dangers. The study discussed in this Chapter has attempted to provide some broad comparisons of cost and some reasonably robust hypotheses to explain these differences. The findings of the study were greeted positively by policy-makers and some of the findings have in turn, at least in part, been employed to provide support for the government proposal to introduce Public Defenders in the summary courts in Scotland on an experimental basis (Scottish Office, 1997; Booth, 1997). There are, however, a number of issues with which this and other studies must grapple if meaningful cost comparisons are to be made and explanations advanced. The subsequent section of this Chapter sketches out these issues and in the course of so doing develops the argument that the essential problem in empirical 'comparative' research does not necessarily lie in comparing more than one jurisdiction. Instead, the fundamental empirical research issues are manifested in the attempt to make *any* comparison of the practice of legal aid spending.

Issues in the construction of 'comparison': jurisdiction's misplaced centrality

Although the research discussed here relates to criminal legal aid, the issues raised go beyond that specific milieu and relate also to civil legal aid. The issues in conducting comparative legal aid research might immediately be understood to involve the comparison between legal jurisdictions. However, the difficulty in making comparisons *between jurisdictions* is only one *incidental* aspect of the problem of comparison and, as I will suggest, one that can be easily over-emphasised. All research which lays claim to social science takes at its heart the task of comparison. Thus, any attempt to describe legal aid spending and practice necessitates consideration, whether explicitly or implicitly, of assumptions about what it means to compare 'like with like' (i.e. 'similarity'). Whether similarity is defined by the category of jurisdiction (the legal limits of the state) or by geography, ethnicity, culture, economy, organisation or any combination of these definitional categories the same difficulties arise. These difficulties are not necessarily eradicated, or even limited, by conducting research within one jurisdiction only. It seems curious, therefore, that research comparing different jurisdictions tends to be labelled as 'comparative' when jurisdiction is only one aspect in the overall task of comparison. True, it may be that the label 'comparative' is merely an innocuous and convenient short-hand for inter-jurisdictional research. However, it perhaps reflects and perpetuates the easy assumption that inter-jurisdictional research is somehow genuinely or more 'comparative' than intra-jurisdictional research. I would suggest that this is not a safe assumption since it is premised on the belief that jurisdiction (and thus legality)[18] is the central definitional category of similarity: the starting point for comparing like with like. Below, I question the idea that legality should be the assumed starting point for defining similarity in legal aid spending and practices; and that the introduction of more than one jurisdiction into a study does not in principle necessarily complicate the activity of comparison. The basic methodological questions which the researcher must ask him/herself are not fundamentally altered by legality. I will use the findings and discussion already presented on criminal legal aid spending as context for this argument.

What is 'a case'?

At first blush this might seem to be an unnecessary question: a 'case' is surely self-evident. The term 'case' is so embedded in legal and popular consciousness that one instinctively knows what it is. Yet there is no codified or accepted definition.

[18] By 'jurisdiction' I mean the legal limits of the state; by 'legality' I mean legal doctrine and institutional legal obligations.

This is not to deny that there is in a sociological sense a 'knowledge' of what is a case as a narrative of interrelated events, or story, but this merely emphasises the inherent social construction of this 'knowledge' (e.g. Cicourel, 1968; Emerson, 1995; Matoesian, 1995; Sudnow, 1964; Tata, 1997; Waegel, 1981). However, the implications of the question 'what is a case?' permeate far beyond the niceties of research methodology. Research attempting to even describe (let alone explain) levels of spending on legal aid necessitates some notion of what constitutes 'a case' as some notion of the basic unit of work. If, as was attempted in the study discussed above, we are to make any kind of sense out of inter- *or intra*-jurisdictional comparative figures of expenditure (even if crudely controlled by population) then the questions of 'volume' and 'units' of work are inescapable. Thus, if comparative research is to be meaningful then researchers are bound to struggle with conceptions of 'a case'.

There are at least three aspects to this endeavour. First, different bodies recording and disseminating data may employ differing, even incommensurable, taken-for-granted conceptions of 'a case'. This variation may coincide with (though not originate from) jurisdiction. For example, it was noted above that compared with both Scotland and England and Wales, the Netherlands fund fewer legally aided criminal cases. It might be tempting to conclude from this that in some sense the Netherlands is in some way less generous than the other two countries. However, the practice of combining cases is seemingly more widespread in the Netherlands. 'Combined cases' involve the aggregation of two or more narrative charge sheets involving the same accused person. These are derived from reports from the police to the prosecutor's office and may describe quite separate incidents which were alleged to have been committed up to two years apart and of quite a different nature. It has in recent years, at least in the major cities, become deliberate policy to conjoin such charge sheets together, and although there have been some moves in this direction in Scotland, the Dutch prosecutors appear to act with greater vigour than their Scottish counterparts. Thus the courts in the Netherlands may dispose of the 'case' in one single hearing whereas the courts in the other two jurisdictions would (from a Dutch perspective) normally split the cases. Secondly, there are differing assumptions underlying the term 'case' between different agencies in the justice process. As we saw above, the police have a different automatic understanding of a case to, for example the courts, or social work departments, prosecutors' offices, etc. To the police a case may be understood as one report of criminal activity. On the other hand, the courts and post-sentence agencies (such as probation, prison, etc.) tend to understand 'a case' as being about one person: one person processed at one time equals one case. How then is the legal aid researcher to identify and classify a unit of work? How this question is answered will have a major impact on the research outcomes. Thirdly, there is no reason to assume any national homogeneity in the way agencies define a case. Instead it might be safer to assume that this will vary geographically, organisationally, ethnically, culturally, and indeed chronologically. So the 'comparative' legal aid researcher has to address not only *inter*- but also *intra*-agency differences of definition.

Comparing roles and functions

In the research study described here, an attempt has been made to compare legal roles and functions in different countries. However, categorising process and functions is far from unproblematic (Blakenburg 1992). For example, earlier in this Chapter we concentrated on the findings relating to 'representation' in the three countries. However, one fundamental comparative question deserves to be tackled explicitly: what constitutes 'representation'? In the Netherlands, for example, an accused person is not required to appear in court, which would be anathema in most English-speaking jurisdictions. If a Dutch accused person does not appear in court then s/he cannot receive legal aid representation. Although some crude comparisons could be made between jury and non-jury courts in Scotland and England and Wales, there are no juries in the Netherlands. The Dutch figures include serious cases which would almost certainly have been heard before a jury court in Britain. In this respect, the comparison between non-jury courts and all Dutch courts surely overestimates Dutch spending.

Comparing 'real' need

Punitiveness and leniency. Until recently it appeared to be conventional penological wisdom to suggest that Dutch sentencing is far more lenient and tolerant than that in other countries, especially the UK (Downes, 1988). It would be tempting to conclude that this explains a generally more 'tolerant' climate which in turn may require lower legal aid spending since a custodial sentence may be assessed as unlikely by legal aid decision-makers, making legal aid unnecessary. However, the evidence for this more lenient penological approach is open to question. The evidence tends to concentrate on the analysis of cross-national rates of imprisonment. The conventional means of comparison of national prison populations is as a number incarcerated per 100,000 of population (e.g. Council of Europe, 1992). These have tended to show a substantially higher rate in Great Britain than that in the Netherlands. However, this is not the end of the story in assessing punitiveness and leniency. Ken Pease has argued that expressing prison population in relation to national population is '. . . useless for all practical and intellectual purposes' (Pease, 1994:125, *sic*). The Netherlands may not be as lenient as their position in the oft-used league tables of imprisonment rates suggest (see Kommer, 1994). In using the number of people imprisoned per 100,000 of the population as the main indicator of punitiveness, the influence of early release legislation and practices (including remission and parole), pre-trial practices and their relationship with 'backdating' to cover a period spent in custody on remand are critical. Given the relatively less generous practice concerning early release from custody in the Netherlands than in Britain, the use of imprisonment rates as a means of calibrating of punitiveness and leniency may therefore be suspect. Reviewing alternative means of comparing 'national punitivess', Pease concludes: 'If compelled to take a position on the current severity of the English/Welsh system, it would have to be that pronounced sentences may be marginally more severe elsewhere in Europe, but that the severity of sentencing after taking account of the effects of discretionary release is, for all offences, save homicide, lower than international practice generally, including those few European comparisons which are possible' (Pease, 1994:125–6).

Furthermore, for some years now commentators (e.g. Dhondt, 1988; van Swaaningen and uit Beijerse, 1993) have detected a major shift in emphasis with a more punitive penal approach in the Netherlands illustrated by a major prison-building programme.

Crime rates. It might be supposed that if there is more 'need' of criminal legal aid then there must be more crime. Although comparing crime rates is a fraught business, there is little evidence to suggest that Scotland suffers a higher 'rate' of crime than the other two countries in the study described earlier (e.g. van Dijk and Mayhew, 1993). Once again, however, in examining crime rates we need to be careful to disaggregate the questions involved. A well as alternative strategies for recording and representing aggregate information about crime, there are a number of questions which need to be disentangled. First, we need to distinguish 'units' of crime. If a researcher finds that there are one hundred thousand crimes committed last year in area A and two hundred thousand committed in area B it then it might seem to follow that there is more crime in area B. Yet, what are the measures of crime? Here we come back to the issue of identifying a criminal unit (or 'case'). Of course, even if this issue can be satisfactorily resolved there is then the issue of population. There may be the attempt to count crimes per 100,000 of population as in the study outlined earlier in this Chapter. However, it is important to recognise that this can only be the crudest control, and that this might be supplemented by looking at particular sub-samples using dimensions such as age, sex, employment, and socio-economic status.

Populations, criminalisation and legal aid need

Geography, age, ethnicity, sex and gender, and socio-economic status may all play a part in determining entry and exit points in the criminal process. Let us briefly consider just one social dimension which can predict entry and exit points: race. In his detailed examination of the relationship between race and sentencing, Tonry (1995) has shown that the emblem of the Reagan and Bush presidencies' 'War on Drugs' (and especially crack cocaine) included US sentencing Federal Guideline legislation which was bound (and indeed was intended) to fall with greater force on racial minorities.[19] If this, as Tonry (1995) suggests, is one illustration of the way in which legislation and enforcement are targeted specifically towards certain (in this case racial) groups, then we should expect eligibility for criminal legal aid to be systematically patterned by certain social dimensions of relative disadvantage and criminal process agencies' professional 'on-the-job knowledge' of criminality and dangerousness. For example, in the 'interests of justice test' operated in Scotland, and England and Wales, eligibility, as we saw earlier, is crucially determined by expectation of the sentencing result. Hood's careful study (1992) of sentencing in the Crown Court in England and Wales has revealed an element of disparity in the way in which different racial groups are sentenced. Free (1996) concludes that racial disparities in the US are largely attributable to rates of arrest and the pre-judicial sentencing stages in the criminal process. If, as research suggests, certain groups are disproportionately retained and treated more seriously by criminal process agencies then we should expect disproportionate legal aid eligibility arising from those groups. In this sense, then, the (comparative) researcher needs to consider how the social reality of legal aid eligibility is determined rather than merely focusing on simple technical eligibility.

Case similarity and need

We saw earlier that the rise in Scottish criminal legal aid appeared to arise from the numbers of summary cases receiving legal aid representation. It was suggested that there may be 'minor' cases receiving legal aid, whereas similar cases had not received legal aid in the past, or, that 'minor' cases had been pursued in the higher sheriff court rather than lower district court. There are, however, fundamental issues in this hypothesis concerning the conceptualisation of the 'seriousness' of cases, or the value or 'worth' of cases (Emerson, 1995). Thinking about what kinds of cases are legally aided necessitates some notion of case similarity. How can cases be compared? Once again, the trans-jurisdictional comparative researcher is faced with issues which do not originate in the study of different countries and are not necessarily diminished through single-country research. The same issue concerning the conception and representation of seriousness or 'worth' of a case is inherent in single-country research.

One possibility is to compare cases on the basis of their headline charges (e.g. 'assault', 'theft', etc. in common law countries, and statutory sections. Indeed, this is the method employed in the collection of official data from administrative sources and was that employed by the study outlined above. The implicit assumption is that similarity can be meaningfully captured by classifying cases on the

[19] As Doob (1995) observed, it seems odd that under the Guidelines ten grams of 'crack' (a drug used in the poor, black inner cities) has the same penal value as one kilogram of cocaine (the drug of choice of the rich and famous). 'The fact that cocaine can easily be made into crack (thus increasing the penal value of the drug in one's possession dramatically) is lost in the Guidelines' (ibid.).

basis of their headline charge. This is, at best, only a very crude way of operationalising case 'similarity'. Before considering the difficulties in this approach it is first useful to recall the purpose of comparison: to grasp which cases (if the charge(s) are proved) are 'likely' to result in a custodial sentence. Thus, in thinking about the relationship between cases and the level of spending the crucial lens through which similarity is viewed is expected sentencing outcome.

Using the headline charge is not, however, a satisfactory way of representing similarity from the perspective of sentencing. First, the headline charge provides the sentencer with very limited information about the circumstances, nature, and thus the relative seriousness of the alleged offence (see e.g. Ashworth *et al.*, 1984; Fitzmaurice and Pease, 1986; Parker, Sumner and Jarvis, 1989; Tata and Hutton, 1998). In the common law jurisdiction of Scotland, for example, the charge of 'theft' can range from theft of unimportant computer disks from an employer to highly organised teams of 'professional' shop-lifting of very high-value goods. 'Housebreaking' can range from the opportunistic theft of a milk-bottle from a doorstep to a pre-meditated night-time domestic break-in and theft of a pensioners' war medals which cause an elderly person enormous distress. 'Assault' can range from a slap in the face to a gang attack. It might be supposed that this is a problem peculiar to common law charges and that statutory charges ensure adequate clarity in terms of seriousness. However, jurisdictions world-wide have struggled to offer sufficient statutory clarity which provides sentencers with sufficient information about the case simply from a headline charge (e.g. Tonry, 1996). Statutory charges inevitably fail to provide adequate information from the perspective of sentencing (as opposed to conviction) about the nature, consequences, motivation etc. (and thus seriousness) of an offence incident.

So far we have limited the discussion to assessing the seriousness of cases involving a single charge. However, most cases involve more than one charge, even if on conviction this figure reduces to around half (Hutton *et al.*, 1996). How should research attempt to capture the seriousness of multi-charge cases? In multi-charge cases the conventional method has been to record cases according to the principal charge. But how is this selected? This is an issue which has received surprisingly little attention (Walker, 1995:28–9; Tata, 1997:298–401).

Administrative bodies typically collect and disseminate data by representing cases in terms of their 'principal charge' or conviction. The principal conviction may be determined by the charge which receives the most severe penalty, or selected by the police who typically provide the source data (e.g. Scottish Office, 1993b; Home Office, 1995).[20] The sentence recorded against each case is the total effective (i.e. net rather than gross) sentence passed. For example, let us imagine a case where the offender has been convicted of both an assault causing severe

[20] There are also fundamental difficulties in determining the most severe sentence, especially where, as in the vast majority of cases in western jurisdictions, the most common penalty is non-custodial.

injury and a breach of the peace. The court passes a custodial sentence of eighteen months for the assault and further sentence of three months to run consecutively with it. Thus, the total net sentence is twenty-one months. Under the principal conviction method this would be recorded as 'assault—twenty one months'. This would indicate that the offender was sentenced to twenty-one months simply for assault, concealing the three months for breach of the peace. The fact that the three months for the public order offence get lost in the statistics may seem to be a small price to pay in exchange for the recording of huge amounts of official data.

However, let us consider another case where the difficulty inherent in the principal conviction method of recording and representing criminal justice data is more acute. An offender may have been convicted for a series of four robberies and four serious assaults inflicted during the course of each robbery. A net sentence of fifty months' imprisonment is passed. This would be recorded as 'Robbery—50 months'. The problem with this method of representing aggregate data is that it is not possible to distinguish between cases where there was a single conviction of robbery and cases where there was a spree of robberies and accompanying assaults and the case is simply represented in official statistics as 'robbery'. Another example is where cases of highly organised multiple theft appear in official statistics together with cases involving a single, opportunist theft of low value. Less straightforward still are cases where there are charges against one person for drug and robbery offences (where an offender may have robbed a chemist of a quantity of drugs and then sold these on to a number of people). How should such a case be recorded using principal conviction method: as a drug case or as a robbery case? Using a principal conviction approach, the choice of how to classify this drugs-robbery case must inevitably be arbitrary.

The problem for a principal charge/conviction method, then, is that it produces very limited, and potentially misleading, aggregate information about the pattern of cases. This is due to a flawed characterisation of 'similarity' which demands that every case be defined and represented on the basis of one conviction only. The reader will recall that in practice a key determination of the decision to grant or refuse legal aid representation is whether the case is sufficiently serious that, if charges are proved, a custodial sentence is a '*likely*' outcome. In practice, how do legal aid decision-makers come to a judgement about 'likely' sentence outcomes? I would suggest that the basis upon which legal aid decision-makers arrive at a decision probably contrasts markedly from a principal charge/conviction approach to interpreting cases. Like other practitioners, legal aid decision-makers attempt to consider the sequence of events in the whole case rather focusing exclusively on one arbitrarily selected 'principal' charge. Elsewhere I have discussed these issues further and offer an alternative method based on researching agencies' conceptions of 'typical whole case stories' (Tata, 1997). Legal aid research which attempts to identify officials' working professional knowledge about the similarity and seriousness of cases would be fruitful. The research would try to tease out the ways in which officials decide, and in particular how they judge the seriousness of a case and its likelihood of receiving a custodial sentence. It would investigate how administrators intuitively construct meaning (for example, in terms of motivation, culpability, etc. of the accused person if the charges are proved) from the file. In this way research would strive to capture routine representations of cases in their social context, 'naturalistically' (Manning, 1992) rather than simply attempting to represent the case as a collection of supposedly discrete independent abstract 'factors' (Tata, 1998).

It was suggested above that there might be a tendency in Scotland towards 'Widgery drift'. Taken together, 'breach of the peace', 'vandalism', and 'other road traffic' cases in 1991/2 accounted for 24 per cent of all cases and 18 per cent of all expenditure. By 1994/5 they accounted for 31 per cent of cases and 22 per cent of expenditure. However, a puzzle remains. Has it been the case that during this period internal SLAB organisational norms about the assumed correct threshold for granting legal aid has been lowered (i.e. have administrators become more generous); or are administrators simply responding to a changing flavour of narratives from the criminal process which present cases as more serious? Without closer attention to the typical and routine characterisations of case similarity (which takes its cues from the way in which the case has evolved and is expected to evolve from its processing by other criminal agencies) it is not possible to answer with any certainty why the numbers of cases receiving legal aid may be increasing (and the legal aid bill rising). Research attempting to capture the informal rules of thumb operated by legal aid decision-makers and their routine, intuitive professional knowledge (e.g. Hawkins, 1992; Baldwin and Hawkings, 1984; Halliday, 1998a; 1998b; Lempert, 1992; Emerson, 1995) may bring us closer towards answering questions about the nature of 'Widgery drift'.

The perils of a jurisdiction-centred approach to 'comparative' empirical research

I have argued that the difficulties encountered in so-called 'comparative' or inter-jurisdictional research are in principle no different from those which must be faced by intra-jurisdictional research. They *may* in practice sometimes be exacerbated by studying two or more countries, but this is only incidental to the fundamental problem of comparisons. The source of the difficulties in comparative legal aid research does not lie in jurisdiction itself, but in practices which may (or may not) coincide with jurisdiction. For example, trying to identify similar roles and functions of the criminal process in different jurisdictions can be especially problematic when using legal aid budget readings. Equally, however, there may be greater variation *within* a single jurisdiction.

However, these difficulties may only appear to be a function of jurisdiction if comparative research assumes legality as the basic or central category of explanation (in this context formal rules, statutory and case law, formal and issued procedures and guidelines). On the other hand, if research also attends to sociological rules and processes (in the context of legal aid spending, concerns such as, inter- and intra-agency relationships; professional knowledge and constructs in decision-making; economic, micro and macro power relations; and social and cultural considerations) then the difficulties of being able to make meaningful comparisons are not found only in comparing different jurisdictions but in making any comparisons at all. Research which privileges legality as its exclusive or defining concern cannot hope to provide meaningful comparisons within a jurisdiction, let alone explain differences between jurisdictions' legal aid spending practices. Ultimately such an approach can only hope to explain spending behaviour in terms of the simple mechanisms of legal requirement. It cannot begin to explain why spending might rise within a jurisdiction, or may be patterned in particular ways.

If meaningful comparison of legal aid is to be feasible then jurisdiction and legality must be only one of a range of explanations for behaviour, rather than the central or basic explanatory category. Consequently, the fundamental problems of the principle of comparison are not complicated by jurisdiction but are connected with questions inherent in the measurement of cases: functions; populations; time periods; criminalisation; and case similarity. The principles which these issues raise are not necessarily avoided or diminished by research which confines itself to a single-jurisdiction study. To locate jurisdiction as the primary or central explanatory category in a comparative study (of legal aid) is only to privilege a legality-centred approach to research which necessarily cannot begin to explain patterns of observed behaviour, whether within or between jurisdictions.

Appendix A

Interests of Justice Factors used in the Decision to Grant Criminal Legal Aid

Scotland	*England and Wales*
a. The offence is such that if proved it is likely that the court would impose a sentence which would deprive the accused of his liberty or lead to loss of his livelihood;	a. The offence is such that if proved it is likely that the court would impose a sentence which would deprive the accused of his liberty or lead to loss of his livelihood;
b. the determination of the case may involve consideration of a substantial question of law, or of evidence of a complex or difficult nature;	b. the determination of the case may involve consideration of a substantial question of law;
c. the accused may be unable to understand the proceedings or to state his own case because of his age, inadequate knowledge of English, mental illness, other mental or physical disability or otherwise;	c. the accused may be unable to understand the proceedings or to state his own case because of his inadequate knowledge of English, mental illness or other mental or physical disability;
d. it is in the interests of someone other than the accused that the accused be legally represented;	d. it is in the interests of someone other than the accused that the accused be legally represented;
e. the defence to be advanced by the accused does not appear to be frivolous;	e. the nature of the defence is such as to involve the tracing and interviewing of witnesses or expert cross-examination of a witness for the prosecution.
f. the accused has been remanded in custody pending trial.	

Source: The Scottish Office, Criminal Legal Aid Review Consultation Paper, SOHHD, November 1993.

7

Legal Aid Reform in France and the Republic of Ireland in the 1990s[*]

MEL COUSINS

Introduction

The comparative study of legal aid schemes has tended to focus on 'leaders' (i.e. those countries with more extensive legal aid schemes) and to ignore the 'laggards'. Cappelletti's study of legal aid, for example, was based on the assumption that the development of legal aid was tied to the modernisation of societies. Accordingly, those countries which did not have extensive legal aid schemes were seen as 'Anachronisms in the Modern World' (Cappelletti, Gordley and Johnson, 1975).

However, there are a number of problematic aspects about this focus. First, it is based on an assumption that more extensive legal aid systems are somehow 'better' at providing access to the law. While this assumption is intuitively appealing, it needs to be tested rather than simply taken for granted. In fact, there have been relatively few studies which have tried to assess the degree of access to the law between countries with different levels of legal aid. Secondly, it is now clear that there are many more countries which have a low or medium level of civil legal aid spending[1] compared to the very small number of countries with extensive schemes. This calls into question the modernisation theory implicit in Cappelletti's approach and suggests that there are a range of other factors which need to be taken into account in analysing the development of legal aid. Finally, the focus on 'leaders' has tended to mean that Catholic countries which generally have much lower levels of legal aid are not included in the analysis.

This Chapter attempts to make an initial step towards redressing this imbalance by looking at two Catholic countries in which public spending on legal aid is in the low to medium category: France and the Republic of Ireland (hereafter

* I would like to thank Don Fleming and Gerry Whyte, Trinity College, Dublin, for their very helpful comments on earlier drafts.

[1] Low public spending means public spending on civil legal aid and advice <0.01% of GDP; medium = 0.01–0.025% of GDP; high = > 0.025% of GDP. While the level of public spending on legal aid in a country cannot be assumed to be precisely correlated to the extent or 'quality' of its service, in the absence of any other reliable indicator in this regard (e.g. case-load), it gives some indication as to the political importance attached to legal aid in a given country in terms of the amount spent on legal aid as a proportion of the countries' Gross Domestic Product.

Ireland). For this purpose a country is considered to be Catholic if a clear majority of the population has been baptised as Roman Catholic for most of the period during which legal aid has developed. On this basis both Ireland and France (Whyte, 1981:139) can be described as Catholic. The Chapter focuses primarily on civil (rather than criminal) legal aid. Ideally, a long-term comparative study of the development of legal aid in both countries should be made (and indeed in other Catholic countries such as Belgium, Italy and Spain). However, the detailed history of the development of legal aid in both France and Ireland remains to be written (for France see Schnapper, 1984 and Crespin, 1995; for Ireland see Carney, 1979). This Chapter focuses on reforms in France and Ireland in the 1990s, and, in particular, on the detailed public discussion as set out in official reports and parliamentary debates.[2]

The theoretical approach adopted follows the Marxist-oriented perspective of Alcock (1976:163). It seeks 'to locate the social basis of the phenomenon of legal aid in the variety of practices historically involved in its formation'. The Alcock perspective on the development of legal aid does not treat any one factor as determinative, but 'treats all phenomenon as the result of the interrelationship of the social factors comprising them, none being the sole causational factor, but all together acting as the structural cause of the existence of the phenomena' (Alcock, 1976:164).

In the first part of this article, I look briefly at the modern history of legal aid in both France and Ireland up to the 1990s, and in more detail at the passage of recent legislation in both countries. In the second part of the Chapter, I move from description to analysis and attempt to identify some of the factors relevant to the way in which legal aid has developed in both countries.

The history of legal aid in France and Ireland

France

In France, legislative provision for legal aid was initially established in 1851 (see Cappelletti, Gordley and Johnson, 1975; Schnapper, 1984; Crespin, 1995). These

[2] For France see Conseil d'État (1991); *Assemblée nationale*: Project de loi no. 1949; Rapport de M. Colcombet, commission des lois, no. 2010; Discussion and adoption 29 and 30 Apr. 1991; Project de loi, modifé par le Senat, no. 2075; Rapport de M. Colcombet, commission des lois, no. 2079; Discussion and adoption 10 June 1991; Project de loi, modifé par le Senat en 2ème lecture, no. 2154; Rapport de M. Colombet, commission mixte paritaire, no. 2155; Discussion and adoption 28 June 1991; *Senat*; Project de loi, adopté par l'Assemblée nationale, no. 310; Rapport de M. Dejoie, commission des lois, no. 338; Discussion and adoption 29 and 30 May 1991; Project de loi, adopté avec modifications par l'Assemblee nationale en 2ème lecture, no. 374; Rapport de M. Dejoie, commission des lois, no. 404; Discussion and adoption 26 June 1991; Rapport de M. Dejoie, commission mixte paritaire, no. 422; Discussion and adoption 28 June 1991. For Ireland see 141 Seanad *Debates* 2124ff.; 142 *Seanad Debates* 47ff.; 1864ff.; 143 *Seanad Debates* 515ff.; 1975ff.; 455 *Dail Debates* 762ff.; 458 *Dail Debates* 406ff.; L5 Select *Committee on Legislation and Security* 171 ff.

provisions obliged the legal profession to provide gratuitous assistance to *indigents*. There was, however, no right to legal aid and no public remuneration of the lawyers involved (although lawyers could, in some cases, recover their costs from the other party to the litigation). The initial legislation applied only to court cases and there was no provision in relation to legal advice. Legal aid bureaux were established to adjudicate on applications for legal aid. These consisted of representatives of the state, the judiciary and the legal professions. The number of persons assisted rose from 3,000 (2.5 per cent of all cases) in 1870 to 20,000 (14 per cent) by 1897 (Crespin, 1995:144). The 1851 legislation remained in force for over 100 years with relatively minor changes. In 1901 the term *indigent* was replaced by the expression 'persons who, due to inadequate resources, cannot exercise their rights effectively'. This, however, had little impact on the operation of the scheme in practice (Crespin, 1995:149). In 1958, at a time when much more extensive legislation was being implemented in countries such as the United Kingdom and the Netherlands, the French scheme was reformed. The reforms provided that, in certain circumstances, a lawyer could obtain his or her costs from a legally aided person who was awarded damages of such a level that he or she would not have been entitled to legal aid.

In 1972 new legislation was enacted by the French Parliament to replace the 1851 legislation. In his speech to the French Parliament, the then Minister for Justice highlighted the four main criticisms of the existing legislation as being (1) the arbitrary nature of decisions in relation to granting and refusing legal assistance; (2) the all-or-nothing nature of such decisions and the lack of any partial legal aid; (3) the fact that almost the entire costs of the scheme fell on lawyers; and (4) the fact that, in adjudicating on applications for legal aid, the legal aid bureaux were, in effect, evaluating the case (Cappelletti, Gordley and Johnson, 1975:423). In response to these criticisms, the new legal aid legislation set out clear criteria in relation to the granting of legal aid, provided for the compensation of lawyers involved in legal aid and introduced a system of partial legal aid. However, the payment to lawyers was not intended to reflect the full market value of their services and was described as an *indemnité* (allowance). The reforms very much retained the shape of the earlier legislation and the main differences involved the sharing of financial responsibilities for legal aid by the state and the clarification of criteria in relation to the granting of legal aid.

The 1972 reforms represented an important development in relation to legal aid. The scheme had a broad scope, both in terms of the proportion of households entitled to legal aid and the types of case covered. In practice, however, it never developed in the way which might have been expected. The proportion of households entitled to legal aid was allowed to decline significantly through a failure to index-link the income thresholds. In practice, about two-thirds of all legal aid cases related to family law and there were significant delays in getting access to legal aid. At the same time, the indemnities paid to the legal profession in respect of legal aid services were also allowed to decline in real terms. This led to calls for reform from the legal profession and to strike action by local bar organisations, itself directly related to the ongoing reform of the French legal profession which led to new legislation in 1990 (Karpik, 1995:390–4). As a result, in December 1989, the government requested the Conseil d'État to carry out a study of legal aid and make recommendations for reform which are considered in more detail below.

Ireland

Legal aid in Ireland developed quite differently from that in France (Carney, 1979). Modern Ireland was initially part of the United Kingdom with the consequence that much United Kingdom legislation also applied in Ireland. On Independence in 1922, there were no particular statutory provisions in force in Ireland relating to civil or criminal legal aid. Up to the 1960s, it appears that criminal legal aid was provided only in relation to murder cases (and even here there appears to have been no statutory basis for the practice). A comprehensive system of criminal legal aid was provided for in the Criminal Justice (Legal Aid) Act 1962. This legislation did not come into force until 1965 due to disagreement with the legal profession as to the fees to be paid. This legislation provided for legal representation by private lawyers where a person's means were insufficient to enable him or her to obtain legal assistance and where 'by reason of the gravity of the charge or of exceptional circumstances, it [wa]s essential in the interests of justice that he should have legal aid in the preparation and conduct of his defence'. The 1962 scheme made no provision for legal advice. It was in effect transformed in the 1970s, first, by a decision of the Irish Supreme Court that persons had a constitutional right to criminal legal aid in certain circumstances, and secondly, by significant increases in the fees paid to lawyers (Cousins, 1996a).

In civil proceedings in contrast there was no State provision of legal aid and advice at all until 1980. In so far as private practitioners did such work on a *pro bono* basis, this was left entirely to their own discretion. The position in relation to civil legal aid began to change in the 1960s with the establishment of the Free Legal Advice Centres (FLACs). From 1969 this organisation of young lawyers and law students both provided legal advice and representation and campaigned for the introduction of a comprehensive scheme of civil legal aid and advice. As part of this campaign, FLAC established the Coolock Community Law Centre in Dublin in 1975 which remains the only service of its kind operating in Ireland.

In 1974, and arising from the FLAC campaign, the then Minister for Justice appointed a committee to advise on the introduction of a comprehensive scheme of legal aid and advice in civil matters. This Pringle Committee reported in 1977 (Committee on Civil Legal Aid and Advice, 1978). The recommendations of the report were very much influenced by arguments put forward by FLAC and comparable organisations. The Pringle Committee Report recommended the establishment of a comprehensive system of civil legal aid and advice under the auspices of an independent Legal Aid Board. Legal services were to be provided both through private practitioners and through a network of community law centres and legal advice centres. The Pringle Committee estimated the overall cost of the comprehensive scheme to be of the order of £2m per annum. It also put forward proposals in relation to a more limited interim scheme if it was considered necessary to introduce such an interim measure. However, no immediate action was taken by the government in response to its recommendations.

Late 1979 saw two significant developments in relation to legal aid in Ireland. In October the European Court of Human Rights found in *Airey* v. *Ireland* (1979) 2 EHRR 305 that Ireland was in breach of its obligations under the Convention of Human Rights. In particular that its failure to provide a scheme of legal aid and advice had meant that an individual's right of access to the courts under Article 6(1) of the Convention had been violated. Two months later the Irish Minister for Justice established a trial civil legal aid and advice scheme on an interim administrative basis. The new civil legal aid scheme differed significantly from the recommendations of the Pringle Committee (Whyte, 1984). In contrast to those recommendations, private practitioners were not involved in providing services at all. Legal aid and advice was to be provided solely through a network of government law centres managed directly by the Legal Aid Board. Whilst the scheme provided for the appointment of advisory committees, including representatives of the community, they had no direct role in the management of the centres. The 1979 civil legal aid scheme excluded a number of areas of legal proceedings (including defamation and debt collection) and set out a range of detailed tests which an applicant had to satisfy in order to qualify for legal aid.

Throughout the 1980s Ireland experienced significant financial and economic difficulties which led to strict controls on public expenditure. This had unfortunate repercussions for the new civil legal aid scheme. In contrast to other public services which already had established levels of spending, it was forced to seek additional funding at a time of fiscal restraint. This led to severe restrictions on the legal aid services being provided. In effect, the vast majority of services related to family law matters, long delays operated in many cases in getting access to legal aid and, at times, services were totally suspended (other than for emergency cases) in order to clear existing backlogs of work.[3] In January 1990 the then Chairman of the Legal Aid Board (who was coincidentally also then Chairman of the Bar Council) and the then President of the Law Society who was a member of the Legal Aid Board both resigned from the Board due to successive governments' failure to provide adequate resources.

There were a number of reasons for the slow development of legal aid in the 1980s. Obviously, the overall economic climate was unfavourable. However, the legal aid service was also faced with a generally unsupportive Department and a succession of Ministers who also showed little support for the service. In addi-

[3] See the successive annual *Reports* of the Legal Aid Board.

tion, neither legal profession campaigned seriously for a more comprehensive legal aid service. While the resignation of the leaders of both professions would suggest the contrary, in fact these resignations were treated very much as personal matters by the two individuals concerned and did not lead to any particular action by either profession. However, in the 1990s there was a changed environment for legal aid in Ireland, and the consequent developments are discussed below.

Developments in the 1990s

France

The Conseil d'État, which in December 1989 had been requested to carry out a study of the legal aid scheme, reported back to the government in April 1990, highlighting the inadequacies of the current scheme and setting out detailed proposals for reform (Conseil d'État, 1991). The Conseil found that criticisms of the existing legal aid scheme came from three different quarters. First, the coverage of legal aid had been allowed to decline from 75 per cent of the population in 1972 to about 34 per cent. Secondly, the legal profession was dissatisfied both with the inadequate level of fees payable and with the inequalities between local bar organisations, some bars providing significantly more legal aid than others. Finally, the study found that the state itself had very little control over the manner in which legal aid was spent. The Conseil Report highlighted the importance of legal aid in ensuring access to justice in a country such as France which had well developed systems of law and social services. However, the Conseil found that the level of spending on legal aid in France was extremely low: 7 FF per person, compared to 30 FF in comparable countries such as Germany, and as much as 98 FF in England and Wales. It also found considerable delays in obtaining access to legal aid in many areas.

The Conseil put forward a range of proposals for reform of the 1972 scheme. In the area of legal aid itself, most of these consisted of a refining and up-dating of the legislation. In particular, the Conseil proposed a move from *indemnification* of lawyers to *remuneration* (i.e. payment for services). However, the Conseil recognised that the level of remuneration would not correspond to that received in private practice and that the legal professions should accept a lower rate as part of a duty of solidarity (*devoir de solidarité*) seen as a counterpart to their legal monopoly. The Conseil also recommended the introduction of a scheme of legal advice. In contrast to the legal aid service which was to be funded by the state, the legal advice service was to operate at a local level and obtain funding from a variety of sources including local government and the state. It proposed the establishment of a National Commission on Legal Aid and Regional Legal Aid Commissions which would be tripartite bodies including representatives of the legal profession, the judiciary and local authorities (the latter in their dual capacity as providers of finance and representatives of users).

The proposals of the Conseil d'État were largely accepted by the government and in April 1991 a Legal Aid Bill was brought forward to implement them. The Bill proposed a significant increase in the level of legal aid so as to increase the number of households covered to approximately 50 per cent. The government also committed itself to significant increases in funding for legal aid. In the area of legal aid itself, the Bill set out a range of proposals to fine-tune the existing service and to reform the system of payment to lawyers. The Bill also contained proposals for the establishment of the system of legal advice to be managed at a local level by Departmental Legal Aid Commissions.

The Bill was adopted by the French Parliament largely in the form in which it had been presented by the government. However, on a number of key issues the Parliament forced changes on the minority Socialist Government. These related to the method of payment of lawyers and the extent of control of lawyers over the legal aid service and, in particular, to the new legal advice service.

First, the Bill made a number of proposals in relation to the payment of lawyers. It proposed to change from the existing system of *indemnité* to one of *contribution* (i.e. a contribution to the cost of providing legal aid rather than *remuneration* as recommended by the Conseil d'État) while recognising that this '*contribution*' would not correspond to market prices because of the duty of solidarity owed by the legal profession. The Bill also provided for the decentralisation of payments and proposed a new method for the assessment of payments based on an hourly rate. While the decentralisation of payments was generally accepted, there was significant opposition to the notion of a contribution rather than remuneration and to the introduction of an hourly system of payment. It appears that the opposition arose because the legal profession feared that hourly payment would lead to the *tarrification* (fixing a scale of costs) of legal costs. Ironically, the introduction of a system of scale payments had been opposed on similar grounds in 1972 (Herzog and Ecolivet Herzog, 1973). Despite the objections of the Government, the Parliament amended the legislation to provide for payment of a '*retribution*' (a compensatory payment towards the cost of legal aid) and to revert to the existing system of a scale list of fees for different type of work rather than payment on an hourly basis. In addition, and against the strong objections of the Minister of Justice, Parliament amended the legislation in relation to the National and Departmental Legal Aid Commissions to provide that the representatives of the legal profession would make up at least 50 per cent of the boards of these bodies.

It is interesting to note that references to the concept of solidarity appeared at a number of points in the debate. The role of the state in funding the legal aid scheme was justified as being on the basis of national solidarity, in contrast to funding responsibilities for the legal advice service which was seen as including a much wider range of actors (*Assemblée nationale rapport*, no. 2010: 21). The concept of family solidarity was invoked to justify taking into account the means of the family for the purposes of the means test (*Assemblée nationale rapport*, no. 2010: 61). Finally, as we have seen, the legal profession were seen as owing a duty of solidarity in relation to reduced fees as a counterpart of the monopoly which they enjoyed in terms of legal representation.

The 1991 legislation required the Government to carry out a study of the operation of the new scheme after three years and to report to Parliament. This study provides some detailed information on the implementation of the legislation (Ministère de la Justice, 1995). The number in receipt of legal aid has increased sharply from 350,000 in 1991 to 580,000 in 1994. Civil and administrative matters accounted for two-thirds of all grants of legal aid with criminal matters accounting for the remainder. Family law remained the principal area giving rise to applications for legal aid, accounting for almost half of all civil matters. The study attempted to identify the reasons for the significant increase in legal aid. It found that the increase in the legal aid income thresholds accounted for over a quarter of the increase. The overall trend in the case-load of the French judicial system was only weakly linked to the increase in legal aid and the study suggested that other relevant factors included the increase in the jurisdictional scope of the scheme (relatively limited impact), increased awareness of the scheme, the unfavourable economic conjuncture (rising unemployment, etc.) and a greater propensity amongst lawyers to advise the clients to seek legal aid (arising from the increased legal aid payments) (1995:19). Overall expenditure on legal aid had, however, increased more slowly than expected (to about 890 million FF in 1994 or about 0.012 per cent of GDP). The study found that the legal advice system had been very slow to develop and that a number of departments had not yet taken any steps to establish a scheme. Reform of this aspect of the legal aid law is currently under discussion as Departmental Legal Aid Commissions operate in only about 20 departments (*Le Monde*, 13 Jan. 1998).

Ireland

A number of factors led to the changed environment for legal aid services in Ireland in the 1990s. First, Ireland's economic position improved which led to easier access to public expenditure for social services. Secondly, elections in 1992 led to the establishment of a new Government in 1993. Responsibility for the Civil Legal Aid Scheme was transferred to a newly established Department of Equality and Law Reform. The new Minister of the Department was perceived to be much more supportive towards the scheme than had been previous Ministers for Justice.[4] Thirdly, the new Government decided to hold a referendum to

[4] In 1997, following the most recent elections, the Department of Equality and Law Reform was abolished and a new Department of Justice, Equality and Law Reform was established. The implications of these changes remains to be seen.

remove the constitutional ban on divorce during its term of office. A similar referendum had previously been held in 1986. Although opinion polls in the early 1990s indicated that a significant majority of the population supported the removal of the ban on divorce, the proposal was soundly defeated in the referendum itself. Many commentators attributed this result, at least in part, to a lack of preparation by the then Government. There was a perception that a range of other legislation, ancillary to divorce, had not been put in place and that this had influenced people in voting 'No'. The new government adopted a policy of putting in place a wide range of legislation in an attempt to ensure that the divorce referendum campaign would focus on the right to remarry. One of the key planks of this approach was to put in place an adequate legal aid scheme as it was clear that the introduction of divorce would lead to significant additional demands on the legal aid service.

Thus there were significant increases in funding for the Civil Legal Aid Scheme from 1993 onwards (to 0.0135 per cent of GDP in 1994 and 0.016 per cent in 1995). The level of funding for legal aid had probably been artificially held down because of the lack of support of previous Ministers. It is likely that some significant increase would have occurred in any case in view of the growing level of family law litigation. To some extent, this can already been seen in the early 1990s where levels of spending already show an increase (from 0.006 per cent of GDP in 1989 to 0.009 per cent in 1992).

The Law Society had been approached in the early 1990s by the then Minister for Justice, in the context of discussions concerning general legislation on the solicitor's profession, with a view to seeing whether the profession would be prepared to make a *pro bono* contribution to the legal aid service. The Law Society immediately established a Committee to consider the issue of legal aid; this effectively resulted in a rejection of the Minister's suggestion and reiterated calls for a statutory legal aid service with increased funding. The Committee did foresee some involvement by private practitioners, but only as supplementary to the existing salaried service. Indeed, the only flurry of activity on the part of the Law Society throughout the 1990s related to the subsequent establishment of such a pilot system in 1993. Initially, the Council of the Law Society approved a proposal from the Minister for Equality and Law Reform that Family Law solicitors might take on one legal aid case on a *pro bono* basis in return for which the Minister indicated that he would substantially increase funding to the legal aid service and include the private profession ((1993) 87 *Gazette*:193). However, when the pilot scheme was introduced the Law Society was highly critical of the limited amount of funding provided (£100,000) and of the fact that the scheme only applied to District Court work. In particular, the Council took the view that the fee of £75 per case was too low (up to the first four cases, with £65 after that). This compared with a Law Society recommended fee of £300 for a custody application in the District Court (Fair Trade Commission 1990). The Law Society considered that the new fees were so inadequate that it recommended that members should not participate ((1993) 87

Gazette:245). However, some solicitors did participate in the scheme and were criticised by the Law Society for doing so ((1993) 87 *Gazette*:293, 333).

In addition to increasing the level of funding, the Government decided to introduce the long awaited legislation to put the scheme on a statutory basis and this was introduced and passed in 1995 prior to the holding of the divorce referendum itself in November 1995. In introducing the Civil Legal Aid Bill in the Senate, the Minister for Equality and Law Reform, Mervyn Taylor, TD, described it as being 'in substance, a family law measure, and for that reason it is a priority measure under the Government's Programme of Legislation'. The Minister described the Bill as 'part of a series of extensive proposals which the government is pursuing in relation to Family Law matters, including the holding of a Referendum on Divorce in 1995' (141 *Seanad Debates*, col. 2124).

In effect, the Bill simply puts the existing Scheme of Civil Legal Aid and Advice into statutory form and there were relatively few changes to the structure of the service. Legal aid services are still provided primarily by salaried lawyers in law centres administered directly by the Legal Aid Board. The 1995 legislation allowed for the continued involvement of private practitioners but it was clear that this was seen as supplementary to the main provision of services by the law centres. Otherwise, the legislation very much reflected the existing limitations set out in the Scheme of Civil Legal Aid and Advice. The Scheme focused solely on advice and representation, and amendments proposing to give the Legal Aid Board a role in relation to research, education and law reform were defeated in the Parliament. Legal representation only applied to representation in the courts although the Bill did allow the Minister to extend this to tribunal representation. An opposition amendment to extend legal aid to social welfare and employment tribunals was successful at committee stage in the Senate but this was reversed by the Government at a later stage of the debate. The means test and the wide range of exclusion for various legal matters remained largely intact although a number of relatively minor provisions were amended or removed.

The 1995 Civil Legal Aid legislation came into effect in October 1996. The involvement of private practitioners continues to face opposition both from the salaried staff employed by the Board and from the Law Society who, despite a significant increase in the proposed fees to £120 per case, continued to feel that this was totally inadequate and that a fixed fee was wrong in principle. However, the Society agreed that participation in the scheme should be left to individual solicitors as 'it seemed that some practitioners would participate in it regardless of the Society's views' ((1996) 90 *Gazette* 319).

Similarities and differences

To conclude the descriptive section of this Chapter, let us consider the similarities and differences between the schemes in France and Ireland. Despite the reforms of the 1990s, both countries still have relatively limited schemes of legal aid and advice in comparison with the Netherlands and the United Kingdom. The legal aid schemes in both France and Ireland are narrowly confined to legal representation and advice and neither has any role in relation to a broader concept of legal research, legal education or law reform. In both countries, family law accounts for the majority of civil legal aid cases, although this is much more the case in Ireland (over 90 per cent) than in France (50 per cent). Both schemes are means-tested and appear to apply to roughly the same proportion of the population. On the other hand there are major differences in the way in which legal aid is delivered. In Ireland, salaried lawyers directly employed by the government appointed Legal Aid Board remain responsible for the vast majority of legal aid work; in France the legal aid service is provided solely through private practitioners who appear to have gained a dominant role in relation to the provision of legal advice.

Analysing the development of legal aid

This section of the Chapter examines recent developments in legal aid in France and Ireland so as to analyse factors relevant to the way in which services have developed. In doing so, I look at both structural factors (such as the underlying economic position, the structure of the legal system, and religion) and the role of key actors (in particular, the state and the legal profession). These two levels, of course, are not independent of each other. The structure of the legal system has implications for the way in which the legal profession acts and, in turn, the legal profession influences the structure of the legal system.

I have argued elsewhere (Cousins, 1996b) that structural factors such as industrialisation, economic development, religion, divorce and political unrest *may* influence the development of legal aid, but that none of these factors is determinative. In relation to religion, I noted that legal aid spending is generally higher in Protestant than in Catholic countries and suggested that this might be related to general cultural factors which had an indirect effect on the development of legal aid. I argued that the legal profession and the public administration have played a key role in the development of legal aid. Here I rehearse some of the arguments in relation to factors explaining the development of legal aid and consider to what extent these general arguments are confirmed or contradicted by this specific study.

Social and economic structures

There is no clear correlation between public spending on legal aid and the wealth (in terms of Gross Domestic Product) of European countries. France has a significantly higher GDP *per capita* than Ireland but both spend about the same on legal aid. While poorer countries, such as Spain and Portugal, are likely to have low levels of legal aid expenditure, one can observe a great variation in levels of expenditure amongst wealthy countries. For example, in 1994–5 Belgium, which has a higher level of GDP *per capita* than the United Kingdom, spent only BF316m on civil legal aid (0.004 per cent of GDP) which is a small fraction of the annual legal aid expenditure in the United Kingdom. The lack of any clear correlation between wealth and legal aid spending combined with the fact that legal aid spending is extremely small in relation to other social services suggests that legal aid has a limited functional importance for European countries. It appears that some wealthy European countries can get on quite well without spending significant sums of money on legal aid.

Alternatively, one might hypothesise that, as legal aid is a social service, spending in relation to legal aid would be related to the level of spending on other social services. However, this is also not the case. In 1993 France spent 31 per cent of its GDP on social security and health services; Ireland spent only 21 per cent (European Commission, 1995). Yet, as we have seen, their levels of legal aid spending are quite similar. Belgium and the United Kingdom spent very similar proportions of their Gross Domestic Product on social security and health (27.6 per cent and 27.3 per cent respectively) yet there are enormous differences between their levels of spending on legal aid.

Even if there is no clear relationship between the level of spending on legal aid and that on social services, can we identify links between the manner in which legal aid is provided and the general structure of social services in a particular country? Esping-Andersen (1990:29) argues that the essential criteria for categorising welfare states are: (1) the quality of social rights; (2) social stratification; and (3) the relationship between state, market and family. The outcome is a typology of three models of welfare state—the social democratic, the corporatist, and the liberal. It has been suggested that Esping-Andersen's typology can usefully be employed in the analysis of legal aid schemes (Regan, 1994). Unfortunately, however, Ireland does not appear to fall easily into any of these three models (Cousins, 1997), a problem which is not resolved by the alternative Castles and Mitchell (1993) analysis of welfare states in English speaking nations. France on the other hand is clearly identified by Esping-Andersen as falling into the corporatist model of welfare state. Esping-Andersen identifies corporatist welfare states as being weak on social rights; focusing on the preservation of status differentials; and being 'perfectly ready to displace the market as a provider of welfare' (1993:27). To what extent does the system of legal aid in France correspond with this model? There appears to be a weak legal right to aid since, despite the long delays which existed prior to the 1991 reforms, there is no indication that individuals were able to assert their right to legal aid through the courts. While French legal aid is focused primarily on the poorest section of the population, there is little evidence of legal aid being socially stratified like other French social services. For example, many social insurance schemes have historically been linked to particular occupations. In contrast, the legal aid scheme falls much more into the tradition of residual *aide sociale*. In terms of the relationship between the state, market and family, the market clearly plays a dominant role in the provision of legal aid. Thus, while there are some points of similarity, it is not at all clear that the French legal aid system would fit neatly into the corporatist model of welfare state. Regan's (1994) examination of legal aid in Sweden and Australia also found a less than perfect match with Esping-Andersen's typologies (Goriely, 1994).[5] Thus, while the social policy approach utilised by Esping-Andersen in analysing different welfare regimes may be helpful in terms of analysing legal aid, it is suggested that any clear link between typologies of legal aid and Esping-Andersen's welfare regimes is yet to be demonstrated.

Religion

While the sociological implications of religion have received considerable study, particularly in relation to the impact of religion on economic development and politics, the role of religion in relation to social policy has received very little attention. In a recent article, Castles (1994) has undertaken a preliminary study of the impact of Catholicism on various aspects of social policy. However, those aspects have tended to be ones in which the Catholic Church had clearly identifiable policies, such as the development of the welfare state and the role of women in the labour force.

It has been noted by several authors that legal aid schemes tend to be slower to develop in Catholic countries than in Protestant countries (Abel, 1996; Cousins, 1996b). However, the reasons for this have not been investigated in any detail. In the present case study, we can clearly see that the development of legal aid in Ireland is closely linked to the growth in family breakdown and, specifically, to the introduction of divorce in 1995. Given that the Irish legal aid scheme is almost totally a family law scheme, it is clear that the growing demand for the scheme arose from increasing family law litigation. Specifically, the introduction of the Legal Aid Bill in 1995 was part of the government's overall strategy to ensure the passage of the Divorce Referendum. The Catholic nature of Irish society was clearly one of the reasons (although not the only one) for the much later development of significant levels of family litigation in comparison with other European countries.

However, this explanation does not apply in the French case. A nationwide survey in 1958 concluded that 91 per cent of the population had been baptised in the Catholic faith (quoted in Whyte, 1981:139). Despite this at least nominally Catholic nature of the French population there has historically been a much

[5] In the case of Australia this may, in part, arise from the fact that Australia is misclassified by Esping-Andersen (Castles and Mitchell, 1993).

greater level of secularism in French politics and policy. In fact, it appears that the level of marriage breakdown in France has, historically, been quite high. For example, in 1950 there were 11 divorces per 100 marriages in France compared to 8 in the Netherlands and 7 in the United Kingdom (Andersen, 1980:21). However, this did not lead to the development of legal aid, despite the fact that legal representation is necessary in order to obtain a divorce. A possible explanation for this is considered below.

Legal system

This section examines the relationship between legal aid schemes and the legal systems in different countries. One point can be disposed of initially. There appears to be no relationship between the population density of lawyers in a country and the amount spent on legal aid. In France there are almost 2,000 people per lawyer, compared to about 800 in Ireland (McIntosh and Holmes, 1991). Yet spending on legal aid is very similar. The Netherlands has one of the lowest population densities of lawyers in the EU (2,500 people per lawyer) and yet has one of the highest levels of legal aid spending.

Secondly, there is no clear relationship between the overall level of litigation in a country and the development of legal aid. It might be thought that countries with higher levels of litigation would tend to have more extensive legal aid schemes. If anything, the opposite is the case. For example, Blankenburg's (1995; 1997) analysis of case-loads in civil law countries indicates that the Netherlands (a legal aid leader) has a low case-load, a factor which Blankenburg attributes to the development a range of out-of-court institutions which avoid litigation. In contrast countries with much less extensive legal aid schemes, such as Belgium and Germany, have high case-loads, with France coming in between. While it is always difficult to compare case-loads, it would appear that the Republic of Ireland has a higher civil case-load than does Northern Ireland (which, as part of the United Kingdom, has a much more extensive system of legal aid). In 1993 for instance there were about 6,600 civil proceedings brought per 100,000 people in the Irish Republic, compared to about 3,000 in Northern Ireland. The Republic figures are disproportionately high by reason of the inclusion of about 100,000 licensing and debt enforcement cases, proceedings of a kind which are generally not dealt with in the court system of Northern Ireland. If these proceedings are excluded the number of civil proceedings per 100,000 people in the Republic falls to about 3,500.

Is there a relationship between the type of legal system (i.e. civil or common law) and spending in legal aid? This appears to be the case in the area of criminal legal aid. In Ireland, more public funding has always gone to the criminal legal aid scheme than to civil legal aid and similar tendencies can be seen in the United Kingdom, Canada and Australia. In contrast, only a small proportion of

French legal aid spending goes on criminal legal aid, and a similar tendency can be seen in the Netherlands and Germany.

The situation in relation to civil legal aid appears to be more complex. Francis Castles and his colleagues have developed the concept of 'Families of Nations' in analysing social policies (Castles, 1993). In particular, Castles has drawn on work by Zweigert and Kötz (1987) in relation to different legal families. Studies have, for example, been carried out in relation to the influence of different legal families on divorce rates (Castles and Flood, 1993) and children's rights (Therborn, 1993). These authors have argued that, in general terms, differences in divorce rates and in the development of children's rights can, in part, be explained or at least categorised according to different types of legal families. The different types of families of relevance to our study are:

1. Anglo/American (including the United Kingdom, Ireland, Australia, Canada (except Quebec) and the United States);
2. Romanistic (including France, Belgium, Luxembourg, the Netherlands, Spain, Portugal, Italy and Quebec);
3. Germanic (including Germany, Austria and Switzerland);
4. Nordic (including Sweden, Denmark, Finland and Norway).

At first sight, this breakdown does not seem to be of much assistance in analysing legal aid since, for example, the Anglo/American family includes countries with very high levels of legal aid (the United Kingdom) and very low levels (the United States). The same applies in relation to the Romanistic family which includes both the Netherlands and Belgium. However, looking at the situation in more detail, perhaps this breakdown may be of assistance. If we look at the Nordic family, there does seem to be a general tendency to have reasonably developed legal aid schemes in these countries (Johnsen, 1994). In addition, these countries have tended to be the leaders in developing other forms of assistance to individuals seeking to enforce rights, such as ombudsman schemes. In contrast, the Germanic countries generally appear to have more limited legal aid schemes.

In the case of Anglo/American countries, one could argue that because the United States separated from the United Kingdom at such an early stage, and because its law and legal professions developed in such different ways, it may not be useful to categorise this country in the same group (at least for present purposes). Looking at the other countries in this group, they generally have low to medium levels of development of legal aid, only the United Kingdom having exceptionally high spending in this area. This suggests that perhaps the United Kingdom is also an exception to this group. This exceptionalism might be explained by the greater wealth of the United Kingdom, the development of a welfare state after World War II and the strength of the legal profession in shaping legal aid policy.

The Romanistic family generally involves countries with quite low levels of legal aid spending. Important exceptions are the Netherlands and, to a lesser extent, Quebec. Perhaps one of the reasons for this mismatch is a misclassification of countries within the different groups. It has been suggested that the categorisations developed for the purposes of comparative legal study may not be useful from a sociological (or social policy) perspective (Cotterrell, 1997). Nonetheless, there is at least enough evidence to warrant further investigation of whether or not different legal families may have their own legal aid regimes.

It appears that the French legal aid system, despite its apparently low level of funding, is much more successful in delivering legal aid to persons involved in family law proceedings than is the Irish system. For example, in 1994 36 per cent of the parties to a divorce were legally aided in France. This contrasts with the Irish situation where in 1994 legal aid certificates were granted in relation to 3,600 family law matters compared to a total of 17,000 family law applications in that year. It must, of course, be remembered that the Irish legal aid scheme also involves the provision of legal advice, something which has only been introduced in France. The difficulties in relation to ensuring comparability of figures must also be borne in mind in comparing this data. However, the degree of difference between the two strongly suggests that the French legal aid scheme is able to deliver representation in a much higher proportion of cases for approximately the same level of spending as a proportion of GDP.

This would suggest either that legal services in France are significantly cheaper than in Ireland or that the French legal profession is prepared to subsidise legal aid services to a much greater extent. While comparisons are difficult, it would appear that the relevant costs in France may be lower in relative terms than those in Ireland. The Conseil d'État report in 1990 refers to legal costs of between 350 and 400 FF per hour. In contrast, in 1994 the Irish Law Society sought payments of I£65 an hour in respect of legal aid services ((1994) *Gazette*:91). In addition, it was clearly accepted that the French legal profession would, on a basis of a duty of solidarity, accept a significantly lower level of payment than the going market rate. This duty of solidarity is referred to on numerous occasions in both the Conseil d'État report and in the Parliamentary Debates on the legal aid legislation. It is interesting to note that, in contrast, as long ago as 1977 the legal profession representatives on the Irish Committee on Civil Legal Aid and Advice dissented from the Committee's recommendation that private practitioners should be prepared to accept a percentage reduction in their fees in recognition of the fact that legal aid is a social service and that they would be guaranteed payment of their fees. In a reservation, these representatives argued that they did not 'see why the work which is done for the less fortunate members of our community should be remunerated on a level which is less than that which would be applicable to the more fortunate members of the community' (Committee on Civil Legal Aid and Advice, 1978:170).

While the concept that the legal profession might reduce their fees in such a situation is not, of course, unknown in other countries, it is unlikely to be presented as being on the basis of solidarity. Solidarity is a concept which emerged in French social thought towards the end of the last century, and has since been used in social policy in France (Donzelot, 1984). It is also utilised in Catholic social thought. Its basic principles were not inconsistent with late nineteenth-century Catholic social thought (Dorr, 1983) although it appears that Catholic (or at least Vatican) social thinking did not use the term until much later. Clearly, solidarity is not a concept which applies to all Catholic countries as the Irish case shows. It would, however, be interesting to investigate whether the legal professions in Continental Catholic countries, such as France, Belgium, Spain and Italy (i.e. the bulk of the Romanistic family) are prepared to make a greater contribution of their resources towards the provision of legal aid and whether this explains, to some extent, the seemingly low level of public spending on legal aid in these countries. This is not necessarily to suggest that these legal professions are necessarily more altruistic than others but rather than the early introduction of a statutory obligation to provide legal aid may have created a situation whereby an obligation to contribute to legal aid is more widely accepted. One factor of specific relevance to Ireland is that the Department of Justice which has been responsible for the legal aid service has traditionally had little knowledge about or interest in concepts such as efficiency and cost-effectiveness. The Department's main concern was to be able to control the legal aid service, both in terms of its overall cost (which was easy as it was cash-limited) and in terms of the types of case it might take on (so as to exclude test cases and representative actions) (Dalton, 1989). The Department had little interest in whether or not the scheme itself was run efficiently.

Key actors

In the French case, the key actors were the state and the legal profession. The government was, effectively, forced to act in 1991 in relation to legal aid because of the dissatisfaction of the legal profession with the existing situation. The report of the Conseil d'État drawn up by a commission consisting of civil servants (including members of the judiciary) and lawyers was largely accepted by the Government and formed the basic shape of the Legal Aid Bill. In its passage through the French Parliament, the Bill was altered to strengthen the provisions in relation to the payment of the legal profession and to strengthen their role in relation to legal advice. Although non-governmental organisations were consulted by the Conseil d'État, there is little indication that they had any significant say in shaping the final outcome. There is also little sign that the shape of the legal aid system would have been substantially different had the right-wing opposition parties, rather than the then Socialist Government, been in power. Many opposition speakers during the debates broadly welcomed the Bill (although it was criticised on many grounds) and few opposition speakers put forward any clear alternatives to the basic approach proposed by the government.

The development of legal aid in France is consistent with Karpik's (1994) sociological interpretation of the history of the (or more correctly a) French legal profession. Karpik argues that in the nineteenth century the profession of *avocat* adopted a logic based on an *économie de la modération* which excluded pure market principles and emphasised the *désintéressement* of the profession. This is not inconsistent with provision of gratuitous legal aid under the 1851 Act. Karpik argues that in recent decades the profession has moved towards a much more market-influenced approach with two major reforms of the French legal professions in 1971 and 1990. The legal aid reforms in 1972 and 1991—introducing and then extending payment for legal aid services—are consistent with this interpretation.

The key actor in the Irish case was ostensibly the state. The Legal Aid Bill, originally drafted by the Department of Justice, largely replicated the original Scheme of Civil Legal Aid and Advice (itself drafted by the Department). Over the period since 1980, all major Irish political parties have been in government at some stage and there is no indication whatsoever that any of the parties would have adopted a significantly different approach to that outlined in the 1995 Bill. During the Dail Debates on that Bill, the opposition parties opportunistically put forward proposals which they had themselves refused to entertain while in government (such as the broadening of the scope of the legal aid service to include research, education and law reform and the inclusion of tribunal representation). Non-governmental organisations, such as the Free Legal Advice Centres and Coolock Community Law Centre, were very influential in shaping the parliamentary debate. However, the views of the organisations had little impact on the final content of the Act. Indeed, one of the key tenets of such groups, community involvement, disappeared entirely with the Act although it had been present in the original administrative scheme.

The Law Society and Bar Council were noticeable by their absence in the debates on the Bill. The Law Society's own monthly journal made almost no comment at all on the proposal. Although a significant number of parliamentarians are members of the legal profession, there is no indication in the debate that any informal briefing had been carried out by either the Law Society or the Bar Council. However, I would argue that the failure to act by the Law Society and the Bar Council does not make them unimportant actors. Both organisations are key players in the development of any legal service. Accordingly, their failure to act represented a particular course of action.

The Law Society, the larger and much more active of the two bodies, has, despite occasional rhetorical calls for improvements in civil legal aid, consistently displayed a lack of interest in the area. Arguably, this arises from a fear amongst certain sections of the Law Society that a growth in legal aid amongst the private profession would lead, first to a dragging down of overall civil legal costs, and secondly, to a greater level of involvement by the state in the operation of the private profession. Accordingly, the Law Society has effectively acquiesced in the establishment of a two-tier legal system with a small salaried service for those who cannot afford the fees of private practitioners.

Conclusion

We have seen that there are a number of similarities between the French and Irish civil legal aid schemes—in particular both have comparatively low levels of public funding (of the order of 0.015 per cent of GDP) and both concentrate on family law. Both are confined to traditional legal advice and representation and do not involve any educational, research or reform role. There are, however, also significant differences.

The French scheme was originally established almost 150 years ago. It has retained its total reliance on the private profession as providers of services. The Irish scheme is a much later developer and relies principally on a salaried service. The indirect impact of Catholicism can clearly be seen in Ireland where the scheme developed later than in other European countries, largely because family law litigation also developed later. In contrast, no such clear link can be seen in the French case. It is noteworthy that the French scheme delivers representation to a much higher proportion of people and it appears that the scheme is subsidised to a much greater extent by the French legal profession. This is perhaps related to the early establishment of a system of gratuitous legal aid on a statutory basis which has now created an environment whereby a duty of solidarity is expected of and (more or less willingly) accepted by the legal profession. Whether any relationship exists between this duty of solidarity and Catholicism must be a matter for further research.

In both France and Ireland, the key actors have been the state and the legal profession. In the French case, the legal profession have effectively traded off low fees for a legal monopoly. In contrast, the Irish profession have largely failed to act thereby allowing the development of a two-tier system with a private market for those who can afford the services and a public salaried model for those who cannot.

In overall terms, the study of legal aid reforms in France and Ireland is consistent with the theory that the phenomenon of legal aid is the result of the inter-relationship of a complex range of social factors (including group interests) and that there is no one causational factor. There are no clear links between the legal aid schemes and the wealth of either country, nor the structure or size of its social services, the size of its legal profession nor level of litigation. The lack of any evidence of a link between Catholicism and legal aid in France suggests the need for caution in positing any general theories about the impact of Catholicism on the development of legal aid. This study does suggest that there may be links between the type of legal system and the development of legal aid and that this issue would merit further research. Finally, the findings of this study are consistent with the argument that the state and the legal profession tend to be key players in the development of legal aid.

8

Why Do Legal Aid Services Vary Between Societies? Re-examining the Impact of Welfare States and Legal Families

FRANCIS REGAN

Introduction

Recent comparative legal aid research presents us with a puzzle. While a number of fascinating patterns have been identified between different societies' legal aid services, little progress has been made in explaining their origins or appreciating their significance. For example, the proportion of the population eligible for legal aid varies widely between groups of societies as does the range of services. Most of the population are, for example, usually eligible in Northern Europe but in English-speaking societies it is usually targeted at the poor. Meanwhile, the latter often provide surprisingly extensive services for problems that are unlikely to end in court while the Continental schemes usually assist their citizens primarily in relation to court cases. Why do these patterns exist? And are they significant? That is, do schemes differ in the way they assist their citizens to defend and assert their legal rights, or 'mobilise the law'? If so what, if any, are the policy implications for the future development of legal aid?

Recent attempts to answer these questions have met with limited success. Blankenburg (1991) and Cousins (1992) attempted, for example, to explain differences in expenditure upon legal aid services in European societies. While they examined links between legal aid and the level of welfare state development and differences between adversarial and inquisitorial procedures, they concluded no such relationships existed. Are the patterns, therefore, entirely due to accidents of history and internal national developments, or can they be partly explained in terms of larger, even global, influences?

This Chapter re-examines the impact of welfare states and legal families on legal aid. Instead of examining expenditure I compare schemes in terms of the core policy values of dependence and self-reliance expressed in their services (Rein, 1976). Rather than internal to legal aid, I argue that the blend of these values in a given society reflects those of its welfare state and legal 'family'. In societies with social democratic welfare states and civil law origins, for example, legal aid generally gives more emphasis to citizens' dependence on lawyers and, primarily, for court cases. Meanwhile, societies with liberal welfare states and common law origins generally give more emphasis to citizens' self-reliance for court cases and for problems outside court. In practice, these are not either/or choices. Most societies promote both values to some extent, the difference lies in the particular blend.

In the Chapter, therefore, I identify and explain differences between a specific group of legal aid schemes. Rather than examine all industrialised schemes I focus solely on the group of highly developed, or 'first-tier', schemes where post-War reforms extinguished all remnants of charitable legal aid, replacing it with publicly funded assistance for a wide range of legal problems. Interestingly these schemes exist in Northern Europe and English-speaking societies with their distinct welfare state and legal family traditions. In the first part of the Chapter I summarise the often ignored literature explaining the variety of ways citizens 'mobilise the law', describe the range of services provided by the 'first-tier' schemes and interpret the data in terms of welfare state and legal family influences. I conclude by considering a number of policy implications. First, however, I explain my approach in more detail.

Comparing legal aid policy

This Chapter draws on comparative policy research methods. That is, while recognising the need to identify distinct national developments I also identify patterns and similarities between societies and explain them by drawing on theory. In the process I aim to achieve a balance between 'the extremes of universalism and particularism' (Rose, 1991:447; Higgins, 1984). There is, however, a bewildering array of data available for comparison. What particular aspect is to be compared? In other words, what template will be used to create order from apparent chaos? One starting point is to acknowledge that public policies reflect dilemmas and conflict over policy values (Rein, 1976:13; Higgins, 1981:175). Legal aid policy is, for example, not simply a question of how much governments pay lawyers to assist the citizens of a society. Instead, seen in terms of policy values, it is a question of the degree to which governments promote dependence on publicly funded lawyers as well as individual self-reliance. Needless to say, legal aid scheme services usually promote dependence and self-reliance but in varying blends. But the varying blends have dramatic consequences as I explain below.

The particular blend of values expressed in a society's legal aid services are not accidents, nor do they affect that policy alone. Instead they reflect critical choices made through history about the role of government in developing the 'good society'. Two competing 'models' of government are recognised in the literature. On one hand, where the role of government is 'to manage the lives of people and steer society', policies generally emphasise dependence on the state and professionals. Alternatively, where governments 'maintain the social equilibrium and merely provide a framework for social self-management and individual self-definition', policies emphasise self-reliance (Damaska, 1986:11).

These emphases not only influence legal aid. They also lie at the core of welfare states and legal families. For example, because Northern European governments are generally 'managers', welfare programmes are highly developed. In addition, because of the 'civil law' traditions, law is highly integrated into the state, emphasising implementation of government policy (Damaska, 1986:11). Meanwhile, in English-speaking societies with their less developed liberal welfare the model of government corresponds more closely to maintaining social equilibrium. The common law family also focuses more on resolving conflicts and individual rights rather than implementing government policy (ibid. 11). In sum, the combination of highly developed welfare states and civil law traditions in Northern Europe leads to more emphasis on dependence on the state. And the combination of liberal welfare state and common law traditions in the English-speaking societies results in more emphasis on self-reliance.

These values are not obvious if we focus only on services for court cases, or even types of law, such as criminal or family law, as other studies have done. But they can be detected if we analyse the *complete range* of legal aid services offered in the 'first-tier' schemes. In the Northern European schemes for example, most of the citizens can depend on the state for 'in litigation' services, as Cohn (1943) referred to them, for the costs of court cases. The English-speaking societies, however, target these services at the poor and most of the population are expected to fend for themselves. But while the latter societies often offer extensive 'outside litigation' services to assist their citizens with legal problems that are unlikely to end in court (Cohn, 1943), the Northern European schemes rarely do so. In other words a fascinating pattern of dependence and self-reliance can be identified when the complete range of legal aid services are compared.

Needless to say, the policy implications of such an analysis must be carefully considered. In brief, overemphasising either value leads to difficulties. Self-reliance easily degenerates into neglect if, for example, legal problems are of such complexity that people are unable to deal with them on their own. At the same time dependence on professionals runs the danger of undermining people's capacity competently to respond to their own legal problems.[1] While it may be tempting, therefore, to conclude that one emphasis is 'better' than another this is inappropriate. Instead societies should recognise the potential for assisting their citizens to defend and assert their legal rights in a variety of ways. In reality, as I explain in the next section, citizens in fact require different sorts of assistance to respond to different sorts of legal problems in different sorts of ways.

[1] Indeed this is precisely the concern about post-War welfare policies. That is, that some create unhealthy dependence on the state and welfare professionals, while others abandon much of the population to their own resources. See Kymlicka and Norman (1994).

Legal mobilisation and legal aid services

Legal aid commentators often forget that only a fraction of the citizen's legal problems arrive at court. It is therefore important to consider how and why citizens choose to 'mobilise' the law before analysing the legal aid services designed to assist them. Legal mobilisation occurs not just when citizens contact lawyers or use the courts, instead it is 'when a desire or want is translated into a demand or an assertion of rights' according to Zemans (1983:700). It can therefore occur with or without a lawyer, and in or out of court.[2] Drawing on empirical and theoretical research, Zemans proposed a 'rational decision-making model' to explain how and why citizens mobilise the law. She argues that individuals make rational decisions in light of a range of influences including the seriousness of the issue, the amount of effort required to pursue the other party, the cost of pursuing the issue with lawyers and the courts, and the potential cost to ongoing relationships of pursuing the problem. As a result they respond to legal problems in a variety of ways including avoiding and 'lumping it', negotiation and other self-help strategies. Finally, on rare occasions and often as a last resort, they consult lawyers.

The citizens do not fail to mobilise the law if they resort to other strategies. Lawyers and courts are neither the most common response, nor do they exhaust the possible responses. Indeed the opposite is more correct. Citizens may consider or 'mobilise' the law when they choose to avoid a legal problem, or resolve it themselves without the help of lawyers. In practice, they may, for example, negotiate with a neighbour about repairing a fence based on knowledge of the relevant law, or negotiate with another party to a motor vehicle accident on the basis of the law covering this event. The fact that the problem does not come to the attention of lawyers or courts simply means that citizens have chosen at various points not to enter the formal legal system. It does not mean that law has not been mobilised. Indeed the norms of law may have been used in many ways and on many occasions.

This model suggests that responding to legal problems is a complex process. In sum it involves numerous decisions about *if and how to mobilise the law* which may involve decisions to avoid, bypass, prevent or even threaten litigation, not just to initiate it. The complexity of this process has profound implications for how we conceive what we could call the 'ideal range of legal aid services'. What would this consist of?

As long ago as the 1940s Cohn argued that legal aid services should, ideally, pursue two distinct but complementary purposes. If not they would inadequately assist the citizens. First, schemes should provide legal advice and representation

[2] Legal mobilisation therefore includes, but is not restricted to, what is referred to as 'bargaining in the shadow of the law'.

to assist citizens in their court cases, or what Cohn referred to as 'in litigation' services (1943:253). These services are required in order, for example, to protect individual liberty in criminal cases. But schemes should ideally also provide a range of 'outside litigation' services in order to assist citizens to choose if and how to mobilise the law (Cohn, 1943:253). As Pound noted early this century, citizens in modern societies experience numerous problems of everyday life where the law is used against and by them (1906). These problems include rent and tenancy matters, financial problems, contracts or family disputes, and wills and estates. Many are unlikely to end in court but they are important not just because of that possibility but also because they are numerous and cause great concern.

For Cohn, Zemans and others, there are no either/or choices here. Two types of legal aid services are required in order to assist the citizens effectively to mobilise the law.[3] One without the other is inadequate. Citizens are abandoned to the mercy of the courts if 'in litigation' services are inadequate, but equally they are abandoned to their own knowledge of the law if 'outside litigation' services do not exist to assist them to choose if and how to respond to common legal problems. Do legal aid schemes pursue these two goals by offering the two types of services?

Surprisingly, there is a long but unrecognised history of doing so. From late last century some societies unambiguously pursued these complementary goals. The League of Nations study 'Legal Aid for the Poor' (1927) for example, describes how early this century many schemes assisted the poor with 'in litigation' services, including advice and representation in relation to serious criminal, matrimonial and civil court cases. Responding to concerns to ensure the poor were represented in court, legislation was often used to mandate the private legal profession to assist, albeit without payment. Or in policy value terms, the poor were encouraged to depend on the legal profession. As I explain below, dependence on lawyers was accentuated when governments used these schemes as the basis of the publicly funded legal aid in the post-War period.

What is less well understood, however, is that late last century a complementary form of legal aid emerged in many societies. Schemes offering 'outside litigation' services were established or expanded in Sweden, England, the USA and Germany to assist citizens with the less serious but more common legal problems of everyday life (League of Nations, 1927). Often established by educational, religious and trade union organisations, or municipal governments, rather than the private legal profession or governments, these schemes provided advice and assistance in a wide range of civil and matrimonial problems unlikely to end in court cases. The purpose of these services was to inform and educate the citizens about their options in order to assist them to make decisions about legal problems (ibid. 254). In practice, this meant advising clients about their options for mobilising the

[3] Nevertheless, as I explain below, Cohn, a lawyer, not unexpectedly regarded 'in litigation' as more important than 'outside litigation' services.

law in different ways or avoiding legal action altogether. Assistance included not only writing letters to clarify issues, or reading documents to explain details, but also negotiations to settle existing actions or to avoid litigation, and sometimes initiating litigation despite having tried to avoid it. The Swedish Regulations for the remarkably comprehensive municipal 'Legal Aid Institutions' of 1919 illustrate the point. While legal aid was offered for court cases an additional object was 'to provide the [poor], *inter alia*, with advice and information, assist them in drawing up documents, [and] in settling disputes by amicable agreement' (League of Nations, 1927:237–8).[4]

These 'outside litigation' services therefore promoted citizens' capacities to decide if and how to mobilise law, not just initiate or avoid litigation.[5] Or to use the language of policy values, they not only promoted reliance on professionals, but also the citizens' capacities to deal, to some extent at least, with their own legal problems.

The two types of services survived to the present day although they fared very differently depending on the type of society. 'Outside litigation' services, for example, gradually disappeared until World War II when they flourished in response to demand from the armed forces in a number of societies,[6] declined again in the post-War period and reemerged, albeit transformed, in some societies in the 1970s. Meanwhile 'in litigation' legal aid received massive injections of public funding in many societies in the post-War period. Paradoxically, where 'in litigation' services expanded most, 'outside litigation' services faltered and vice versa. In order to understand this paradox it is necessary to explore the relationship between welfare states, legal families and legal aid.

Welfare states and 'in litigation' legal aid

While many commentators have discussed the impact of welfare states on post-War legal aid schemes, including Cappelletti (1975) and Abel (1985), a number of aspects of the relationship remain to be considered. In this section I argue that welfare states were an essential pre-condition of the post-War schemes, that they shaped important features of 'in litigation' services and as a result, citizens' access to these services varies widely between societies.

[4] The League of Nations Report includes a detailed discussion of these institutions: ibid. 254–7.

[5] The legal aid literature often distinguishes between two types of legal aid services: those for litigation and avoiding or preventing litigation. Blankenburg (1991) for example, distinguishes between litigation and litigation avoidance services and mechanisms. However such a distinction does not allow for the fact that some advice and assistance may ultimately result in a person initiating, not avoiding, litigation. Similarly NLAAC's (1990) distinction between 'legal services' and 'preventive services' fails to recognise that sometimes the latter may not prevent but ultimately may stimulate litigation. These classifications fail to appreciate that mobilising the law requires information at different stages in the decision-making process and that a range of decisions are made in response to legal problems.

[6] For the USA see Blake (1951), for Australia see Harkins (1976) and Regan (1996).

The rise of welfare states was in fact one of the essential preconditions for the emergence of the post-War publicly funded legal aid schemes. Without the former, governments would have continued to rely on the volunteer efforts of the legal profession. But legal aid was merely one example of the new publicly funded welfare programmes. Cappelletti (1975) and Abel (1985), for example, recognised that the post-War legal aid reforms were part of a profound transformation in the role of governments from often minimal intervention to actively promoting citizens' well-being. This was achieved by funding a range of welfare programmes, including health, housing, income maintenance and legal aid. Funding for the latter overcame the problems of the charitable schemes which failed to assist all who needed help due to relying upon private legal profession volunteers (Cappelletti, 1975; Cohn, 1943; Herbert, 1919). The welfare state schemes, by contrast, paid lawyers to represent citizens in court, especially the poor, and ushered in an era where legal aid became part of a bundle of rights of citizenship.

Welfare states also shaped the post-War legal aid schemes in other ways. Abel (1985), for example, pointed to the social control functions of welfare bureaucracies where welfare rights, including legal aid, were more to do with inhibiting class warfare than promoting the liberal ideal of equal justice. But Abel failed to appreciate that welfare state influences also profoundly shaped legal aid in other ways.

The rise of welfare states was not only a precondition of the post war legal aid schemes. They also decisively shaped legal aid eligibility criteria and the range of services. In the 'first-tier' schemes, for example, the existing private profession charitable schemes were replaced with publicly funded and organised schemes. In most cases responsibility for co-ordination and management shifted from the private legal profession to national public agencies that were allocated substantial public funds to compensate lawyers representing legal aid clients in court. More importantly, eligibility criteria were revised in two ways in order to improve effectiveness. First, 'generosity' increased because of less strict means tests. As a result, the proportion of the population eligible for 'in litigation' services dramatically increased. 'Comprehensiveness' also improved substantially thereby extending 'in litigation' services to a vastly increased range of cases and types of courts.

While these changes in the first-tier schemes were similarly dramatic they were by no means identical across societies. Generally speaking, welfare eligibility reforms decisively shaped those of legal aid. In social democratic Sweden and the Netherlands, for example, not only did 70 per cent of the population come to depend on the state for 'in litigation' services, but they could do so for most legal problems. Meanwhile in liberal Australia and Canada, reforms commenced from a lower starting point and consisted of ensuring eligibility for the poor alone, although for most legal problems. In other words, legal aid eligibility was extended not because it was special but because it was not. It was one of many programmes undergoing similar reforms (Esping-Andersen, 1990).

The Swedish reforms in the early 1970s illustrate the social democratic reform process. Prior to 1973 legal aid in Sweden consisted of a number of separate and poorly co-ordinated schemes (Bruzelius and Bolding, 1975). While they offered varying services and applied inconsistent eligibility criteria these schemes ensured the poor were not abandoned to their own devices in court. On the contrary, 'indigent or low salaried people were entitled to legal aid' (Bruzelius and Bolding, 1975:567). As a result, in 1968, for example, in more than 40 per cent of all completed civil cases in the lower courts the plaintiff and/or the defendant received legal aid (Bruzelius and Bolding, 1975:564). These arrangements were widely criticised, however, and not just because of administrative/co-ordination weaknesses. There were also political concerns about legal aid eligibility (ibid 1975). The problem was that legal aid was *only* for the poor at a time when most other Swedish welfare programmes included all or most of the population (Esping-Andersen, 1990; Marklund, 1986). As a result, the 1973 legal aid reforms were designed to bring legal aid into line with other welfare programmes.

> It was generally regarded to be unfair that persons with a higher income could not qualify for legal aid at all, and the system in practice was heavily criticized. Citizens who were neither indigent nor well-off were at a disadvantage according to public opinion. Thus, a party, in order to be able to litigate, needed to be either very rich or rather poor, or to have the support of some organisation. It was pointed out by many critics of the prior system that the party who had been granted the privilege of free legal proceedings, and thus assistance by counsel, had an undue advantage over the adversary who lacked this privilege (Burzelius and Bolding, 1975:567).

It is no coincidence, therefore, that eligibility for 'in litigation' was extended to include most of the population and most legal problems in first-tier schemes. This was also the nature of reforms in England and Wales in 1949 (Goriely, 1996a) and the Netherlands in 1967 (Goriely, 1992).

Legal aid reforms also coincided with periods of welfare reform in liberal first-tier societies. While they mimic the form of the social democratic societies reforms the scale is very different. In sum, the liberal reforms transformed grossly inadequate to adequate welfare that was targeted at the poor. The Australian reforms, for example, occurred in the 1970s during a period of substantial welfare reforms responding to a rediscovery of poverty. Similarly, legal aid reforms in the USA were part of the Johnson administration's 'War on Poverty' in the mid 1960s (Johnson, 1978). The Canadian reforms also occurred in a period of welfare reforms designed to address the problems of the poor (Zemans (ed.), 1979).

Table 8.1 summarises eligibility for 'in litigation' legal aid in the first-tier schemes in 1992/3. Leaving England and Wales to one side for the moment, the table highlights the fact that in these societies, a person's prospects of being granted 'in litigation' legal aid depends on the nature of welfare in the society in

Table 8.1: Eligibility for 'In Litigation' Legal Aid and other welfare programmes in 'First-Tier' Schemes, 1992/93

Country	Eligibility criteria for most welfare programmes[a]	Eligibility Criteria for 'In Litigation' Services: Generosity[b] and Comprehensiveness[c]
1. Sweden 2. The Netherlands	most of the population eligible for most welfare programmes	most of population eligible for most types of court cases
3. England and Wales	majority of the population eligible for most welfare programmes	majority of population eligible for most cases in court but not tribunals
4. Australia 5. Canada 6. USA	welfare targeted at the poor and for a narrow range of programmes	minority of population eligible and large range of cases excluded

Source: Adapted from Cousins (1993); Goriely (1992); Huxtable (1994); Klijn & Huls (1994); Regan (1994b).
[a] Based on Esping-Andersen's (1991) classification of welfare states.
[b] Generosity is the proportion of the population estimated to be eligible for 'in litigation' services.
[c] Comprehensiveness is the range of legal problems for which 'in litigation' services are offered.

which they live. The more generous and comprehensive welfare programmes are, so too are 'in litigation' legal aid services. For example, not only did most Swedes qualify depending on the cost of the case, but there were also few restrictions on the type of cases for which aid was available. By contrast, Australians not only had to be poor to qualify, their case also had to fall within a relatively narrow range of cases. Eligibility for legal aid in a common problem, divorce proceedings, further illustrates the point. In the early 1990s, Swedes on relatively high incomes involved in a costly divorce case may have qualified, but not in Australia where legal aid for divorce was abolished in the 1970s for rich and poor alike in all but exceptional cases.[7]

Table 8.1 also reflects the degree to which citizens are able to depend on publicly funded programmes and have to be self-reliant. In the social democratic schemes, for example, the citizens can depend on publicly funded lawyers to represent them in court cases in the same way as they depend on other professions for other welfare programmes. They are not abandoned to their own resources in court. By contrast, in the English-speaking societies (apart from England and Wales) eligibility is restricted to the poor and most citizens are left to their own

[7] However, welfare cuts, including legal aid, have also occurred in Sweden. In 1997, the Swedish government introduced major legal aid reforms including the expectation that most Swedes would utilise 'legal expense insurance' for many legal problems prior to applying for legal aid. One aim was to reduce the cost of grants of legal aid in divorce proceedings (Sverne, 1997).

devices for this and other welfare programmes. Most of the population are therefore expected to be self-reliant in relation to legal problems in court, regardless of their capacity to do so.[8]

England and Wales, however, require separate comment due to their apparently anomalous position. In fact this is an example of a society gradually changing the balance between policy values, from emphasising dependence on the state to an emphasis on self-reliance. In the 1950s and 1960s England had much in common with other social democratic societies' generous and comprehensive welfare programmes (Esping-Andersen, 1990). But eligibility criteria for welfare, including legal aid, have declined substantially since that time under Conservative governments in the 1980s and 1990s. As a result, while approximately 70 per cent of the population was eligible for legal aid in 1950, this had declined to less than 50 per cent by the early 1990s (Goriely, 1992).

Finally, a renewed emphasis on self-reliance in welfare programmes, including legal aid, can be detected in all the first-tier societies in the 1980s and 1990s. While both the social democrat and liberal societies cut legal aid eligibility in order to reduce dependence on the state, the starting points and consequences were very different. In the Netherlands, for example, the means test was severely cut in 1994 in order to cut public expenditure. In Sweden, meanwhile, legal aid was abolished for most family law cases in court in 1997 and individuals were instead expected to rely on private legal expense insurance wherever possible (Sverne, 1997). In other words, the social democrat schemes cut eligibility for the non-poor, expecting them to be become more self-reliant. The poor meanwhile remain able to depend on the state.

The changes in Northern Europe were minor, however, compared to the savage eligibility cuts for 'in litigation' legal aid in the liberal societies in the 1990s. The poor are, as a result, less able to depend on the state for 'in litigation' services than at any time since the reforms occurred. Funding cuts in Australia in the mid-1990s resulted in eligibility cuts. Similar contractions of eligibility and funding cuts also occurred in Canada in the early 1990s (Zemans, 1994; Kuras, 1994). The most savage decline, however, was in the USA where legal aid in civil and family law cases has been drastically reduced in the 1990s as Congress steadily introduced eligibility restrictions as well as 'defunding' the national Legal Services Corporation, as Kilwein explains in this volume. As a result, even the poor in the USA are now regularly forced to be self-reliant in civil and family law court cases. The state-based public defender legal aid programmes for criminal cases have to a large degree, however, avoided these cuts due to a constitutional right to a fair trial in such cases.

[8] Further research is needed to determine whether the pattern is replicated in other societies. Research could also assess the impact of other potentially important factors including: variations in the type of cases for which 'in litigation' legal aid is granted; the penetration of legal expense insurance and its relationship with legal aid; and the effect of procedural rules on legal aid e.g. the 'costs' rule where the losing party may have to pay the other party's costs.

In sum, for this group of societies, eligibility is similar for 'in litigation' services and welfare generally.[9] The most developed welfare states ensure most of the population have access to 'in litigation' services for most legal problems. The least developed welfare states, by contrast, target these services at the poor and restrict the range of problems for which aid is available. The impact of welfare states on 'outside litigation' services is, however, more complex than for 'in litigation'. The next section explains why this is so and examines the consequences for citizens' capacities to mobilise the law outside court cases.

The paradox of welfare states

While the post-War welfare state legal aid schemes dramatically reduced the number of citizens appearing in court unrepresented, they often extinguished 'outside litigation' legal aid, sometimes permanently. Paradoxically, these services declined at least partly because of the rise of welfare state schemes.

Over the last five hundred years the dominant priority in legal aid reforms has been 'in litigation' services, or to assist the poor in court (Cappelletti, 1975; Cohn, 1943). Late in the nineteenth century, legal aid progressed beyond court-ordered, voluntary arrangements in many societies when the private legal profession established, or were 'persuaded' by governments to establish schemes to assist the poor in serious criminal and matrimonial court cases. The publicly funded welfare state schemes in the second half of the twentieth century built upon but extended these priorities by including a wide range of court cases and often extended eligibility to include the middle class as well as the poor. But, as I have explained, 'in litigation' services have not always been the sole, or dominant, priority.

In the late nineteenth century attempts were also made in a number of societies to assist citizens to mobilise the law outside the courts. Schemes offering 'outside litigation' services were established to assist citizens, especially the poor, with legal advice, information and minor assistance, including reading documents, drafting letters, and negotiations with other parties (Cohn, 1943). The emphasis was on the ordinary non-criminal legal problems of everyday life, rather than serious court cases. While a lawyer may regard these schemes as being insignificant or superfluous to court cases, they complemented the private profession schemes by providing additional means for citizens to mobilise the law.

Interestingly, these schemes were established in a number of societies at approximately the same time and for similar reasons. Shortly after private

[9] Apprently anomalous data for other societies needs to be closely examined. Norway, for example, is generally regarded as a highly developed welfare state along with other Nordic societies, yet legal aid is targeted at the poor according to Johnsen (1994). However, this does not necessarily undermine the model. As Marklund (1988) pointed out, Norway is in many ways the Nordic welfare state laggard, having consistently relied more on the private market and less on public programmes than the other Nordic societies.

profession schemes were established, their weakness was recognised—they ignored most legal problems except for serious court cases. Their strength was also a weakness. The Swedish case illustrates one of the responses to this realisation. From the 1870s a number of Swedish towns appointed 'Poor Man's Advocates' to 'assist the poor members of the community both in and out of court for a small fee' (League of Nations, 1927:248) In time, these advocates proved ineffective because they were private lawyers with a duty to assist the poor as part of their work rather than working full-time for the poor. In 1920 the Swedish Government transformed these arrangements by funding towns to establish legal aid Bureaux employing lawyers to provide legal aid in and out of court (League of Nations, 1927:253–60). Under the Free Legal Proceedings Act 1919, the aim was to 'giv[e] an indigent member of society as far as possible the same facilities for gaining access to the courts as the more well-to-do and thus placing him in a position to assert and defend his rights without any hindrance of a financial nature' (ibid. 249–50). The Bureaux were not confined, however, to assisting the poor in court. Instead they undertook all legal work up to and including court cases, including advice, reading and writing letters, negotiations and conciliation.

> The work of the legal aid institutions consists, first of all, in simply supplying *explanations on points of law* to persons wishing to obtain information on the legal principles governing such-and-such a point. In addition, they act in an *advisory* capacity in a wider sense and help persons wishing to know how to proceed in defence of their interest.
>
> The institutions also give their assistance in drawing up legal documents, applications to the authorities, etc. and in other branches of notarial business.
>
> The extra-judicial legal aid provided by the institutions is not confined to this. An applicant often addresses himself to an institution because he wishes to take proceedings against somebody or to defend proceedings taken against himself by another persons. In these cases, the first step to be taken by the institutions is to make as full an inquiry as possible and to get in touch with the opposing party (ibid. 254).

Not surprisingly, court cases comprised only a fraction of the work. In 1923 the Stockholm Bureau, for example, assisted 24,326 people but only 1,294 cases went to court. By contrast, advice and information was sufficient in 3,975 cases, a further 3,290 were assisted by way of minor assistance including letters. A further 1,257 involved conciliation without litigation (ibid. 259).

The contrast between the Stockholm Bureau and the private profession schemes in other societies at the time was dramatic. When Garrison, an American lawyer, visited Sweden in the late 1930s, he was astonished by the rationale and work-load of the Stockholm Bureau (1940). He drew attention first, to the wide variety of services available in Sweden compared to his home city of Milwaukee. Instead of providing legal aid solely for court cases, as was the case in Milwaukee, assistance was available in the variety of forms noted above. Secondly, he was surprised to find aid was available to people of 'small means', not just the poor. Finally, he noted that the contrasts with the USA were due to the state taking responsibility for legal aid funding. Funds were used to employ lawyers to undertake legal aid work and as a result people did not have to rely solely on the private profession who were often reluctant to undertake extensive amounts of free work in view of the impact on their income (Garrison, 1940:295).

Schemes offering 'outside litigation' services also developed elsewhere. In England, for example, the voluntary 'Poor Man's Lawyer's Associations' were established in the late nineteenth century alongside the private profession scheme assisting the poor in serious matrimonial and criminal court cases (Goriely, 1996a). In 1925 there were twenty-five Poor Man's Lawyer's centres in London and ten in other cities but this grew to fifty-five in London and seventy in other cities by 1939. The centres used volunteer lawyers to provide advice and minor assistance to the poor. While some centres assisted with negotiations and minor court cases, others had insufficient resources to do so (ibid. 219). Nevertheless, these centres 'generated substantial workloads and reported similar areas of work: housing, maintenance and affiliation, workmen's compensation, social security, employment and debt' (Finlay, 1926, in ibid. 219).

These services also emerged in other societies. Sometimes governments established schemes employing lawyers to offer 'in' and 'outside' litigation services simultaneously. In Australia, for example, the South Australian Public Solicitors Office established by that state's government in the 1920s employed a lawyer to represent the poor in court in serious criminal and matrimonial matters. But he also provided an extensive volume of legal advice and minor assistance to all who required it, including the non-poor, in interviews and in letters to those who were unable to attend for interviews. He also negotiated on behalf of clients in relation to debts and other disputes. As was the case in Sweden, the 'outside' not 'in' litigation services dominated the work-load (Regan, 1996). Meanwhile, in the USA 'outside' litigation was often the only form of assistance offered by the charitable schemes, according to Herbert (1919). Blankenburg highlights in this volume the rapid and extensive development of these schemes in Germany early this century.

Finally, 'outside litigation' legal aid schemes flourished during World War II in response to the needs of defence force personnel and their families. In some societies the defence forces established voluntary schemes where serving lawyers offered advice and minor assistance. Other schemes utilised the services of full-time defence force legal staff to work solely for the defence force personnel and their families while the private legal profession also established schemes to assist the defence forces (Blake, 1951; Abel, 1985). The schemes did not, however, survive the transition to peacetime, at least partly because of antagonism towards them from the private legal professions (Regan, 1996).

As I have explained, the post-War legal aid reforms emphasised improving 'in litigation' services. The rise of these services, however, often had a detrimental effect on 'outside litigation' services and while it may not be a causal relationship there are reasons to suggest the two are linked. First, the private legal profession lobbied governments to expand 'in litigation' services but rarely did so for 'outside litigation' services. The former were, for the profession at least, undoubtedly more important, and not just financially. When Cohn examined the need for legal aid in England in the early 1940s, for example, he expressed the profession's priorities in a memorable comment:

> Ever since legal aid for the poor became a recognised necessity, legal aid in litigation has stood in the foreground of interest. Legal aid outside litigation is a later development. Even to-day it is everywhere still in the experimental stage. This may be partly due to the fact that former centuries were accustomed to consider litigation as the most important side of the law. But it is undoubtedly largely due to the fact that legal aid in litigation is more important. With legal aid outside litigation but not in litigation the poor man is like a soldier sent to battle, fully trained, but without arms (1943: 253–4).

It is not surprising, therefore, that the English legal aid scheme established in 1949 included provision for legal advice and assistance, but that they were not funded until 1960 (Goriely, 1996a). While the government may have run out of money and time, the profession were not strong supporters of such services.

A second partial explanation for the decline of 'outside litigation' services lies in a strength of welfare states. Welfare states centralise and streamline programmes in order, among other things, to provide nationally consistent, high-standard professional services across societies (Damaska, 1986). But as a consequence, community, religious, voluntary and municipal organisations that previously provided volunteer services often disappeared. Sometimes they disbanded themselves in the belief that their work was done, but sometimes, as part of the 1960s and 1970s reforms, welfare states extinguished schemes specialising in 'outside litigation' services.

Societies with highly centralised state structures and generous welfare states were usually the most destructive. That is, where the model of government is 'to manage the lives of people and steer society' (Damaska, 1986). But as a result, they often gave an almost exclusive priority to 'in litigation' services. One consequence is that community-based legal aid appears to have been extinguished along with the 'outside litigation' services. Events in Sweden, with its highly developed welfare state and generous 'in litigation' services, are perhaps the clearest example of the process. As a result of numerous complaints and inquiries over the course of the century, the central government gradually assumed responsibility for all legal aid in Sweden (Bruzelius and Bolding, 1975). This included the administration of the inadequate private profession schemes for court and the municipal bureau providing 'in' and 'outside litigation' aid. In the process the latter all but disappeared. The Swedish reforms of 1972, for example, gave priority to 'in litigation' and recent data suggests that court cases continue to dominate (Lin,g 1994; Regan, 1994b). Ironically, the innovative nineteenth-century Swedish 'outside litigation' scheme was extinguished by the rise of the welfare state scheme.

While the 'outside litigation' services were not extinguished in all the developed welfare states, the evidence suggests they are usually a low priority. The

Netherlands scheme, for example, provides advice and information to assist citizens to avoid litigation (Goriely, 1992; Blankenburg, 1995). However, neither the breadth nor volume of services appear to match those often provided in the English-speaking societies.

Interestingly, the decline of 'outside litigation' was temporary in some societies. In the English-speaking societies, for example, it disappeared with the rise of the large, welfare state legal aid schemes, but re-emerged, transformed, in the late 1960s and 1970s. While continuing the traditions of the Swedish and English organisations from late last century, the contemporary organisations expanded services to include not just advice and minor assistance but also legal education and training, and law reform projects (Regan, 1996).[10] Or to use the language of policy values, they offer a wide range of services actively to assist their citizens to respond, at least to some extent, to their own legal problems. But is there in fact a relationship between legal families and 'outside litigation' services?

Reconsidering legal families

Legal aid researchers have overlooked the fact that 'outside litigation' services are most effective in liberal societies and surprisingly underdeveloped in the social democratic societies. The liberal emphasis on self-reliance is therefore positive, not just negative. The common law emphasis on individual rights combined with the liberal emphasis on self-reliance prompts governments to assist individuals to respond to their own legal problems outside court. In order to explain why this is so, I sketch key features of the two legal families, explain why they promote or inhibit 'outside litigation' services, and illustrate my argument using the first-tier schemes' services in the early 1990s.

The differences between the two legal families of the civil and common law are extensive, according to commentators. Differences include their procedure, origins and traditions, and the role of judges and lawyers (Zweigert and Kötz, 1987; David and Brierley, 1985).[11] It would be puzzling, therefore, if legal aid

[10] These services are also offered by different types of organisations. For example, sometimes they are offered by community-based groups including the Community Law Centres in England and Wales (Stephens, 1991), Legal Clinics in Canada (Kuras 1994), and the Community Legal Centres in Australia (OLAFS, 1991). But sometimes public legal aid organisations offer them alongside 'in litigation' services. In the USA, for example, the Legal Services Corporation fund programmes in this way (Huxtable, 1994) as do the Australian public sector Legal Aid Commissions (Regan, 1996).

[11] For the purposes of this Chapter I avoid the debate about classifications of legal families, an issue which has received considerable attention in the literature. See for example: Zweigert and Kötz (1987) and David and Brierley (1985). Instead I highlight differences in the values and traditions of the common and civil law, an issue upon which there is substantial agreement. As a result, some of these debates dissipate. For example, Scandinavian legal systems are often regarded as misclassified if included in the civil law family. But Strömholm comments that 'Generally speaking, there can be no doubt that Scandinavian law is, in terms of historical development and actual contents, far more closely akin to Continental law than to common law' (1987:33).

services did not vary also. Nevertheless, researchers, including Cousins (1992) and Blankenburg (1991), have concluded that variations in European societies' legal aid cannot be explained by those in legal families. Some relevant legal family differences have not, however, been examined.

Comparative law scholars rarely ask, for example, if the citizen's opportunities to mobilise the law differs between legal families. Instead they usually focus on legal procedures, specific laws and institutions such as courts and other features of interest to lawyers and judges (Zweigert and Kötz, 1987; David and Brierley, 1985). A historical and political perspective, however, suggests that subtle but important differences between the families affect the likelihood of 'outside litigation' services flourishing and surviving over time. A summary of the recent development of the two families explains why this is so. In brief, 'outside litigation' services flourish where law has a degree of autonomy from the state, where it is relatively uncertain rather than codified, and where the role of lawyers and judges emphasises protecting individuals against the coercive interference of the state. These are features more closely associated with the common law.[12]

One key to understanding why the civil and common law families differ is to appreciate their development over the last four hundred years. The eclipse of monarchies and the rise of centralised, bureaucratic nation states, for example, had a dramatic but quite distinct impact in England, the birthplace of the common law, and France, the birthplace of the modern civil law family. In France, the post-revolutionary codification of law partly responded to the lack of uniform law in the society, but it was also part of civil and legal institutional reforms designed to increase and centralise the power of the state. Finally, codification was designed to contain the power and independence of the French judiciary and legal profession (Damaska, 1986). As a result, the law, judiciary and legal professions were in effect integrated into the state administration. According to Nettl:

> In Europe the tradition of law is essentially an emanation of the state—or rather, it became incorporated into the state when the latter institution 'took over' the sovereign powers of individual rulers. Thus the law on the Continent has traditionally been the profession of the state *par excellence*. To a greater or lesser extent, judges, prosecutors, and others connected with the administration of justice regard themselves as state servants; the law they enforce is a distinct and, on the whole, narrowly defined as well as carefully codified system intimately connected with the judicial function of the state . . . Law as such has little autonomy of its own (1968:384, quoted in Rueschemeyer, 1988:307).

The state also exercised extensive control over legally educated professionals in France and societies where the civil law was 'received', including the

[12] Another partial explanation lies in the civil and common law interpretation of the legal values of 'certainty and predictability'. The emphasis on codification, or more certain and predictable law in the civil family generally offers the citizens less opportunity to prove their case is different and worthy of special consideration. The common law case method, by contrast, is more open to the possibility that each case contains within it new possibilities to develop law in that area. See e.g. David and Brierley, 1985:98–9.

Netherlands and Scandinavia (Abel, 1988). This included control of the content of legal education, regulating the size of legal 'professions' and controlling fee schedules. In France, for example, the state strictly controlled the division of the legal professions until 1971 when the *avocat* and *avoué* professions were fused. The previous distinction was at least partly 'between an officer of the court subordinated to the state and an independent practitioner totally committed to representing a client' (Abel, 1988:20; also see Boigeol, 1988). In Scandinavia the legal profession was created by the state to serve the state's administrative requirements and an independent profession emerged only late in the nineteenth century (Johnsen,1988:56; 1994:303; Rueschemeyer, 1988:308). Indeed, lawyers have traditionally occupied all core civil service positions in Germany and Scandinavia, 'and still [do], to a significant extent', according to Rueschemeyer, (1988:307). Finally, in contrast to the common law tradition of selecting the judiciary from the ranks of practising lawyers, the civil law judiciary are career public servants. As a result, legally trained professionals in the civil law family often regard themselves as 'servants' of the state, not independent professionals standing between the state and its citizens. As I explain below, the integration of law and the state has profound and surprising consequences for the citizens wanting to mobilise law outside court.

The eclipse of the monarchy in England, by contrast, ensured that common law lawyers and judges emphasised autonomy *from* the state. The 'glorious' revolution of 1688 continued the process of centralising administration and law in England that began earlier in the millennium but the results were in marked contrast to those in France. In England, the successful alliance of the judiciary and parliament against the monarchy restricted rather than replaced the latter's power. The result was a greater degree of independence of the law, courts, and legal personnel from, instead of their integration into, the state than in France (David and Brierley, 1985:67). As a consequence the common law lawyers and judiciary have more of an independent, constitutional character than the administrative emphasis in the civil law.

While both the French and English revolutions promoted the ideals of individual rights and freedom, the emphasis was different. Whereas France emphasised protection *by* the state, England's law and legal personnel 'serv[ed] to protect the citizens against the arbitrary inroads of absolute authority' (Zweigert and Kötz, 1987:202). The comparative law scholar, Chloros, observes for example, that:

> . . . it can be argued that the philosophy of the Common Law, the scale of values which it attempts to express, is one of rights rather than duties, of emancipation rather than control, of responsibility rather than paternalism. For the Common law was profoundly influenced by the tug-of-war between the English King and Parliament . . . Evidence of this is not only the Magna Carta and the Bill of Rights, but also the stress which ordinary English case-law and statute place upon the right of the individual to dispose of himself and of his property to the exclusion of every other interest (1978:14).

While these traditions represent differences in emphasis rather than either/or distinctions, they have important implications for the citizen's opportunities to mobilise the law. This can be illustrated by considering where and how legal problems are processed in the two families. In brief, because of the civil law state's degree of control of law it rarely promotes the citizens capacities to mobilise the law outside, or encourages alternatives to, the courts. As a result, independent, community-based organisations, such as community mediation centres, are not sanctioned. Instead, civil law societies are more likely to develop alternatives *within* state structures. In addition, the civil law societies are also likely to utilise legal personnel to process legal problems because they are expected to be responsible for this work. While lay people often assist judges in courts in the civil law family, lay judges do not sit on the bench without 'legal' judges, as occurs in England (Damaska, 1986). Similarly, volunteers rarely process legal problems problems in community-based mediation agencies in the civil law societies, but do in common law societies. Finally, legal personnel are unlikely to promote alternatives to the courts because of their privileged position of controlling legal work.

In the common law societies, by contrast, the citizens have more opportunities to mobilise the law because it is not as integrated into the state. Alternatives to the courts are tolerated and even encouraged, including community-based mediation and other non-state mechanisms. The private legal profession and judiciary are also more tolerant of alternatives including the independent community-based mediation agencies for neighbour disputes and family law cases that have been established in many common law societies over the last twenty years and staffed by social workers, lawyers and other professionals and laypeople.

The common law emphasis on individual rights has one other important consequence for outside litigation services. Not only can the citizens attend non-court agencies to resolve legal problems, they can also obtain information and undertake education about the law in these societies. Basic legal education is provided in secondary schools while training courses and printed materials assist citizens to respond to everyday legal problems. 'Do-it-yourself' (DIY) kits exist for a wide range of everyday problems including land transfers, powers of attorney, and wills. DIY kits are widely available in the USA, Canada, Australia and England (Huxtable, 1994). Common law citizens are less likely, therefore, to have to choose either to deal with their own legal problems or to use lawyers, courts or other government agencies. Instead, they can make use of a range of agencies staffed by a range of personnel. And they are assisted, to some extent, to respond themselves.

Finally, while part of the reason Napoleon emphasised clarity when the codes were drafted was in order to allow the citizens to mobilise the law themselves (Zweigert and Kötz, 1987:85–6), the effect has probably been the opposite. 'In litigation' legal aid is a priority because the law 'belongs' to the state—it is an administrative function undertaken on behalf of its citizens. Legal problems are, therefore, resolved by the state in courts presided over by legal professionals. Paradoxically, however, state control of law also means the citizens are unlikely to be offered 'outside litigation' services because this is a state activity. Advice, information and education services are more likely to flourish where the law is more uncertain, changing and ambiguous, and where there is a stronger emphasis on individual rights, as is true in the common law.

The evidence from the first-tier legal aid schemes supports the argument outlined above. In sum, 'outside litigation' legal aid services, advice, information and assistance unrelated to court proceedings, education and training are more extensive in the common than civil law schemes. The 'first-tier' schemes' emphases for 1992/3 are summarised in Table 8.2.

The small but nevertheless significant common/civil law differences in Table 8.2 suggest that citizens' capacities to mobilise the law 'outside litigation' vary substantially. In order to illustrate the differences I examine these schemes in turn. The Swedish scheme, for example, primarily assists people with court cases (Ling, 1994; Regan, 1994b; Johnsen, 1994). As a result, 'outside litigation' services are not a priority, as demonstrated by the relatively low volume of legal advice, the absence of other services, including legal education and training, and the fact that no plans exist to introduce these services in Sweden (Sverne, 1997). Finally, and more generally, legal education and training in the form of classes, DIY kits, pamphlets and other publications and training courses are absent in the society generally, not just the legal aid scheme. In other words, the Swedish legal aid scheme, and legal system generally, emphasise dependence upon legal professionals and little assistance is offered if citizens wish to mobilise the law themselves.

The case of the Netherlands is more complex. There is no doubt, for example,

Table 8.2: 'Outside Litigation' Legal Aid Services and Legal Families

Legal Family	Country	Emphasis on 'Outside litigation' Legal Aid Services[a]
Civil law	Sweden	1. Low priority on legal advice, no other services
	The Netherlands	2. High priority on legal advice, very low priority on education and training
Common law	England	3. High priority on legal advice, low priority on legal education and training
	Australia, USA and Canada	4. High priority on legal advice and education and training

Sources: Goriely (1992), Cousins and O'Hara (1992), Huxtable (1994), Regan (1994b), Johnsen (1994).

[a] 'Outside litigation' services include legal advice and information by way of interview and over the telephone, legal education and training.

that 'outside litigation' services are offered in that society. But the emphasis on dependence on professionals persists and there is little emphasis on services to assist individuals to resolve their own legal problems. The Dutch legal aid agencies, the public *Buros voor Rechtshulp* and the community-based *raadslieden* and 'law shops', offer advice and information about the law and undertake a small amount of law reform work (Cousins, 1993:160; Goriely, 1992:816; Huls, 1994). Advice and information is rarely offered over the telephone, making it far less accessible than in Australia or other liberal societies. More importantly, legal education and training services are rarely available. As Cousins and O'Hara point out, legal aid legislation does not require the scheme to 'fulfil an education and information role' and while some *Buros voor Rechtshulp* offer education services this is by no means a consistent priority (1992:66). The significance of this point is clearer if we reconsider Zemans's model of legal mobilisation.

In some respects, Dutch society is highly developed in terms of the Zemans model (1983). As I have shown, 'in litigation' legal aid services are generous and comprehensive. Extensive legal advice and information services also assist the Dutch to respond to legal problems. Blankenburg argues, for example, that the Netherlands has a remarkable litigation 'avoidance infrastructure' involving a large number of sources of help for people to respond to, and avoid, legal problems (1994).[13] Nevertheless, there is little emphasis on services to promote people's capacities to solve their own legal problems in the form of classes, publications, DIY kits or training courses. They are not a priority for the Netherlands legal aid scheme or the society generally. In other words Dutch legal aid gives a high priority to 'outside litigation' services where the citizens depend on legal and other professionals, but there is little emphasis on actively promoting self-reliance.

The USA, Canada and Australia's 'outside litigation' services are, by contrast, extensive. Legal advice and education and training are readily available from legal aid agencies but also in the society generally in the form of DIY kits, pamphlets, booklets, classes and training courses (Huxtable, 1994; Regan, 1996).[14] While they are not as extensive in Britain, this can be partly explained by the private legal profession's historically dominant position in legal aid (Goriely, 1996). In sum, the profession is unlikely to develop an extensive range of 'outside litigation' services because it is unlikely to generate income. As a result 'outside litigation' services are only offered in England and Wales by the 50 Community Law Centres (Cousins and O'Hara, 1992). Nevertheless, legal

[13] The 'avoidance infrastructure' is certainly extensive. Not only do lawyers not have a monopoly on giving legal advice but there is also a long history of community-based agencies offering legal and other forms of advice. The 90 *raadslieden*, for example, are similar to but predate the British Citizens Advice Bureau by more than 50 years (Goriely, 1992:807).

[14] This is also true for Canada. See Huxtable (1994) and Kuras (1994).

education and training is widely available in Britain in the form of DIY kits, booklets, pamphlets and classes.[15]

While policy values explain why 'outside litigation' legal aid services are more extensive in common law than civil law schemes a number of other possible explanations must also be considered. A 'replacement effect' may, for example, be at work. That is, the common law schemes may in a time of welfare cutbacks offer these relatively cheap services to replace the expensive 'inside litigation' services. There is some truth in such an explanation. The Australian LACs, for example, expanded their 'outside litigation' services as their capacity to fund 'in litigation' declined due to budget cuts (LAFS, 1994:1). However, this explanation is, on its own, inadequate for two reasons.

First, it fails to explain the political agitation by legal aid activists in the common law societies to establish these services in the 1960s and 1970s. They did not aim to compensate for the inadequate 'in litigation' services; instead they believed that 'outside litigation' services were integral to legal aid because they empowered citizens to use the law themselves. Secondly, if a replacement effect was the sole reason for these services flourishing in the common law schemes then they should have emerged in civil law schemes over the last ten years as budgets declined and eligibility criteria were tightened. Recent studies of civil law schemes demonstrates, however, that this is not the case (Johnsen, 1994; Cousins, 1994). In other words, 'outside litigation' services have not flourished in the civil law schemes.

Finally, it must be acknowledged that certain civil law family features reduce the need for 'outside litigation' services. The government in these societies, as I have explained, can be understood as managing society. As a result, some legal problems that are resolved in courts in other societies are regarded as administrative problems in civil law societies. The so-called 'no fault' accident and workers compensation insurance schemes in Scandinavia, for example, were designed so most cases could bypass court and be processed administratively (Strömholm, 1988; Oldertz and Tidefelt, 1988). As a result the need for 'outside litigation' services in these cases was dramatically reduced. Nevertheless, while some classes of 'legal' problems have been transformed in this way, numerous everyday civil and family legal problems continue to be resolved in courts utilising legal procedures. The civil law societies have not established administrative mechanisms to resolve all legal problems and disputes. 'Outside litigation' services are not, therefore, an anachronism in the civil law societies; instead the potential exists for individuals to be assisted to resolve their own legal problems.

15 Evidence from other societies appears to reflect a similar pattern. Societies with common law origins, including Ireland (Cousins and O'Hara, 1992) and Canada (Huxtable, 1994) offer more extensive 'outside litigation' services than those with civil law origins, including France (Cousins and O'Hara, 1992) and Norway (Johnsen, 1994).

Conclusion

The puzzle in recent comparative legal aid research can be partly explained in terms of the impact of policy values of dependence and self-reliance that underpin models of government, their welfare states and legal families. As a result, some societies assist their citizens to mobilise the law in court but offer little help, outside court while others offer little help for court but more assistance outside court. In addition, societies generally emphasise either 'in litigation' or 'outside litigation' services, not both.

Interestingly, the discussion suggests little has changed since Cohn argued that legal aid services can and should pursue two complementary purposes. A combination of 'in' and 'outside' litigation services was required in the 1940s and still is. But as Cohn might have predicted, due to a number of reasons, including the mixed benefits of welfare states, the power of the legal profession and the impact of legal families, no society currently pursues both purposes adequately.

Nevertheless, Cohn's insight continues to offer guidance for legal aid debates in the late 1990s. For example, at one level the argument for these two types of services could be viewed as trivial, even perverse. It could be argued, for example, that court cases far outweigh the importance of 'outside litigation' services. The latter are not comparable, according to this view, to protecting a person's liberty if they face a possible jail sentence. The policy implication of this perspective is, therefore, to direct legal aid funding solely to services for court cases and abandon others because they divert money away from this superior purpose.[16] This is an important argument to consider in view of rising pressures on legal aid budgets and cuts to services. From one perspective it is also compelling. Schemes could assist more people in court if all funds were solely used for court cases. But whether 'outside litigation' services should be abolished in order to shore up 'in litigation' is another question altogether. An alternative perspective is to recognise that citizens experience many types of legal problems and as a result different types of legal aid services are required. It is not an either/or choice. The policy implication is, therefore, that both should be maintained and, ideally, improved not sacrifice one in order to enhance the other.

This conclusion also suggests perspectives with which to consider the future development of legal aid. Ideally schemes might look something like the best of

[16] This argument was recently made by the private legal profession in two Australian states. The Bar Association in South Australia argued that the 'access' services as they were referred to, drained money away from the more important work of assisting citizens in court cases. Their submission to a parliamentary review of legal aid highlighted the importance of legal aid in criminal trials in particular due to the risk to citizens liberty if they are unrepresented (Parliament of South Australia, Statutory Authorities Review Committee, 1996). Similarly, in 1995, The Law Society of Western Australia argued that the LAC in that state should abandon all community legal education activities in order to return to the core business of legal aid, which was understood as representing people in court cases (Goldie, 1996:296).

the two clusters of schemes analysed in this Chapter, offering generous and comprehensive 'in litigation' services and extensive 'outside litigation' services. The implication for existing civil and common law schemes is that they could, for their citizens sake, learn from each other's strengths and weaknesses. The civil law schemes could, for example, extend their 'outside litigation' services while the common law could improve eligibility for 'in litigation' services. It seems unlikely this will happen, however, in view of the historical origins of the respective blends of policy values and the more general current fad to 'downsize' government.

Part Three

Emerging Themes

9

Studies of Legal Needs and Legal Aid in a Market Context

JON JOHNSEN

Introduction

All Western countries use the market as the main mechanism for delivering professional legal services. Legal experts form the private profession—lawyers in private practice. However, the market also impacts on the formation and function of legal aid schemes in many ways. But how exactly does it do this?

This Chapter examines recent legal aid research and considers one aspect of this relationship, namely the research on 'legal needs'. I focus on two problems applicable to all societies:

a. first the meaning and importance of *legal needs research* as part of a general strategy for legal services research, and for mapping premises for legal aid reform. I concentrate on a methodological question: can we develop empirical notions of legal needs, or are all attempts at such a conceptualisation inherently normative?
b. the possibility of developing a *systematic approach* to legal services research. I describe the major mechanisms by which the legal services market influences legal aid schemes and relate legal needs' studies to some general perspectives on legal services. I also describe some constitutive assumptions about legal aid research tacitly adopted by many studies, because by making those assumptions explicit we might improve the quality of legal aid research.

Why is it important to revive and refine legal needs research? Why should we understand such studies in a broad context and recognise them as an inseparable part of a research strategy aimed at mapping the major mechanisms of the legal services system? Legal services research has been closely linked to policy reform, especially policy designed to improve services to the poor. Such studies are linked to fundamental ideas about fair distribution of justice and equal protection before the law (Zemans, 1983). Some reformists have looked upon legal aid itself as a political tool that might trigger reforms in several fields including housing, family, consumer issues, welfare and criminal justice. Others have looked upon citizens' use of law as an important element of political participation in a democratic society (Zemans, 1983). Providing legal services also means improving access to welfare services for more people, which can diffuse dissatisfaction and political opposition that otherwise might develop into revolutionary movements (Garth, 1980:134–5).

However, legal services also influence the way welfare schemes actually work for the underprivileged. When politicians transform political interests and demands into law through their decision-making in elected assemblies, they also transform group interests into individual legal 'positions' of rights, claims or discretionary entitlements. The law usually leaves it to the citizens as individuals to enforce such positions through the legal and bureaucratic machinery (Zemans, 1983). The common interests that make political reform viable are disbanded, and the reform's effectiveness then depends on the capacity of the entitled to utilise the law.

A paradox therefore emerges for welfare law. The intention is to help the poorest and diminish class and social differences; yet the welfare improvements depend on actual use. A few schemes have mechanisms for automatic implementation but most presuppose some sort of legal activity from the people with entitlements. If they lack the skills and drive to utilise their legal positions, such schemes become ineffective. As a result, welfare schemes tend to become least effective for groups that suffer most from poverty because legal skills are unevenly distributed within societies. This too often results in those groups' political neutralisation (Johnsen, 1980:25–7).

Ineffective legal aid therefore opens the way for symbolic politics where politicians enact reforms that ideologically satisfy the needs of the poor but at the same time recognise they will become ineffective due to inadequate legal aid schemes. Legal needs research can of course play a critical role in uncovering such strategies.

If people are unable to assert their legal positions on their own, legal services become crucial to the effectiveness of all areas of law. For the poor, the quality of legal aid schemes is therefore paramount. As a result, knowledge about *how* people use their legal positions is important. We need to understand the factors that motivate both their use and non-use of law.

However, we must distinguish between use and non-use *that matters* to people, and those where people are *indifferent*. Legal need studies have aimed at this complex task. In particular the non-use—often labelled 'un-met legal needs'—became an important research issue in the sixties and seventies when many jurisdictions developed their legal aid schemes.

Unfortunately, when the expansion came to an end and many jurisdictions 'downsized' legal aid the interest in legal needs studies also diminished. Methodological problems were also evident. It proved difficult to operationalise 'legal needs' in ways that produced reliable empirical studies using meaningful quantitative methods. Statistics on legal needs are of limited value in seeking reform if the concept itself appears controversial, the definitions used appear arbitrary, and different operationalisations produce widely varying results.

Still, none of these arguments cast serious doubt on the value of research which promotes a reliable understanding of legal needs that reformers can use in shaping legal services and legal aid. When legal aid declines it is even more important that the problems that matter most are covered first. Therefore, good legal needs studies are as important to legal aid policy as ever and I believe it is possible to improve their methodology along the lines discussed in this Chapter.

Finally, a word about my analytical approach in this Chapter. Although I focus on studies of the legal needs of the poor, I think it is necessary to situate such studies in a broader context because the market mechanisms apply to all groups. Although all segments of society might benefit from legal services, lawyers as a profession mainly target the affluent. Poor people represent a less profitable market and governments therefore establish legal aid schemes to improve legal services to them. But without thorough insights into the way legal services work for those in an advantaged financial situation we cannot thoroughly understand the operation of legal aid to the poor, or their needs.[1] My perspective therefore considers legal aid to the poor as part of the general mechanisms for delivering legal services.

The two major issues addressed in this Chapter clearly imply criticism of existing legal aid research. I would have liked to include a critical summary of some of the major studies. However, space does not allow for this apart from my analysis of the concept of legal needs, where I include a short evaluation of some major studies. When I propose my systematic approach, therefore, I mainly present my own views and leave it to the reader to apply them to existing and future research. While my arguments are adapted from my Norwegian book (Johnsen, 1987)[2] they have also been developed in response to research published over the last decade.

Policy values, reform models and empirical understanding

The foundation of my approach is the relationship between research and politics in the field of legal services. Some questions relate to challenges in the formation of legal aid policy and will receive attention below, while others are general and relate to the overall relationship between law and society research and policy. With one exemption, I will not deal with the latter, but since legal aid research emphasises reform, it is appropriate to make a few brief remarks about the relationship between policy values, reform ideas and empirical theories about legal needs:

[1] A major premise for Norwegian legal aid policy has been to avoid developing legal aid schemes that provide a better service for the groups covered than for groups that must hire lawyers on ordinary market terms (Johnsen, 1994:307–8, 325).

[2] I have not included detailed references to this work, since they probably will be of limited use to English-speaking readers.

Policy values All reform strategies are founded on values about how society ought to function. Legal services and legal aid are no exception. In public debate we find values that are held by a large part of society as well as those that are controversial and subject to conflicting interests. Empirical research cannot decide between such values. However, it ought to be aware of the dominant values relating to the formation of legal aid policy and attempt to shape its analysis to make it relevant to most of them. Although research cannot *decide* what values society ought to use in structuring legal aid, it can thoroughly map the existing values about legal services and identify areas of consensus and controversy. To undertake such a programme, however, it is necessary to develop concepts that relate to existing perceptions of needs among politicians, professionals and the poor.

Problem-creating mechanisms All reform proposals are based on perceptions of reality that conflict with the reformer's values. Such perceptions may or may not be accurate. One of the important tasks of empirical research is to provide reformers with a comprehensive and detailed picture of the legal needs and the actual operation of legal services. Of course nothing prevents research from producing reform models according to the values of the opposition groups. However, such models may have bleak prospects of being implemented.

Reform models Reform analysis ought to provide alternatives to the existing system. An important research task is to develop models that promise to improve reality in line with prevailing values.

These three elements of reform analysis are interdependent, as shown in Figure 9.1.

Attitudes towards legal aid reforms will depend on values, empirical understanding and the visions of reform models. A change in values might also change

Figure 9.1: Interdependence Between Policy Values, Empirical Data and Reforms

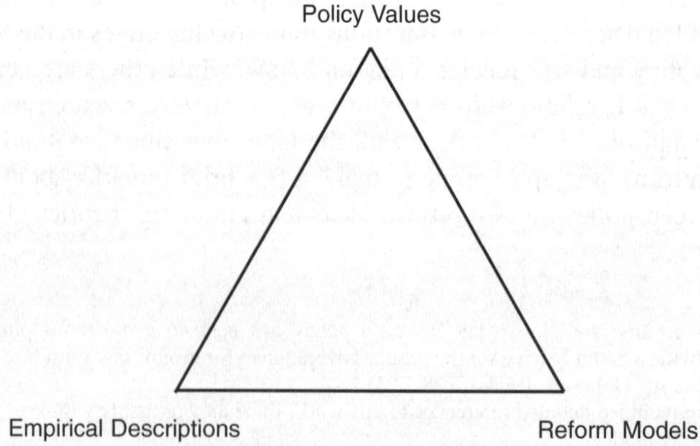

the attitude to reform. As mentioned above, influencing society's values towards legal aid through empirical research is difficult. However, research might significantly alter influential groups' *empirical understanding* of how the existing system works. Changes in perception might also change the attitude towards reform when values and reform models remain constant. Similarly, a change in the perception of *reform models* might change attitudes towards reform even if values and empirical understanding remain the same. If all legal aid reform models seem costly and ineffective, reform may be viewed negatively even if politicians regard the existing system as highly inadequate. However, if research documents a cheap and effective alternative model, it may trigger reforms.

There are many tasks for empirical research. They include plotting the gap between standards which have been set and the actual situation, as well as developing, analysing and evaluating different delivery models that may be effective in meeting needs. But policy-making seldom presents as an either/or task: instead, compromises and priority decisions frequently occur. Research can therefore encourage more rational policy decisions by identifying the values and standards which, although different in their general framing, overlap in practice. Research can also improve the prospects for evaluating the pros and cons of various reform models through applying *different* standards of 'needs'. It can also present the opportunity for all relevant interest groups to assess the welfare benefits of the proposed strategies and estimate the resources necessary to implement them. Finally it can serve an important democratic function of identifying and highlighting the 'hidden needs' standards of deprived groups that lack the ability to channel their policy demands into public debate.

In the remainder of this Chapter, however, I focus on the empirical corner of the triangle in Figure 9.1 rather than the reform models.

Conceptualising legal needs

The legal needs literature is vast. Among the early, well known studies were Abel-Smith, Zander and Brooke (1973) from the UK; Eskeland and Finne (1973) from Norway; Messier (1975) from Canada; Cass and Sackville (1975) from Australia; Schuyt, Gronendijk and Sloot (1976) from the Netherlands; and Curran (1977) from the USA. Among recent studies are the Comprehensive Legal Needs Study (CLNS) conducted by the American Bar Association (see Cantril, 1996 for references and a summary) and Blacksell, Economides and Watkins (1991) from the UK—although the latter try to avoid the term 'legal needs' in their analysis (see below).

As mentioned above, 'legal needs' studies try to find out when people might resort to using the law. But we must distinguish between two major meanings of 'legal needs'. Sometimes we mean 'needs' that relate to *substantive law*, for example, better protection against violence, reduced taxation, more liberal social benefit regulations. An alternative interpretation, and the one I use in this Chapter, is the 'need' for *legal services* that relates to an opportunity to utilise legal positions according to the law *currently in force*. The latter interpretation does not presuppose change in the substantive law, however, it does not in itself prevent normative interpretations. Statements about 'legal needs' might still imply that society has a duty to provide the service in question.

Several scholars have expressed scepticism about 'legal needs' research, including Marks (1977), Griffiths (1980), Zemans (1982), Campbell (1983), Paterson and Nelken (1984) who sum up the UK debate, and Blacksell, Economides and Watkins (1991). The main objections concern the assumption implicit in this research that when we label something a legal 'need', we also presuppose that society must fulfil that need. Griffiths argued, for example, that legal needs research might serve three main ends. Such studies may be part of the *implementation* of legal services reforms. Secondly, they might also try to answer questions about the *necessity* of such reforms. Thirdly, they might be used as a vehicle for improving our general understanding of *how law actually functions in a society* (Griffiths, 1980:20–30).

Griffiths does not object to research mapping the volume and extension of legal aid reforms which I highlighted in the model-development corner of Figure 9.1. However, he opposes the other two forms of research. He regards the empirical corner of the triangle as unviable because 'legal needs' necessarily refer to something different from actual use of legal services. The concept might relate, for example, to subjective experiences of need, or to judgements made by a third party. But 'needs' in this sense do not correspond to observable behaviour. We cannot, therefore, measure 'needs' by mapping demands for or actual prices of legal services:

> . . . there is no such thing as an empirical need or no such thing as an empirical 'legal problem' or empirical 'legal services'. These concepts are all ways of expressing judgements about how the world ought to be. To say that legal services should be made available to some groups in some situations because they have a need for such services, is merely to say they ought to have the services because they ought to use them (ibid. 30).

For Griffiths, legal needs research is inadequate to answer the value questions in legal aid policy. Merely by labelling a condition a 'legal need' we are implying that the need should be satisfied. He then argues that we do not rectify legal problems by legal services alone. Law merely constitutes one of *several* problem solving strategies available. Nor are lawyers the only professionals that can supply legal services. Legal needs research therefore implicitly favours one sort of problem solving over others without attempting actual comparisons. The research therefore legitimates legal services reforms without considering alternatives (ibid. 33–5).

Other researchers have advocated similar views. In their recent study, Blacksell, Economides and Watkins refuse to apply a 'legal needs' concept, since using that language 'presuppose[s] that legal solutions are superior to any other in the resolution of conflict. Instead we prefer to think in the terms "territorial justice" and "legal contact" [. . .]—and the *opportunities* of access—rather than imputing *a priori* values as to their use, or non use, by potential clients and claimants' (1991:11).[3]

Their main objection to the 'needs' concept, therefore, concerns its lack of political flexibility. Nevertheless, I think some sort of 'legal need' concept is necessary in legal services research and do not agree that such policy implications necessarily follow. A 'legal needs' concept can identify problems that appear solvable through the use of legal services *with no presumption about obligations to deliver such services.* If we conceptualise in this manner, however, we must distinguish sharply between the *existence* of legal needs and their *fulfilment*. The existence of legal needs might be subject to empirical research, while the question of fulfilment ultimately rests on value choices that we cannot address empirically. Ideologies about justice, fairness, rules of law, etc. determine answers to such questions. What then is a more appropriate and empirically measurable definition of 'legal needs'?

An outline of a definition

There are two essential features of an empirical definition of 'legal needs'. First, the substance of the 'need', or the *legal expertise*, and secondly, the 'need-condition', that is, the *human state* to which the 'need' relates.

Legal expertise means a person's insights about the law and the legal system. We can distinguish between three major elements:

doctrinal knowledge or expertise in the normative content of the law;
application insights—expertise in researching, documenting and constructing legal meaningful facts;
tactical experience—expertise about the actual structure and functioning (*modus operandi*) of the legal system and in forwarding claims to, and invoking actions from, that system (Johnsen, 1987:41–3).

This outline necessarily leaves several questions open. For example, what levels of knowledge are required? And how broad? Nor are the three elements exhaustive. What about communication and negotiation skills, empathy and ethics? Such skills and attributes might also significantly contribute to legal expertise. However, while other elements may be included it is difficult to envisage a viable definition of legal expertise with any of these three core elements missing.

What about the '*need condition*'? 'Need' in ordinary language points to some

[3] Blacksell, Economides and Watkins (1991) refer to Lewis (1973) and Paterson and Nelken (1984), Coates and Rawstron (1971) and Mayhew and Reiss (1969). However, I do not think they succeed in avoiding the legal needs concept. See my criticism in Johnsen (1992:423–31, esp 423–5).

sort of lack of legal expertise—some state of deficit, desire or want. The 'deficit' concept implies a value statement that the existing situation is negative or unwanted in some sense. This deficit concept can be developed further by considering its two meanings. First we can argue that legal aid will change the existing situation in a way that reduces the deficit, that it will result in a *welfare improvement*. Such statements are of course prognostic in character. That is, they presume that a specific type of result will occur if we supply a particular service. Such statements are also empirically testable.

Applying the second meaning, we can develop a normative concept, or value statement, claiming *someone ought to receive*, or *possesses a legitimate demand for* legal aid. This meaning implies statements of moral, political and legal character. Empirical methods are of limited use to such analysis but normative disciplines like law, ethics and religion might make some contribution in this area. Most of the criticism of legal needs research relates to attempts to define needs through normative value laden empirical research. Griffiths, for example, argues: 'Thus the concept of need in legal needs research is based on an idea of the benefit of legal services that pretends objectivity, but which is in fact an extension to the whole population of lawyers' idealised notions concerning the judgement of prudent members of the middle classes' (1980:35).[4]

He argues that legal services research 'should concern itself with the distribution of actual use of lawyers' services, the difference that such services make to outcomes of various individual situations, and the costs and effects of various redistribution schemes' (ibid. 36).

But Griffiths fails to see the potential of the first model of the concept of 'legal needs' described above: this approach works well in research that attempts to map 'the differences legal services make to the outcome of various individual situations', and also in the study of the general welfare effects of such services.

Conceptual flexibility

If we focus on the first model, we still find several ambiguities, and considerable scope for discretionary choices. However, my aim here is only to show that it is

[4] Griffiths (ibid. 35–6) substantiates his argument as follows: 'First, they are not any kind of fact at all but rather concealed ideas about policy, and thus to invoke them in support of a policy is to beg the question. Secondly, legal needs research has in fact not figured in the major policy decisions that have been made about the distribution of legal services, for example, the decision to recognise a right to counsel in criminal cases. The terms of that debate were justice—fairness and equality—not need.'

He also criticises legal needs studies for being 'profoundly justificatory of existing arrangements; it takes the correctness of those arguments for granted as the basis of an argument for increasing the output of the very product that is currently being produced. No wonder that the organised bar enthusiastically finances such research!' I might add that the Norwegian bar showed a deep scepticism to the findings of the Scandinavian action research studies, referred to below. The studies showed a reality they did not recognise from their own practices, and they felt that the results threatened their hegemony as the main providers of legal service to all segments of society. See Johnsen (1987:79–145) and my article about Norwegian legal aid policy forthcoming in the *International Journal of the Legal Profession*.

possible to construct a meaningful empirical concept about legal needs so we can view the indicators as a *framework* to develop and adjust according to the research tasks in question.

If we identify 'welfare improvements' in some form as the major indicator for 'legal needs' some questions arise. For example, should welfare improvements be *substantial*? Should even minor gains count, or do we only accept gains above a certain level? We must also keep in mind that empirical mapping of needs does not in itself result in a public obligation to respond to such needs. Researchers might identify standards of *seriousness*, for example, where particular needs are prioritised using standards from the existing legal aid ideologies. And from a reform perspective it would be wise to map and describe 'needs' according to a range of different legal aid ideologies in a society. Such strategy might call for a needs concept that also incorporates minor welfare improvements. One example is the provision of legal advice to clarify specific legal questions which may be causing concern. We might subject our empirical findings to *different* tests of seriousness according to existing policy ideologies. Such tests might leave parts of the existing needs outside the scope of legal aid policy. However, this strategy is likely to introduce a more comprehensive picture of the prioritisation dilemmas than one that attempts to measure only the types of needs that policy-makers want their schemes to cover. If studies only map needs according to dominant policy values, they will not show the problems that are not being addressed nor their welfare significance. As a result, such studies might conceal important needs from the policy debate.

When we use a broad definition of legal needs, we can also ask about the difference between *legal needs* and *legal problems*. Whenever the use of legal expertise might lead to improved welfare it is reasonable to talk about 'legal problems' as well as 'needs'. If the person with the problem only uses her or his own legal knowledge to solve a question, we might label it a legal problem, but not a legal need since external expertise is superfluous. However, the difference is a matter of degree. Some legal problems might be solved by the problem holder, but with a less satisfactory outcome and more stress. 'Legal needs' are then the legal problems that the problem holder cannot solve effectively by his or her own means.

A problem holder might make their own assessment of needs for legal expertise using *internal* criteria of 'legal needs'. Others, including members of the local community, welfare agencies, lawyers, legal aid bureaucrats or politicians, might also evaluate the problem applying *external* criteria. Of course, the content of both internal and external criteria might vary depending on how they formulate their concept of needs. Empirical studies are important in order to elucidate both internal and external criteria.

We can research the welfare effects in several ways. When people decide whether to see a lawyer, they make their 'needs' assessment from *prognoses* of what effect legal expertise might have on the problem. However, their evaluation might differ from the prognosis made by a legal expert. We might also assess the impact of assistance after an *outcome* has been recorded. Studies of outcomes may reveal that the welfare effects of expert assistance differ significantly from prognostic judgements.

It is also important to distinguish between *legal needs* and *demand*. A 'demand' presupposes that a problem holder actually asks for help. It also usually presupposes a 'need'—few people will ask for legal assistance unless they think it will be of some use. Problem holders usually assess their needs from their own understanding of the law, supported by their personal and informal network. However, they might miscalculate according to external definitions set by various professionals, for example politicians, lawyers or researchers.[5]

The *supply* of legal expertise in society, however, corresponds neither with the needs nor with the demand. While we might accept that legal needs exist as long as *any* form of expert legal help might effect the problem, supply depends on how we organise legal services. But whether society has created a service that covers all such problems is a different question altogether. Therefore, in attempting to answer this question we must map both legal needs and demands which existing legal services do not respond to systematically.

Legal expertise can also be used to solve legal problems according to the law in force and to press for law reform. Of course, the distinction is blurred in some respects. Pleadings for a court precedent are both an 'according-to-law' activity and, if successful, an action that might change the law. Still it is useful to distinguish between needs that relate to assistance for utilising the present legal reality and those that suggest the need for new law.

As I explain in the next section, researchers have utilised different strategies when conducting legal needs studies.

Research strategies

As mentioned above, several projects in different countries have attempted to map legal needs. Most of them have used *interviews* in some form as their major data-gathering tool. Scandinavian legal research, however, deviates from this pattern by primarily using *action research* methods. Interesting differences in methodology and in the empirical perceptions of legal needs emerge when using action research combined with interviews, as in Scandinavia. In this section I outline and compare these two major approaches.

1. Interview studies The interview studies in the sixties and the seventies focused especially on mapping the respondent's *previous* legal needs. The

[5] Zemans has criticised previous legal needs research, often labelled the 'access to justice approach', both for mapping needs only from external criteria and for producing an incomplete picture of the factors that influence demand (1982:990–1).

methodology used in these studies varied. Some attempted to map *all* of the respondents' past needs, regardless of when they occurred (Curran, 1977; Cass and Sackville, 1973). Others focused on a *specific time-span*, asking about problems experienced during the last seven years (Abel-Smith, Zander and Brooke, 1973) five years (Cass and Sackville, 1973) or two years (Schuyt, Gronendijk and Sloot, 1976). Yet others asked about the *last* legal problem experienced.

Some interview projects asked respondents to state *all problems* experienced during the chosen period, while others used checklists to cover *selected main types* of problems, recording those thoroughly. Some used a combination of these techniques (Schuyt, Gronendijk and Sloot, 1976; Cass and Sackville, 1973), while others were limited to checklists (Curran, 1977; Abel-Smith, Zander and Brooke, 1973).

A range of differing interview techniques were also used. In some cases unstructured interviews were used to emphasise detail, while in others structured questionnaires were administered with strictly ordered questions. In some instances direct questions were asked about the legal problems experienced, while in other research the questions related to situations with a 'high' occurrence of legal problems and asked whether the respondent had experienced such problems. Still other studies used combinations of interview techniques.

Some projects limited the mapping of problems to those diagnosed by the respondent. Such an approach does not include problems where legal issues have not been identified by the respondent despite being relevant according to external criteria. Other studies asked respondents if they had consulted a lawyer or other legal expert. Finally, Sykes (1969–70) enlisted six lawyers to evaluate the legal aspects of the described problems according to external criteria, while Schuyt, Gronendijk and Sloot (1976) used lawyers as interviewers supplementing the respondent's diagnosis with external criteria.

Studies from the nineties adopted similar practices. Blacksell, Economides and Watkins, for example, seem to have mapped their respondents' own perception of a 'legal need' to mean the need for a consultation with a solicitor or an adviser in a Citizen Advice Bureau (1991:213–14).[6] They appear not to have systematically mapped or measured problems by external standards.

The American Bar Association's CLNS developed a comprehensive questionnaire containing sixty-seven specific sets of circumstances and asked if anyone in the respondent's household had experienced such situations during 1992. The project consulted 'virtually all legal needs surveys (primarily at the state level) conducted over the last two decades', and aimed at covering 'a broad range of matters for which legal representation might be appropriate'. When a positive response was received the interviewers asked further questions to clarify that a

[6] 'The third section [of the questionnaire] was designed to assess the extent to which people may have thought about consulting a solicitor over an issue, but decided against doing this for some reason. If this situation had occurred, the respondents were asked if they had gone to anyone else for advice, and whether the issue had ever been resolved' (Blacksell, Economides and Watkins, 1991:213–14).

legal issue had been raised and to determine what course of action had been taken by the respondent. However, the project took care not to ask the respondents to determine the legal context of the situation. Nor did it ask if the household experienced the situation as serious. 'Legal needs' were determined by external criteria only and developed in consultation with a panel of experienced lawyers. Evaluation was based on whether the household might have benefited 'from the assistance of a lawyer, a small claims court, or other forum within the civil justice system'. The study therefore measured 'the frequency with which circumstances occur in people's lives, rather than the frequency with which people "want" legal help or think they may need it' (Cantril, 1996:1, 35). The study cautions that a person's ability to handle a difficult set of circumstances depends on a complex mix of personal, social, economic and environmental factors. Furthermore, it was not assumed that the help needed is either 'legal', 'non-legal' or both (ibid. 3).

2. *Action research studies* By contrast, Scandinavian legal needs studies have used action research as the main methodology. For example, see Eskeland and Finne (1973), Johnsen (1978), Lid (1980), Haugen and Vigerust (1992), and Sejr (1977). Johnsen (1987:255–74) also presents a general approach to, and analysis of methodology questions in action research.

The action research studies use legally competent interviewers who offer extensive assistance in mapping legal aspects of the respondents' legal problems. They use interviewing techniques which lawyers apply in counselling sessions with clients. In addition, they employ extensive check-lists constructed from earlier experiences in delivering legal services to similar groups. These projects encourage respondents to go through their problems thoroughly before the interview. They are requested to present all problems which they think may benefit from an evaluation by a legally competent person. Respondents usually evaluate their needs for legal counselling only after the interviewers make their initial diagnosis of the problem.

The action research methodology evolved from the projects' offer of legal assistance for all professionally identified problems. Therefore they evaluate the problems both according to the internal 'legal needs' criteria of the respondents and the external criteria of the project as applied by the professional conducting the survey. These studies usually label problems as 'legal needs' only when they pass both these standards.

Action research studies use the data produced through their own legal counselling and representation as the main source of analysis. But one of the differences with the interview studies is that they map the case stories thoroughly. Besides interviewing, such projects *handle* all problems that satisfy both internal and external criteria. This methodology produces a rich and precise source of material about the factual and legal structure of the problems and the behaviour of the legal machinery. The *case handling data* appear as the major source of information about legal needs. The interviews therefore function primarily as the detector of needs, not as the major source of information about their content.

When the problems have been mapped and handled, the projects typically evaluate the registered problems according to different prevailing 'legal needs' standards. They usually sort out the problems that pass the means and merits test of the judicare schemes and compare them with the ones that fall outside the schemes. They also apply various standards for needs' seriousness proposed in reform debates in order to show the precise effects of alternative reform models.

3. Comparisons What are the strengths and weaknesses of the two approaches? While the interview studies tend to produce more representative data, action research requires a legal services apparatus for handling the registered problems, which is costly and complicated to establish. Developing national statistically representative samples is resource-intensive. Action research also requires an extended data-gathering period, since both the problem solving process and the outcome constitute major material for the research.

When studies essentially record legal problems and needs from the respondent's own account, they map legal needs according to internal criteria. The respondent's own perception of a 'legal problem' and a 'legal need' determine results. These projects do not systematically confront the respondents' perception with other data. Attempts to evaluate what services may have been needed are problematic, particularly in cases where the respondent has not sought legal advice. Internal criteria will differ between respondents, and make any assessment of the services required difficult to gauge. However, when the respondent's perception is supplemented with evaluations from legal experts the relevance of the research for reform purposes increases. These experts are likely to perform external evaluations according to set criteria and, as a result, systematise internal perceptions of 'needs' with a common standard.

Action research studies actively and consciously influence their respondents' perception of needs. They generally register as needs all problems that are actually dealt with. This usually implies a close link between the respondent's internal needs criteria and the project's external needs evaluation. Action research studies map the legal expert's evaluation as well as the respondent's, and often also the perception of the other party. Such studies record with considerable precision the relationship between the welfare problems experienced by the respondent and specific parts of the legal system's regulations, organisation and case handling. In this way they parallel medical studies that map people's health problems according to the worries they report compared to studies done by doctors who treat patients. In sum, action research produces a richer and more accurate picture of what legal assistance actually means to the respondents' welfare than the interview studies.

Both interview studies and action research are, however, vulnerable to *under-reporting*. When asked about past problems, people forget details. They are also likely to experience emotional barriers to reporting sensitive cases. So far surveys have usually measured problems experienced *in the past,* not the amount and structure of unsolved problems that presently exist. But we could expect people to be more concerned about their current problems than those in the past. Often they also have vague memories of, and are less willing to talk about, past problems. In the interview study by Blacksell, Economides and Watkins, more than two-thirds of the reported solicitor contacts had taken place during the last five years and more than one-third during the last twelve months (1991:155–6). Taken at face value, a dramatic rise from 7 per cent to 36 per cent in the use of lawyers would have been expected during the last year. These findings suggest extensive under-reporting from previous years. Asking about present problems, as the action research studies do, reduces under-reporting. Offering legal services also reduces the barrier against reporting sensitive problems, since respondents might improve their welfare by participating.

By offering legal assistance, the action research studies have attempted to map the present unmet legal need, not previously experienced problems. They produce *new information* about the structure and content of the needs through their professional case handling. Action research therefore provides a broader basis for the evaluations of different policy options.

Some interview projects have measured respondents attitudes towards *hypothetical legal problems* presented to them. Such studies produce limited information about their respondents' actual legal needs, since it is difficult to tell how frequently the hypothetical situations actually occur.

As mentioned, some studies only ask if the respondent has experienced *situations* where legal problems frequently occur. They ask whether the respondent has experienced divorce, bought a house, had a traffic accident, etc. (Curran, 1977; Cantril, 1996). However, none of these studies can guarantee to cover all situations with a high occurrence of legal problems. They consciously ignore all situations where they consider legal problems are less likely to occur. If we consider that legal problems are likely to occur in a range of situations not identified in these studies most of the legal needs might still go unnoticed.

Finally, research that limits its mapping to check-lists of stipulated problems obviously will not systematically register problems that fall *outside* the list. However, under-reporting is a risk even in projects combining check-lists with open questions about legal needs. Problems relevant to external needs criteria might fall outside the respondents' understanding and remain undetected by the interviewer.

I have examined the academic viability of legal needs studies above because I think they are indispensable in developing a proper understanding of how the legal services system—legal aid included—actually covers the legal problems that people experience. I will now develop this argument by presenting a general framework for legal services and legal aid research that might help generate knowledge about legal services in a systematic fashion. Besides clarifying the usefulness of legal needs studies, a systematic approach might help develop empirical findings into more general assumptions or theories about the role of legal services and legal aid.

A Systematic Approach to Legal Needs Research

Western societies use the market as the main mechanism for distributing legal services.[7] Markets function mainly according to the economic principles of supply and demand. Legal aid policy attempts to modify the market mechanism with the aim of making legal services available to the poorer part of the population (Abel, 1985).

Legal aid policies which modify the market differ significantly between societies. In the *judicare* system the public buy services from the private profession to assist the poor. In a *salaried* legal aid system the public puts up separate service systems that deliver either free or affordable services to the poor. The dominance of the market in legal services also means that market mechanisms heavily influence the operation of both judicare and salaried legal aid.

However, Western societies usually provide a legal counsellor, either free or at a greatly reduced cost, in serious criminal and other types of cases where there is a risk of loss of liberty. Such legal aid regulations eliminate the direct effects of supply and demand on the use of legal expertise in criminal cases. Nevertheless, market mechanisms have many indirect effects.

A model of the social processing of legal problems

It is important to understand and analyse the need for legal services and legal aid in a broad social context because legal problems and legal needs are not static phenomena. They arise, exist and disappear. We should therefore study them as elements in continually developing processes. This perspective is developed in Figure 9.2.

1. Problem generating factors Figure 9.2 assumes that legal problems result from major social processes. We might label them *problem generating factors*. Examples of these factors are industrialisation, urbanisation, structural reorganisation of trade and industry, environmentalism, racism, and changing gender roles. Within these categories three aspects are important.

First, the *dynamics* of social change are important factors in generating legal

[7] See Abel and Lewis (1988–9) for extensive documentation.

Figure 9.2: Legal Problem Processes

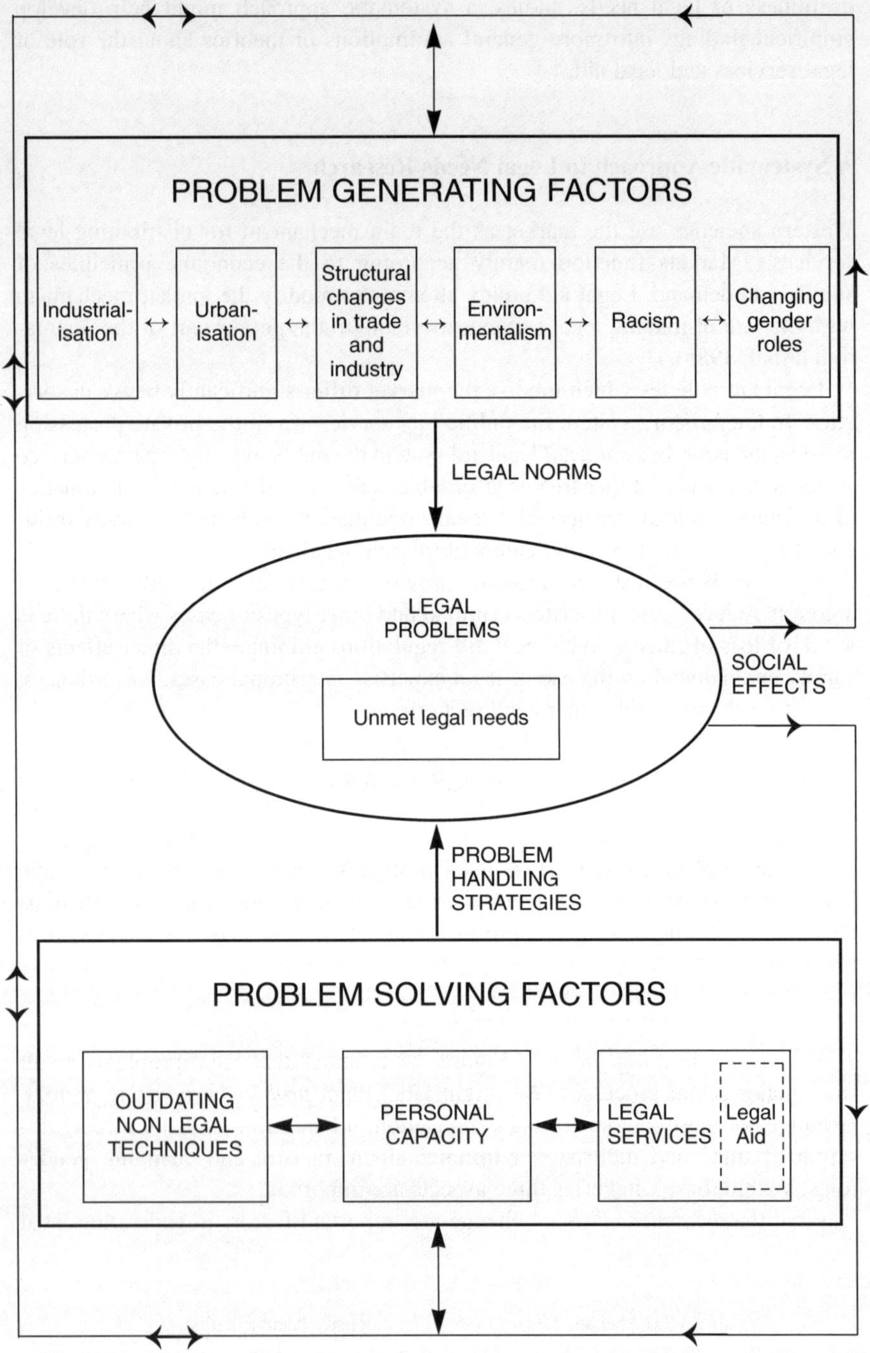

problems. For example: when agricultural families are transformed from a rural barter economy to one of urban wage-earners and market-oriented consumerism, the structure of their legal problems also changes, both in numbers and in content. When the main aim of the household's production is to satisfy its own needs, and the exchange of goods and services take place informally within the local community, law has a limited influence on people's everyday life. However, when production for the market becomes the main goal the meaning of law changes drastically. Market transactions become essential to people's welfare. They also must sell their products on the market, and satisfy their consumer needs from these sales. For all transactions, they must comply with complicated legal regulations. If they lose their earning capacity, they must depend on private or public pensions and welfare schemes governed by complex legal rules rather than being able to draw on informal care and support.

Society's attempt at *governing* or at least *influencing* such processes therefore becomes essential. Political institutions use the legal system as an important vehicle for handling social change. They issue a flow of provisions, containing market regulations, welfare reforms, property regulations, industrial statutes, and educational programmes. Politicians also change bureaucratic and legal institutions and their powers to adapt to change. The structure and development of legal norms and legal institutions therefore contribute significantly to the production of legal problems.

Finally, individuals adapt to social and legal changes in many ways. These strategies also influence the production of legal problems since some adoption strategies produce more legal problems than others. When, for example, craftsmen or small farmers face new regulations about book-keeping, they might just neglect the instructions, decide to cope with them on their own or hire an accountant to handle the book-keeping material. The choice will probably significantly influence both the resulting number of legal problems and their legal content.

2. Problem solving factors As Griffiths (1980) has demonstrated, resort to legal services is only one way of handling legal problems. We can distinguish between three major types of *problem solving factors* as shown in Figure 9.2.

First, people handle numerous legal problems on their own. They buy and complain about consumer goods, transfer property, divorce and negotiate building licences without expert assistance. Sometimes they would have been better off if they had used external assistance but they achieve acceptable results in numerous cases. *People's own capacity* to solve legal problems is obviously therefore an important problem solving factor. As mentioned above, we might argue about identifying as legal needs difficult problems handled alone without legal assistance. Leaving aside this issue, people's own problem solving capacity constitutes one of the determining factors for identifying the amount of *unmet legal needs* in society.

The structure of the *legal services system* determines the amount and type of legal problems it solves. Which institutions legitimately belong to the 'legal services system' is a matter for debate. Strictly speaking, we might limit it to lawyers and public institutions with legally trained staff who deliver legal services as their main task. However, we might also include all institutions and persons that actually contribute to legal problem solving, like consumer offices, citizens advice bureaux, public administration, professionals including doctors, priests, architects, accountants and economists, as well as interest organisations, local community leaders, neighbours, friends and family. The effectiveness of the legal services system constitutes a second major factor in the amount of unmet legal need in society.

Legal problems can also disappear or be transformed into other types of problems without active attempts at legal problem solving. The passage of time makes some claims obsolete. For example, an application for continuing medical benefit becomes irrelevant if the claimant dies. We can label such processes as *outdating factors*. They obviously also influence the amount of unmet legal need.

Finally, it is important to distinguish between individual strategies that influence the *problem-generating process*, and problem solving techniques that presuppose that a legal problem *has materialised*. Of course they are interrelated. Accountants might also help by solving legal problems that appear from incomplete book-keeping, and experience from such problem solving might lead the client to adopt a different strategy in the future. For example, small farmers might decide to hire accountants instead of neglecting the book-keeping regulations if they experience trouble with tax authorities. The major consideration behind a need for legal planning is the desire to avoid legal needs in the future by adopting the most appropriate strategy for prevention.

3. The model The model in Figure 9.2 combines these major elements. The upper part suggests factors that create legal problems, while the lower part shows major problem solving factors. These factors overlap to some extent. For example, urbanisation and changing gender roles interrelate. The effect of expert legal advice also depends on the client's capacity to understand and communicate his problems. We might sometimes find it difficult to distinguish between passivity as an informed strategy and passivity due to legal ignorance, which constitutes an outdating factor. However, research projects might refine such concepts when needed for empirical research.

The model suggests that legal questions arise in society due to a combination of complex social processes and society's attempts at influencing them through law and legal institutions. Legal questions become legal problems at the point where it requires *effort* for the problem holder to solve them, either by his or her own legal capacity or with assistance from the legal services. Unsolved legal problems constitute un-met legal needs until they become outdated legal problems. The un-met legal needs therefore appear as the *difference* between the effects of the problem creating and the problem solving factors.

Thc model has both a static and a dynamic interpretation. From a static perspective, it describes legal problems and un-met legal needs at a specific point in time. However, it also describes ongoing processes. Studying legal needs at a set point in time reveals an incomplete picture of the existing needs. It does not capture the legal needs' *turnover*. Some legal problems are quickly outdated within weeks or months, while others might last for years if the holder is unable to solve it. Studies of legal problems and un-met legal needs over time, therefore reveals the *dynamics* of the primary factors in the creation and resolution of legal problems. However, the existing studies have given limited emphasis to dynamic aspects.

Only a proportion of the legal problems existing in society result in un-met legal need. Numerous legal questions will be solved by problem holders, either alone or with help from the legal services system.

One of the consequences of legal problems and un-met legal needs is that they produce detrimental welfare effects. They influence the welfare of numerous groups in society, including the person with the problem, the problem holder's family and his or her local community. They also impact on the effectiveness of law as governing and dispute-resolving tools. Both legal problems and un-met legal needs act as barriers to the effectiveness of law as a means of achieving social goals.

The model assumes several *feedback* processes:

a. The social consequences of legal problems and unmet legal needs might impact on problem handling factors. New experiences with law and legal problems might lead individuals to adapt differently to the law in the future and to change their methods for handling legal problems. The legal services system might also change its operation due to feedback that suggests that available resources might be more effectively prioritised. If problem holders perceive the legal services system as ill equipped to handle problems, more of these problems might be channelled into other types of services.
b. The social impact of legal needs might also feed back upon society's attempts to govern problem creating factors. If a legal regime produces huge un-met legal needs with detrimental welfare effects, governing bodies might find it appropriate to change the law to reduce problems. For example, in some countries, as divorce rates increased administrative schemes and 'do-it-yourself' packages replaced obligatory lawyer-assisted, court-based responses.
c. Legal needs do not always mediate between problem generation and problem handling. Processes may be scrutinised by both individuals and the legal services system resulting in the development of preventative measures to address anticipated legal problems. Alternatively, when society either enacts new law and regulations or changes and renews legal institutions, the governing bodies might also anticipate the resulting legal needs and try to shape changes in a way that minimise them.

d. The model also allows for feedback processes between the different problem generating factors themselves. As I explained above, structural change, industrialisation and urbanisation are interdependent processes. Similarly, problem handling processes are also interrelated. If people's own problem solving capacity increases, their need for legal services diminishes. On the other hand, if we improve legal services, problems which would otherwise have been either solved by individuals or become outdated may be identified as 'legal problems'.

Whether the empirical assumptions that I derive from the model actually exist, and to what degree, are matters for research. Vital parts of the model are still poorly researched and understood. Most research on problem handling factors focuses on the structure and operation of the legal services system and on legal services to the poor. Research has paid less attention to people's own capacity to handle legal problems and the effects of outdating factors. Neither have the welfare consequences and distributive effects of legal problems and un-met legal needs received enough attention. Studies of problem creating factors seem to concentrate on the occurrence and structure of the legal problems and needs, less on the social and political dynamics that form the problem creating processes. Research has also largely ignored the different feedback processes.

By studying legal need from a process perspective, we might develop a better understanding of its dynamics. Legal problems and legal needs appear and disappear in a continuous stream. Studies at a set point in time will reveal only an incomplete picture of the process. A range of complex factors generates legal problems and the problem solving process is also complex. We might influence poor people's handling of legal problems in several ways. These dynamics also form patterns of action that might be of value in a reform perspective. Legal aid appears as just one of many strategies for reducing legal needs for poor people.

We might also attempt to improve their own problem solving capacity; for example through better information, education, and organising or improving support systems. We might also target problem creation, by adjusting regulations and bureaucratic practices or by teaching individuals and groups better prevention strategies.

Demand for legal services and legal aid

I have suggested that the demand for legal services will differ from the un-met needs. Whether an unsolved problem leads to demand depends mainly on the problem holders' evaluation of the problem and his or her attitudes towards seeking help. Two major factors that I call *strain-off factors* determine which needs actually result in demand.

First, we might ask to what extent people themselves perceive problems as legal and begin considering whether to seek legal assistance. Do they diagnose the legal aspects of their problems, and to what extent? When a tenant receives notice of an unforeseen rent increase, for example, she might experience it as a pure economic problem or she might start to wonder whether the landlord has a legitimate legal claim. We might label this as a *legal diagnosis* strain-off factor.

Secondly, when people experience a legal problem according to internal criteria, they must somehow decide whether to use legal services. If they try to make rational choices, they must weigh possible positive welfare consequences of seeking legal assistance against negative ones. That is, they make a *legal services calculation*. These mechanisms are added to the model in Figure 9.3.

Figure 9.3: Strain-Off Mechanisms

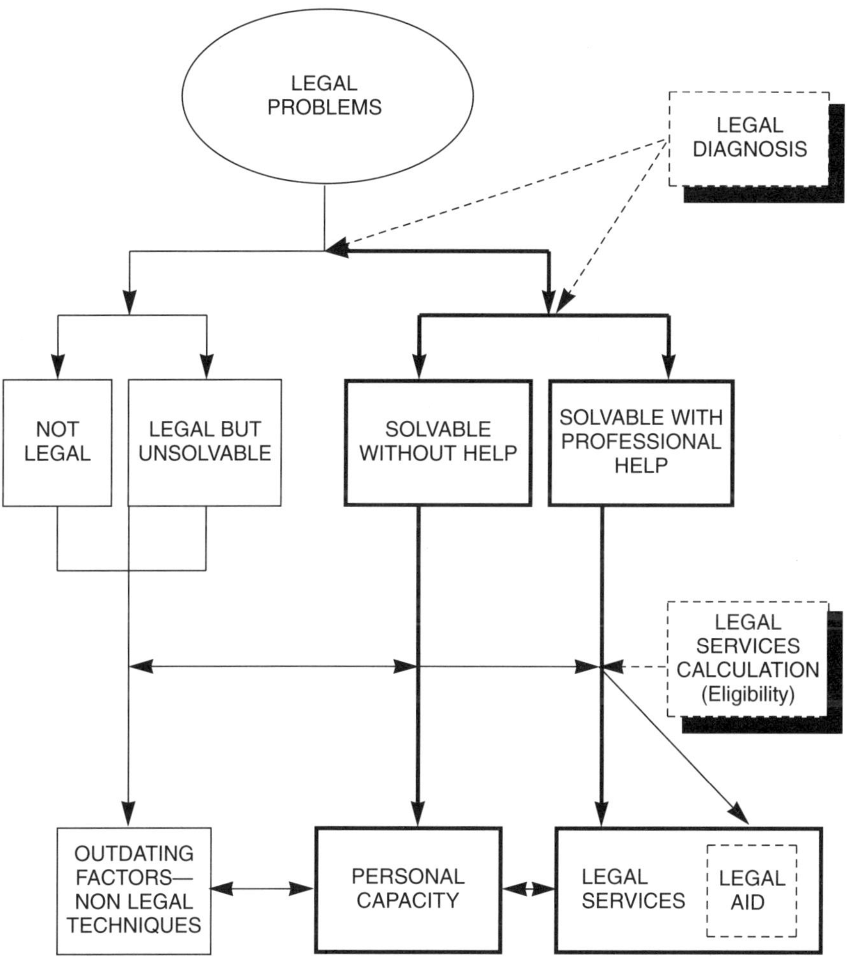

1. Legal diagnosis First I examine the strain-off effects of the legal diagnosis. It is important to distinguish between internal and external definitions of legal needs. In order to become a legal problem the person with the problem must recognise its potential legal nature. People's capability to make a reliable assessment of their own legal problems therefore impacts on their demand for legal services and legal aid.

We can divide the required diagnostic skills into two major components. To what extent

a. do people perceive their problems as having legal aspects? and
b. are they aware of existing legal services institutions and legal aid schemes?

However, problems that are legal according to an external definition may not appear as such to problem holders themselves. It is reasonable to assume that professionals will label many problems as 'legal' that the individuals themselves do not perceive as such due to lack of legal competence or differences in the definition of legal problems. It is then unlikely that they will consider handling them by legal means. For example, if people are unaware of the complaint procedures against administrative decision-making, they might regard a refusal of an application as an unjust fact of life, not as a problem that might have a legal remedy.

Of the problems perceived as legal, we must assume that problem holders will regard many as 'unsolvable'. Such a diagnosis seems adequate if they cannot gain any welfare improvements from applying legal insights. However, the problem holder might also misjudge both the legal prospects and the legal services available. Problems that would have profited from legal strategies might become labelled as legally unsolvable, due to insufficient legal diagnosis. 'Not legal' and 'unsolvable' problems will become subject to outdating factors and might disappear over time. The problem holder might also resort to non-legal problem solving techniques.

We might expect problem holders to separate solvable problems into two categories: those solvable with legal assistance and those solvable by the problem holder alone. Of course, problem holders might misjudge their legal service diagnosis as well. They might misjudge both their own problem solving capacity and the complexity of the problem. They might also regard problems as 'solvable' without sufficient reason. Misjudging might lead to strategies that ultimately fail and produce losses or unwarranted claims for legal services.

If legal needs research only maps those problems that people themselves diagnose as legal, it will overlook all the problems that people would label legal if they had access to an expert opinion. Similarly, there are problems which respondents label as legal, but which would have been labelled non-legal had they had such access. The less legally educated the respondents, the greater the risk of such misconceptions. The danger of misjudging therefore appears highest for the poor.

2. Legal services calculations Problems that appear solvable according to a legal diagnosis also undergo further evaluation. Rational problem holders will try to predict the consequences of taking legal action. The problem holder might record both positive and negative possible welfare effects. We cannot expect them to put effort into solving problems or seeking legal assistance unless their calculations show that the advantages of taking some sort of action outweigh the disadvantages. An evaluation of positive and negative factors that include welfare gains and losses will take place. I do not pretend to identify an exhaustive list of possible factors in a legal services calculation, but rather point to some main examples:

Welfare losses are expenses of various kinds, such as lawyer fees, documentation expenditures, loss of income, travel costs and costs to the opposing party. Lost time is also common. Legal problem solving consumes time whether it is assisted or not. The problem holder must consider the questions, strategies and argumentation thoroughly and often include arguments with an opposing party. If assisted, they must spend time on counselling sessions with the counsellor.

Handling legal problems also means stress. Uncertainty, both about the outcome and about the process itself, are common. Being involved in legal quarrels compromises self-image for many people. A social stigma is often attached to legal problems and the problem holder might risk social or economic sanctions from the opposing party. Resorting to law might escalate conflicts, and non-legal opportunities for problem solving might be lost.

Welfare gains include improvements of all sorts. They might result from new acquisitions and from the prevention of losses, for example, by successfully defeating a claim for compensation. Economic gains will often appear as a major motive for taking legal action. However, cases about child custody, libel and items dealing with sentimental and emotional issues will also bear on other welfare values. Welfare gains might also result from legal planning. To construct a building will result in some costs in the short run, but over time become important to the welfare benefactors. Although legal counselling might not lead to specific gains or losses, eliminating uncertainty may in itself be a significant relief. Legal action might also offer the opportunity to sanction an opposing party.

People will carry out their calculations according to the individual characteristics of the problem in question and with a varying number of legal services institutions in mind. We might expect them to consider each institution separately. The local lawyer, an advice bureau, a consumer office: all will impact differently on the calculation (Mayhew and Reiss, 1966:309–18; Mayhew, 1975:401–6). They will make a calculation using the understanding and information they actually possess about the legal structure and complexity of the problem in question, their own capacity to solve it and the character and availability of legal services. If their understanding is inadequate, miscalculations and misconceptions will occur. We might experience demand for help in hopeless or irrelevant cases and lack of demand in relevant and important cases. Of course, considerable uncertainty is likely to be attached to evaluation of the different factors in the calculation.

Strain-off factors therefore influence demand. Problem holders' legal diagnoses determine whether they will become aware of a legal problem at all. If not, we cannot expect demand for legal services to occur. We might regard them as a *potential* demand for legal services that might surface if the problem holder's perception of them changes. Their legal services calculation might lead problem holders to conclude that they will not profit from legal services even when needs exist. Such problems might also become channelled into other types of problem solving or end up as 'unsolvable' problems. Only when the problem holder diagnoses the problem as legal, and thinks the use of legal services profitable, can we expect demand for legal services to occur.

Legal aid will also influence the legal services calculation. If a problem holder qualifies for legal aid, this might alter the cost incentive significantly. Also the calculation of the legal aid eligibility must be made from the problem holders actual understanding of the coverage of the schemes. If knowledge is poor, miscalculations will occur. However, if problem holders find it worthwhile to consult an advice service, such misconceptions are likely to be corrected.

It is important to recognise strain-off factors in legal aid research. If we use actual demand to register legal needs, we will miss all problems that are not brought to the legal service system. People only channel a very limited number of the legal problems they experience to legal services. We also build a very incomplete picture if we rely wholly on the problems that appear legal according to the problem holders' internal criteria, as several legal needs studies have done. In addition we might expect internal criteria to vary significantly between problem holders. We register their perception of legal problems instead of the problems that would profit from legal expertise.

Supply of legal services and legal aid

According to market theory, demand and supply have different elasticity. If supply is elastic it will adapt to demand; if it is inelastic demand must adapt. But what factors influence the supply of legal services? My two previous models describe mechanisms that determine demand. Supply will depend on the structure and capacity of the legal services system. Figure 9.4 identifies several factors that are important in determining the elasticity of the system.

Figure 9.4 suggests that the number of legal experts in a society influence the capacity of the legal services system. This number depends on the turnover in the legal profession and is strongly influenced by the output of legal education. Several factors determine this figure including the general demand for higher education, the number and capacity of law schools, and competition from other professions.

Although law schools constitute a main input factor for the amount of legal expertise in society, they are not the only one. As the model suggests, there are other ways to gain legal expertise, although it is usually more specialised and limited. Other professionals might gain limited legal expertise as part of their training. Doctors learn about the social insurance and medical benefits system,

Figure 9.4: Factors Influencing the Capacity of Legal Services and Legal Aid

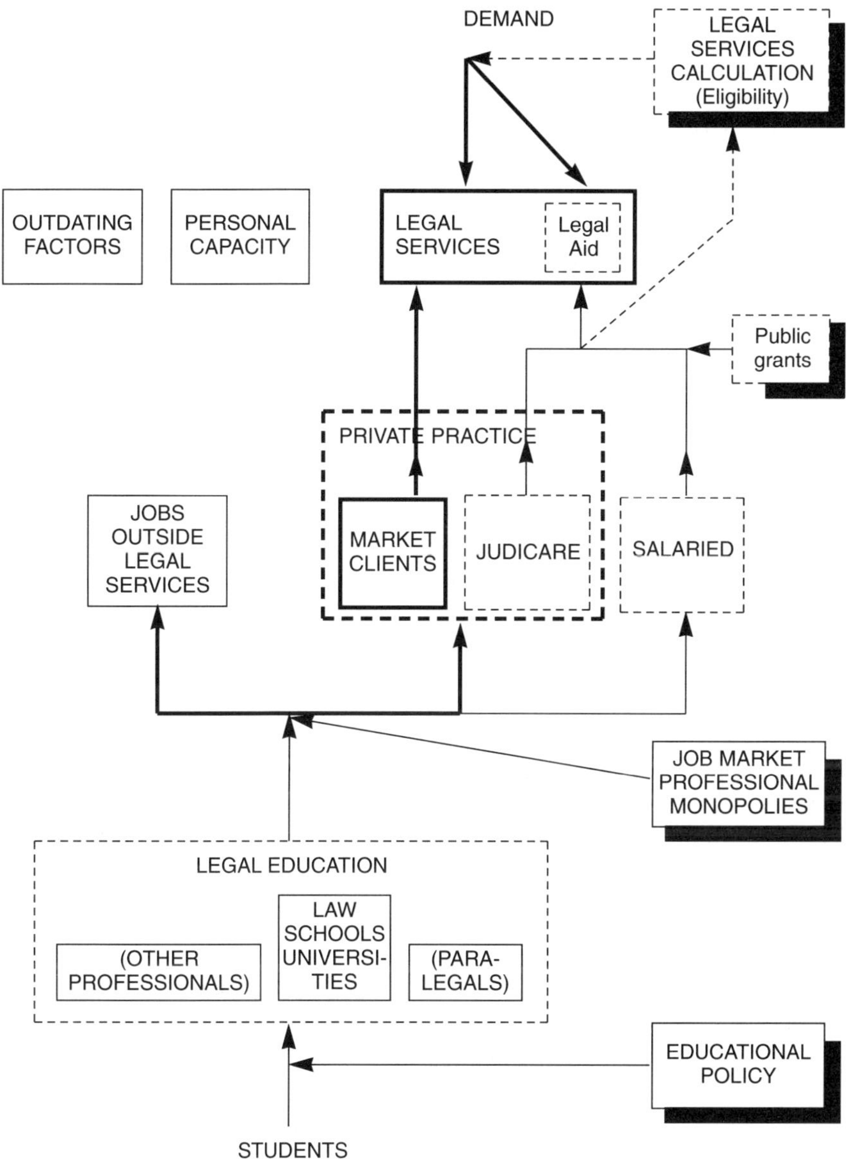

socialworkers about social benefits, accountants about accounting regulations and tax law, estate agents about property transfer regulations, and architects about zoning laws. On-the-job training also qualifies for legal advice services. Several countries have separate education for paralegals. However, monopoly regulations that favour university trained lawyers are likely to hamper the development of alternative legal services institutions (see Abel and Lewis (1988–89) for extensive documentation and discussion of lawyer monopolies in different jurisdictions).

Not all legal experts service the public as legal advisers. In many countries, business, interest organisations and public administrators employ jurists or lawyers. Some also work in the courts or in police and prosecution agencies, and some find non-legal jobs. The structure of the labour market for legally trained professionals therefore influences the capacity of the legal services system. As I mentioned above, monopoly regulations might restrict supply from non-legal professions and from jurists with the same training (Johnsen, 1994:331).

The market mechanism obviously impacts on the distribution of lawyers between legal services and other jobs. The job with the best income prospects will attract most recruits. However, increased numbers entering the profession might decrease income, making alternatives more attractive. Private practice generally pays better than salaried jobs in most countries. Particularly experienced and skilled lawyers will earn more in private practice than in salaried jobs.

The main factors that determine the capacity of the supply of legal services appear inflexible to shift in demands, at least in the short term. The professional monopolies, formal or informal, that exist in most countries also result in a permanent state of supply deficit, especially to the economically weak. For poor people who depend on legal aid, additional barriers exist.

Judicare schemes usually pay less than the market price, some much less. Those commissions generally appear less economically attractive to private practitioners than market clients. The supply of judicare therefore largely depends on their capacity after they have met the demand from paying clients. Of course, the supply also depends on the grants governments are willing to allocate to legal aid. Traditionally, judicare schemes are open in the sense that no limit exists on the number of certificates that the legal aid authorities will issue. The fee level and the eligibility criteria are the main vehicles to control lawyer use and thereby costs (Johnsen, 1994:324–35). The recent development of contracting means new ways for governments to influence the capacity and quality of legal aid schemes.

Salaried legal aid offices compete for lawyers with other legal jobs outside and within private practice. Both the wages paid by other employers and the earning prospects of becoming a self-employed lawyer will impact significantly on the wage level and grants necessary to hire a sufficient amount of qualified staff. For lawyers in salaried offices, the comparison with the income level in private practice is especially related, since few obstacles exist to crossing over. Like judicare, the capacity of salaried legal aid depends on government's willingness to pay. Charity might also contribute.

The model assumes that the supply of legal services impacts on people's legal services calculations. It seems meaningless to ask for legal services if no offer exists. This observation also has implications for legal aid. If access is limited and the service poor, problem holders might decide not to use them even when they think they qualify. Demand tends to conform to supply.

It is not plausible that the existing legal needs among the poor are a major factor in shaping legal services or legal aid. The market mechanisms point at the *balance* between lawyers' capacity and paid commissions as the major determining factor for the supply of legal aid. But it is difficult to envisage the legal needs of the poor influencing this balance.

Therefore, we cannot interpret the needs either from demand or from supply. If we try, we might conceal the need that is present and miss the opportunity to map the mechanism that actually determines how poor people handle their legal problems and important prospects for improvements.[8]

Legal needs research and legal aid policy

I have outlined an empirical approach to legal needs research and discussed some of the methodology challenges for such research. I have criticised previous studies and tried to show that we can improve legal needs research. My discussion has already implied several substantiating arguments for conducting legal needs research according to the principles I have proposed. We might add others as well.

Like Zemans (1983) I think that access to legal services is linked to fundamental ideas of justice and political participation in democratic societies. However, the meaning of legal aid as a means for political emancipation for poor people is controversial. Only within criminal legal aid has a broad consensus on minimum standards developed. Civil legal aid appears vulnerable to shifts in both the economy and political ideology. The schemes become unreliable both as problem solving tools for the poor and as alternative employment fields for lawyers.

We know that the resources available to legal aid are limited and that budgets are presently being reduced in many jurisdictions. Many schemes face severe cuts and some termination. All informed people know that the needs are vast and the existing supply highly insufficient. Does it make sense to study and document needs if it appears obvious that they cannot be met?

Judicare schemes use a major share of their resources on criminal aid and

[8] Zemans presents a model of legal mobilisation that includes many of the mechanisms described in my model (1982:1001). Her thorough and extensive article analyses many of the factors that I have pointed out as important. However, her mobilisation perspective means a focus on barriers to individuals' use of the law, while I place more emphasis on the different social mechanisms and services that society might activate to solve more legal problems. While space does not allow for an extensive comparison, I recommend her article.

family and matrimonial matters. Most legal need studies show that those problems only constitute a limited share of the un-met needs. Housing, debts, social benefits, compensation and consumer matters seldom receive comparable attention. In terms of effectiveness, to get the most out of each legal aid dollar spent, the prioritising of cases and problem areas often seems irrational.

In times of decline it seems as sensible as ever to steer legal aid towards problems that produce the highest welfare gains. Although research cannot decide the underlying value questions about what sort of needs to cover and to what extent, most politicians emphasise effective use of resources when they have made their choices. They want as much legal aid or welfare gains as possible for the money spent.

Such rationality presupposes an intimate understanding of the existing needs. Without thorough legal needs research, it becomes difficult to make rational priority decisions about how to structure legal aid within a set resource limit. For proponents of improved legal aid, documenting weaknesses in the existing system by pointing to serious un-met needs seems imperative.

Research that points to demand or actual use as the benchmark for organising and prioritising legal aid might mask important needs and legitimise insufficient systems and unfair allocations of the services available. Convincing legal needs research might alter the politicians' perception of the needs and the dynamics of the existing legal aid system. If we apply a systematic perspective, we might also identify alternative ways of covering legal needs that do not prioritise legal aid for individuals. We might, for example, gain more from allocating more resources to such strategies as advice centres, legal eduction campaigns, improved public legal education and law reform work.

10

Quality Legal Services: The Dog That Did Not Bark

ALAN PATERSON AND AVROM SHERR

Introit

One of the most striking developments in the international arena of legal services in the past decade relates to the quality of work done by legal aid lawyers and how this has become a topic of central concern. It is a curious phenomenon, not simply because the concern for quality has been such a latecomer to the legal services arena, nor again because its global manifestation has varied so widely between jurisdictions with similarly developed legal aid programmes, but also because for much of the time the enthusiasm for the quality pursuit has come from without the profession. This Chapter examines the meaning of quality, the measures which have emerged as proxies for quality and how these measures have been operationalised. It then details the global experience of the quality concern among the countries with the most developed legal aid programmes, before turning to examine why quality of service is currently more of an issue in some jurisdictions than in others.

Quality: the background

Until comparatively recently in the legal services sector, 'quality' as a concept was understood in its traditional meaning of superiority or excellence (Sherr *et al.*, 1994). However, in the last ten years or so this meaning has been challenged by developments derived from the manufacturing industry. The first perceived quality to mean 'fitness for the purpose', i.e. the extent to which the service attains a set standard. The second, and more recent, trend stems from Total Quality Management and views quality as the extent to which the supplier has met the client's needs (Peters and Waterman, 1982). This in turn has led to a consumerist approach which unashamedly places the clients in the active role of rejecting services which are of unacceptable quality to them (Greene, 1989; Pfeffer and Coote, 1991). On any of these last approaches, quality must be viewed within the specific context of the legal services being evaluated. Thus, if we were to think in terms of a continuum of performance by a lawyer between the atrocious and the excellent (Figure 10.1) a quality service could fall almost anywhere between threshold competence and excellence (Sherr *et al.*, 1994:19).

As Garth (1983:669) observed, the challenge of resourcing poverty legal services confronts us with the impracticality of a uniform standard of competence or quality of performance throughout every sector of professional activity. Whatever the state's original intent in funding poverty legal services in the 1950s, it must be doubtful whether the state now expects that in funding legal aid they are entitled to receive a quality of performance from legal aid lawyers at the excellence end of the continuum—though corporate clients will expect just that from elite law firms. Indeed, today's resource pressures entail a substantial risk that either the funders or the suppliers of poverty legal services will be tempted by economic incentives only to fund or deliver services below threshold competence—what are known in the United Kingdom as 'inadequate professional services' (Sherr *et al.*,1994:19).

If reaching a consensus as to the meaning of 'quality' seems a chimera, it might be anticipated that measuring it would prove no easier, and so it has transpired. Indeed it would not be far short of the mark to state that the search for cheap, simple and easy ways of operationalising proxies for quality has become the postmodernist equivalent of the philosopher's stone for today's professional managers. Quality evaluation work in the medical and legal worlds of professional practice has tended to focus on four main measures or proxies for quality: *Inputs, Structures, Process and Outcomes*. A well rounded quality evaluation will draw on several of these together (Sherr *et al.*, 1994). *Input* measures have the attraction of being relatively easy to collect. Inevitably, being indirect measures of quality at best, they also generally have the least to offer. Typical examples in the medical world are staffing levels and staff costs—in the legal world examples have included educational attainment, professional qualifications, membership of accredited specialist panels, continuing professional development seminars attended, work experience and status in the legal community. *Structural* measures concentrate on the environment in which performance takes place. They range

EXCELLENCE

COMPETENCE PLUS

THRESHOLD COMPETENCE

INADEQUATE PROFESSIONAL SERVICES

NON-PERFORMANCE

Figure 10.1: The Performance Continuum

from resourcing levels to record-keeping procedures, and from staff development policies to complaints procedures. As will be seen, these are just the kinds of quality control and assurance measures which are finding favour with today's professional managers, e.g. the *English Practice Management Standards* (Law Society, 1993) or aspects of international quality assurance programmes such as ISO 9000 or Investors in People. However, structural measures, while assisting efficient practice management, only facilitate quality of performance in other aspects of professional practice—they do not ensure it.

Process measures focus more directly on the behaviour of professionals, examining the efficiency with which the work is done and its compliance with check-lists or standards of performance. They have had the greatest provenance in the medical world, where it is estimated that by the late 1980s several thousand input or process performance indicators were in operation in the British National Health Service (Performance Indicator Group, 1987).[1] There are rather fewer process measures for lawyers though file audit against set checklists is becoming established. It is, for example used by the English Legal Aid Board, who have published detailed checklists, known as transaction criteria (see below).

Outcome measures have also had a greater provenance in educational and medical spheres than in the legal world. In the first there are e.g. the nationally published league tables of pupil examination performances at schools in the UK, or of Oxford University undergraduates' final degree results (the 'Norrington table').[2] Equally, avoidable deaths, morbidity rates, re-infection and re-admission rates, and survival-recurrence rates are everyday fare for today's hospital administrators. Legal equivalents have been slow to arrive and those that have emerged have provoked controversy in the profession. Part of the problem is that examination of outcomes in individual cases is a very different matter from collecting evidence on a lawyer or law firm's outcomes over a substantial number of cases. The first, in the shape of peer review, is understood by lawyers, but very expensive to implement on a wide scale. The second requires a statistical approach which considers general patterns in aggregate case results. While the data is cheaper to collect than by peer review, it assumes that the factors which influence the outcome of an individual case are too complex to be captured by a handful of performance indicators. To this extent, the approach accepts the lawyers' argument that each case is unique. However, the statistical approach is predicated on the assumption that by controlling for all the other key factors which will influence the outcome of a series of cases, if a sufficient sample is taken, systematic

[1] A number of these are contained in the hospital performance league tables which began to be published in 1994, e.g. the percentage of patients seen within 30 minutes of their appointment time, the percentage of accident and emergency patients assessed within 5 minutes of arrival or the response times for ambulance crews to emergency calls. Other similar measures include length of bed stay, and throughput per bed (the 'hot-bed rate').

[2] Critics, of course, have pointed to the fact that such tables are inadequate measures of the absolute quality of educational institutions since they fail to measure the 'added value' imparted by educational institutions to students of lesser ability.

variations in outcomes from a normal distribution of results must be due to differences in the quality of the lawyering. It follows that outcome measures require large sample sizes—which, except for a handful of firms with substantial case-loads, renders their use in the case of many individual firms problematic (Goriely, 1997a). Initial work for the English Legal Aid Board identified four sets of possible outcome measures (Moorhead, Sherr and Paterson, 1994):

Average case cost appears straightforward, and has been utilised by legal aid administrators around the globe. The reality is more complex. Is it the cost to state funds that is the relevant figure, or the rate of return judged by amount gained for every pound or dollar invested? If the former, presumably it is not gross cost which is relevant, but costs net of client contribution (including the clawback from winnings, if any). Furthermore, a low average figure is not necessarily a good sign. Equally, though there may be a link between efficiency and cost, higher than average costs in a firm may be due to non-comparable factors e.g. different case-loads or a greater concentration of more complex cases e.g. in the medical negligence field.

Time taken at first sight also appears to be a useful performance measure. The measure is predicated on the assumption that, if other factors can be held constant, firms or providers of services which consistently take longer than others to handle similar case-loads at otherwise similar standards of quality are providing a poorer service. This should hold as true for the time taken to reach a trial or settlement date as for hospital waiting lists. Yet speed is not in the interests of every litigant—skeleton defences can buy valuable time, a delayed guilty plea may ensure weeks of freedom on bail for an accused who knows that ultimately incarceration is the likely outcome. One side's delay may be the other's duration. Moreover, delays in hearings are likely to vary between court districts due to the operation of 'local legal cultures' (Church, 1978). It is therefore necessary to distinguish between the time actually spent by lawyers in relation to a case and the elapsed time from the date when the prosecution began.

Results or success rates are commonplace performance indicators in the medical world, e.g. mortality rates, re-admission rates, long-term survival or recurrence rates. Even here the indicators will frequently require interpretation. For the legal realm the problems of defining 'success' are considerably greater. Excluding medical negligence cases, the overwhelming majority of personal injury cases result in some sort of settlement. It would be unwise, however, to equate the mere fact of settlement with a quality service. In divorce cases, is the lawyer who extracts the maximum settlement for his or her client at the cost of bitterness and rancour between the parties which affect the children necessarily delivering a higher quality service than the lawyer who settles for less but smooths the way to an amicable parting? Alternatively, in a criminal case it is not intuitively obvious that a lawyer who gains a community service order for his or client is doing a better job than one who obtains probation or even a modest fine. There is, moreover, a rather different approach to result, namely **impact**. Here the emphasis is utilitarian, and highlights outcomes achieved for whole communities through law reform, community development, community legal education, test cases and mass actions. For its proponents, the impact approach provides a better quality of outcome than individual casework since it is more 'fit for the purpose' and 'meets the needs' of clients better. This, however, involves political judgements as to the true purpose of legal aid or the real needs of the public, which are inevitably controversial.

Finally, there is **client satisfaction**. Rooted in the consumerist approach to quality, this measure relies on clients' perceptions of the quality of service that they have received. However, it has long been recognised in the service quality field that what the client perceives may differ from the view of the specialist. Some key factors e.g. the proper price for the job, the length of time which it should take, and what should constitute an acceptable outcome, are matters on which clients—especially first-time or 'one-shot' clients—are peculiarly dependent on the advice of professionals.[3] It follows that client satisfaction surveys which tap into aspects of client care are valuable and have a role to play in quality assessment. Where the surveys go on to look at results achieved, the ability of professionals to influence client perceptions through 'image management' (Rosenthal, 1974:109–12) renders them less useful as an objective measure of quality. As Goriely has observed (1997a) client satisfaction scores tend to produce relatively undifferentiated responses.

Methods of assessment

The quality measures outlined above can be operationalised in the case of lawyers in a variety of ways. **Self assessment** is an integral part of many quality assurance schemes,[4] but only as a starting point. Lawyers are as prone as other mortals to misperceptions as to how they do their work, or even something as apparently straightforward as the time spent on different activities in the working day (Sherr, 1990). **Peer assessment or review** is widely hailed as the best approach to assessing the quality of service provided by professionals. However, it should not be accepted uncritically. Peer review which consists of reputation in the legal community or surveys of professional opinion as to the performance of other lawyers is an unreliable approach to quality measurement. It may rely on nebulous or unarticulated criteria and lays the door open to bias or prejudice.[5] To operate effectively,

[3] In the eyes of several writers on professionalism, the difficulties confronting clients in assessing the quality of legal services afforded to them are but an illustration of the knowledge gap between professionals and laypersons (Johnson, 1972; Perkin, 1989).

[4] For example, the Teaching Quality Assessments of law schools in the United Kingdom in the 1990s have been based on self-assessment documents.

[5] This is precisely the criticism made by women and minority lawyers of certification of specialisation programmes for American lawyers which relied on the views of 'peers' who consisted of white, middle-class, ageing lawyers (Paterson, 1986:699).

peer review requires that the 'peers' use either observation or file-audit techniques. They must be drawn from appropriate sub-specialisms—medical negligence specialists are not good assessors of the work of high street personal injury lawyers with a steady diet of 'pavement-tripping' cases. They must also operate an agreed, and relatively detailed quality framework or set of standards, and receive training in the application of the framework or standards.[6] Since, inevitably, it is very expensive to operate peer review on a large scale it is best used in conjunction with other approaches. The third method is **objective assessment**. This includes a wide range of data-gathering techniques: input measures of lawyer educational attainment or experience in cases handled; check-lists of process standards; outcome measures and the use of '**dummy or model clients**'. The last approach enables the lawyers under scrutiny to be presented with the same 'client' whose case can be structured to contain salient points to test aspects of the lawyers' expertise. Although this technique has been used in tests with doctors in the Netherlands (Rethans *et al.*, 1991) and lawyers in the United States and the United Kingdom (Sherr *et al.*, 1994:10; *Which?*, 1995; *Which?*, 1997) its use is controversial, in part because of the ethical issues (e.g. deception) which can be associated with it.

Quality: the global experience

What then is the global experience of the quality pursuit? Does it represent a significant step forward in the enhancing Access to Justice—possibly even becoming an additional 'wave' to the three waves of Access to Justice identified by Cappelletti and Garth (1978) or is it merely a passing fad? To understand this it is necessary to look at each of the developed jurisdictions in turn.

The USA

The first jurisdiction where we find significant discussion and research in the quality of legal service provision in recent times is the United States. The quality concerns arose following the implementation of the rulings of the US Supreme Court in *Gideon* v. *Wainwright* 372 US 335 (1963) and *Argersinger* v. *Hamlin* 407 US 25 (1972) which established the constitutional right to counsel in criminal cases where there was a threat of imprisonment. This led to a gradual expansion of service provision to those unable to afford a lawyer. However, the fact that the right to counsel for indigent accuseds came from Court rulings and not from legislation meant that there was no federal agency in charge of providing indigent

[6] Peer review through the systematic specification of standards for practice in particular fields and the measurement of actual performances against these standards by peers has now become established in the USA amongst the medical profession, engineers and accountants in response to external pressure e.g. from the SEC or insurance carriers (ALI/ABA, 1988). In the United Kingdom it is used in the educational sphere—the HMI inspectors for schools and QAA assessors for universities.

defence. It was, and remains, a matter that is largely handled at either county or state level. Inevitably, there have been major resource problems in trying to implement the Court's rulings. The predominant programmes—assigned counsel (on a no-fee, low-fee basis) or salaried public defenders (staff model) have each come in for criticism—sometimes severe—on quality grounds (Goriely, 1996). However, it is contract schemes (where the lawyers have entered into a contract with the legal aid authorities, to deliver all or a set portion of the legal aid services in a particular geographic area) which appear to have received the most criticism on quality grounds. From the start of experiments in contracting out indigent defence services in the late 1970s severe misgivings have been voiced by the commentators on quality grounds. Research in Clark County, Washington found contract lawyers provided a poorer quality service than the public defender scheme they were replacing in terms of effort, a greater propensity to plead guilty early, and a reduced willingness to use investigators or expert witnesses (Lefstein, 1982). Three years later another study of contracts which had replaced assigned counsel schemes found that the contractors took less time per case, made fewer appearances, and in other ways provided a lower quality of service than the service they had replaced (Houlden and Balkin, 1985). Indeed, a whole range of studies of contracted services by the Spangenberg Group during the 1980s (Smith, 1993a; Goriely, 1996; Spangenberg and Beeman, 1995) found evidence of systematic underbidding (since contracts were almost universally awarded on the basis of price alone), low use of expert witnesses or investigators, case overload, and the widespread replacement of programmes with experienced attorneys by contracts serviced by recently qualified law graduates and marginally competent attorneys. In short, the commentators have been unanimous: whatever the theoretical merits of contracts for indigent services, their actual use has been repeatedly marked by a devaluation of quality (Singsen, 1991; Huxtable, 1993; Spangenberg and Spence, 1995; Goriely, 1996).

On the civil side, judicare or publicly funded legal aid delivery by the private profession has never been particularly widespread in the United States. Until the 1960s civil legal aid was broadly provided through the *pro bono* work of individual lawyers and through legal aid societies. The quality of service delivered by these means or through lawyers operating on a contingent fee basis seems not to have attracted particular attention. However, the establishment of the Office of Legal Services within the Office of Economic Opportunity in 1965 saw the advent of a radical, community legal services initiative with salaried staff the focus of which was predominantly collective rather than individual (Johnson, 1978; Huxtable, 1993:42; see Chapter 1, above). This work was taken over by the Legal Services Corporation in 1975 but under the presidencies of Reagan and Bush it came under sustained attack from the conservatives. From 1980 to the present date the attacks have continued unabated, severely reducing the efficacy of the programme and its funding and forcing it to become more focused on individual casework (see Chapters 1 and 2). As part of the struggle several major studies have been designed to compare the cost-effectiveness and quality of different legal services models. Perhaps inevitably in such a political context the findings have been hotly contested. The most comprehensive study was the first, The Delivery Systems Study (LSC, 1980). The study compared judicare and contract schemes involving private practitioners with staff attorney schemes on four criteria: cost, quality, client satisfaction and impact. All three models were found to be adequate in terms of quality as judged by peer review, although overall a mixed model of provision (i.e. combinations of staff and judicare or staff and contracts) was found to be the most successful in terms of all the criteria examined. The Delivery Systems Study was criticised for not comparing programmes in the same locality and failing to contrast like with like. As a consequence the Private Law Firm Project was set up in 1983 (Bergmark, 1994) to overcome this defect by comparing contracts with private practitioners with local staff programmes in five cities. Unfortunately the results of this project have never been properly reported and what has emerged has been savaged by the commentators. However, independent studies of two of the cities (Orange County and Jacksonville) revealed that the contract lawyers were unable to match the quality standards or (in Jacksonville's case) the outcomes achieved by the staff attorneys (Goriely, 1996; Pleasence, Maclean and Morley, 1996:99; Meeker, Dombrink and Quinn, 1991). The final study (in San Antonio) like that in Orange County focused on family cases randomly assigned between a staff model, a contract model and a voucher or judicare model of provision. It results have been bitterly contested and must be regarded as inconclusive at best (Goriely, 1996). As in San Antonio, the researchers sought to use client satisfaction questionnaires to test quality. The rates of return were so poor that nothing could be made of the data. In San Antonio a panel of three family specialist attorneys was used to review case files against a 'service deficiency scale' which was drawn up by, and designed for, specialists (Meeker *et al.*, 1991:623). Perhaps not surprisingly the panel rated none of the delivery models as better than average.[7] The experiment therefore failed to implement peer review in a sensible fashion and fell into the trap so clearly flagged up by Garth (1983) of judging the performance of legal services lawyers against the quality standards to be expected of specialists or corporate lawyers with fewer budgetary constraints.

This review shows that the quality of legal service delivery in the USA has become an issue for research and comment on the criminal side, due in part to inadequacies of funding, but in the main to the crude way in which local contracts for indigent representation have been allocated on price alone with no regard to quality. On the civil side it has been triggered, not by criticism as to the quality of service provided by staff attorneys employed by the Legal Services Corporation (LSC)—the quality monitoring of LSC programmes was largely

[7] In terms of the continuum of performance in Figure 10.1 this would presumably be 'competence plus' at best.

abandoned by the Reagan boards (Singsen, 1991)—but as a result of a politically motivated desire to replace the LSC programme by a contract model of provision (ibid. 58). However, as in the criminal sphere, quality concerns have emerged where contracts have been awarded predominantly on considerations of price.

The response of the administrative authorities to these quality concerns has been minimal. This is perhaps not surprising, since on the criminal side there is no federal authority with a remit to intervene. When quality was all too often sacrificed in favour of economy by a myriad local or state administrators,[8] they were united only by their shortage of funds, and not by a policy on adequate provision of service. On the civil side the LSC did introduce improved systems for supervision and training for staff lawyers (Tull, 1994) but the republican administration (and now Congress) favoured contracts, not from a desire to improve quality, but as a vehicle to attack the staff programmes. Only the courts could be said to have taken cognizance of the problem. First, in their willingness to strike down a range of contract programmes on quality and other grounds (Spangenberg and Beeman, 1995) and secondly, in their consideration of the test to be applied where an appeal is lodged by the accused on the grounds of the 'ineffective assistance of [defence] counsel'. Until 1984 the federal courts ruled that the standard to be proved before an appeal could be successful on this ground was that the performance of the defence counsel must have been so poor as to make the proceedings a 'farce and a mockery'. However, in the case of *Strickland* v. *Washington* 466 US 668 (1984) the Supreme Court ruled that for appeals to succeed on this ground in the future, it need only be shown that the performance of the defence counsel had not been reasonably competent. In practice, however, it is unclear how much of a liberalisation the change of wording has been.

The American Bar Association has undoubtedly been the most active player in relation to the quality of legal services in the USA. First, in tackling the issue of quality amongst defence attorneys, and those operating under contracts in particular, in its 1990 and 1992 formulations of its *Standards for Criminal Justice: Providing Defense Services*. These set out detailed lists of quality-assurance requirements, including provisions governing staff work-load, experience, qualifications, compensation levels, support services, infrastructure and facilities and procedures for handling ethical issues such as conflict of interest or confidentiality. Here the ABA was building on its own earlier work on Standards for the Defense Function and the work of specialist pressure groups in the profession. For example, the National Legal Aid and Defenders Association (NLADA) similarly sought to curb the threat to quality posed by contracts in its 1984 *Guidelines for Negotiating and Awarding Indigent Defense Contracts* (see Spangenberg and Beeman 1995; Tull 1994).

Secondly, on the civil side the ABA in 1986 adopted its *Standards for*

[8] By 1995 more than half of the States had organised some form of state-wide indigent defence programme (Spangenberg and Beeman, 1995).

Providers of Civil Legal Services to the Poor. Like the Transaction Criteria of the English Legal Aid Board of a later era, these set out the functions and activities which are deemed to be essential to the production of quality legal work in areas such as litigation, negotiation, advice and counsel (Tull, 1994). Thirdly, the ABA has been at the fore in defending the LSC and its staff programmes against the sustained Republican attack, and by insisting on the validity of comparative research between contract and staff models. These are worthy achievements and the Law Practice Management Section of the ABA has a long and honourable track record of articulating practice management issues for the whole profession. Yet it is difficult not to conclude that the ABA has ultimately found it no easier than its counterpart organisations in other jurisdictions to push proactively for ongoing quality assurance and quality-testing measures. From the heady days of the American Law Institute/American Bar Association (ALI/ABA) Model Peer Review System (1981) and the ALI/ABA Law Practice Quality Guidelines (1985) the reformers seem to have lost their way. Thus an ALI/ABA conference in 1987 on Law Practice Quality Evaluation was marked by doubt on the part of many of the attending lawyers that the quality-evaluation techniques applied in other professions could be applied to them. Moreover, unlike the UK notion of a threshold competence beneath which the practitioner is guilty of 'inadequate professional services', there has been a tendency for American statements of standards to become high-level, aspirational precepts. Yet, as Garth observed (1983), to go down the route of a uniformly high standard of competence risks pricing legal services out of the means of the poor or those on middle incomes. In short, the bulk of the profession has been hostile to having competence measures imposed on them and neither the federal authorities nor the ABA have been keen to take a lead. To quote Martyn: 'performance review involving outside regulation of law practices is an unworkable idea at present. In the absence of clear public outrage demanding official action, it is also unlikely to occur' (1989:227).

England and Wales

The avowed pursuit of quality is now so closely associated with the legal aid regime in England and Wales that observers would be forgiven for assuming that 'value for money' was the key element in the Legal Aid Board's Mission Statement. It was not always thus. In the first half of the century, when around the world legal aid was seen as a *pro bono*, charitable obligation of the profession, little interest was expressed in quality. Even the legal aid societies were despised for their entrepreneurialism and competitiveness, rather than any alleged incompetence. Indeed, quality did not come to the fore as an issue in relation to the provision of poverty legal services in England and Wales until a decade ago. This was all the more curious because there had been a series of research studies which suggested that there were quality issues bearing on the provision of legal aid services in England which required to be addressed (Baldwin and McConville, 1977; Bridges *et al.*, 1975;

Sanders *et al.*, 1989; McConville and Hodgson, 1993; McConville *et al.*, 1994). Only the last of these provoked a response from the legal aid authorities. Instead the expansion of the scope and coverage of legal aid was seen as the principal challenge for reformers. But even as the liberal critics were pushing for new and better forms of legal services (including the establishment of the first UK law centres) the civil servants were growing increasingly uneasy as the costs of the legal aid programme rose ever higher. At first they resorted to the easy tactics of refusing to expand the scope of legal aid, e.g. to cover tribunals, or failing to uprate eligibility limits for applicants or remuneration rates for lawyers, but in 1986 they resorted to the first real cuts in eligibility (Goriely and Paterson, 1996).

In the same year, the government determined that in future legal aid should produce the best possible value for money spent as result of the Scrutiny Report (Zander, 1988:67). The Efficiency Scrutiny Team, to give it its full name, consisted of four civil servants who in the space of four short months in 1986 produced a radical blueprint to transform the provision of legal services. The Team's proposals, which included contracts with non-solicitor agencies, such as the CABx, were ahead of their time and duly perished after a welter of criticism, not least from the grass-roots voluntary agencies. However, its influence lingered on through the legal aid White Paper of 1987, and in particular the recommendation that a quasi-autonomous Legal Aid Board should take over the administration of legal aid from the Law Society. The Board was charged with ensuring that civil legal aid was delivered at proper levels of quality,[9] and to explore whether contracts with advice agencies might supplant elements of the Green Form (legal advice and assistance) scheme.

These three elements (quality, value for money and contracts) were brought together at an early stage by the concept of franchising, which was floated by the Board in 1989. In essence, franchising was a scheme whereby legal aid firms would be given financial rewards in exchange for contracting to meet certain specified quality standards (LAB, 1993; LAB, 1994:34). Following a pilot project in Birmingham, franchising proper was launched in 1993 with the first franchise contracts awarded in 1994. Under the contracts, firms agreed to adhere to a set of Practice Management Standards (covering a personnel plan, a business plan, accounting systems, staff supervision, file-review procedures and a complaints procedure). Compliance with these standards was assessed in a pre-franchise audit. These *structural* measures of quality, modest though they were in terms of what was considered best practice in industry and commerce at the time, required many of the firms applying for franchises[10] to improve their business efficiency. Five years on, they are viewed by

[9] In July 1988 the Lord Chancellor wrote to the new Board indicating that its 'overall aim should be to ensure that legal advice, assistance and representation . . . should be provided in ways which are effective and give the best possible value for money'.

[10] Franchises were awarded in 9 different categories of work: family, crime, personal injury, housing, debt, employment, welfare benefits, consumer and immigration. Firms could apply for franchises in several categories.

franchise-holders as one of the most positive benefits of franchising. Franchising also requires compliance with *process* measures of quality—the Transaction Criteria. These were sets of steps which would be expected to be completed in different types of cases. The criteria were compiled by the researchers (Sherr, Moorhead and Paterson, 1994) from a study of client files, textbooks and practice manuals. The draft criteria were then sent to expert practitioners and other interest groups for comment and revision. The resulting 'check-lists' were therefore an amalgam of empirical work and expert knowledge and opinion. Compliance with the transaction criteria by franchise firms is assessed by audits (both before and after the awarding of a franchise) of a random sample of their files.

These process measures have attracted far more criticism than the structural measures. From the outset practitioners objected to the notion that quality could be gauged from an audit of files which measured compliance with a check-list rather than the adequacy of the advice given or the action taken. The Legal Action Group complained that the criteria appeared to have been drafted for the standard situation with the aim of reducing professional discretion and flexibility (Smith, 1993b:11).[11] Indeed the accusation was made that the criteria encouraged routinisation and standardisation of practice (Harman, 1994). Similarly, Sommerlad (1995) claimed that the criteria will contribute to de-skilling and commodification of the legal aid practitioner, while Goriely (1994:168) fears that they may encourage a mechanistic approach to lawyering, or even enshrine poor standards. In fact the compilers of the transaction criteria had foreseen many of these criticisms (Sherr *et al.*,1994:24) and had adjusted the criteria accordingly, although accepting the charge that they might lead to a degree of standardisation. It was felt, however, that in most cases it would lead to a levelling up rather than a levelling down in standards. Secondly, the research team behind the transaction criteria were convinced that irrespective of the Legal Aid Board's (1994:35) oft restated policy on the point, any experimentation with contracts to provide legal aid might lead eventually to exclusive contracts and tendering.[12] Such scenarios have a history of leading to a 'race to the bottom' in quality terms. In the eyes of the researchers, transaction criteria, properly applied and audited, constituted a robust yet affordable approach to establishing a quality floor, as opposed to the highly expensive option of peer review, much favoured by critics such as the Law Society and the Legal Action Group.[13] The need for such a quality floor was reinforced by

[11] The Legal Action Group has generally been somewhat cool on the topic of franchising in general. Curiously, LAG recommended something very similar to franchising (contracts to select practitioners to provide services of a defined standard) in their evidence to the Royal Commission on Legal Services in England and Wales (Hansen, 1992).

[12] Whatever the Board's position, it has always been clear that an alliance between the Treasury and the Lord Chancellor's Department would be likely to prevail on the issue.

[13] In 1996–7 the Legal Aid Board employed 39 auditors to carry out franchise audits, including transaction criteria audits at a cost of approximately 600,000 pounds sterling. In that year they conducted audits of in excess of 15,000 case files (answer to Parliamentary question 17/7/97). Given the respective salaries for unqualified auditors and fee rates for specialist solicitors required for peer review, it is difficult to see how peer review could match these expenditure parameters.

the experience of jurisdictions such as Australia and the United States (Goriely, 1997a, 1997b) where contracting was introduced largely without adequate quality control measures, to the detriment of levels of service provision.

How successful franchising has been depends partly on which perspective is taken. Solicitors and external critics have generally been happier with the practice management standards than the transaction criteria, whilst generally accepting the value of the audit process (LAB, 1998a:11). The LCD seems to have viewed it as a useful stepping stone to fixed-term contracts, while the Board has been satisfied by the fact that by January 1998 2,200 or so solicitors' offices and other organisations in England and Wales (out of a total of about 11,000 offices receiving legal aid payments at that time) had obtained a franchise in at least one category of legal work (LAB, 1997:34).[14] The transaction criteria research team, nevertheless, acknowledged the force of Harden's observation that 'Goodhart's Law' entails that even reliable proxies for quality may cease to be so once they are articulated and measured (1992:65). Since 1994, therefore, the hunt has been on for new quality proxies.

Unfortunately, time is running out. With the Lord Chancellor's Department backing a variant on franchising in the shape of block contracts (Bevan *et al.*, 1994; LCD, 1995; 1996; LCD, 1998) and the latest Lord Chancellor supporting exclusive contracts at fixed prices (Irvine, 1997; LCD, 1998:31; LAB, 1998a:5), the pressure is mounting to get the quality floor securely in place now. Most of the concentration has fallen on outcome measures. As in North America, this has focused primarily on result achieved, cost, client satisfaction and time taken. As we saw earlier, each of these measures has complications associated with them. However, the experience of the outcome measures research team working for the Board has been one of problems compounded by (a) the need to take large samples to eliminate random factors, (b) a shortage of available data on the Board's computer system, and (c) dissensus in the profession over objective measures of result achieved (Goriely, 1996).

In the absence of available computer data, the only option for assessing outcomes is peer review, possibly combined with model clients. Throughout the era of franchising, the Board has offered to use peer review as a method of gauging quality as an appeal mechanism where a franchise is to be withdrawn. However, the mechanism would only operate where the removal was caused by the firm failing consistently to attain an acceptable compliance rate with transaction criteria. In practice this mechanism has never been invoked. On the other hand, the Board has included both peer review and model clients in its current research project relating to block contracting in the field of non-family civil advice and assistance work (Orchard, 1997).

If the Legal Aid Board has shown a steady commitment to quality, what of the profession? Unlike the ABA, the Law Society's interest in quality of service

[14] Information for 1998 obtained from the Legal Aid Board.

provision emerged only slowly and at a comparatively late stage. Their reluctance to give official cognisance, as a disciplinary matter, to examples of incompetence or poor quality reflected on the Society's view of the public interest. Gradually, however, it became accepted that incompetence or negligence could, in severe cases, amount to misconduct. The growth of the consumerist society brought with it a rise in complaints concerning competence or service. When allied to a Government which was sympathetic to change, the Law Society began to give ground. In 1986 the first Written Professional Standards were produced, including a 'requirement' that clients should receive information on costs from their solicitors at an early stage. In 1988 the concept of Inadequate Professional Services was introduced by legislation, designed to provide remedies for service complaints by clients. Panels of recognised specialists were established by the Law Society and in 1991 the client care rule was implemented, requiring solicitors to communicate effectively with their clients from the earliest stage, and to have a complaints procedure. This in turn was followed by another quality enhancing move: mandatory Continuing Professional Development, and a quasi-endorsement of BS 5750 (the British equivalent of ISO 9000) as a quality system for lawyers. Throughout this period a series of publications on quality were emerging from the Society, including the *Solicitors Office Manual* (1990a), *Best Practice* (1990b) and *Quality: A Briefing for Solicitors* (1991).

Critics, however, were swift to point to signs of ambivalence by the profession such as (1) the repeated surveys which have shown that the client care rule is often ignored by the profession (Harris, 1994; NAO, 1992), (2) the Law Society's refusal to spell out the content of IPS, and (3) the introduction of a provision in the promotional rules to the effect that solicitors could self-certify themselves as specialists. In effect, the Society gave the game away in its own publication *Quality: A Briefing for Solicitors* (1991). There they admitted that their first serious consideration of quality and quality systems had come with the publication of the White Paper in 1987 and franchising proposals in 1990.

In relation to the latter, the Society, after initial misgivings, embraced the concept of Practice Management Standards (1993) which became mandatory for firms seeking a franchise from the LAB and optional for others. This was but the latest in a long line of legal aid reforms which the Society initially resisted and subsequently co-opted (Paterson and Nelken, 1984a, 1984b).[15] In 1997 the Society launched its own system of auditing the PMS, which they entitled LEXCEL. However, in relation to transaction criteria the Society resolutely refused all offers to take them over, far less co-opt them. Indeed, PMS aside, this has been the general response of the Society to franchising. In the face of such

[15] So successful was the co-option in this case that the Society have long since lost sight of the fact that the original idea for Practice Management Standards came from the Board rather than themselves.

intransigence the Board in recent years has by-passed the Society, seeking instead the direct support of legal firms.

The Netherlands

Quality as an issue in relation to legal services in the Netherlands is a comparative newcomer. As in the UK, lawyers (advocates) in private practice have long conducted the bulk of legal aid work there but, unlike the UK, the payment was by way of fixed fees paid in advance. Faced with the same financial constraints as other jurisdictions with developed legal aid programmes, the Dutch Ministry of Justice froze legal aid remuneration at 1981 levels, with no inflationary adjustment. During the next decade the profession grew more incensed at the rates of pay but the Ministry of Justice were not prepared to move. The Order of Advocates seems tacitly to have acknowledged that the remuneration rates might be encouraging 'corner cutting' since in its lobbying for a hourly payment system it argued that this would not only be fairer, but would also improve quality (Goriely, 1992:812). The profession's perceptions were shared by the staff jurists working in the Dutch *Buros Voor Rechschulp* since, by the mid-1980s, they were working with the local bar associations to draw up lists of competent advocates to whom they could refer clients. The Ministry of Justice approved of this activist policy in relation to quality. While they saw the advantages of staff jurists assessing the quality of private lawyers, they did not think this went far enough. Certification of specialisms might have attracted them, but the Dutch bar had only developed a handful of specialist panels. In most fields, as in the UK, advocates could simply designate themselves as specialists. The Ministry were even more concerned with the generalists—particularly those working in sole practices or small law firms—because of the high volume of legal aid work conducted by such firms. The fear was that generalists would struggle to provide a good quality service in all areas of legal aid practice (Huxtable, 1993). In 1985 the Ministry proposed to the bar that legal aid contracts should be introduced which would cash-limit the budget, provide additional remuneration to the bar and set basic quality requirements. This last condition would be met either by an experience requirement (having done a specified minimum of cases in the specialist field to which the contract related), having attended a recognised course or being a recognised specialist in the field. The contracting proposals were vehemently opposed by the Order of Advocates, though not for their imposition of quality-assurance standards. In the end the Ministry dropped the proposals, in part influenced by the fear that, as in the USA, tendering for contracts might have a deleterious effect on quality (Huxtable, 1993). Nevertheless, the new Legal Aid Act of 1994 allows for contracts for advice and assistance in certain geographical areas. More significantly, the Act contains quality provisions not dissimilar to those in the contracting proposals. The new regional Legal Aid Councils were empowered to establish conditions for the registration of legal aid practitioners. To become registered, advocates would have a minimum and a maximum number of legal aid cases which they could undertake in a year, they would have to meet certain expertise requirements and they would have to organise their offices in particular ways (Goriely, 1992). As will be clear, all of these were input or structural measures of quality, thus limiting their efficacy.

Quality expectations for advocates and firms were deliberately left vague since Ministry officials expected them to evolve over time. The Dutch, like the Australians and the Scots, were watching the English franchising experiment with close interest to see what lessons were to be learned (Huxtable, 1993). Accordingly, each Council was given discretion on an annual basis to lay down the exact conditions for registration, subject to approval by the Ministry of Justice. In the first year, all the Councils adopted the same criteria except that in The Hague. Thus, all of them required that advocates should do a minimum of ten cases a year (this was to ensure that they had some experience and some relationship with the Council) and a maximum of 250 cases a year (to preserve quality by preventing advocates from taking on an excessive work-load, as well as guarding against monopolisation). The office organisation standards were very minimalist, merely requiring access to the office during working hours, that it be staffed by someone during these hours and that arrangements for sick leave and holiday cover be in place.

Very early on research was commissioned to study the impact of the registration requirements (Leeuwen, Klijn and Paulides, 1996): first, in case they led to a reduction in participating advocates, particularly those with considerable experience and knowledge, and secondly to try to identify how the registration requirements might help to improve quality. On the initial question the researchers found that the Councils had indeed some grounds for concern. It emerged that one-third of the bar did less than ten cases a year and that 1 per cent did more than 250 cases a year. Worryingly, legal aid lawyers were found to be less specialised than those who did little or no legal aid. They also appeared to be spending less time on legal aid cases than they had before. Most worrying of all, at least 6 per cent of all legal aid cases appeared to be being undertaken by advocates who by their own admission had no expertise or experience of the relevant field of law. This finding leant support to a trend that had already become apparent of the Councils specifying that in addition to the general requirement of ten cases a year, lawyers could only undertake certain areas of legal aid work if they had done a fixed minimum number of cases *in those areas* (Schoenmakers, 1994).

The researchers asked legal aid lawyers what they made of the quality criteria contained in the Act. In general, they did not receive much support from the Bar, but not because the advocates objected to quality criteria being applied to them. Rather they did not agree with the ones contained in the Act. Thus, there was little support for the general minimum number of legal aid cases requirement (since it overlooked the situation of advocates who handled few legal aid cases in a field but had an extensive non-legally aided practice in that field). This view seems to be shared by the Councils, since in 1997 several of them quietly dropped the requirement. However, the upper limit of 250 has been retained, as have the office requirements. Despite this researchers and well informed commentators have formed the impression that the Councils have not been as enthusiastic in exploring possible quality criteria as they might (Leeuwen *et al.*, 1996:149). Nevertheless the researchers found that the advocates would support quality criteria based on specialisation and professional training (e.g. measures that focus on a minimum percentage of time spent in a legal field—whether doing legal aid or private cases—setting a maximum number of areas of law in which legal aid work can be done, and attendance at relevant continuing professional development courses: Leeuwen *et al.*, 1996:102).[16] This would require a greater willingness on the part of the Bar to share information with the Councils than has hitherto been evident. However, informal relations between the profession and the Councils seem to be improving and plans are emerging for quality controls to be set in conjunction with the professional group after consultation with them. In the end much will depend on the profession's willingness to get involved in the quality improvement process. If enhanced rates of compensation are linked to tougher measures for quality accreditation, this may influence the profession's approach to the issue.[17]

Scotland

The Scots' interest in quality has come very late in the proceedings. Its legal aid programme is very similar to that in England and Wales. Not surprisingly, therefore, like the authorities in the Netherlands and Australia, the Scottish Legal Aid Board watched the English franchising experiment with keen attention. Although attracted by the notion of enhanced quality assurance there was much suspicion of the bureaucracy and expense involved in monitoring transaction criteria. Moreover, the concentration of the top one hundred legal aid suppliers in the central belt of Scotland (Paterson, 1994) meant that a system which hinged on the availability of specialist legal aid firms spread geographically across the country was viewed with some scepticism. A further problem was that the legal aid legislation in Scotland was far less enabling than its English counterpart. Neither franchising nor pilot projects with non-solicitor agencies were feasible in Scotland without legislation, for which there was little parliamentary time. An uneasy period ensued, the Law Society of Scotland expecting the Scottish Board to take quality measures and the Board not being sure what it should do and not having the power to do it in any case. The Scottish Board eventually translated some of

[16] It is noteworthy that although the profession has supported a move from weaker input proxies for quality to stronger proxies, they remain input measures. There has been no groundswell of professional support for random file audit or peer review of outcomes.

[17] Information derived by the authors from Peter Levenkamp, the Head of the Legal Aid Department of the Ministry of Justice, 1997.

the transaction criteria into voluntary guidelines appropriate for Scots solicitors. The break in the impasse came from an unexpected source. Faced with a criminal legal aid budget which was rising exponentially, well beyond inflation or productivity, and which now accounted for nearly 70 per cent of total legal aid spending, the Government decided to act. Unconvinced—at that time—by the option of introducing fixed fees, they took advantage of a small comparative research project (Goriely, Tata and Paterson, 1997) which demonstrated that the *per capita* criminal legal aid spending in Scotland exceeded that of England by 50 per cent and of the Netherlands by 900 per cent, to introduce provisions in a Crime and Punishment Bill permitting the Board to set up a pilot experiment with public defenders. The quality of the work done by the Public Defence Solicitor will be monitored by comparison with that of the private profession. The details are still being worked out, but it is likely that the researchers will draw on outcome measures similar to those used in Canadian contracting studies, namely: average case cost, time spent on the case, client satisfaction and result. Part V of the Crime and Punishment (Scotland) Act 1997 introduces a requirement that in future all criminal legal aid lawyers and firms will have to be registered with the Board. Curiously, this proposal was not based on the registration of legal aid lawyers recently introduced in the Netherlands, though this was well known to the Board. Instead registration will require compliance with a Code of Practice including, inter alia, attendance at relevant continuing legal education courses, a weaker form of the Practice Management Standards, ethical standards for criminal lawyers and performance standards relating to quality of service (SLAB, 1997). Again it has not yet been decided how the Code will be monitored, but serious consideration is being given to the use of peer review and outcome measures similar to those being developed for the English Legal Aid Board (Goriely, 1996). The latest reform proposals for civil legal aid (SOHHD, 1998:32) refer to both contracting and a civil Code of Practice. Again, peer review and attendance at relevant continuing professional development courses are suggested as quality criteria. In short, the Scots proposals contain a balance of input, process and outcome measures. Time will tell whether that balance is the right one.

New Zealand

The New Zealand programme is not without interest. It has a staff component but remains essentially judicare. Its tight budgetary controls and detailed statistical returns has enabled it to operate with a soft cap in recent years because of the Legal Services Board's ability to predict with some accuracy (until 1997) the overall spending. This has perhaps led to an over-concentration on cost rather than quality. The assumption has been that average case cost broken down by district (though not by type of case) coupled with auditing of grants and files will suffice. The limited quality controls include: regular progress reports on cases; Board audits of case grants and case handling; client satisfaction with the quality of the work done; and obtaining feedback from judges in cases which have not been handled effectively (Smith, 1997). Peer review, albeit in an impure form, plays a role in a further quality assurance measure. Only the more talented lawyers are allowed to handle the more serious criminal cases. Thus lawyers are stratified into five tiers and promotion up the tiers of lists is achieved after consultation by the Law Society with senior counsel and judges. The system depends on the jurisdiction being small enough for all the lawyers to know each other, but it lacks objectivity and opens the door to prejudice. The Legal Services Board of New Zealand considers that more needs to be done to enhance quality of performance. In their paper *Legal Aid Delivery Reform* (LSB, 1996) they report a survey showing that 18 per cent of criminal legal aid lawyers believe that the service provided in criminal legal aid cases is consistently of a lower quality than in other fields. The Report notes the absence of formal quality controls by the Board and the 'apparent unwillingness on the part of District Law Societies and the judiciary actively to monitor' quality in supply. The absence of such monitoring is understandable, they say, because there is no legislative or regulatory framework which establishes appropriate and fair processes of performance monitoring and review for lawyers. The board plans to embark on a quality assurance programme based on certain quality indicators, yet to be developed, but which will start with benchmark comparisons between classes of lawyer and types of cases from location to location. The Board utilises a few outcome measures, as can be seen, but are acutely conscious that most of their measures are input-focused (Smith, 1997).

Australia

New Zealand's much larger neighbouring jurisdiction, Australia, has been no more active in the pursuit of quality. This is somewhat curious given the characteristics of its legal aid system. Australia moved away from law society control of judicare as early as 1973 with the establishment of the Australian Legal Aid Office. Before long this was broken up and regional Legal Aid Commissions (LACS) were established in each state. Like British Legal Aid Boards, the LACS are appointed by the states but semi-independent of them in operation, though not in funding. Each LAC has staff lawyers who provide a significant measure of the poverty legal services in each state (85 per cent of initial advice, 56 per cent of criminal work and 15 per cent of civil work: Goriely, 1996). Given the considerable autonomy which they enjoy over the distribution of their funds and the allocation of staff lawyer resources, it might be thought that the LACS would have experimented with projects designed to enhance quality of service and value for money. However, this has not been the case. True, there were some attempts to compare the cost-effectiveness of the private profession and the staff lawyers, but each was more politically contentious than the last (Goriely, 1996). As dogma took over, only relative cost was scrutinised, never aspects of quality. Other factors which may explain this surprising neglect of the quality issue include the corollary of a decentralised approach, the abandonment of national policy-making, and the never-ending concerns over the capped budget which focused attention on rationing and prioritisation rather than quality (Crockett, 1994; Cramsie, 1997); and the hope that the existence of salaried lawyers and Community Law Centres as well as the private profession would assist in maintaining the quality of service provided by public and private lawyers alike. This latter argument seems to have been partly vindicated by experience. The Commissions have been able to take account of specialisms and expertise in both sectors in allocating work between them (Cramsie, 1997), but this is more akin to a division of labour rather than a quality assurance programme. It may be that staff lawyers have been able to gauge the quality of the private profession's work, or vice versa, but no systematic data is available on the issue. As in Scotland and the Netherlands, the authorities have been watching the English franchising experience with interest, but in only two states have there been limited projects where quality assurance has performed an overt role (Pleasance *et al.*, 1996:103). In 1994 the Victoria LAC introduced a one-year pilot scheme franchising summary criminal work. The franchise firms were granted contracts based on their agreement to implement practice management standards and to maintain detailed records in their files which would be audited on a quarterly basis. This experiment paralleled a project in Victoria where tenders to undertake 'significant' cases were restricted to lawyers who were accredited members of specialist panels set up by the professional body in Victoria. Members also had to meet specifications akin to the practice management standards. Finally, Queensland introduced tendering for duty lawyer services in 1994. Only practitioners accredited with the Queensland Law Society duty lawyer accreditation procedures could apply. Successful tenderers got exclusive contracts which, however, entailed the Commission conducting unannounced spot checks on quality of performance.

Canada

At first blush the Canadian legal aid programme looks very similar to that of Australia. A mixed delivery system with judicare and staff elements, it is dually funded by the federal and provincial governments, decentralised and administered by quasi-independent bodies in each province. To reinforce the parallel, in most provinces a cap on expenditure has now been introduced. However, the similarities are more apparent than real. The provinces are far more disparate in their provision than their Australian counterparts. Some are purely staff models, some (including Ontario) are primarily judicare models, while the remainder have a genuinely mixed provision. The private profession, in the shape of law societies, has charge of several of the judicare programmes which has given them an interest to resist the spread of the staff model. For the Australian profession, the way forward has been by low-profile negotiations with the Commissions to agree the division of labour between them and the staff lawyers in particular fields of practice. The turf wars in Canada have been more complex, with the profession seeking to preserve judicare where they could, even though the average case costs of the judicare model have generally proved to be higher than in the staff model (Zemans, 1994; Goriely, 1996). The struggle has been fiercest in British Columbia, but also apparent in Quebec and Ontario. As Fremont acidly observes, politics will not allow the more cost-effective staff model of Quebec to be expanded at the expense of the private profession. 'In the end, it seems that the "rational" choice of suppressing the private sector of the legal aid system in favour of an expanded staff system is completely counterbalanced by the "ideological" choice of appearing to be, if not downsizing the State, at least to be restricting the costs involved' (Fremont, 1994:236).

Unlike Australia, comparisons between the staff and judicare models used quality indicators, even from the earliest days. In part it seems to stem from the private profession's belief, perhaps based on what they knew of the American experience, that public defenders were inferior lawyers. The private profession therefore insisted that quality measures be used in the monitoring of the two models. The principal indicators they used were outcome measures: time spent on each case, rates of guilty pleas, conviction rates and sentences imposed. Unfortunately for the private profession, the four evaluations in which quality was measured (the Burnaby project in 1991, the British Columbia evaluation in 1984, the Manitoba evaluation in 1987 and the Saskatchewan evaluation in 1988) all reached the same conclusions (Dept. of Justice, 1993:34).

a. staff lawyers spend less time per case than private lawyers;
b. staff lawyers tend to plead clients guilty more often than do private lawyers;
c. similar proportions of staff and private lawyer clients are convicted;
d. staff lawyers' clients draw fewer jail terms than private lawyers clients.

The studies also drew on two further outcome measures: client satisfaction surveys on comparisons of cost per case. The former revealed relatively high satisfaction rates for both models of delivery, the latter, as we have seen, tends to suggest that staff models are no more expensive and probably cheaper than judicare models (Dept. of Justice, 1993; Goriely, 1996). The researchers found the determination of the quality of legal services complicated, the more so because the private profession in Canada had proved no more adept than its contemporary counterparts in reaching a consensus on how quality might be assessed (Dept. of Justice, 1993).[18] As elsewhere, if a lawyer was admitted to the Bar, the quality of his or her work was assumed to be beyond question. Client complaints or repeated requests for change of counsel might trigger reactive measures by legal

[18] The Canadian Bar Association's Civil Justice Task Force, '*Systems of Civil Justice Report*', (1996) noted that the profession was not structured in a way that allows it to regulate issues of competence. The Association is considering a number of initiatives in the field including: more hands-on regulation for competence, discipline for service complaints, mediation in complaints, mandatory CLE, and developing standards for specialisation.

aid managers on a case-by-case basis, but this was a rare event. Staff lawyers, or those employed in community clinics have grown more used to having their performance evaluated. Thus in Manitoba the staff have a performance appraisal system covering file maintenance, client satisfaction and casework. The staff and their supervisors both play a role in the scheme (Huxtable, 1993:24).

Although there have been a number of limited experiments with contracting legal aid services to the private Bar in Canada, none have involved serious quality control measures. During the 1990s there have been two further studies of quality of service in legal aid in Canada. In 1996 the Canadian Department of Justice conducted a study into the Expanded Duty Counsel Project in Manitoba (Currie, 1996). The researcher used the now well established outcome measures of time spent per case, conviction rates, rates of incarceration, case cost and client satisfaction. The second earlier study was an evaluation of the Ontario judicare programme in 1991. The Review (Meredith *et al.*, 1991) found that the supervision of judicare lawyers in the programme was minimal, or as they put it, the same as that exercised by the Law Society over all lawyers. Although 84 per cent of Area Directors of the programme were satisfied with the existing mechanisms to ensure quality, only 21 per cent of lawyers were so satisfied. Such programmes as there were to improve the quality of the judicare legal services (a Mentor programme, a Research Facility and Specialist Panel)[19] were of limited use. The study found that judicare lawyers were less experienced, more junior in status and located in smaller firms than non-legal aid lawyers. Perhaps as a result, surveys of participating and non-participating lawyers found that over a third of each group considered that the competence of the judicare lawyers was worse than that of non-legal aid lawyers. Despite these concerns the Ontario Plan failed to take steps to address the quality issue. Thus the Ontario Legal Aid Review conducted in 1996 comments in its Executive Summary (OLAR, 1997:6) 'much more serious attention needs to be paid than has been the case in the past to issues of performance monitoring and quality assurance across the whole range of delivery models'. The Review recommends that the services provided by legal aid lawyers should be subjected to appropriate quality assurance mechanisms and that standards should be set for lawyers wishing to be on panels to accept legal aid certificates.

In sum, the Canadian profession has made relatively little headway in monitoring for quality. However, there are increasing signs (Civil Justice Task Force, 1996; OLAR, 1997) that the profession and the legal aid authorities in particular have seen the argument for moving from occasional quality assessment to regular quality monitoring and control. As in similar jurisdictions the incentive to look at quality in legal aid came from the threat of the staff model and public defenders in

[19] There are several specialist panels for judicare lawyers in Ontario, including criminal law, domestic violence, mental health and immigration work. To get in requires mandatory training (Huxtable, 1993: 30).

particular. Funders in pursuit of cost-effectiveness used quality assurance to counter private profession arguments for no change.

Recapitulation: why did the quality dog not bark sooner?

It should be clear from this international excursus that the pursuit of quality arrived late in the legal services field. The conundrum is why it took so long to emerge. Until the Second World War, legal services to the indigent were delivered largely through the vehicle of the 'charitable' model: by volunteer lawyers acting on no- or low-fee basis (Cappelletti, Gordley and Johnson, 1975; Paterson, 1993). Despite the fact that it was commonplace for these services to be delivered by the more junior and inexperienced members of the legal profession, 'learning at the expense' of their clients, as a latterday critic might assert, the quality of service delivered seems to have attracted little comment. It seems probably that several factors contributed to the silence on quality. First, as the demand for legal services grew with the social welfare legislation of the early twentieth century, most reformers were more concerned with establishing any service at all than worrying about its quality. Secondly, to many lawyers the question of quality of work was one which they took for granted. For them part of being a professional was that they determined the legal needs of the public and how they would be met (Johnson, 1972; Perkin, 1989). They were lawyer-centred, not client-centred. Their contractualist perception of professionalism contained not only an obligation to deliver a competent service but also a public service ethic, in return for their high social status and a reasonable income safeguarded by constraints on competition (Paterson, 1996). They expected indigent clients to be not only 'deserving' with respect to the morality of their case, but grateful for the lawyer's help, not carping as to the quality of service they received. Thirdly, the inability of 'one-shot' clients—and most indigent clients at that time would be first-time clients—to gauge the quality of work done for them, and their lack of power and status in any event, also rendered complaints about quality less likely.

Even if these explanations account for the lack of quality concerns in the charitable era of legal aid, why did things not change with the advent of the judicare model wherein the state made payments to the private profession? It was not as though there was ever a halycon period when the treasury authorities in countries with developed legal aid programmes were unconcerned at increases in expenditure. Why did cost-effectiveness not become an issue until the 1980s? Perhaps because it was always politically much easier to introduce hidden cuts by failing to increase eligibility limits (Goriely and Paterson, 1996) than by tackling the profession head-on in the sensitive area of their professional competence. In countries where judicare prevailed, the profession, even if it did not administer legal aid (as it did in the United Kingdom) exercised a hegemonic influence over the definition of a quality service. Attempts by the state to interfere in that area might well have been seen as a threat to the independence of the profession.

Accounting for change: why the dog barked

How then are we to account for the emergence of quality as a key issue in relation to the provision of poverty legal services in recent years?

Curiously, the strongest influence seems to be erosion of professional autonomy in relation to the provision of poverty legal services. Of itself, however, this is an insufficient explanation. Thus the emergence of salaried poverty legal services can be traced back to the USA in the 1880s, and they have existed in different parts of the world ever since. Yet until very recently organisations employing poverty lawyers have had few published quality standards. True, the employed lawyers have been subject to controls, but these have been primarily bureaucratic norms and formal review, rather than explicit quality guidelines. The variant of salaried legal services lawyers attached to community law centres in theory also exposed the legal professionals to community control by community representatives on the centres' management committees (LCF, 1980). In practice, community control has been more honoured in the breach than the observance, at least in the UK, and there have been few attempts by management committees to monitor the quality of service provided by their qualified staff.[20]

Nevertheless, one factor which seems to have contributed to the emergence of the quality pursuit is the transfer of responsibility for legal aid from the professional bodies to quasi-independent commission in most of the jurisdictions we have surveyed. Given the difficulties experienced by lay persons in assessing the quality of legal services, we might expect such bodies to be uneasy about the quality of services for which they are paying. Where the bodies were established at a time when value for money was becoming a significant Treasury concern, as in the case of the English Legal Aid Board and the Dutch Legal Aid Commissions, the unease was translated into an active quest for quality. Yet, again, the argument cannot be pressed too far, since such third-party funders have sometimes been as slow as the profession to embrace the quality pursuit, for example in Australia, and to a lesser extent in Scotland and New Zealand.

Whatever the truth of the suggestion that quality only comes to the fore when professional autonomy is eroded, it is clear that the impetus for the quality pursuit was rarely the result of proactive initiatives from the profession. Why should this be the case when quality lies at the heart of professionalism? Maybe therein lay the problem. It takes a bold professional body to initiate mandatory reforms

[20] The Law Centres' Federation—the professional association for law centres in the UK—did receive funding from the Nuffield Foundation to look into the quality and value for money provided by English law centres, but little came out of it.

designed to improve the quality of service offered by their members, for such reforms have costs. While voluntary codes of practice or statements of good practice are perfectly acceptable, they are necessarily limited in their efficacy. Most lawyers take their competence for granted. They resent any attempt by their professional body to coerce the membership to virtue in this field—allegedly in the name of the public interest—especially if they consider that the proper role of the professional body is to act as a trade union for its members. (Perversely, of course, because they view issues of quality as central to professional autonomy, lawyers resent even more attempts by third-party bodies to bring about improvements in this area). A casual reading of the literature might suggest that the private profession has taken a proactive stance on quality in legal aid cases, e.g. when public legal services have been poorly funded (as with public defenders in the USA) or when a staff model is introduced to a judicare jurisdiction for the first time (as with public defenders in Scotland). In reality, such a perception is misconceived. The professions have tolerated widespread underfunding of legal aid delivered by the private profession, e.g. in the shape of the charitable model or civil judicare in the last fifteen years in the United Kingdom, Australia, Canada and the Netherlands. Again the introduction of the staff model on the civil side in the USA, Canada, Australia, New Zealand, the UK and the Netherlands failed to provoke complaints as to the quality of service of the staff attorneys. It seems that the private profession have only wrapped themselves in the quality flag when they have perceived a threat to their market share from state salaried or contracted lawyers, e.g. public defenders in the USA and Scotland.

Much the same ingredients of erosion of professional autonomy and a reactive legal profession are contained in the assertion that the pursuit of quality has come from deregulation and the reworking of the 'traditional' concept of professionalism which has been taking place in the last fifteen years (Paterson, 1996). According to such neo-contractualist thinking, this 'renegotiation of professionalism' by the forces of consumerism and commercialism has forced the professions onto the back foot, requiring them to deliver greater quality and access in an attempt to stave off the state's and the public's attacks on their anti-competitive practices. Put another way, the profession has felt compelled to deliver higher standards of quality and competence to clients and potential clients (the wider public) in order to preserve the benefits on its 'side' of the tacit contract, which is professionalism (Paterson 1996), such as status and professional autonomy.

If the renegotiation of professionalism accounts for an increased emphasis on quality, why should this be particularly marked in relation to legal aid? On one hand because the large-scale funders of legal services—legal aid commissions and insurance companies—have responded to exponential rises in costs over the years by an increasing interest in value for money. Secondly, in both cases the funding agency is acting as a proxy for the individual client. With deregulation of the legal profession came the growing awareness of the market's ability to control for quality and the vacuum into which third-party funding bodies could step if they chose—to act as proxy for the client in ensuring the quality of publicly funded legal services. The English Legal Aid Board's introduction of franchising is but the most celebrated example of this trend. As franchising gives way to block contracting with an assured quality floor, we can see that the Board is establishing in tangible form, at the level of the individual firm, the professionalism contract that has been renegotiated at the societal level in the last decade. A similar process has seen the private profession embrace aspects of quality e.g. BS 5750, ISO 9000 and Investors in People in an attempt to compete on quality rather than price.

Conclusion

What then are we to conclude as to the significance of the quality pursuit that we have been following from a global perspective? Is it really the Fourth wave of Access to Justice or merely a passing fad? Certainly, the heady attractions of the cachet or marketing edge conferred by BS 5750, ISO 9000, TQM or Investors in People seems to have palled amongst UK solicitors. But as we have seen, the driving force behind the quality pursuit has often stemmed from outside the profession, and these pressures are unlikely to go away. Quality, at least in the sense of 'value for money' may indeed now be the fourth wave of access to justice. Whatever the eventual fate of civil legal aid, public funding will remain on the criminal side. In an era of growing awareness of formal human rights, it would be rash to predict a substantial reversion to the charitable model of legal services provision, even if mandatory *pro bono* can now be discussed in polite legal circles (Boon and Abbey, 1997). However, any government money spent on public legal services will be subject to an efficiency scrutiny. Even in jurisdictions where there is no 'hard cap' or fixed spending limit for public legal service, it seems likely that all will eventually succumb to a form of 'soft cap' (Smith, 1997a) where expenditure is kept within very tightly controlled parameters. Despite the difficulties associated with measuring quality and competence, the politics of global legal services markets in which staff lawyers vie with the private profession will ensure that value for money is rarely off the agenda. If the jealousies of the private profession do not ensure an ongoing focus on quality, the concerns of third-party funders to assess the quality of the services which they are purchasing seem likely to do so. In the face of a renegotiated power balance between the state, the public and the profession, the last may well decide that quality—an essential building block in twentieth-century conceptions of professionalism (Paterson, 1996)—should be co-opted back into professional control. Otherwise, the prospect of external regulators defining professional standards on a long-term basis will surely place any meaningful self-regulation in terminal jeopardy.

11

*Responding to New Demands: Legal Aid and Multi-Party Actions**

DON FLEMING

Introduction

Twenty years ago Cappelletti and Garth argued in the *Access to Justice* volumes that one of the challenges facing legal systems was to go beyond a focus on individuals. Mechanisms were required whereby groups as well as individuals could press their claims or defend their legal rights: otherwise, while equality before the law might be a reality for individuals, it would not be for groups (1978). First, mechanisms were needed to provide legal representation for groups, including indigenous peoples, victims of disasters and consumer groups affected by faulty products, to gain access to the courts. But group or 'multi-party' actions, as they came to be known, also faced problems being heard in court because procedural rules were usually designed for individual cases. Cappelletti and Garth argued that the necessary reforms included contingency fees to allow legal representation for groups and class actions to allow courts to recognise and hear group cases.

Despite the optimism of the late 1970s, these sort of reforms have not been embraced around the globe. While the USA implemented them, other societies were slower to act. For example, Great Britain had no form of contingency fee

* This Chapter is a revised version of paper presented at the 2nd Meeting of the International Legal Aid Group, Edinburgh 18–20 June 1997. In the spirit of the International Legal Aid Group the research process for this paper was truly a co-operative exercise. I wish to record my thanks to National Legal Aid (NLA), the Directors of the Australian legal aid commissions, in particular, to Chris Staniforth and Mike Cramsie, the five respondents in the 'community' sector and Ms Margery Nicholl of the Law Council of Australia. Once again I am indebted to Ms Debra Wheare of the federal office of Legal Aid and Family Services (LAFS) for her willing and ever-professional assistance. I am also indebted to the Centre for Research into Public Sector Management at the University of Canberra for its assistance. In particular, Ms Kylie McIntosh worked closely with me via email in compiling the research data when I was in Germany in May and June 1997. Jason Field from the Human Rights and Equal Opportunity Commission and the Australian Law Reform Commission also willingly co-operated. Once again I am also indebted to my colleagues Neil Andrews, for his knowledge of legal developments affecting indigenous Australians, and Francis Regan. The significance of the necessity to draw again upon the commitment of these organisations and people to improving access to legal aid in Australia is something I have tried to convey throughout this paper. I also wish the express my appreciation to Professor Dr H. G. Petersen, Ruth Bader and Rico Janke at the Australia Centre at the Universität Potsdam for their assistance in May and June 1997 when I wrote the paper on which this Chapter is based.

until the 1990s. In Australia national legislation was introduced in the early 1990s to allow class actions for federal courts but most of the states and territories are yet to do so. Meanwhile, the federal system of government resulted in two Australian states reforming legal profession rules to allow contingency fees while others have resisted this pressure.[1] The experience elsewhere was similarly patchy. In Canada class action legislation was first introduced in Quebec in 1978, but was restrictively applied by the courts until the early 1990s (Day, Balen and McCool, 1995:43–4). In 1992 a class action scheme was enacted in Ontario but its scope appears to be limited by financial constraints (ibid. 44–6). Statutory provision for class actions now also exists in several European countries including France, Germany and the Republic of Ireland (ibid. 48–9).[2] One of the reasons for the slow pace of global reform was that multi-party actions created enormous problems. For example, they were by definition usually long-running and complex cases that soaked up vast amounts of court resources. In addition, there was the problem of funding. These cases involve legal firms in an extensive commitment of time and resources over long periods of time. Private firms were therefore reluctant to take on multi-party actions unless there was a very high prospect of success. They were even more reluctant if contingency fees were not available. But what other sources of funds could be used, particularly if contingency fees were not available?

One solution, especially in the absence of contingency fees, was to utilise public funds. The resources of national legal aid schemes could be used to fund the actions. Publicly funded agencies were ideally placed to expand their responsibilities to fund these actions where other private sources were absent. Ironically, however, the pressure for multi-party action reforms emerged at the time when many societies began to lose faith in legal aid. As the authors in this volume have shown funds, were reduced and tighter eligibility tests introduced in one society after another in the 1980s and 1990s. So how have the declining legal aid schemes responded to this new demand? And what can we learn from these experiences about the challenges facing legal aid and the legal services industry generally?

In this Chapter I present a case study of one national legal aid scheme's response to the rise of multi-party actions. I examine the recent evidence for Australia between 1993 and 1996 and demonstrate that legal aid has funded a small number of multi-party actions and that they are creating headaches for legal aid administrators in a time of declining resources. By summarising some of the recent cases I not only show that they are important but also that they might not have gone before the courts without legal aid funding. I conclude that multi-party

[1] This period was one of unparalleled change in the legal services industry. Increased internal competition and de-regulation have seen speculative actions assume a new and wider prominence. South Australia and NSW introduced legislation authorising and regulating contingency fee agreements in 1993. Other states are likely to follow suit since contingency fees were promoted by the previous government's Access to Justice Advisory Committee (1994).

[2] Although not in Sweden.

actions place new complex demands on legal aid and are likely to continue to do so in the future. They have the potential to result in either severe restrictions on the availability of legal aid in other types of cases or in legal aid being withdrawn from some types of these actions. The more general lesson from this case study is that governments, legal aid administrators and the legal profession in all societies need to pay more attention to the problems created by multi-party actions, and especially their impact on legal aid.

The Chapter begins by presenting the results of an investigation of the recent experience of multi-party actions in Australian legal aid. It concludes with some observations about this experience and its implications for legal aid internationally.

The project methodology and data

The aim of the project was to report on the recent presence, management and significance of 'mass' or multi-party civil, criminal and family law actions in Australia. In view of time and other constraints I focused solely on the recent experience, that is 1993–6. Given the absence of a taxonomy or administrative protocols for describing multi-party actions in Australian legal aid, the first task was to define the subject-matter. For this purpose a simple working definition which enabled identification of the relevant cases was developed. 'Multi-party actions' were defined as:

- test cases to resolve/potentially resolve similar claims of multiple potential litigants, or defences of multiple accused;
- litigation undertaken by groups or individuals in the wider public interest, e.g. environmental, consumer, administrative law proceedings;
- proceedings involving multiple plaintiffs with similar causes of action against a single/common class of defendants;
- representation of multiple defendants in criminal proceedings arising out of a common/related incident; and
- proceedings under any relevant group proceedings, class, representative actions legislation.

Gaining access to reliable national data in relation to these sort of cases poses great difficulties. While national legal aid data exists it does not classify cases according to group or individual clients (LAFS, 1997). Data from the legal profession industry is similarly inaccessible. While the Australian Bureau of Statistics began conducting surveys of the legal services industry in the late 1980s it is essentially macro-level productivity data (ABS, 1995). Finally, it is at least fifteen years since reliable national or regional data was published about trends in the sociology of the legal profession and legal practice. As a result I focused almost exclusively on legal aid agencies data.

There are three discrete segments in the Australian legal aid system—the eight regional legal aid commissions, 150 community legal centres and over 100 offices of the Aboriginal and Torres Strait Islander Legal Services (ATSILS) (Fleming 1994). I approached thirty-one agencies and asked them to report on their experiences of multi-party civil, criminal and family law proceedings in the past three years. These included Legal Aid and Family Services (LAFS) the federal government office responsible for legal aid funding and administration and the regional legal aid commissions which together comprise the existing inter-governmental national legal aid scheme.[3] This scheme is the major provider of legal assistance in Australia (Fleming, 1994). The other twenty-two agencies were 'specialist' community legal centres or 'public interest advocacy' agencies and they were chosen because it was known or seemed likely that their specialist focus had generated involvement in multi-party action and other proceedings.[4] However, this selection of 'community' agencies is by no means perfect. For example, it ignored the presence of any one-off multi-party proceedings in the 120 'generalist' community legal centres.[5] On the basis of the patterns of the late 1980s a few one-off cases almost certainly exist (NLAAC, 1990). In national terms, however, they are not a significant presence, and the case types are likely to replicate those revealed in this research. Finally, although I was not able to include the ATSILS in the list of respondents due to time and other constraints, as is revealed below, the responses to the survey pointed me in the direction of recent developments in multi-party actions affecting indigenous Australians.

The initial response to the project was mixed. Only five of the twenty-two 'community' agencies replied and none recorded any relevant experience of multi-party actions. All but one of the regional legal aid commissions replied to the survey. Their replies provide the basis of the administrative and management

[3] The regional legal aid commissions exist in each Australian state and territory. They are: Legal Aid Office (ACT) (LAOACT)), Legal Aid Commission of New South Wales (LACNSW), Legal Aid Commission of the Northern Territory (LACNT), Legal Aid Office (Queensland) (LAOQ), Legal Services Commission of South Australia (LSCSA), Legal Aid Commission of Tasmania (LACT), Victoria Legal Aid (VLA) and Legal Aid Western Australia (LAWA). For an introduction see Fleming (1994).

[4] They were: the Public Interest Advocacy Centre, Environmental Defenders Office (NSW), Environmental Defenders Office (Vic), Nth Queensland Environmental Defenders Office, Environmental Defenders Office (Qld), Environmental Defenders Office (SA) Inc, Environmental Defenders Office (WA) Inc, Environmental Defenders Office (Tas) Inc, Environmental Defenders Office (ACT) Inc, Environmental Defenders Office (NT), HIV/AIDS Legal Centre, NSW Disability Discrimination Legal Centre, National Children's & Youth Legal Centre, Disability Discrimination Law Advocacy Service, Brisbane Welfare Rights Centre (Disability Discrimination Centre), Cairns Community Legal Centre Inc (Disability Discrimination Centre), Norwood Community Legal Centre (Disability Discrimination Centre), Sussex Street Community Law Centre (Disability Discrimination Centre), Northern Community Legal Service (Disability Discrimination Centre), The Canberra Welfare Rights and Legal Centre (Disability Discrimination Centre) & Darwin Community Legal Service Inc (Disability Discrimination Centre). For a discussion of the differences between 'specialist' and 'generalist' community legal centres see LAFS (1991).

[5] This Chapter focuses on legal proceedings but it is acknowledged that strategic action like education, law reform and prevention in the 'community' legal aid sector have multi-party features.

data reported in Table 11.1 below.[6] The LACNT also alerted me to developments in the Aboriginal 'stolen children' cases explained below, which were being managed by the Northern Australian Aboriginal Legal Aid Service (NAALAS). Generally, however, the legal aid commissions' replies were minimalist in content and description. They were presented in the language of 'insiders', and did not really inform 'outsiders' about the reality of the multi-party experience. LAFS also replied to my questions, and gave me up-to-date information about developments in Commonwealth legal aid policy.

The mixed initial responses produced several counter-responses on my part. I approached National Legal Aid, the legal aid commissions' peak body and explained the shortcomings in the commissions' replies. With its support I again approached LACNSW, LAWA and LAOQ with requests for copies of statements of claim and additional details about the multi-party experience. LACNSW and LAWA were particularly forthcoming. Copies of court documents in the WA *Homeswest* cases, the *Copper 7 IUD Products* litigation, the atomic-testing cases and details of other cases explained below were supplied. I also sought information from NAALAS about the *Stolen Children* cases and made related inquiries about this question to the federal Human Rights and Equal Opportunity Commission. Finally, several firms of solicitors known to be practising in the field of multi-party actions, including Cashman and Partners in Sydney and Slater and Gordon in Melbourne, were approached, but without success.

In the end the project was reasonably successful, given the systemic constraints noted above. Some data is now available on the presence and management of multi-party actions in the national legal aid scheme as well as some of the details of recent experience in regional and cross-regional experience multi-party civil litigation. Finally, the project generated some details of recent multi-party actions by Australian indigenous peoples. These outcomes are reported below.

The presence and management of multi-party actions

The data tells us a lot about how legal aid is responding to multi-party actions. First, multi-party proceedings are not a major part of the national legal aid

[6] The legal aid commissions were asked seven primary questions: 1. in 1993/6 how many applications were received/approved/referred for legal aid in civil, criminal and family law mass action type proceedings? 2. Was the presence of mass action-type proceedings a special consideration in applications approved/referred? Why? 3. Were applications received/approved/referred affected by the presence/absence of legislation/Rules of Court facilitating the conduct of mass action-type proceedings? 4. Did standard civil, criminal and family law financial guidelines apply to applications for legal assistance in mass action-type proceedings? If no, how did the applicable eligibility criteria differ? 5. Was a standard approach taken to the imposition/payment of contributions? 6. Details of outcomes in mass-type proceedings in which legal assistance was granted in 1993/6? 7. Did the Commission at the time have a policy in relation to grants of legal assistance in mass action-type proceedings? Does it now?

scheme. The legal aid commissions reported that less than 100 applications for legal aid in multi-party proceedings were approved over the period 1993/96 (see Table 11.1). When it is granted, aid is primarily in one type of law—the majority, approximately 95 per cent, were for the purposes of legally aided civil proceedings. Only the LSCSA reported granting legal aid in multi-party criminal proceedings where aid was granted in five applications involving a total of thirty-five accused variously facing trial for murder, conspiracy, attempted murder and prison riot (LSCSA 1997). The pattern of applications nationally is also far from uniform. There were, for example, no applications for multi-party legal aid in LACNT or LACT (Table 11.1). The small number of approvals in other jurisdictions reflect a low application rate. On the other hand the NSW experience is quite distinctive, involving a total of ninety applications over the three years (Table 11.1). Nevertheless, without legal aid funding these multi-party actions would have faced great difficulty in proceeding to court.

The generally low profile of multi-party proceedings is reflected in the management response to such actions. Most agencies in the national legal aid scheme have not developed special guidelines, contributions formulae or policies for these proceedings (Table 11.1). The exception is LACNSW which, because of a relatively high number of applications, has made special provision for the administration of multi-party proceedings. A 'Common Interest Unit' which processes applications in matters where there is 'a common interest in the outcome amongst various applicants' has been established, according to Mike Cramsie, the Managing Director. The unit employs two lawyers and an administrative officer. Special consideration is given to applicants for legal aid in multi-party civil proceedings and this manifests itself in several different ways. For example, a more flexible approach is taken to the application of financial eligibility criteria. In practice this means that the presence of an applicant in a multi-party application whose personal income and assets exceeds standard allowances will not necessarily lead to refusal of legal aid. Instead the application is assessed on a collective basis. On the other hand LACNSW may reach the view that applicants for multi-party legal aid constitute a class of people who are able to afford the likely cost of the proceedings. The standard AUS$40 application fee is not demanded of applicants whose claims are representative of a wider class of people whose interests stand to be protected by the proceedings. The LACNSW took this approach in the '*Caravan Park*' case described below.

The LACNSW standard 'merits' test is also varied. Applicants for multi-party legal aid are required to satisfy the usual requirement that they 'have reasonable prospects of success in the proceedings'. The potential benefits arm of the 'merits' test is, however, broadened to: 'take into account the benefit that may accrue, not only to the applicants but to the wider public for whom legal aid is designed to assist, being the financially and socially disadvantaged in NSW and Australia'.

LACNSW decision-making in relation to multi-party applications also factors

Table 11.1: Multi-party actions in the Australian national legal aid scheme 1993–6

Agency	Applications			Special Rules of Court etc	Standard guidelines	Standard contributions	Policy on multi-party actions
	Received	Referred	Approved				
LAWA	NA	NA	12	No	Yes	Yes	No
LSCSA	2 civil	2 civil[a]	–				
	5 crim	–	5 crim	No	Yes	Yes	No
LAOQ	–	–	20 civil	No	Yes	Yes	No
LAOACT	4 civil	–	4 civil	No	Yes	Yes	No
LACNT	NR	NR	NR	No	Yes	Yes	No
LAOACT	nil	nil	nil	*	NR	NR	NR
VLA	*	*	*	*	*	*	*
LACNSW	90 civil	40 civil	50 civil	Yes	No	No	Yes
LAFS	NA[b]	NA	NA	–	Yes[c]	Yes[c]	No

Source: Information supplied by legal aid agencies
* Not supplied
NA Not available
NR Not relevant
[a] LSCSA no longer funds civil actions in cost recovery jurisdictions.
[b] Anecdotal evidence suggests multi-party applications in 1993/6 under the Commonwealth statutory industrial relations, sex and racial discrimination and native title legal aid schemes. See description of these provisions in NLAAC, 1990:44–5.
[c] A number of the Commonwealth statutory and non-statutory legal aid schemes are designed for collective and interest group proceedings. The existing guidelines for assistance and contributions have the flexibility required for multi-party actions.

in the availability of grouped proceedings. Where group proceeding law does not apply and there is a high probability of plaintiffs obtaining favourable individual settlements, legal aid is unlikely to be approved for a multi-party action. Conversely, where group procedures exist legal aid may be granted for a multi-party action, even though the monetary value of individual claims is low.

Multi-party actions in the national legal aid scheme

The data in Table 11.1 does not tell us, however, about the actual experience of multi-party actions in the national legal aid scheme. This experience is not well known outside the regional legal aid commissions. There are various reasons for this. In the case of LACNSW Cramsie notes that as 'common interest matters are only a small proportion of the work conducted by the Commission, our annual reports do not adequately detail the successes in these matters' (1997). Similar circumstances apply to the other commissions. Their 'bread and butter' is the provision of legal assistance, duty lawyer services and legal advice to *individual* litigants and accused. Other factors such as the absence of a research culture, work pressure, concerns about client confidentiality and the professional reticence of lawyers have contributed to non-publication of the multi-party experience in the national scheme. In this context the presentation of the recent Australian data below fulfils two objectives. It elaborates upon the basic data in Table 11.1 and it also establishes something of a public benchmark for the purposes of subsequently constructing a complete picture of the scope of multi-party proceedings in the Australian legal aid system. The experience over 1993/6 can be divided into two categories: within and across regions.

The multi-party experience in the regions

The first category is the multi-party experience in the regions. Table 11.1 shows that LACNSW is the major regional player in the national scheme. Over 1993–6 it provided legal aid in eight significant civil multi-party actions. LACNSW also administers a scheme in which small grants of legal aid are available in proceedings challenging developments likely to negatively impact on the natural environment. In 1995 and 1996 LACNSW made financial grants of between $500–$20,000 to applicants in thirty multi-party environmental cases (Cramsie, 1997).

The eight legally aided civil multi-party actions cover a wide range of matters and together they demonstrate the importance of such actions. One case has its origins in the mid to late 1980s when 141 people who had been treated at the Chelmsford Private Hospital in the 1970s applied for legal aid. These former patients sought to take action for damages against the hospital and associated medical practitioners in respect of personal injuries sustained during 'deep sleep therapy'. LACNSW granted assistance to several applicants to initiate Supreme Court proceedings. In 1995, one of these applicants finally succeeded in a High Court appeal maintained by the NSW Medical Defence Union against an earlier decision of the NSW Supreme Court.[7] The Medical Defence Union is now settling the claims of all the original applicants for legal aid. It is also settling similar claims against the Chelmsford Private Hospital by approximately 300 other former patients who undertook proceedings with the aid of private solicitors instructed on a speculatory basis (Cramsie, 1997).

Six of the other LACNSW multi-party actions related to consumer protection. The first concerned an immigration status scam in the early 1990s. Twenty people approached a solicitor in order to try to obtain permanent residency in Australia. The solicitor told them he could guarantee permanent residency under the 'employer nomination scheme' but in fact this was not possible, and the clients suffered financial loss. LACNSW funded an action in the Federal Court which upheld the clients' claim finding that 'the solicitor charged them excessively . . . in many cases very little work was done and where applications were lodged, they had little hope of success and were ultimately rejected'. Damages were awarded

[7] *NSW Medical Defence Union* v. *Crawford* S20571994 95/043 unreported.

in favour of the applicants against the solicitor. These proceedings are seen by LACNSW as having an immediate impact in obtaining damages for the applicants. But they also have a salutary longer-term impact on lawyers and migration agents tempted to exploit the social vulnerability of ordinary immigrants seeking changes to migration status.

Two of the consumer protection cases concerned residents' rights. In the *Caravan Park* case a group of caravan park residents had purchased site occupancy rights from the owner. The agreement provided that only limited rent increases were permissible for a period of eighteen years. It also provided that any new owner of the caravan park would be required to novate the occupancy agreement. The caravan park was subsequently sold and the new owner was not notified of the existence of the site occupancy agreement. It declined to acknowledge that it was bound by the agreement, and sought to redevelop the caravan park in a manner inconsistent with the rights of the long-term residents. LACNSW has provided legal aid to these residents to bring an action for breach of contract against the former owner for damages. The *Caravan Park* case is yet to be determined. The second residents' rights case is the 'Retirement Village' proceedings in which LACNSW granted legal aid to seventeen residents of a retirement village to obtain review of a rental increase. The proprietor, Christian Enterprises Ltd, had advised the village residents of its intention to increase individual weekly licence fees from AUS$27 to $70. The residents applied for Supreme Court declarations that the proprietor was bound to comply with the rental increase procedures contained in the Retirement Village Industry Code of Practice. In November 1996 the Supreme Court granted the applications. At the time of writing, Christian Enterprises Ltd has appealed and the residents have been granted additional legal aid to respond (Cramsie, 1997).

Three of the consumer protection actions related to consumer credit. In the *Gordon Investments Time-share* case LACNSW received seven applications for legal aid from people who borrowed money to purchase timeshares in a Port Macquarie, a seaside resort. The applications appear to have emanated from a community legal centre which represented a total of ninety-five time-share borrowers. Grants of legal aid were approved to four applicants to take action against the lender Gordon Investments for non-compliance with the consumer protection provisions of the Credit Act 1984 (NSW). The action has so far progressed through the NSW Commercial Tribunal, the Supreme Court and Court of Appeal and the High Court. The consumers have succeeded in their substantive action. The proceedings have been remitted to the Commercial Tribunal to fix the penalty which Gordon Investments should pay for its breaches of the Credit Act. Legal aid has been granted to all the time-share borrowers represented by the community legal centre for the purposes of this determination. Gordon Investments company has ceased trading and the improper sales of its time-shares stopped (Cramsie, 1997).

Aid has also been granted in cases involving large groups of applicants. In the

Home Fund Loans cases LACNSW received 775 applications for legal aid from borrowers in the public 'Home Fund' scheme. The applicants sought to contest key aspects of the credit arrangements in the scheme. Legal aid was granted to two applicants as representatives of the 750 applicants who belonged to the United Borrowers Association of Australia (UBAA). It was also provided to another applicant to represent non-UBAA borrowers. The proceedings are currently before the High Court for resolution of legal issues of the application of Crown immunity to state-related commercial companies. LACNSW also granted legal aid to fifty applicants in the *State Bank* case to represent the interests of customers in opposing the State Bank's application to reinstate approx AUS$450m in credit charges. The Bank had lost this money when it failed to comply with the disclosure provisions of the Credit Act. The total number of credit contracts affected by the application was 250,000. As a result of these proceedings the State Bank was ordered to pay a penalty of $5m and to pay costs totalling $550,000 of the legally aided respondents (Cramsie, 1997).

LACNSW also provided legal aid to assist 700 women steel workers who took proceedings against an employer alleging that its hiring practices discriminated against the employment of women. These proceedings were successful, and women were subsequently employed as steelworkers. Women steelworkers were however subsequently retrenched in disproportionate numbers as a result of the application of a policy of 'first hired, last fired'. Further legally aided discrimination proceedings were undertaken. These proceedings were eventually settled in a manner favourable to the applicants (Cramsie, 1997).

LAWA, LAOQ and the LAOACT also funded intra-regional multi-party actions. In 1995 LAWA undertook a representative action on behalf of 118 Sino-Vietnamese people who had landed unlawfully in Australia aboard MV 'Albatross'. At the time they landed it appears it was legally possible for them to apply for refugee status. The federal immigration authorities, however, declined to facilitate any applications for migration status, and refused the detainees access to independent legal advice. New legislation was promulgated affecting the rights of illegal immigrants to apply for refugee status. This legislation had been foreshadowed but was not in force when the Sino-Vietnamese people first arrived. It had the effect of prohibiting illegal entrants from applying for refugee status whilst detained in Australia. The immigration authorities relied on these provisions to deny the legitimacy of the subsequent applications for refugee status. LAWA funded proceedings in the Federal Court on the basis that federal migration authorities were legally obliged to provide the detainees with the necessary forms for refugee status applications. The proceedings also sought to establish that the migration authorities should have permitted the detainees access to a solicitor so that they could be fully advised of their legal rights.[8] The representative action went to the High Court where the applicants were unsuccessful on appeal.

[8] *You Fang & Ors* v. *Minister for Immigration and Ethnic Affairs & Anor* (1996) 135 ALR 583.

LAWA also provided multi-party legal aid in the '*Homeswest*' cases. Homeswest is the public housing authority of the West Australian government. State legislation made pursuant to the terms of the Commonwealth-State housing agreements conferred security of tenure upon indigent public tenants subject to proof of breach of their lease agreements. In the early 1990s Homeswest began to evict its non-paying tenants under s. 64 of the Residential Tenancies Act 1987 (WA) (RTA). Section 64 enabled landlords to terminate a tenancy without giving reasons on sixty days' notice. Over 1993/96 LAWA provided legal aid to four public tenants affected by s. 64 notices to bring proceedings to challenge the legality of the Homeswest eviction decisions. One set of legally aided proceedings took the form of judicial review proceedings in the WA Supreme Court. In these proceedings the applicants argued that the status of Homeswest as a public housing authority means that it denies procedural fairness to its tenants if it decides to evict tenants without providing either reasons or the opportunity of administrative protest. The applicants also argued that it is against public policy for a public housing authority to have resort to law primarily intended for use by private landlords, according to the Director of Legal Aid WA (1997). At the time of writing, these actions are pending trial. In two related cases LAWA has provided legal aid in Supreme Court proceedings to review the legality of orders for termination and possession obtained by Homeswest in the Small Disputes Division of the WA Local Court while judicial review proceedings in respect of s. 64 notices were pending.

The Queensland LAO has provided legal aid in four multi-party asbestosis actions. It has also provided legal aid in five multi-party medical procedure applications. Four of these applicants are in the *Tubal Litigation* matters which are yet to be determined (LAOQ, 1997). The other medical procedure action was the *Depo Medrol Epidural* case which has recently been resolved in favour of the applicant. The LAOACT is also involved in the *Debendox* case but at the time of writing I have no information about these proceedings.

The cross-regional multi-party experience

The second category of multi-party experience in the national legal aid scheme is the cross-regional proceedings. There are at least two major multi-party civil proceedings which have been funded by the legal aid commissions on a cross-regional basis. The research indicates that there is no inter-commission protocol governing these types of national multi-party actions (LACNSW, 1997) but there are cost-sharing agreements of some kind which are documented by exchanges of letters. The multi-party civil proceedings are the *Copper 7 IUD Products* litigation and the *Atomic radiation* cases.

1. The *Copper 7 IUD Products* litigation is the major multi-party action jointly funded by the legal aid commissions. Copper 7s were intra-uterine contraceptive

devices (IUDs) first marketed in Australia in 1974 by a US medical goods manufacturer which is now a subsidiary of Monsanto. In 1989 Australian women who had formerly used the Copper 7 IUDs began proceedings alleging negligence against the manufacturer, Monsanto and the Australian distributor seeking damages and compensation and declaratory relief in respect of alleged breaches of the consumer protection provisions of the Trade Practices Act 1974 (Cth). The Australian Government is also a respondent to the proceedings.

The plaintiffs' essential claim is that in 1970 when the Monsanto subsidiary acquired rights over the Copper 7 IUD technology it knew or soon realised that women who used this product risked infertility. Since 1968 published medical research had indicated women using IUDs were more likely to contract pelvic inflammatory disease (PID). The risk posed to fertility by the contraction of PID has also generated a substantial body of contemporary medical opinion which suggested that IUDs were not an appropriate form of contraception for women who had never had children. The plaintiffs' case is that the manufacturer disregarded this evidence and resolved to bring the product to market by April 1971. It was prevented from doing so in the United States by the regulatory requirements of the its Food and Drug Administration. Different and less stringent regulatory requirements applied in Australia. The plaintiffs' allege that the manufacturer and its local agent misled and deceived the Australian regulatory authorities, the medical profession, family planning services and consumers as to the safety, efficacy, design and integrity of the Copper 7 IUD products. The plaintiffs also allege that the manufacturer subsequently misled all these parties as to the consumer protection measures it had adopted. The Australian Government is alleged to have been negligent in the discharge of its regulatory and related public functions.

The plaintiffs sued personally, and in a representative capacity on behalf of all Australian women who have used Copper 7 IUDs since 1974 or who may do so in the future. Approximately 200 Australian women whose fertility, reproductive well-being or health was damaged by use of Copper 7 IUD products have received legal aid from the regional agencies.[9] The proceedings were issued in the Federal Court and are being heard in the NSW Supreme Court under the federal cross-vesting legislation. Nine lead cases were selected for the hearing which commenced in the Supreme Court on 29 January 1996. The impact of the case on the courts and legal aid is illustrated by the fact that it was estimated the case would take forty-one weeks of hearings including twenty-eight weeks of oral evidence (Cramsie, 1997). At the time of writing the case has not been completed. The proceedings are being conducted by Cashman & Partners, a firm of Sydney solicitors associated with the Public Interest Advocacy Centre.

[9] Although only LAWA (7), LACQ (16) and LACNSW (9) provided numbers of legally aided claimants.

2. The *Atomic Radiation* cases. In the 1950s and 1960s Australia permitted the British Government to test and explode atomic bombs and nuclear devices at Maralinga and the Monte Bello islands. In the late 1980s several ex-servicemen and widows issued High Court proceedings claiming damages for personal injury arising out of exposure to radiation. The plaintiffs claim that the Australian Government was negligent in its administration of the conduct of the tests and explosions, in breach of statutory duty and failed to properly instruct service personnel in the safe performance of their duties.[10] Alternative claims were made on the grounds of strict liability, breach of occupier's duty and trespass to the person. The Australian Government denied all liability. It also claimed initially that the proceedings were statute-barred, although leave appears to have been granted in 1992 to allow the plaintiffs to proceed.

The complete details of cross-regional participation in the *Atomic Radiation* cases are unfortunately not available. However, it is known that thirty applications for legal aid were received by the LACNSW, aid was granted to three claimants in substantive proceedings and to another seven to obtain leave to extend the time to initiate proceedings. Applications were refused for eleven and the balance have not, at time of writing, been determined. Other legal aid commissions have also made related grants of legal aid but the details are not available.

Three of the *Atomic Radiation* cases were recently presented as test cases in the NSW Supreme Court. While two of these actions failed the third, a legally aided plaintiff, was successful and costs were awarded against the Australian Government. This allowed the LACNSW to recover expenditure of AUS$1.05m (Cramsie, 1997). Other *Atomic Radiation* cases are yet to be determined.

Multi-party actions by Australian indigenous peoples

Finally, a number of important developments have recently taken place in the context of civil multi-party actions on behalf of Aboriginal and Torres Strait Islander peoples. Some cases have been legally aided. In the early 1990s *Mabo* case the High Court transformed the modern law of indigenous customary title in Australia.[11] This spawned further litigation which impacted upon the potential legal rights of many indigenous peoples and communities who were potential claimants for hitherto unrecognised rights over unalienated Crown lands.[12] The changes to Australian land law prompted by *Mabo* and the political reaction of all interested parties is likely, in the future, to involve indigenous peoples in new defences of their human rights.[13]

[10] Statement of claim, *J R Coleman* v. *The Commonwealth of Australia* S156/1988 2–9.

[11] *Mabo (No. 2)* v. *Queensland* (1992) 175 CLR 1.

[12] *Western Australia* v. *Commonwealth* (1995) 183 CLR 373; *The Wik Peoples* v. *The State of Queensland & Ors; The Thayorre People* v. *The State of Queensland & Ors* (1996) 134 ALR 637.

[13] These changes included the establishment of a National Native Title Tribunal. A statutory scheme also provides legal aid for parties to Tribunal proceedings, including in test cases raising important questions about the Native Title Act 1993 (Cth) or other Commonwealth law.

One important multi-party action which affected the interests of Australian indigenous peoples were the '*Stolen Children*' cases. These proceedings related to the officially sanctioned practice of forcibly removing indigenous children from their families. A recent national human rights inquiry has found that this practice began 'in the first days of European colonisation . . . Indigenous children were kidnapped and exploited for their labour. Governments and missionaries [later] targeted Indigenous children for removal so that they could be employed in service to colonial settlers' (Human Rights and Equal Opportunity Commission (HREOC), 1997:2).

In the twentieth century the major actors in forcible removal were the public welfare agencies and church groups. Whilst removal sometimes had charitable objectives the human rights inquiry found that since 1937 at least it was part of co-ordinated public policies intended to absorb indigenous people into white society (HREOC, 1997:2–3). The report which was presented to the Australian Government in April 1997 includes the finding that since at least 1946 the 'policy of forcibly transferring indigenous children to non-indigenous institutions constituted genocide, contrary to binding international law' (HREOC, 1997:8).

In 1996, two Aboriginal plaintiffs were assisted by NAALAS to bring proceedings in the High Court against the Australian Government claiming damages for their forcible removal as children. The plaintiffs claimed that their removal was unlawful as it breached fundamental human rights and implied and express constitutional rights. In particular, a breach of an implied right to legal equality, freedom of political discourse and freedom of association and movement and the express constitutional right to freedom of religion.[14] The High Court handed down judgment in mid-1997, finding in favour of the Australian Government. It held that the legislative powers contained in s. 122 of the Australian Constitution were not impliedly constrained by the human rights considerations which the plaintiffs had contended.[15]

Other multi-party litigation has been commenced by Aboriginal people. In Queensland in 1996 an Aboriginal man named *Fisher* commenced a multi-party action against the State Government in respect of funds allegedly misappropriated from its Aboriginal savings and welfare account funds. These funds were established in the late nineteenth century and continued into the 1960s. In effect they were publicly administered trust funds into which wages earned by Aboriginal people subject to institutional controls were paid. The *Fisher* claim seeks declarations that the Queensland Government is in breach of trust and fiduciary duty,

[14] 'Reliving the days they took the children away' *Age* 30 Jan. 1996; 'Blacks claim law created a "master race"' *Sydney Morning Herald* 13 Feb. 1996; 'Aboriginals suffered "a holocaust"' *Canberra Times* 14 Feb. 1996; 'Past white views irrelevant: QC' *Age* 14 Feb. 1996; 'Time to retrieve their lost rights' *Age* 16 Feb. 1996; 'Aborigines entitled to damages, court told' *Australian* 14 Feb. 1996; 'Aborigines in test case over child removal' *Age* 12 Feb. 1996.

[15] *Kruger* v. *The Commonwealth of Australia*: *Bray* v. *The Commonwealth of Australia* (1997) 146 ALR 126.

and claims compensation and damages. It was anticipated that a comparable action would be taken by the Foundation for Aboriginal and Islander Research. Both these actions have the potential to benefit thousands of indigenous people and their families in Queensland.

Conclusion

The principal value of this research has been to compile and consolidate something of the experience of multi-party actions in Australian legal aid in 1993–6. At a general level it serves to confirm that the phenomenon of 'mass' torts which first emerged in the United States in the early 1980s (Hensler and Peterson, 1993:961–2; Nocera, 1995; Weinstein, 1995) is now entrenched in the Australian legal system, as in the legal systems of comparable Western countries. It also suggests that legally aided actions are currently one vehicle for victims of 'mass' torts and other collective civil wrongs and abuses to pursue legal redress. The value of such cases cannot be ignored, especially in view of the restrictions on contingency fees in many Australian states and territories. Without legal aid some of these cases would not have commenced let alone been finalised in the courts.

Nevertheless, much remains to be done if legal aid is going to be able to better respond to multi-party actions. For example, the legal aid agencies have done little to develop policies and procedures to process these resource intensive, complex and long-running cases. Furthermore, the research suggests there is little co-ordination between legal aid agencies in relation to such cases. If more cases emerge in the future the agencies would benefit from a more co-operative approach to developing policies and procedures.

The research does, however, prompt a number of questions. For example, from a management point of view, the research does not answer the question of why legal aid is necessarily the most appropriate option to fund such cases. Why should scarce public resources give priority to these civil actions and not the large number of other individual civil actions? Similarly, from a consumer point of view there are now a range of private legal profession and private industry options for pursuing legal actions including speculatory actions, contingency fee agreements or even legal insurance. These are all parallel forms of popular access to lawyers' services which experienced significant developments in Australia over the period 1993–6 (Access to Justice Advisory Committee, 1994).

Even if a society decides that public funds should support multi-party actions it does not necessarily follow that they should be legal aid funds. Alternative funding sources might be more appropriate in a time of scarce resources. For example, the previous Commonwealth Government established a national fund to pay the costs of special cases of national significance including test cases. Such a fund might also be the best vehicle for multi-party actions rather than to try to make legal aid administrators reshape their activities. There is no logical reason why legal aid should necessarily move beyond granting aid to individuals and good reasons why special funds and alternative organisations might be a better way to proceed.

The results are also a timely reminder of the legacy of inadequate investment in the technology of research and development in Australian and other societies' legal aid. Those in the industry and researchers tend now to take this situation for granted, but it remains a serious problem if we are ever to achieve the national understanding necessary to adapt legal aid services in a rapidly changing legal services industry. Australian legal aid managers have much to learn from the recent experience of their counterparts in England and Scotland in effective administration of multi-party actions (Day, Balen and McCool, 1995: 76–81; Scottish Law Commission, 1994; (Cmnd. 3291)). This 'negative' result of the project and its processes may also contain lessons for those currently reconsidering public outlays on legal aid, whether in Australia or elsewhere. If we cannot describe what is happening it is dangerous to make changes to parts of the legal system, including promoting multi-party actions, that are likely to impact on legal aid.

The project, its outcomes and processes reminds us of the ever-present necessity to understand legal aid and its management in the context of national law and government. The presence and management of legally aided multi-party actions in Australia was influenced by the introduction of grouped proceedings provisions in the Federal Court in 1991[16] and the rule changes that allowed contingency fees in some states. Future demand and management of multi-party actions will continue to be influenced by comparable contextual factors.

Finally, the research reminds us that Australia and other societies have yet to find a workable institutional solution which locates legal aid in the machinery of the welfare state. In Australia since 1977 there have been five national legal aid advisory bodies, and various earlier configurations of LAFS. An important systemic lesson of this Chapter is that Australian or any other societies' legal aid can only be improved in the context of a body responsible for the oversight of the national legal services system. Legal aid and its managers would have a role in this body. However, it is to ignore the historical failure of governments to integrate legal aid, the trend of 'access to justice' policy and the post-1970s transformation of law and public administration to continue to see legal aid as the centrepiece of the ongoing problems of popular access to law. Multi-party actions force us to confront yet again the fact that legal aid is only a small part of all the legal services needed and delivered in a society.

[16] Federal Court of Australia Amendment Act 1991 (Cth) inserted PART IVA into the Federal Court of Australia Act 1976 (Cth).

Table of Cases

Australia

European Community/Union

United Kingdom

United States of America

Table of Statutes and Regulations

Australia

Canada

Germany

Ireland

Netherlands

Sweden

United Kingdom

United States of America

Bibliography

Abel, R. ed. (1982) *The Politics of Informal Justice*, vol. 2, New York: Academic Press

—— (1985) 'Law Without Politics: Legal Aid under Advanced Capitalism', *UCLA Law Review*, 32:474

—— (1988) 'Lawyers in the Civil World', in: Abel, R. & Lewis, P. eds. *The Civil Law World* (Lawyers in Society, vol. 2), Berkeley: UCLA Press

—— ed. (1995) *The Law and Society Reader*, New York: New York University Press

—— (1996) 'The Paradoxes of Legal Aid', in: Paterson, A. & Goriely, T. eds. *Resourcing Civil Justice*, Oxford: Oxford University Press

—— & Lewis, P. eds. (1988–89) *Lawyers in Society*, 3 vols., Berkeley: UCLA Press

Abel-Smith, B. & Titmuss K. eds. (1987) *The Philosophy of Welfare: Selected writings of Richard M. Titmuss*, London: Allen & Unwin

Abel-Smith, B., Zander, M. & Brooke, R. (1973) *Legal Problems and the Citizen*, London: Heinemann

Access to Justice Advisory Committee (1994) *Access to Justice: An Action Plan*, Canberra: Australian Government Publishing Service

Access to Justice Working Group, California State Bar (1996) *And Justice for All: Fulfilling the Promise of Access to Civil Justice in California*, San Francisco: California State Bar

Agnew, S. T. (1972) 'What's Wrong with the Legal Services Program', *American Bar Association Journal*, 58:930

Alcock, P. (1976) 'Legal Aid: Whose Problem?' *British Journal of Law and Society*, 4:151

Alfieri, A. (1987–88) 'The Antinomes of Poverty Law and a Theory of Dialogic Empowerment', *Review of Law and Social Change*, 16:666

Allbeson, J. & Smith, R. (1984) *We Don't Give Clothing Grants Any More*, London: Child Poverty Action Group

Allen-Jones, J. E. (1938) 'Legal Aid for the Poor', *Law Times*, 186:296

American Bar Association (1971) *The Corporation for Legal Services: A Study*, prepared by ABA Section on Individual Rights and Responsibilities and Standing Committee on Legal Aid and Indigent Defendants, Chicago: ABA

American Law Institute/American Bar Association, Committee on Continuing Professional education (1981) *A Model Peer Review System*, Pennsylvania: ALI/ABA

—— (1985) *Law Practice Quality Guidelines*, Pennsylvania: ALI/ABA

—— (1988) *Law Practice Quality Evaluation*, Pennsylvania: ALI/ABA

Andersen, M. (1980) *Sociology of the Family*, Harmondsworth: Penguin

Ashworth, A., Genders, E., Mansfield, G., Peay, J. & Player, E. (1984) *Sentencing in the Crown Court: Report of an Exploratory Study*, Oxford: Centre for Criminological Research Occasional Paper No. 10

Ashworth, A. (1996) 'Legal Aid, Human Rights and Criminal Justice', in: Young, R. & Wall, D. eds. *Access to Criminal Justice*, London: Blackstone Press

Australian Bureau of Statistics (1995) *Legal and Accounting Services, Australia 1992–93*, Australian Bureau of Statistics: Canberra. (Catalogue no. 8678.0)

Australian Government (1995) *Justice Statement*, Canberra: Australian Government Publishing Service

Baldwin, J. (1996) 'Consumers' Access to Justice: Small Claims Procedures in the County Courts', in: Office of Fair Trading, *Developments in Consumer Redress—Report on a Symposium on 27 September 1995*, London: Office of Fair Trading

—— & Hill, S. (1988) *The Operation of the Green Form Scheme in England and Wales*, London: Lord Chancellor's Department

—— & McConville, M. (1977) *Negotiated Justice*, London: Martin Robertson

—— Wikeley, N. & Young, R. (1992) *Judging Social Security: the Adjudication of Claims for Benefit in Britain*, Oxford: Clarendon Press

—— Wilkeley, N. & Young, R. (1996) 'Adjudication in Local Offices', in: Galligan, D. ed. *A Reader on Administrative Law*, Oxford: Oxford University Press

Baldwin, P. (1990) *The Politics of Social Solidarity: Class Bases of the European Welfare State 1875–1975*, Cambridge: Cambridge University Press

Baldwin, R., & Hawkins, K. (1984) 'Discretionary Justice: Davis Reconsidered', *Public Law*, 570

Bamberger, C. E. (1966) 'The Legal Services Program of the Office of Economic Opportunity', *Notre Dame Lawyer*, 41:847

—— (1989) 'Statement to the Committee on Legal Aid in the Netherlands', *Rechtshulp*, 10:2

Barron, A. & Scott, C. (1992) 'The Citizen's Charter Programme', *Modern Law Review*, 55:526

Basten, J. (1987) 'Legal Aid and Community Legal Centres' *Australian Law Journal*, 61:714

Basten, J., Graycar, R., & Neal, N. (1983) 'Legal Centres in Australia', *University of New South Wales Law Journal*, 6:163

Beirne, P. & Nelken, D. (1997) 'Introduction', in: Beirne, P. & Nelken, D, eds. *Issues in Comparative Criminology*, Aldershot: Dartmouth

—— eds. (1997) *Issues in Comparative Criminology*, Aldershot: Dartmouth

Bellow, G. (1977) 'Turning Solutions into Problems: The Legal Aid Experience', *NLADA Briefcase*, 34:103

—— (1994) 'Legal Services in Comparative Perspective', *Maryland Journal of Comparative Legal Issues*, 5:371

Bergmark, M. (1994) 'The role of Competition in Making Grants for the Provision of Legal Services to the Poor' in: *Legal Aid in the Post Welfare State Society*, Proceedings of the International Conference on Legal Aid, The Hague

Besharov, D. ed. (1990) *Legal Services for the Poor: Time for Reform*, Washington: AEI Press

Bevan, G., Holland, A. & Partington, M. (1994) *Organising Cost-Effective Access to Justice*, Social Market Foundation Memorandum, no. 7, London: Social Market Foundation

Beveridge, Sir W. (1942) *Social Insurance and Allied Services*, Cm. 6404, London: HMSO

Blacksell, M., Economides, K. & Watkins, C. (1991) *Justice outside the City: Access to Legal Services in Rural Britain*, Essex: Longman

Blake, M. (1951) 'Legal Assistance for Servicemen', *American Bar Association Journal*, 37:9

Blankenburg, E. ed. (1980) *Innovations in the Legal Services*, Cambridge: Oelgeschlager, Gunn & Hain

Blankenburg, E. (1981), 'Legal Insurance, Litigant Decisions and the Rising Caseload of Courts: A West German Study', *Law & Society Review*, 16:601

—— (1985) 'Evaluation des ersten Jalves Beratungshilife', in: Zeitschrift für Rechtspolitik (ZRP), 39

—— (1992) 'Comparing Legal Aid Schemes in Europe', *Civil Justice Quarterly*, 11:106

—— (1994) 'The Infrastructure for Avoiding Civil Litigation: Comparing Cultures of Legal Behaviour in the Netherlands and West Germany', *Law and Society Review*, 28:789

—— (1995) 'Access to Justice and Alternatives to Courts: European Procedural Justice Compared', *Civil Justice Quarterly*, 14:176

—— (1997) 'Civil Litigation Rates as Indicators of Legal Cultures', in: Nelken, D. ed. *Comparing Legal Cultures*, Aldershot: Dartmouth

—— & Kaupen, W., eds. (1978) *Rechtsbedürfnis und Rechtshilfe*, *Jahrbuch für Rechtssoziologieund Rechtstheorie*, vol. 5, Wiesbaden: Westdeutscher Verlag

—— & Reifner, U. (1981) *Rechtsberatung*, Luchterhand: Neuwied

Boigeol, A. (1988) 'The French Bar: The Difficulties of Unifying a Divided Profession', in: Abel, R. & Lewis, P. eds. *The Civil Law World* (Lawyers in Society, vol. 2), Berkeley: UCLA Press

Boon, A. & Abbey, R. (1997) 'Moral Agendas? Pro Bono Publico in Large Law Firms in the United Kingdom', *Modern Law Review*, 60:630

Booth, J. (1997) 'Cost of state lawyer plan challenged', *Scotsman*, 22 Nov.

Bradway, J. (1939) 'National Aspects of Legal Aid', *Annals*, 205:101

Brakel, S. J. (1982) 'Legal Services for the Poor in the Reagan Years', *American Bar Association Journal*, 68:821

Bridges, L., Suffrin, B., Whetton, J. & White, R. (1975) *Legal Services in Birmingham*, Birmingham: University of Birmingham, Institute of Judicial Administration

Brownell, E. (1951) *Legal Aid in the United States*, Rochester: Lawyers Cooperative

Bruce, S., van Moorst, E., & Panagiotidis, S. (1992) 'Community Legal Education: Access to Justice', *Alternative Law Journal*, 17:278

Brunner, L. (1906) 'Die deutschen Arbeitersekretariate im Jahre 1905', *Correspondenzblatt der Generalkommission der Gewerkschaften Deutschlands*, 25:485–501

Bruzelius, A. & Bolding, P. O. (1975) 'An Introduction to the Swedish Legal Aid Reform', in: Cappelletti, M., Gordley, J. & Johnson, E. Jr eds. *Towards Equal Justice: A Comparative Study of Legal Aid in Modern Societies*, New York: Dobbs Ferry

Buck, M. R. (1976) 'The Legal Services Corporation: Finally Separate, But Not Quite Equal', *Syracuse Law Review*, 27:611

Bull, G. and Sergeant, J. (1996) *Alternative Methods of Delivering Services*, London: Policy Studies Institute

Bureau of Justice Statistics (1988) *Criminal Defence or the Poor, 1986*, Bulletin (September) Washington DC: Department of Justice

Burrage, M. (1989) 'Revolution as a Starting Point for the Comparative Analysis of the French, American and English Legal Professions', in: Abel, R. & Lewis, P. eds. *Comparative Theories* (Lawyers in Society, vol. 3), Berkeley: UCLA Press

Bushnell, G. E. Jr (1995) 'The President's Message', *ABA Journal*, 6 Jan.

Cabinet Office (1992) *The Citizen's Charter: First Report*, Cm. 2101, London: HMSO

Cahn, E. S. & Cahn, J. C. (1964) 'The War on Poverty: A Civilian Perspective', *Yale Law Journal*, 73:1317

Cameron Committee (1946) *Report of the Committee on Legal Aid in Scotland*, Cmd. 6925, Edinburgh: HMSO

Campbell, J. (1987) *Nye Bevan and the Mirage of British Socialism*, London: Weidenfeld & Nicolson

Canadian Bar Association (1996) 'Systems of Civil Justice Report', Canadian Bar Association, Toronto, <http://www.algonquinc.on.ca/cba/syseng.html>

Cantril, A. H. (1996) *Agenda for Access: The American People and Civil Justice. Final Report on the Implications of the Comprehensive Legal Needs Study Consortium on Legal Services and the Public*, Chicago: American Bar Foundation

Cappelletti, M. ed. (1984) *Accès à la Justice et l'Etat Providence*, Paris: Mouton

—— & Garth, B. eds. (1978/9), *Access to Justice*, (3 vols.) Milan: Dott A Giuffre

—— Gordley, J. & Johnson, E. Jr eds. (1975) *Towards Equal Justice: A Comparative Study of Legal Aid in Modern Societies*, New York: Dobbs Ferry

Carey Miller, D, & Beaumont, P. eds. (1993) *The Option of Litigating in Europe*, London: United Kingdom National Committee of Comparative Law

Carlin, J. Howard, J. & Messinger, S. (1966) *Civil Justice and the Poor*, New York: Russell Sage Foundation

Carney, C. (1979) 'The Growth of Legal Aid in the Republic of Ireland', *Irish Jurist*, 14:61, 211

Castles, F. ed. (1993) *Families of Nations: Patterns of Public Policy in Western Democracies*, Aldershot: Dartmouth

Castles, F. (1994) 'On Religion and Public Policy: Does Catholicism make a Difference?' *European Journal of Political Research*, 25:19

Castles, F., & Flood, M. (1993a) 'Law, Religious Belief and Modernity', in: Castles, F. ed. *Families of Nations: Patterns of Public Policy in Western Democracies*, Aldershot: Dartmouth

—— (1993b) 'Why Divorce Rates Differ: Law, Religious Belief and Modernity', in: Castles, F. ed. *Families of Nations: Patterns of Public Policy in Western Democracies*, Aldershot: Dartmouth

—— & Mitchell, D. (1993) 'Worlds of Welfare and Families of Nations', in: Castles F. ed. *Families of Nations: Patterns of Public Policy in Western Democracies*, Aldershot: Dartmouth

Cass, M. & Sackville R. (1975) *Legal Needs of the Poor*, Australian Government Commission on Inquiry into Poverty, Canberra: Australian Government Publishing Service

Chesterman, J. (1996) *Poverty Law and Social Change: The Story of the Fitzroy Legal Service*, Melbourne: Melbourne University Press

Chloros, A. G. (1992) 'Common Law, Civil Law and Socialist Law: Three Leading Systems of the World, Three Kinds of Legal Thought', in: Varga, C. ed. *Comparative Legal Cultures*, Aldershot: Dartmouth

Christie, M. (1990) *Breach of the Peace*, Edinburgh: Butterworths

Church, T. (1978) *Justice Delayed*, Virginia: National Centre for State Courts

Cicourel, A. (1968) *The Social Organisation of Juvenile Justice*, New York: John Wiley & Sons

Clarke, P., Brooks, T. & Machray, C. (1988) *Focus on Health Care: Surveying the Public in Four Health Districts*, London: Royal Institute of Public Administration

Clarkson, C. & Morgan, R. eds. (1995) *The Politics of Sentencing Reform*, Oxford: Oxford University Press

Coates, B. E. & Rawstron E. M. (1971) *Regional Variations in Britain: Studies in Economic and Social Geography*, London: Batsford

Cohn, E. (1943) 'Legal Aid for the Poor: A Study in Comparative Law and Legal Reform', *Law Quarterly Review*, 59:250, 359

Committee on Civil Legal Aid and Advice (1978) *Report*, Dublin: Stationery Office

Conseil d'État, (1991) *L'aide juridique: pour un meilleure accès au droit et à la justice*, Paris: Documentation Française

Cooper, J. (1994) 'English Legal Services: A Tale of Diminishing returns', *Maryland Journal of Comparative Legal Issues*, 5:264

Cooper, R. R. (1996) 'The President's Message', *ABA Journal*, 6 Apr.

Cooper, S. (1963) 'Sneok Piquante' in: Sissons, M. & French P. eds. *The Age of Austerity*, London: Hodder & Stoughton

Coote, A. ed. (1992) *The Welfare of Citizens: Developing New Social Rights*, London: IPPR/Rivers Oram Press

Cotterrell, R. (1997) 'The concept of Legal Culture', in: Nelken, D. ed. *Comparing Legal Cultures*, Aldershot: Dartmouth

Council of Europe (1992) *Prison Information Bulletin*, June, Strasbourg: Council of Europe

Council on Tribunals (1981) *Annual Report 1980–81*, HC 89, London: HMSO

—— (1987) *Annual Report 1986–87*, HC 234, London: HMSO

Cousins, M. (1993) 'Civil Legal Aid in France, Ireland, the Netherlands and the United Kingdom: A Comparative Study', *Civil Justice Quarterly*, 12:154

—— (1994) 'The Politics of Legal Aid: A Solution in Search of a Problem?', *Civil Justice Quarterly*, 13:111

—— (1996a) 'At the Heart of the Legal: The Role of Legal Aid in Legitimating Criminal Justice', in: Young, R. & Wall, D. eds. *Access to Criminal Justice*, London: Blackstone

—— (1996b) 'The Politics of Legal Aid: A Solution in Search of a Problem', in: Paterson, A. & Goriely, T. eds. *Resourcing Civil Justice*, Oxford: Oxford University Press

—— (1997) 'Ireland's Place in the Worlds of Welfare Capitalism', *Journal of European Social Policy*, 7:223

—— & O'Hara, G. (1992) *Access to the Courts in Four European Countries*, Dublin: Free Legal Advice Centres

Cowan, D., ed. (1998) *Housing: Participation and Exclusion*, Aldershot: Dartmouth

Coyle, P. (1995) 'Rights or Responsibilities?', *ABA Journal*, Apr. 82

Crampton, R. C. (1976) 'Promise and Reality in Legal Services', *Cornell Law Review*, 61:670

Cramsie, M. (1997) 'A broad overview of Legal Aid in 1997', in: *Legal Aid: How much justice can we afford?*, Proceedings of the International Conference on Legal Aid at Edinburgh, vol.1

Crespin, H. (1995) *Les frais de justice au dix-neuvième siècle*, Paris: LGDJ

Crockett, A. (1994) 'Legal Aid in Australia', in *Legal Aid in the Post-Welfare State Society*, Proceedings of the International Conference on Legal Aid, The Hague

Curran, B. (1977) *The Legal Needs of the Public*, Chicago: American Bar Foundation

Curran, B. (1996) *Agenda for Access: The American People and Civil Justice: Findings of the Comprehensive Legal Needs Study*, Chicago: American Bar Foundation

Currie, A. (1996) *The Legal Aid Manitoba Expanded Duty Counsel Project*, Ottawa: Canadian Ministry of Justice

Dalley, G. & Berthoud, R. (1992) *Challenging Discretion: the Social Fund Review Procedure*, London: Policy Studies Institute

Dalton, T. (1989) 'The Civil Legal Aid Scheme: Scope and Operation', *Gazette*, 83:137

Damaska, M. (1986) *The Faces of Justice and State Authority*, New Haven: Yale University Press

Darbyshire, P. (1997) 'An Essay on the Importance and Neglect of the Magistracy', *Criminal Law Review*, Sep. 627

David, R. & Brierley, J. (1985) *Major Systems in the World Today*, London: Stevens & Sons

Davies, P. & Freedland, M. (1993) *Labour Legislation and Public Policy: A Contemporary History*, Oxford: Clarendon Press

Day, M., Balen, P. & McCool, G. (1995) *Multi-Party Actions: A Practitioner's Guide to Pursuing Group Claims*, London: Legal Action Group

Denning Committee (1946) *Second Interim Report of the Committee on Procedure in Matrimonial Causes*, Cm. 6945, HMSO: London

Department of Social Security (1993) *Annual Report of the Social Fund Commissioner for 1992/93 on the Standards of Reviews by Social Fund Inspectors*, London: HMSO

Dhondt, J. (1988) 'Holland: Is the Penal Honeymoon Over?', *Prison Report*, 1988, 6

Donzelot, J. (1984) *L'invention du social*, Paris: Fayard

Doob, A. (1995) 'The United States Sentencing Commission Guidelines: If you don't know where you are going you might not get there' in: Clarkson, C. & Morgan, R. eds. *The Politics of Sentencing Reform*, Oxford: Oxford University Press

Dooley, J. A. & Houseman, A. W. (1984) *Legal Services History*, Washington: National Legal Aid and Defenders Association Management Project

Dorr, D. (1992) *Option for the Poor: A Hundred Years of Vatican Social Teaching*, Dublin: Gill & Macmillan

Downes, D. (1988) *Contrasts in Tolerance: Post-War Penal Policy in the Netherlands and England and Wales*, Oxford: Clarendon Press

Doyle, N. & Harding, T. (1992) 'Community care: Applying Procedural Fairness', in: Coote, A. ed. *The Welfare of Citizens: Developing New Social Rights*, London: IPPR/Rivers Oram Press

Duff, P. (1997) 'Diversion from Psychiatric Care: Who Controls the Gates?', *British Journal of Criminology*, 37:15

—— & Findlay, M. (1997) 'Jury Reforms: of Myths and Moral Panics', *International Journal of the Sociology of Law*, 25:368

Elson, A. (1946) 'The Rushcliffe Report', *University of Chicago Law Review*, 13:131

Emerson, R. M. (1995) 'Holistic Effects in Social Control Decision-Making', in: Abel, R. ed. *The Law and Society Reader*, New York: New York University Press

Eskeland, S. & Finne, J. (1973) *Rettshjelp*, Oslo: Pax

Esping-Andersen, G. (1990) *The Three Worlds of Welfare Capitalism*, Cambridge: Polity Press

European Commission (1995) *Social Protection in Europe 1995*, Luxembourg: Office of the Official Publications of the EC

Fennell, P., Harding, C., Jörg, N. & Swart, B. eds. (1995) *Criminal Justice in Europe: A Comparative Study*, Oxford: Clarendon Press

Fadden, R. *et al.* (1992) 'Community Legal Centres: National Overview 1992', *Alternative Law Journal*, 17:283

Faine, J. (1993) *Lawyers in the Alice: Aboriginals and Whitefellas' Law*, Annandale, NSW: Federation Press

Fair Trade Commission (1990) *Report of Study into Restrictive Practices in the Legal Profession*, Dublin: Stationery Office

Falk, J. & Pollard, S. (1973) 'Political Interference with Publicly Funded Lawyers: The CRLA Controversy and the Future of Legal Services', *Hastings Law Journal*, 24:599

Fionda, J. (1995) *Public Prosecutors and Discretion: A Comparative Study*, New York: Clarendon Press

Fitzmaurice, C. & Pease, K. (1986) *The Psychology of Judicial Sentencing*, Manchester: Manchester University Press

Fleming, D. (1994) 'The Mixed Model of Legal Aid in Australia', in: *Legal Aid in the Post-Welfare State Society*, Proceedings of the International conference on Legal Aid, The Hague

Flora, P. & Alber, J. (1981) 'Modernization, Democratization and the Development of Welfare States in Europe', in: Flora, P. & Heidenheimer, A. J. eds. *The Development of Welfare States in Europe and America*, London: Transaction

Flora, P. & Heidenheimer, A. J. eds. (1981*) The Development of Welfare States in Europe and America*, London: Transaction

Fox Piven, F. & Cloward, R. A. (1971) *Regulating the Poor: The Functions of Public Welfare*, New York: Vintage

Free, M. (1996) *African Americans in the Criminal Justice System*: *Current Issues in Criminal Justice*, vol. 13, New York: Garland

Fremont, J. (1994) 'Reassessing the Mixed Legal Aid Model in Quebec', in *Legal Aid in the Post-Welfare State Society*, Proceedings of the International Conference on Legal Aid, The Hague

Galanter, M. (1974) 'Why the "Haves" Come Out Ahead', *Law and Society Review*, 9:95

Galligan, D. ed. (1996) *A Reader on Administrative Law*, Oxford: Oxford University Press

Garment, L. (1997) *Crazy Rhythm*, New York: Random House

Garrison, L. (1940) 'Legal Service For Low Income Groups in Sweden', *American Bar Association Journal*, 26:215, 293

Garth, B. (1980) *Neighbourhood Law Firms for the Poor*, Alpen den Rijn: Sijthoff & Noorhoff

Garth, B. G. (1983) 'Rethinking the Legal Profession's Approach to Collective Self-improvement', *Wisconsin Law Review*, 639

Genn, H. & Genn, Y. (1989) *The Effectiveness of Representation at Tribunals*, London: Lord Chancellor's Department

George, W. (1976) 'Development of the Legal Services Corporation', *Cornell Law Review*, 61:681

Gibson, F. (1997) *When the Battle's Lost and Won, Legal Aid in Civil Matters in New South Wales 1992–94: Outline of a Community Legal Centre Campaign*, Kingsford: Kingsford Legal Centre

Goldie, C. (1996) 'Will Lawyers Ever Learn?' *Alternative Law Journal*, 21:296

Goriely, T. (1992) 'Legal Aid in the Netherlands: A View from England', *Modern Law Review*, 55:183

—— (1994a) 'Debating the Quality of Legal Services', *International Journal of the Legal Profession*, 1:159

—— (1994b) 'Why Do Some Societies Have Civil Legal Aid While Others Don't?' Paper to the Third European Conference on Legal Profession, Rouen, France

—— (1994c) 'Rushcliffe Fifty Years On', *Journal of Law and Society*, 21:545

—— (1996a) 'Law for Poor: The Relationship Between Advice Agencies and Solicitors in the Development of Poverty Law', *International Journal of the Legal Profession*, 3:215

—— (1996b) *Introducing Outcome Measures*, Report for the Scottish Legal Aid Board, Edinburgh: Scottish Legal Aid Board

—— (1997a) 'Contracting', in *Legal Aid: How much justice can we afford?*, Proceedings of the International Conference on Legal Aid, Edinburgh, vol. 1

—— (1997b) *Legal Aid Delivery Systems*, LCD Research Series no. 10/97, London: Lord Chancellor's Department

—— & Paterson, A. (1996) 'Introduction: Resourcing Civil Justice', in: Paterson, A. & Goriely, T. eds. *Resourcing Civil Justice*, Oxford: Oxford University Press

—— Tata, C. & Paterson, A., (1997) *Expenditure on Criminal Legal Aid*, Report for SOHHD, Edinburgh: Scottish Office Central Research Unit

Gray, A. (1994) 'The Reform of Legal Aid', *Oxford Review of Economic Policy*, 10:51

Greene, R. ed. (1989) *The Quality Pursuit*, ABA Law Practice Management Section, Chicago: American Bar Association

Gregg, P. (1967) *The Welfare State: An Economic and Social History of Great Britain from 1945 to the Present Day*, London: Harrap

Griffiths, J. (1980) 'A Comment on Research into "Legal Needs" ', in: Blankenburg, E. ed. *Innovations in the Legal Services*, Cambridge: Oelgeschlager, Gunn & Hain

Habermas, J. (1980) *Theorie des kommunikativen Handelns*, Frankfurt: Suhrkamp

Halliday, S. (1998a) 'Researching the "Impact" of Judicial Review on Routine Administrative Decision Making', in: Cowan, D. ed. *Housing: Participation and Exclusion*, Aldershot: Ashgate Dartmouth

—— (1998b) 'Administrative Justice, Administrative Process, and the Social Construction of Knowledge', Paper Presented to the Annual Meeting of the Law & Society Association, Aspen, Colorado, 2–7 June

Hansen, M. (1997) 'Loosening Congress' Purse Strings', *ABA Journal*, Apr. 28

Hansen, O. (1992) 'A Future for Legal Aid?', in: Thomas, P. ed. *Tomorrow's Lawyers*, Oxford: Blackwell

Harden, I. (1992) *The Contracting State*, London: Open University Press

Harkins, J. P. (1976) *Federal Legal Aid in Australia*, Canberra: Attorney General's Department

Harman, S. (1994) 'Franchising: the Preliminary Audit', *Legal Action*, 9 Jan.

Harris, N. (1994) *Solicitors and Client Care*, London: National Consumer Council

Hart, A. C. (1988) 'Criminal law policy in the Netherlands', in: van Dijk, J., Haffmans, C., Ruter, F., Schulte, J., Stolwijk, S., eds. *Criminal Law in Action: An Overview of Current Issues in Western Societies*, Deventer: Kluwer

Haugen, M. S. & Vigerust, E. (1992) 'Det udekkede behov for rettshjelp—et ulost problem', *Juss-Buss Report no. 59*, Oslo: University of Oslo, Institute for Sociology of Law

Haveman, R. (1973) *A Decade of Federal Anti-Poverty Programs*, New York: Academic Press

Hawkins, K. (1984) *Environmental Regulation and Enforcement: Regulation and the Social Definition of Pollution*, Oxford: Clarendon Press

Hawkins, K. ed. (1992) *The Uses of Discretion*, Oxford: Clarendon Press

Hawkins, K. (1992) 'The Use of Legal discretion: Perspectives from Law and the Social Sciences', in: Hawkins, K. ed. *The Uses of Discretion*, Oxford: Clarendon Press

—— & Baldwin, R. (1984) '*Discretionary Justice: Davis Reconsiders*', *Public Law*, Winter:570

Hayek, F. A. (1944) *The Road to Serfdom*, London: Routledge & Kegan Paul

—— (1973) *Law, Legislation and Liberty: A New Statement of Liberal Principles of Justice and Political Economy*: vol. 1—*Rules and Order*, London: Routledge

Hensler, D. & Peterson, M. (1993) 'Understanding Mass Personal Injury Litigation: A Socio-Legal Analysis', *Brooklyn Law Review*, 59:961

Herbert, R. (1919) *Justice and the Poor*, New York: Charles Scribnor's Sons

Herzog, P. & Herzog, B. E. (1973) 'The Reform of the Legal Profession and of Legal Aid in France', *International Comparative Law Quarterly*, 22:462

Hirschman, A. O. (1970) *Exit, Voice and Loyalty: Responses to Decline in Firms, Organizations and States*, Cambridge, Mass.: Harvard University Press

Hogg, Q. (1947) *The Case for Conservatism*, West Drayton: Penguin Books

Holthius, H. (1993) 'The Role of the Public Prosecutor in the Netherlands', in: NACRO, *International Comparisons in Criminal Justice: the London Seminars*, Dec.

Home Office (1975) *Racial Discrimination*, Cm. 6234, London: HMSO

—— (1995) 'Cautions, Court Proceedings and Sentencing: England and Wales 1994' *Home Office Statistical Bulletin* Issue 18/95, London: Government Statistical Service

—— (1996) 'Notifiable Offences: England and Wales, July 1995 to June 1996' *Home Office Statistical Bulletin* Issue 18/96, London: Government Statistical Service

Hood, R. (1992) *Race and Sentencing: A Study in the Crown Court*, a Report for the Commission for Racial Equality, Oxford: Clarendon Press

Horowitz, D. L. (1977) *The Courts and Social Policy*, Washington: The Brookings Institution

Houlden, J. & Balkin, J. (1985) 'Quality and Costs Comparisons of Private Bar Indigent Dense Systems', *Journal of Criminal Law and Criminology*, 79:176

Houseman, A. W. (1991) 'Poverty Law: Past and Future', in: Lardent, E. F. ed. *Civil Justice: An Agenda for the 1990s*, Chicago: ABA

Hutton, N., Paterson, A., Tata, C. & Wilson, J. (1996) *A Sentencing Information for the Scottish High Court of Justiciary: Report of the Study of Feasibility*, Scottish Office: HMSO

Huxtable, P. (1994) *An Examination of Foreign Legal Aid Schemes, With Implications for Australia*, (Churchill Fellowship Report), Bunbury: Legal Aid Commission of Western Australia

Illich, I. (1977) *Disabling Professions*, London: Boyars

Irvine, Lord (1997) Speech to Solicitors' Annual Conference, 18 Oct.

Jayasuriya, L. (1996) 'Citizenship and Welfare: Rediscovering Marshall', *Australian Journal of Social Issues*, 31:19

Johnsen, J. T. (1978) 'Udekkede rettshjelpbehov I to nordnorske lokalsamfunn', *Rettshjelp I utkantstrok* : 11, Oslo: University of Oslo, Institute for Sociology of Law

—— (1980) 'Problems in Planning Legal Services', in: Blankenburg, E. ed. *Innovations in the Legal Services*, Cambridge: Oelgeschlager, Gunn & Hain

—— (1987) *Retten til juridisk bistand*, Oslo: Tano

—— (1988) 'The Professionalisation of Legal Counselling in Norway', in: Abel, R. & Lewis, P. eds. *The Civil Law World* (Lawyers in Society, vol. 2), Berkeley: UCLA Press

—— (1992) 'Rural Justice: Country Lawyers and Legal Services in the United States and Britain', *Law and Social Inquiry*, 17:415

—— (1994) 'Nordic Legal Aid', *Maryland Journal of Contemporary Legal Issues*, 4:301

Johnson, E. Jr (1978) *Justice and Reform: The Formative Years of the American Legal Services Program*, New Brunswick: Transaction Press

—— (1981) 'Lawyers' Choice: A Theoretical Appraisal of Litigation Investment Decisions', *Law and Society Review*, 15:567

—— (1985) 'The Right to Counsel in Civil Cases: An International Perspective', *Loyola*, 19:341

Johnson, T. (1972) *Professions and Power*, London: Macmillan

Jörg, N., Field, S. & Brants, C. (1995) 'Are "Inquisitorial" and "Adversarial" Systems Converging?', in: Fennell, P., Harding, C., Jörg, N. & Swart, B. eds. *Criminal Justice in Europe: A Comparative Study*, Oxford: Clarendon Press

Karabian, R. (1972) 'Legal Services for the Poor: Some Political Observations', *University of San Francisco Law Review*, 6:253

Karpik, L. (1995) *Les avocats: Entre l'Etat, le public et le marché*, Paris: Gallimard

Katz, J. (1982) *Poor People's Lawyers in Transition*, New Brunswick: Transaction Press

Katz, M. B. (1990) *In the Shadow of the Poorhouse: A Social History of Welfare in America*, New York: Basic Books

Keys Young (1997) *Review of Community Legal Centres in South Australia*, Milson's Point: Keys Young

Kilwein, J. C. (1997) Congressional Hearings on Legal Services (unpublished research)

Klaus, W. R. (1972) 'Legal Services Program: Reply to Vice President Agnew', *American Bar Association Journal*, 58:1178

Klien, R. & Spangenburg, R. (1993) *The Indigent Defense Crisis*, Washington DC: American Bar Association

Klijn, A. (1981) *De balie geschetst*, WODC 24, The Hague

—— & Huls, F. (1994) 'The International Legal Aid Scene: A Concise Comparison', in: *Legal Aid in the Post-Welfare State Society*, Proceedings of the International Conference on Legal Aid, The Hague

Kommer, M. (1994) 'Punitiveness in Europe: A Comparison', *European Journal on Criminal Justice Policy and Research*, 2:29

Krislov, S. (1973) 'The OEO Lawyers Fail to Constitutionalize a Right to Welfare: A Study in the Uses and Limits of the Judicial Process', *University of Minnesota Law Review*, 58:211

Kuras, J. (1994) 'Access to Poverty Law Specialists: Ontario's Community Legal Clinics', in: *Legal Aid in the Post Welfare State Society*, Proceedings of the International Conference on Legal Aid, The Hague

Kymlicka, W. & Norman, W. (1994) 'Return of the Citizen: A Survey of Recent Research in Citizenship Theory', *Ethics*, 104:352

Lardent, E. F. ed. (1991) *Civil Justice: An Agenda for the 1990s*, Chicago: ABA

Law Centres Federation (1980) *Law Centres: A Practical Guide*, London: LCF

—— (1991)*What is a Law Centre?* London: LCF

Lawrence, S. E. (1990) *The Poor in Court: The Legal Services Program and Supreme Court Decision Making*, Lawrenceville, NJ: Princeton

Law Society (1990a) *Solicitors' Office Manual*, London: Law Society of England and Wales

—— (1990b) *Best Practice*, London: Law Society of England and Wales

—— (1991) *Quality: A Briefing for Solicitors*, London: Law Society of England and Wales

—— (1993) *Practice Management Standards*, London: Law Society of England and Wales

Law Society of Upper Canada, Ontario Legal Aid Plan (1992) *Community Legal Clinics Annual Report 1991–1992*,Toronto: Law Society of Upper Canada

Law Society of Upper Canada, Committee on Governance Restructuring (1996) *Change Through Leadership*, Toronto: Law Society of Upper Canada

Law Society of Upper Canada (1997) *Ontario Legal Aid Plan: Annual Report 1996*, Toronto: Law Society of Upper Canada

League of Nations (1927) *Legal Aid for the Poor*, Geneva: League of Nations

Leeuwen, S., Klijn, A. & Paulides, G. (1996) *De toegevoegde kwaliteit*, Arnhem: Gouda Quint

Lefstein, N. (1982) *Criminal Defense Systems for the Poor*, Washington DC: American Bar Association

Legal Action Group (1992) *A Strategy for Justice: Publicly Funded Legal Services in the 1990s*, London: Legal Action Group

Legal Aid and Family Services (1997) *Legal Aid in Australia 1995–96 Statistical Yearbook*, Canberra: Attorney General's Department

Legal Aid Board (1989) *Second Stage Consultation on the Future of the Green Form Scheme*, London: Legal Aid Board

—— (1993) *The Franchising Specification*, London: Legal Aid Board

—— (1994) *Annual Report 1993–94*, London: HMSO

—— (1997) *Annual Report 1996–97*, London: HMSO

—— (1998a) *Reforming the Civil Advice and Assistance Scheme: Exclusive Contracting—The Way Forward*, London: Legal Aid Board

—— (1998b) *Focus* 25

Legal Aid Commission of Western Australia (1992) *Legal Aid in Western Australia: State Services Study*, Canberra: Australian Government Publishing Service

Legal Aid Task Force (1985) *Legal Aid Task Force Final Report*, Canberra: Australian Government Publishing Service

Legal Services Board (1996) *Legal Aid Delivery Reform*, Briefing Paper, Minister of Justice, New Zealand, Dec.

Legal Services Corporation (1980) *The Delivery Systems Study*, Washington DC: LSC

—— (1994) *Annual Report*, Washington DC: LSC

Legrand, P. (1996) 'European Legal Systems are Not Converging', *International and Comparative Law Journal*, 45:52

Lempert, R. (1992) 'Discretion in a Behavioural Perspective: The Case of a Public housing Eviction Board' in: Hawkins, K. ed. *The Uses of Discretion*, Oxford: Clarendon Press

Lenzner, T. (1971) 'Legal Services Fights for the Poor, But Who Fights for Legal Services', *Jurist Doctor*, 1:9

Lewis, N. & Birkinshaw, P. (1993) *When Citizens Complain: Reforming Justice and Administration*, Buckingham: Open University Press

Lewis, N., Seneviratne, M. & Cracknell, S. (1987) *Complaints Procedures in Local Government*, Centre for Criminological and Socio-Legal Studies, University of Sheffield

Lewis, P. (1973) 'Unmet Legal Needs' in: Morris, P., White, R. & Lewis, P. eds. *Social Needs and Legal Action*, London: Martin Robertson

Lid, B. (1980) 'Fangers rettshjelpbehov', *Juss-Buss Report no. 15*, Oslo: University of Oslo, Institute for Sociology of Law

Linblom, P. H. (1985) 'The Protection of Diffuse, Fragmented and Collective Interests in Civil Litigation in Sweden', *Scandinavian Studies in Law*, 30:103

Lindsay, M. (1991) 'Complaints Procedures and their Limitations in the Light of the "Pindown" Inquiry', *Journal of Social Welfare and Family Law*, 13:432

Ling, O. (1994) 'Legal Aid Costs in Sweden', in *Legal Aid in the Post-Welfare State Society*, Proceedings of the International Conference on Legal Aid, The Hague

Lord Chancellor's Department (1986) *Legal Aid Efficiency Scrutiny*, London: HMSO

—— (1995a) *Legal Aid: Targeting Need*, Cm. 2854, London: HMSO

—— (1995b) *Looking to the Future: Mediation and the Ground for Divorce*, Cm. 2799, London: HMSO

—— (1996) *Striking the Balance: The Future of Legal Aid in England and Wales*, Cm. 3305, London: HMSO

—— (1998) *Modernising Justice* Cm. 4155, London: HMSO

Low Pay Unit (1990) *Crime without Punishment: The Story behind Wages Council Underpayment*, London: Low Pay Unit

Lowe, R. (1994) 'Lessons from the Past: The Rise and Fall of the Classic Welfare State in Britain 1945–76', in: Oakley, A. & Williams, A. S. eds. *The Politics of the Welfare State*, London: UCL Press

Lubove, R. (1986) *The Struggle for Social Security 1900–1935* (2nd edn.) Pittsburgh: University of Pittsburgh Press

McBarnet, D. (1979) *Conviction*, London: Macmillan

McCarthy, P. *et al.* (1992) *Grievances, Complaints and Local Government*, Aldershot: Avebury

McCarthy, P. & Simpson, B. (1993) 'Effective Complaining in Local Government Services', *Consumer Policy Review*, 3:39

McConville, M. & Hodgson, J. (1993) *Custodial Advice and the Right to Silence*, Royal Commission on Criminal Justice, Research Study no. 16, London: HMSO

—— Bridges, L. & Pavlovic, A. (1994) *Standing Accused*, Oxford: Clarendon Press

McConville, M., Sanders, A. & Leng, R. (1991) *The Case for the Prosecution*, New York: Routledge

McIntosh, D. & Holmes, M. (1991) *Civil Procedures in EC Countries*, London: Lloyd's of London/Davies Arnold Cooper

Makin, K. (1998) 'Law Society to Give Up Legal Aid', Toronto Globe and Mail, 28 Feb

Manning, P. (1992) 'Big Bang Decisions: Notes on a Naturalistic Approach', in: Hawkins, K. (ed.) *The Uses of Discretion*, Oxford: Clarendon Press

Marklund, S. (1988) *Paradise Lost? The Nordic Welfare States and the Recession 1975–1985*, Lund: Arkiv

Marks, R. (1977) 'Some Research Perspectives for looking at Legal Need and Legal Delivery Systems: Old Forms Or New?' *Law And Society Review*, 11:191

Marshall, T. H. (1949) 'Citizenship and Social Class', reprinted in: Marshall, T. H. ed. *Sociology at the Crossroads and Other Essays*, London: Heinemann, 1963

—— ed. (1963) *Sociology at the Crossroads and Other Essays*, London: Heinemann

Martyn, S. (1989) 'Standards of Quality', in: Greene, R. ed. *The Quality Pursuit*, ABA Law Practice Management Section, Chicago: American Bar Association

Matoesian, G. (1995) 'Language, Law and Society: Policy Implications of the Kennedy Smith Rape Trial', *Law and Society Review*, 29:669

Mayhew, L. (1975) 'Institutions of Representation: Civil Justice and the Public', *Law and Society Review*, 9:401

—— & Reiss, A. (1969) 'The Social Organisation of Legal Contacts', *American Sociological Review*, 34:34

Meeker, J., Dombrink, J., & Quinn, B. (1991) 'Competitive Bidding and Legal Services for the Poor: An Analysis of the Scientific Evidence', *Western State University Law Review*, 18:611

Meredith, C., Forsyth, J., Zemans, F. & Cassels, G. (1991) *Comprehensive Review and Evaluation of the Certificate Component of the Ontario Legal Aid Plan*, Ottawa: Abt Associates of Canada

Messier, C. (1975a) *Les Mains de la Loi. Une Problematique des Besoins Juridiques des Economiquementes du Quebec*, Montreal: Commission des Services Juridiques

—— (1975b) *In the hands of the Law* (*Summary Report*) Montreal: Commission des Services Juridiques

Ministère de la Justice (1995) *Bilan des trois premieres années d'application de la loi relative à l'aide juridique*, Paris: Ministère de la Justice

Moody, S. & Tombs, J. (1982) *Prosecution in the Public Interest*, Edinburgh: Edinburgh University Press

Moorhead, R. (1998) 'Legal Aid in the Eye of a Storm: Rationing, Contracting and a New Institutionalism', *Journal of Law & Society*, 25:365

—— Sherr, A. & Paterson, A. (1994) 'Judging by Results', *International Journal of the Legal Profession*, 1:191

MORI (1993) *Electricity Services: The Customer Perspective*, report prepared for the Office of Electricity Regulation, London

Morris, P., White, R. & Lewis, P. eds. (1973) *Social Needs and Legal Action*, London: Martin Robertson

Mosher J. (1997) 'Poverty Law: A Case Study', in: Ontario Legal Aid Review (1997) *Report of the Ontario Legal Aid Review: A Blueprint for Publicly Funded Legal Services*, Toronto: Ministry of the Attorney General

Mossman, M. J. (1983) 'Community Legal Clinics in Ontario', *Windsor Yearbook of Access to Justice*, 3:375

Moynihan, D. P. (1970) *Maximum Feasible Misunderstanding*, New York: Free Press

Murray, C. (1984) *Losing Ground: American Social Policy 1950–1980*, New York: Basic Books

National Association of Community Legal Centres (1996d) *Submission to the Senate Legal and Constitutional References Committee Legal Aid Inquiry*, Sydney: National Association of Community Legal Centres

—— (1996b) *Annual Report 1995/6*, Sydney: NACLC

—— (1997) *Annual Report 1996/7*, Sydney: NACLC

National Association of Citizens Advice Bureaux (1995) *Annual Report 1994/95*, London: National Association of Citizens Advice Bureaux

National Audit Office (1992) *The Administration of Legal Aid in England and Wales*, London: HMSO

National Consumer Council (1989) *Ordinary Justice: Legal Services and the Courts in England and Wales: A Consumer view*, London: HMSO

—— (1991) *Out of Court: A Consumer View of Three Low-cost Arbitration Schemes*, London: National Consumer Council

—— (1993) *Ombudsman Services: Consumers' views of the Office of the Building Societies Ombudsmen and Insurance Ombudsman Bureau*, London: National Consumer Council

National Council of Social Service (1923) *Annual Report*, London: National Council of Social Services

National Inquiry into the Separation of Aboriginal and Torres Straight Island Children from their Families, Australia (1997) *Bringing them Home*, Sydney: Human Rights and Equal Opportunity Commission

National Legal Aid Advisory Committee (1990) *Legal Aid for the Australian Community*, Canberra: Australian Government Publishing Service

Neal, D. ed. (1984) *On Tap, Not on Top: Legal Centres in Australia 1972–82*, Clayton: Legal Service Bulletin Co-Operative

Nelken, D. ed. (1997) *Comparing Legal Cultures*, Aldershot: Dartmouth

Nelson, D. (1969) *Unemployment Insurance: The American Experience 1915–1935*, Madison: University of Wisconsin Press

Nocera, J. (1995) *Fortune*, 16 Oct.

Noone, M. A. (1992) 'Imperatives for Community Legal Centres', *Alternative Law Journal*, 17:120

—— (1997) 'Mid-life Crisis: Australian Community Legal Centres', *Alternative Law Journal*, 22:25

—— (1998) 'Australian Community Legal Centres; The University Connection' in: Cooper, J. & Trubek, L. eds. *Educating for Justice: Social Values and Legal Education*, Aldershot: Dartmouth

North Kensington Neighbourhood Law Centre (1971) *Annual Report 1971*, London: North Kensington Neighbourhood Law Centre

Note (1983) 'Special Project: The Legal Services Corporation: Past, Present and Future', *New York Law School Review*, 28:593

O'Brien, W. (1967) 'Why Not Appoint Counsel in Civil Cases? The Swiss Approach', *Ohio State Law Review*, 28:1

Office of Economic Opportunity (1971) *Report of the Office of Economic Opportunity Commission on California Rural Legal Assistance Inc.*, Washington DC: OEO (unpublished report)

Office of Fair Trading (1991) *Consumer Redress Mechanisms*, London: Office of Fair Trading

Office of Legal Aid and Family Services (1991) *Community Legal Centres: A Study of Four Centres in New South Wales and Victoria*, Canberra: Attorney General's Department

Oldertz, C. & Tidefelt, E. (1988) *Compensation for Personal Injury in Sweden and Other Countries*, Stockholm: Juristforlaget

Ontario Legal Aid Review (1997a) *Report of the Ontario Legal Aid Review: A Blueprint for Publicly Funded Legal Services*, Toronto: Ministry of the Attorney General

—— (1997b) *Submission by Clinic Funding Committee* (unpublished)

Ontario, Ministry of the Attorney General (1965) *Report of the Joint Committee on Legal Aid*, Toronto: Queen's Printer

—— (1974) *Report of the Task Force on Legal Aid*, Toronto: Queen's Printer (Mr Justice John Osler, Chair)

Ontario Task Force on Legal Aid (1978) *Report of the Commission on Clinical Funding*, Toronto: Queen's Printer (Mr Justice Samuel Grange, Commissioner)

Openbaar Ministerie (1995) *Annual Report 1994: The NPPS on the Move*, Openbaar Ministerie: The Hague

Orchard, S. (1997) 'Contracting: The English Proposals' in: *Legal Aid: How Much Justice Can We Afford?*, Proceedings of the International Conference on Legal Aid at Edinburgh, vol. 2

Parker, H., Sumner, M. & Jarvis, G. (1989) *Unmasking the Magistrates*, Milton Keynes: Open University Press

Parliament of South Australia, Statutory Authorities Review Committee (1996) *Review of the Legal Services Commission* (Part 1), Adelaide: Parliament of South Australia

Parliament of the Commonwealth of Australia (1997) *Inquiry Into the Australian Legal Aid System: First Report*, Senate Legal and Constitutional References Committee, Canberra: Australian Government Publishing Service

Paterson, A. (1979) 'Legal Advice and Assistance', *SCOLAC*, 34: 105

—— (1986) 'Specialisation and the Legal Profession', *New Law Journal*, 25 July, 697

—— (1990) *Professional Competence in Legal Services*, London: National Consumer Council

—— (1993) 'Financing Legal Services', in: Carey Miller, D. & Beaumont, P. eds. *The Option of Litigating in Europe*, London: United Kingdom National Committee of Comparative Law

—— (1994) 'Access, Legal Aid and Rural Scotland' in: *Legal Aid in the Post-Welfare State Society*, Proceedings of the International Conference on Legal Aid, The Hague

—— (1996) 'Professionalism and the Legal Services Market', *International Journal of the Legal Profession*, 3:137

—— & Goriely, T. eds. (1996) *Resourcing Civil Justice*, Oxford: Oxford University Press

—— (1984a) 'Evolution in Legal Services: Practice Without Theory', *Civil Justice Quarterly*, 3:229

—— & Nelken, D. (1984b) 'The Evolution of Legal Services in Britain', *Windsor Yearbook of Access to Justice*, 4:101

Department of Justice (1993) *Patterns in Legal Aid* (2nd edn.), Ottawa: Canadian Department of Justice

Patterson, J. T. (1967) *Congressional Conservatism and the New Deal: The Growth of the Conservative Coalition in Congress 1933–1939*, Lexington: University of Kentucky Press

—— (1994) *America's Struggle Against Poverty 1900–1994*, Cambridge: Harvard University Press

Pearson, J. B. (1971) 'To Protect the Rights of the Poor: The Legal Services Corporation Act of 1971', *Kansas Law Review*, 19:641

Pease, K. (1994) 'Cross-National Imprisonment Rates: Limitations of Method and Possible Conclusions', *British Journal of Criminology*, 34:116

Performance Indicator Group (1987) *Performance Indicators for the National Health Service*, Consultation paper no. 2, London: Department of Health

Perkin, H. (1989) *The Rise of Professional Society*, London: Routledge

Peters, T. J. & Waterman, R. H. (1982) *In Search of Excellence*, New York: Harper & Row

Petterson, G. *et al.* (1995) *Users' Views of the CAB Service*, London: National Association of Citizens Advice Bureaux

Pfeffer, N. & Coote, A. (1991) *Is Quality Good for You?* London: Institute for Public Policy Research

Pleasance, P., Maclean, S. & Morley, A. (1996) *Profiling Civil Litigation*, London: Legal Aid Board Research Unit

Plowden V. (1993) 'Right to Complain', *Childright*, July:14

Pollock, S. (1975) *Legal Aid: The First Twenty-five Years*, London: Oyez

Pound, R. (1906) 'Causes of Popular Dissatisfaction with Administration of Justice', *American Bar Association Review*, 29:395

Quadagno, J. (1994) *The Color of Welfare: How Racism Undermined the War on Poverty*, New York: Oxford University Press

Radbruch, G. (1919) 'Das Recht im sozialen Volksstaat', in: *Die Gemeinnützige Rechtsauskunft*, 95

Regan, F. (1994a) 'Legal Resources Development in Uganda', *International Journal of the Sociology of Law*, 22:203

—— (1994b) 'Are There "Mean" and "Generous" Legal Aid Schemes?', in: *Legal Aid in the Post-Welfare State Society*, Proceedings of the International Conference on Legal Aid, The Hague

—— (1996) 'Criminal Legal Aid: Does Defending Liberty Undermine Citizenship?', in: Young, R. & Wall, D. eds. *Access to Criminal Justice: Legal Aid, Lawyers and the Defence of Liberty*, London: Blackstone Press

—— (1997) 'The Politics of Priorities', in: *Legal Aid: How Much Justice Can We Afford?* Proceedings of the International Conference on Legal Aid, Edinburgh, vol. 2

Reifner, U. (1982) 'Individualistic and Collective Legalisation: Theory and Practice of Legal Advice for Workers in Pre-fascist Germany', in: Abel, R. ed. *The Politics of Informal Justice*, vol. 2, New York: Academic Press

Rethans, J., Drop, R., Sturmans, F. & Vleuten, C. (1991) 'A Method for Introducing Standardized (Simulated) Patients into General Practice Consultations', *British Journal of General Practice*, 41:94

Richardson, M. and Reynolds, S. (1994) 'The Shrinking Public Purse: Civil Legal Aid In New South Wales, Australia', *Maryland Journal of Contemporary Legal Issues*, 5:349

Ridley Committee (1945) *Report of the Inter-Departmental Committee on Rent Control*, Cm. 6621, London: HMSO

Robb, J. R. (1970) 'Controversial Cases and the Legal Services Program', *American Bar Association Journal*, 56:329

—— (1971) 'Poverty Lawyers' Independence: Battle Cry for Justice', *New Mexico Law Review*, 1:215

Robinson, T. (1978) *In Worlds Apart: Professionals and their Clients in the Welfare State*, London: Bedford Square Press

Rose, R. (1991) 'Comparing Forms of Comparative Analysis', *Political Studies*, 39:446

Rosenberg, G. N. (1991) *The Hollow Hope: Can Courts Bring About Social Change?*, Chicago: University of Chicago Press

Rosenthal, D. (1974) *Lawyer and Client: Who's in Charge?*, New York: Russell Sage Foundation

Rowan, J. (1993) 'Legal Aid in New Zealand', *New Zealand Law Journal*, Nov.:396

Rowe, T. (1984) 'Predicting the Effects of Attorney Fee Shifting', *Law and Contemporary Problems*, 47:139

Royal Commission on Legal Services (1979) *Final Report*, London: HMSO

Rudden, B. (1992) 'Courts and Codes in England, France and Soviet Russia', in: Varga, C. ed. *Comparative Legal Cultures*, Aldershot: Dartmouth

Rueschemeyer, D. (1989) 'Comparing Legal Professions: A State Centred Approach', in: Abel, R. & Lewis, P. eds. *Comparative Theories* (Lawyers in Society, vol. 3), Berkeley: UCLA Press

Rushcliffe Committee (1944) Written evidence to the Rushcliffe Committee, Public Record Office Files LCO2 3899–3900, London

—— (1945) *Report of the Committee on Legal Aid and Legal Advice in England and Wales*, Cm. 6641. London: HMSO

Sackville, R. (1975) *Legal Aid in Australia*, Canberra: Australian Government Publishing Service

Samuel, E. (1996) 'Criminal Legal Aid Expenditure: Supplier or System Driven? The Case of Scotland' in: Young, R. & Wall, D. eds. *Access to Criminal Justice*, London: Blackstone Press

—— & Adler, M. (1994) *Criminal Legal Aid Case Trajectories*, Nov. 1994, Scottish Office Central Research Unit, Final Draft Report

Sanders, A., Bridges, L., Mulvaney. A, & Crozier, G. (1989) *Advice and Assistance at Police Stations and the 24 Hour Duty Solicitor Scheme*, London: Lord Chancellor's Department

Sarat, A. (1990) ' "... The Law is all over": Power, Resistance and the Legal Consciousness of the Welfare Poor', *Yale Journal of Law and the Humanities*, 2:343

—— & Scheingold, S. A. eds. (1998) *Cause Lawyering*, New York: Oxford University Press

Scheindlin, S. A. (1974) 'Legal Services Past and Present', *Cornell Law Review*, 59:960

Scheingold, S. A. (1974) *The Politics of Rights: Lawyers, Public Policy, and Political Change*, New Haven: Yale University Press

—— (1984) 'The Dilemma of Legal Services', *Stanford Law Review*, 36:891

Schnapper, B. (1984) 'De la charité à la solidarité: L'assistance judiciaire française 1951–1972', *Revue d'histoire du droit*, 105

Schoenmakers, H. (1994) 'No Compassion: The Quality of Legal Aid Under the New Legal Aid Act in the Netherlands', in: *Legal Aid in the Post-Welfare State Society*, Proceedings of the International Conference on Legal Aid, The Hague

Schuyt, K. (1980) 'Dilemmas in the Delivery of the Legal Services', in: Blankenburg, E. ed., *Innovations in the Legal Services*, Cambridge: Oelgeschlager, Gunn and Hain

—— Gronendijk, K. & Sloot, B. (1976) *De weg naar het recht*, Deventer: Kluwer

—— Gronendijk, K. & Sloot, B. (1978) 'Rechtsprobleme oder Private Scwierigkeiten. Die Inanspruchname von Rechtshilfe in den Niederlanden' in: Blankenburg, E. & Kaupen, W. eds., *Rechtsbedurfnis und Rechtshilfe. Jahrbuch für Rechtssoziologieund Rechtstheorie*, Band V Opladen 109 vol. 5, Wiesbaden, Westdeutscher: Verlag

Scottish Law Commission (1994) *Multi-Party Actions: Court Proceedings and Funding*, Cm. 3291, Edinburgh: HMSO

Scottish Legal Aid Board (1997) *Registration and Code of Practice*, Consultation Paper Issued by the Scottish Legal Aid Board, Edinburgh: Scottish Legal Aid Board

Scottish Office (1993a) *Criminal Legal Aid Review: Consultation Paper*, Edinburgh: HMSO

—— (1993b) *Criminal Proceedings in the Scottish Courts 1992*, Scottish Office Statistical Bulletin, Nov.

—— (1994) *Criminal Proceedings in Scottish Courts 1994*, Scottish Office Statistical Bulletin CRJ/1995/9 (revised 1997)

—— (1996) *Crime and Punishment*, Cm. 3302, Edinburgh: HMSO

—— (1997) *White Paper on Legal Aid and Public Defenders*, Edinburgh: HMSO

—— Home and Health Division (1998) *Access to Justice: A Consultation Paper on Civil Legal Aid*, Edinburgh: The Scottish Office

Sejr, L. ed. (1977) *Retshjaelp i Ee lokalområde*, University of Arhus

Sherr, A. (1990) *Solicitors and Their Skills*, Research report, London: Law Society of England and Wales

—— Moorhead, R. & Paterson, A. (1994) *Lawyers: The Quality Agenda*, London: HMSO

Singsen, G. (1991) 'The Role of Competition in the Making of Grants for the Provision of Legal Services to the Poor', *Public Interest Law Journal*, 1:57

Sissons, M. & French P. eds. (1963) *The Age of Austerity*, London: Hodder & Stoughton

Smith, R. (1989) 'Revamping Legal Aid', *Legal Action*, April: 8

—— (1993a) 'Competitive Tendering', *Legal Action*, June: 8

—— (1993b) 'Transaction Criteria', *Legal Action*, April: 7

—— (1997a) *Justice: Redressing the Balance*, London: Legal Action Group

—— (1997b) 'Clinics in a Cold Climate: Law Centres in England and Wales', *Osgoode Hall Law Journal*, 35:895

—— (1997c) 'You Are Not Alone: Legal Aid in England and Wales' in: Zemans, F., Monahan, P., & Thomas, A., eds., *A New Legal Aid Plan for Ontario: Background Papers*, Ontario.: York University Centre for Public Law and Public Policy

Smith, R. H. (1919) *Justice and the Poor*, New York: Carnegie Foundation

—— (1949) 'The English Legal Assistance Plan: Its Significance for American Legal Institutions', *ABA Journal*, 35:453

Social Trends (1994) No. 24, Government Statistical Service, London: HMSO

Society of Conservative Lawyers (1968) *Rough Justice*, London: Society of Conservative Lawyers

Society of Labour Lawyers (1968) *Justice for All*, Fabian Research Series 273, London

Sommerlad, H. (1995) 'Managerialism and the Legal Profession', *International Journal of the Legal Profession*, 2:159

Spangenberg, R. & Beeman, M. (1995) 'Indigent Defense Systems in the United States', *Law and Contemporary Problems*, 58:31

—— & Spence, A. (1995) *Findings Concerning Contracting for the Delivery of Indigent Defense Services*, Report to ABA Standing Committee on Legal Aid and Indigent Defendants, Chicago: ABA

State Bar of California (1996) *And Justice for All*, San Francisco: San Francisco Office of Legal Services

Stephens, M. (1991) *Community Law Centres: A Critical Appraisal*, Aldershot: Avebury

Stone, L. (1990) *The Road to Divorce*, Oxford: Oxford University Press

Strober, G. S. & Strober, D. H. (1994) *Nixon: An Oral History of His Presidency*, New York: Harper Collins

Strömholm, S. ed. (1988) *An Introduction to Swedish Law*, (2nd. edition), Stockholm: Norstedts Förlag

Sudnow, D. (1964) 'Normal Crimes: Sociological Features of the Penal Code in a Public Defender Office', *Social Problems*, 12:255

Sverne, E. (1997) 'Introductory Paper on Legal Aid in Sweden', in: *Legal Aid: How Much Jutice Can We Afford?* Proceedings of the International Conference on Legal Aid, Edinburgh,Vol. 1

Swart, B. & Young, J. (1995) 'The European Convention on Human Rights and Criminal Justice in the Netherlands and the United Kingdom', in: Fennell, P. Harding, C., Jörg, N. & Swart, B. eds. *Criminal Justice in Europe: A Comparative Study*, Oxford: Clarendon Press

Sykes, G. M. (1969–70) 'Legal Needs of the Poor in the City of Denver', *Law and Society Review*, 4:255

Taman, L. (1971) *The Legal Services Controversy: An Examination of the Evidence*, Ottawa: National Council on Welfare

Tata, C. (1997) 'Conceptions and Representations of the Sentencing Decision Process', *Journal of Law and Society*, 24:365

—— (1998) 'The Application of Judicial Intelligence and Rules to Systems Supporting Discretionary Judicial Decision-Making', *Artificial Intelligence and Law: An International Journal*, 6:199

—— & Hutton, N. (1998) 'What "Rules" in Sentencing?', *The International Journal of the Sociology of Law*, 26: 339–64

Therborn, G. (1993) 'The Politics of Childhood: The Rights of Children in Modern Times' in: Castles, F. ed. *Families of Nations: Patterns of Public Policy in Western Democracies*, Aldershot: Dartmouth

Thomas, P. ed. (1992) *Tomorrow's Lawyers*, Oxford: Blackwell

Titmuss, R. (1970) 'Welfare Rights, Law and Discretion', reprinted in: Abel-Smith B. & Titmuss K. eds. *The Philosophy of Welfare: Selected Writings of Richard M. Titmuss*, London: Allen & Unwin, 1987

Tomasic, R. (1975) *Australian Legal Aid*, St. Leonards: Law Foundation of New South Wales

Tombs, J. & Moody, S. (1993) 'Alternatives to Prosecution: the Public Interest Redefined', *Criminal Law Review*, 357

Tonry, M. (1995) *Malign Neglect: Race, Crime and Punishment in America*, New York: Oxford University Press

—— (1996) *Sentencing Matters*, New York: Oxford University Press

Trattner, W. I. (1994) *From Poor Law to Welfare State: A History of Social Welfare in America* (5th edn.) New York: Free Press

Tremblay, P. R. (1990) 'Towards a Community-Based Ethic for Legal Services Practice', *UCLA Law Review*, 37:1101

Tull, J. (1994) 'Assessing Quality and Effectiveness in Legal Services Programs for the Poor', in: *Legal Aid in the Post-Welfare State Society*, Proceedings of the International Conference on Legal Aid, The Hague

Turner, A. F. (1982) 'President Reagan and the Legal Services Corporation', *Creighton Law Review*, 15:711

US Bureau of the Census (1996) *Statistical Abstract of the United States 1996*, 116th edition, Washington DC

US Congress (1995) *Hearings Before the Subcommittee on Commercial and Administrative Law of the Committee on the Judiciary, House of Representatives*, 104th Congress Washington: GPO

Varga, C. ed. (1992) *Comparative Legal Cultures*, Aldershot: Dartmouth

van Dijk, J., Haffmans, C. *et al.* eds. (1988) *Criminal Law in Action: An Overview of Current Issues in Western Societies*, Deventer: Kluwer

van Dijk, J. & Mayhew, P. (1993) *Criminal Victimization in the Industrialized World: Key findings of the 1989 and 1992 International Crime Surveys*, The Hague: Netherlands Ministry of Justice

van Kersbergen, K. & Becker, U. (1988) 'The Netherlands: A Passive Social Democratic Welfare State in a Christian Democratic Ruled Society', *Journal of Social Policy*, 17:477

van Leeuwen, S. *et al.* (1996) *De toegevoegde kwaliteit*, WODC 151, The Hague: Netherlands Ministry of Justice

van Swaaningen, R. & uit Beijerse, J. (1993) 'From Punishment to Diversion: The Debate on Non-Custodial Sanctions and Penal Reform in the Netherlands', *British Journal of Criminology*, 33:136

van Tulder, F. (1990), *De prijs van de weg naar het recht*, SCP, The Hague: Social Cultural Planning Bureau

van Vliet, A. (1990) 'Juvenile Complaints: The Dutch Way', *Childright* , 65:17

Wagel, W. (1981) 'Case Routinization in Investigative Police Work', *Social Problems*, 28:263

Walker, M. (1995) 'Criminal Justice and Offenders', in: Walker, M. ed. *Interpreting Crime Statistics*, Oxford: Clarendon Press

Walker, M. ed. (1995) *Interpreting Crime Statistics*, Oxford: Clarendon Press

Wall, D. (1996) 'Legal Aid, Social Policy, and the Architecture of Criminal Justice: The Supplier Induced Inflation Thesis and Legal Aid', *Journal of Law and Society*, 23:549

Weinstein, J. B. (1995) *Individual Justice in Mass Tort Litigation*, Illinios: Northwestern University Press

Weissman, H. ed. (1969) *Justice and the Law in the Mobilization for Youth Experience*, New York: Association Press

White, R. (1973) 'Lawyers and the Enforcement of Rights', in: Morris P., White R. & Lewis P., eds. *Social Needs and Legal Action*, London: Martin Robertson

Whyte, G. (1984) 'And Justice for Some', *Dublin University Law Journal*, 6:88

Whyte, J. (1980) *Catholics in Western Democracies*, Dublin: Gill and Macmillan

Williams, K. (1992) 'Legal Centres Across Australia', *Alternative Law Journal*, 17:293

Woolf, H. (1996) *Access to Justice: Final Report to the Lord Chancellor on the Civil Justice System in England and Wales*, London: Lord Chancellor's Department

Young, R. (1996) 'Will Widgery Do?', in: Young, R. & Wall, D. eds. *Access to Criminal Justice*, London: Blackstone Press

—— & Wall, D. (1996) eds. *Access to Criminal Justice*, London: Blackstone Press

Zander, M. (1975) 'Costs of Litigation: A Study in the Queen's Bench Division', *Law Society's Gazette*, June 25, 680

—— (1978) *Legal Services for the Community*, London: Temple Smith

—— (1988) *A Matter of Justice*, London: IB Tauris & Co

Zarefsky, D. (1986) *President Johnson's War on Poverty: Rhetoric and History*, University City: University of Alabama Press

Zemans, F. ed. (1979) *Perspectives on Legal Aid*, London: Frances Pinter

Zemans, F. (1994a) 'Legal Aid Services in Ontario in the Nineties', in: *Legal Aid in the Post-Welfare State Society*, Proceedings of the International Conference on Legal Aid, The Hague

—— (1994b) 'Can Ontario Sustain Cadillac Legal Services?', *Maryland Journal of Legal Issues*, 5:247

—— & Monahan, P. J. (1997) *From Crisis to Reform: A New Legal Aid Plan for Ontario*, Osgoode Hall Law School/York University Centre for Public Law and Public Policy, York, Ontario

Zemans, F. K. (1982) 'Framework for Analysis of Legal Mobilisation: A Decision-Making Model', *American Bar Foundation Research Journal*, 989

—— (1983) 'Legal Mobilization: the Neglected Role of the Law in the Political System', *American Political Science Review*, 77:690

Zweigert, K. & Kötz, H. (1987) *Introduction to Comparative Law* (2nd edn.) Oxford: Clarendon Press

Index